The Politics of White Rights

POLITICS AND CULTURE IN THE
TWENTIETH-CENTURY SOUTH

SERIES EDITORS

Bryant Simon, *Temple University*
Jane Dailey, *University of Chicago*

ADVISORY BOARD

Lisa Dorr, *University of Alabama*
Grace Elizabeth Hale, *University of Virginia*
Randal Jelks, *University of Kansas*
Kevin Kruse, *Princeton University*
Robert Norrell, *University of Tennessee*
Bruce Schulman, *Boston University*
Marjorie Spruill, *University of South Carolina*
J. Mills Thornton, *University of Michigan*
Allen Tullos, *Emory University*
Brian Ward, *University of Manchester*

The Politics of White Rights

RACE, JUSTICE, AND
INTEGRATING ALABAMA'S SCHOOLS

Joseph Bagley

The University of Georgia Press
ATHENS

© 2018 by the University of Georgia Press
Athens, Georgia 30602
www.ugapress.org
All rights reserved
Designed by
Set in 10.25/13.5 Minion Pro by Graphic Composition, Inc., Bogart, GA.

Most University of Georgia Press titles are
available from popular e-book vendors.

Printed digitally

Library of Congress Cataloging-in-Publication Data

Names: Bagley, Joseph, 1981– author.
Title: The politics of white rights : race, justice, and integrating Alabama's schools / Joseph Bagley.
Other titles: Politics and culture in the twentieth-century South.
Description: Athens : The University of Georgia Press, [2018] | Series: Politics and culture in the twentieth-century South | Includes bibliographical references and index.
Identifiers: LCCN 2018015514 | ISBN 9780820354194 (hardback : alk. paper) | ISBN 9780820354835 (pbk. : alk. paper) | ISBN 9780820354187 (ebook)
Subjects: LCSH: School integration—Alabama—History—20th century. | Segregation in education—Alabama—History—20th century. | School integration—Massive resistance movement—Alabama—History—20th century.
Classification: LCC LC212.522.A2 B34 2018 | DDC 379.2/6309761—dc23
LC record available at https://lccn.loc.gov/2018015514

CONTENTS

Acknowledgments vii

Introduction 1

CHAPTER 1. "The NAACP Organized—Why Not You," 1954–1960 12

CHAPTER 2. "Our Most Historical Moment," 1962–1963 43

CHAPTER 3. "Now a Single Shot Can Do It," 1964–1966 77

CHAPTER 4. "More Than a Mere Word of Promise," 1966–1968 109

CHAPTER 5. "Depths of Disillusionment," 1968–1970 146

CHAPTER 6. *Swann* Song, 1970–1973 181

Epilogue. "If Ever Is Going to Happen": 1973–2017 216

Notes 235

Index 277

ACKNOWLEDGMENTS

I am indebted to Rob Baker and David Sehat for their unfailing support; to Brian Landsberg for reading the manuscript and sharing his research; to Chuck Bolton for offering invaluable suggestions and introducing me to my wonderful editor, Walter Biggins; to the anonymous readers for the University of Georgia Press whose assistance was critical; to Walter and the staff at UGA Press, especially Jon Davies and Beth Snead; to freelance copy editor, Chris Dodge; to Patrick Kerwin and everyone at the Library of Congress Manuscript Division; to Steve Murray and everyone at the Alabama Department of Archives and History; to the staff at the Georgia State University Pullen Library, Emory University Woodruff Library, and Auburn University Draughon Library; to all in the GSU and Auburn history departments; to LG, who commented on the manuscript and on life; to everyone who shared their stories with me, especially Solomon Seay and Brian Landsberg; to my wife and family; and to my friends, especially those who reminded me to always look down. I regret that Sol Seay did not live to see the book's publication. I hope it partly fulfills his desire to write a history of school desegregation in Alabama.

MAP 1. Counties, Major Cities, and Regions

The Politics of White Rights

Introduction

Eighty-one-year-old attorney Solomon Seay Jr. sat at his dining room table in February 2012, reflecting on the triumphs and failures of a lifetime of civil rights litigation. One of a very small group of black lawyers in Alabama in the 1950s and 1960s, Seay had helped dismantle Jim Crow segregation. He was the son of a prominent civil rights activist and minister and had been naturally drawn to the fight for racial justice. He had avoided his father's path to the pulpit, though, and his father's commitment to nonviolent protest and civil disobedience, or direct action, the hallmark of what has been called the classical phase of the civil rights movement. Although he and others operated in more than one milieu, as a young attorney Seay gravitated away from the streets and toward the courtroom. He would devote his life to fighting the system from within.

Seay left his native Montgomery for law school at Howard University in 1952. Drafted into the army just a year into his studies, he served in Korea for two years. He finished his degree upon being discharged and returned to his hometown in 1957. There he joined the practice of attorney Fred Gray, who had made a name for himself defending Rosa Parks and arguing a successful civil suit against the city during the 1955 bus boycott precipitated by her arrest. In the early 1960s, Gray partnered with the Legal Defense and Education Fund of the National Association for the Advancement of Colored People in an effort to finally end segregation in the state's public schools. It had been nearly a decade since the U.S. Supreme Court's 1954 *Brown v. Board of Education* decision, and not a single black child had attended school with a white child in Alabama. Not only would it take Gray and Seay another decade in federal courts to even begin to tear down that wall, in the winter of 2012 Sol Seay was still litigating school desegregation cases.[1]

A slim but imposing figure with a razor-sharp mind and serious demeanor, Seay sat that afternoon looking pensively at a stack of file boxes in the corner of the room, by his desk and computer. He wore a black-and-white Mickey Mouse T-shirt, part of an extensive collection begun when a racist school superintendent dismissively referred to Seay as "that Mickey Mouse lawyer from Montgomery," an epithet Seay chose to embrace. As he conjured up a description of the man who had attempted to belittle him with it, Seay's thoughts drifted toward the 1990s, long after the breakthroughs of the 1960s and 1970s that had seen most southern school systems desegregated in tokenized fashion, with a few black students in white schools. In 1995 Seay's health had temporarily failed him. He had been representing thirty sets of plaintiffs in cases that had been splintered from Alabama's landmark statewide school desegregation case, *Lee v. Macon County Board of Education*. "For health reasons, I couldn't carry that load," he allowed, without a hint of regret in his deliberate and raspy baritone. "But I kept one case," he added quickly, as he looked back over to the files by his desk. "I kept Randolph County."[2]

Seay had obtained what he described as "the very best public school desegregation plan that [he] had gotten in any system," a plan that "touched on every facet of education in a public school system," including, for example, the hiring and firing of faculty, administration, and staff; extracurricular activities; and student discipline. He had taken an added interest in the case in 1994 due to the actions of a part-time hog farmer and longtime high school principal named Hulond Humphries, the quintessential practitioner of a crass form of racism and segregationist resistance with which Seay was all too familiar.[3]

Randolph County lies along the Georgia border in northeastern Alabama. Like most counties with a solid white majority, when schools were desegregated, it had not seen whites abandon the public school system for private schools and other public systems with fewer blacks, a process known as white flight. There were exclusively white private schools established to avoid desegregation, now called segregation academies, but Randolph's public school system was integrated and in compliance with court orders in 1995. That February, Humphries was addressing Randolph County High School students at an assembly in Wedowee, Alabama, when he decided to broach a subject that had been deeply troubling him: interracial dating. Twenty years of integrated education had apparently taught some students that what segregationists called "miscegenation"—intimate relationships between blacks and whites, particularly white women and black men—would not lead to the "mongrelization" of the white race and the destruction of Western civilization after all. Interracial couples had become increasingly common.[4]

Humphries considered this to be an abomination to God rather than a sign of improving race relations. He asked the students how many of them planned on taking a date of the opposite race to the upcoming prom. When a substantial number raised their hands, he threatened to cancel it. Junior class president ReVonda Bowen, the child of a racially mixed marriage of eighteen years, boldly stood to provide a blunt and forceful challenge to Humphries's dichotomous understanding of race. Bowen asked, "Who should I bring?" Humphries was undeterred. He told her that this was a perfect illustration of the problem. Her parents, he believed, had "made a mistake" in conceiving her, and he was not going to see any more mistakes made on his watch. He basked proudly in his parry while Bowen sat down and began to cry.[5]

The calls started coming in the next day. Humphries tried to backtrack. He announced that the prom would not be canceled. He claimed that his concern was simply that interracial dating would ultimately lead to violence. But it was too late. Seay filed a motion for further relief in the county's ongoing desegregation case, and Bowen filed a civil suit of her own. The litigation subsequently revealed that Humphries's remark at the assembly was but a taste of a much larger stew. For years he had been calling students into his office to badger them about their interracial relationships, and he had frequently told white girls that white boys would no longer "have them" after they had been with a black boy.[6]

National media attention fell upon Wedowee. White parents organized motorcades in support of Humphries, and black parents organized a boycott of the school system and set up "freedom schools" in local black churches. Bowen received death threats, prompting the FBI to put a guard at her home. The prom was held, though many attended a "protest prom" instead. That summer someone burned down Randolph County High. The school board eventually opted to settle Bowen's civil suit, agreeing to pay $25,000 toward her college education. Seay convinced the court to amend the county's 1970 court-sanctioned desegregation plan, making it the best he had ever obtained.[7]

Seay, the Civil Rights Division of the U.S. Justice Department, and the school board worked out an agreement whereby Humphries was reassigned to an administrative position and barred from school grounds, and Wedowee receded from the national consciousness. Seay stayed on the case for the next eighteen years. After one hearing, he saw Humphries as he was walking out of a restroom, Humphries offered his hand, and Seay reciprocated. As Seay later recalled, Humphries then said, "Well, Seay, I'll be seeing you," and Seay had had no idea what he meant. Seay bemoaned, "The next time around, son of a bitch ran for superintendent and got elected. And that kept me in the lawsuit."[8]

The events in Wedowee in 1995 powerfully illustrated the endurance of racial prejudice. But it was easy to dismiss Hulond Humphries and his kind as caricatures from a bygone era, unfortunate exceptions in a South that had come of age racially and in which out-and-out racism was no longer acceptable, at least publicly. Americans outside the South looked with disdain on a region that seemed to continue to embarrass itself. But white southerners bristled at that judgment. Most did not consider themselves racists. The civil rights era had run its course successfully, they figured; southern whites had repudiated de jure segregation, or segregation by law; blacks had earned their right to vote; and that disreputable period had rightfully drawn to a close. The way most southerners reckoned it, the South was more racially progressive than the rest of the country, because it had been forced to look its problems in the face. They got it partly right.

Racism and white privilege were problems nationwide. Not only did whites from Boston to Los Angeles harbor racist animosity, but also government policies at every level continued to uphold a social, political, and economic order that served the interests of whites throughout the country more readily than blacks. The bulwarks of that order had always been subtle in regions outside the South, hidden, unlike the "Whites Only" and "Colored" signs. Historians have since shone light on these foundations and determined that the South has not been the exception in a story of otherwise steadily advancing American equality. Certainly the openness of Jim Crow was unusual. But by the 1990s Jim Crow was dead, and the pillars of white privilege in the South were becoming much harder to see. Careless racists like Hulond Humphries had become lingering manifestations of a less effective style. A new strategy had been tested, matured, and refined. It was an ethos and a philosophy of power, and it produced results designed to withstand the scrutiny of the law. At the very moment Humphries was bringing shame upon Randolph County, its followers were being challenged in court, with much less attention.[9]

The testing grounds were Alabama's institutions of higher education, which had been desegregated by court order in the 1960s. In 1969 a federal court had given the state the authority to build satellite campuses of its two flagship, predominantly white universities—Auburn University and the University of Alabama—in the cities of Montgomery and Huntsville, respectively. These were intended to serve as local alternatives for white students who might otherwise have chosen to attend either of the state's two public, historically black universities—Alabama State and Alabama A&M—had those schools been given the proper resources. Each of the state's public universities, then, remained nearly all-white or nearly all-black in 1981, when state representative

Joe Knight filed a suit in federal court alleging that the state was still operating a discriminatory higher education system.[10]

Knight v. Alabama moved forward at an excruciatingly slow pace, even by the abysmal standards of school desegregation litigation. Fred Gray and Sol Seay represented Alabama State University. The trial court did not issue a ruling until 1991, when U.S. district judge Harold Murphy determined that the state was obligated to eliminate certain "vestiges of segregation" in higher education. A panel of the Eleventh Circuit Court of Appeals partially reversed Murphy, resulting in a new trial, which culminated in 1995. The court then fashioned a remedial decree similar to the one adopted in the *Lee v. Macon* case nearly thirty years before. Murphy ordered the state to increase black access to predominantly white colleges and to encourage white attendance at historically black ones, using specific, enumerated steps, the implementation of which the trial court would supervise over a ten-year period.[11]

Just before those ten years elapsed, the plaintiffs in *Knight* filed a motion for further relief, which took the case in a new direction. They contended that the chronic underfunding of elementary and secondary schools had prevented the state from fulfilling its obligations under the remedial decree. They argued that the state had been "shielding the property of whites from being taxed to support the education of blacks," thereby "denying black citizens equal access to attend and to complete higher education." The plaintiffs sought an injunction against the enforcement of two amendments to the state's still-operative 1901 constitution known as the "Lid Bill" amendments.[12]

Historians testifying for the *Knight* plaintiffs linked an antipathy toward property taxation to both the 1901 constitution and its 1875 predecessor. Each constitution had been adopted during what white southerners called "Redemption," when white Democrats supplanted the Republican Reconstruction governments that had come to power after the Civil War. Each was intended to entrench white supremacy, especially by ensuring that no white tax dollars would be used for the advancement of former slaves and their progeny. By the 1970s, this particular element of white privilege was in serious jeopardy. With black voting increasing and white flight from public schools becoming total in some areas, whites feared that black elected officials might raise property taxes as a way of funding all-black public school systems. The first Lid Bill, adopted in 1972, thus limited the rates at which certain types of land could be assessed, and it placed absolute caps, or lids, on the amount of tax revenue that could be raised from any property. A second Lid Bill lowered the assessment rates and the caps in 1978. The result was that Alabama in the late 1990s had the lowest per capita property tax revenues of any state in the Union, and it wasn't close.

The *Knight* plaintiffs argued that the effect on revenue-starved black school systems across the state was "crippling."[13]

The state's defense, and its adoption of the Lid Bills in the first place, represented the maturation of what historians have described as a supposedly, though never actually, color-blind politics. The state's attorneys maintained that legislators' opposition to property taxation had nothing to do with race. Joe Knight and Sol Seay understood that it had everything to do with race and certainly was not "color-blind." Historians who have used this term have meant to underscore the superficial race-neutrality of a new segregationist strategy and to expose a pervasive and false sense of racial innocence in white, middle-class America. Using "color-blind" in this way, though, has been potentially misleading, particularly in discussions outside of the historiography. This new politics—intentionally devoid of linguistic racial markers but wholly intended to protect white privilege and white rights—was what we might call color-masked. Unmasking the laws that it produced would be difficult, legally at least, because segregationists had had decades to develop an effective nonracial veneer.[14]

In a 2004 ruling, Judge Murphy agreed in principle with the plaintiffs—the Lid Bills were designed to protect the money of white landowners as public education became increasingly black due to white flight. Heavily citing the expert historians, Murphy described the state's property tax system as a "vestige of discrimination" that was "traceable to, rooted in, and [had its] antecedents in an original segregative, discriminatory policy." The Lid Bills ensured that rural land, almost all of it owned by whites, would always be assessed at "a mere fraction of the property's value," which guaranteed that "no level of millage rates [would] produce minimally adequate property taxes." Tax revenue generated by that land averaged less than one dollar per acre and accounted for only 2 percent of property tax revenue in the state. Murphy acknowledged that the effect on poor, black school systems in these rural areas was indeed crippling.[15]

However, Murphy did not grant the injunction. He argued that the laws themselves were not responsible for segregation, and that the plaintiffs had not demonstrated that they were preventing the state from carrying out its responsibilities as laid out in the 1995 *Knight* decree. They had not proven that the property tax system was preventing poor, black students from attending college. Therefore, Murphy insisted, the *Knight* litigation was not the venue for a challenge to that system. The plaintiffs appealed, but the Eleventh Circuit upheld the decision. And the Supreme Court declined to hear the case. The Lid Bills had done what they were designed to do: withstand a legal test, protect white tax dollars, and protect white rights.[16]

This book is an attempt to explain how characters like Hulond Humphries were marginalized, and how laws like the Lid Bill amendments became the focus of the segregationist fight—or how segregationists learned to tailor what has been called massive resistance to the growing body of desegregation law and the demands of the courts. It is the story of the activist-litigants and attorneys and civil rights organizers and students who struggled to force Alabama to comply with the *Brown v. Board of Education* decision, and it is the story of the politicians, and the fearful white constituents they courted, who doggedly resisted those efforts.

Historians in recent years have broadened their understanding of the civil rights narrative beyond the classical phase of the 1950s and 1960s. One has described a "long backlash" to civil rights, and it is through that lens that we need to examine white resistance to school desegregation litigation. Not only did the roots of so-called massive resistance reach back well before *Brown*, but also the defense strategy crafted by segregationists in the 1950s and 1960s had critical ramifications for the 1970s, 1980s, 1990s, and 2000s. Massive resistance never died; it simply adapted, so using that phrase to characterize only a period of reckless and ultimately self-defeating defiance has had the effect of obscuring the potency of the resistance that followed the adaptation.[17]

Whites massively resisted black advancement from the moment of emancipation. They adapted that resistance to meet challenges presented during the New Deal era and after World War II. Then the *Brown* decision unleashed a decade of rabid attempts to keep any form of desegregation at bay. Historians have recently demonstrated that it was not just *Brown* that fueled this particular phase, but rather the implementation campaign undertaken by the NAACP at the regional and local level. Zeroing in on that campaign and the white reaction to it allows us to see beyond the more bombastic examples of resistance and reveals the beginnings of a crucial shift in the political and legal approach to preparing the segregationist defense.[18]

Nowhere was the transformation more profound and the resistance more obdurate than in Alabama. By the time violent resistance reached its crescendo with the 1963 bombing of Birmingham's Sixteenth Street Baptist Church, most segregationists had begrudgingly and sometimes disgustedly accepted the reality of token school desegregation as the "law of the land." They had espoused a politics of law and order, which was critical to the development of a politics of white rights. "Law and order" has long been recognized as coded political language meant to arouse fears of urban black violence, especially in the 1970s. But it has been a malleable phrase. In the late 1950s and early 1960s, a commitment to law and order meant admitting that massive resistance to desegregation, as such, had failed; that violent resistance was counterproductive and ought to be abandoned; that outright defiance of federal courts was no longer feasible; and that some degree of tokenism was unfortunately inevitable. Crucially, very few whites ever accepted that segregation was morally repugnant and *ought* to be abandoned. "Law and order" became the color-masked creed that allowed resistance to integration to be channeled into more subtle forms.[19]

By the 1970s, whites who espoused a politics of law and order had made what historians now call "strategic accommodations" and had "rearticulated" their resistance. A political movement coalesced around the need to protect *white* rights, especially to freedom of choice and freedom of association. This included the right to avoid attending integrated schools and eventually to avoid funding them too. White flight was an obvious manifestation of this new politics, but even as affluent white suburbs swelled and segregation academies proliferated, lawmakers were at work, having learned from their mistakes. Resistance to dismantling segregation was always about protecting white privilege—especially white political power and white wealth. The Lid Bills were a law-and-order solution designed to meet the threat to these. By placing them in the proper historical context, we can see that, in trying to prevent school desegregation, whites learned how to craft a more effective, color-masked brand of massive resistance, and they began to subscribe to a politics of racial innocence that continues today to deny the pervasiveness of state-sponsored white privilege in Alabama and beyond. At the heart of their ethos is the individualized equivalent of arguing that the Civil War had been fought over states' rights and not slavery. Their resistance, in other words, became all the more powerful by denying its roots.[20]

In a narrative of segregationist strategy, the demagoguery of longtime Alabama governor George Wallace is inescapable. Political historians of the conservative counterrevolution of the 1970s and 1980s have described Wallace as the godfather of a "southern strategy" in the Republican Party. They have demonstrated how politicians from Nixon to Reagan learned from Wallace how to appeal to whites with coded racial messages that were artificially color-blind. The dominant interpretation is now more nuanced. Historians have given credit to local southern whites for mastering the art of coded language before Wallace did. They have added layers of motivation to whites fleeing the Democratic Party, beyond just race. And they have taken the story of grassroots resistance national, from the suburbs of Detroit to the exurbs of Los Angeles, at the western edge of the Sunbelt stretching from the Deep South to the Pacific. By the 1970s, Wallace had learned to master the new color-masked style, as incubated by some of his own protégés, and to adhere to a more mature law-and-order ethos. This adaptation, alongside his defiant segregationist bona fides, allowed him to maintain his position in the vanguard of the defense of white rights.[21]

Scholars have also wrangled with *Brown*'s significance, and telling Alabama's story provides crucial insight here as well. Many have taken a favorable view of the decision and its legacy. Former Civil Rights Division director and legal scholar Brian Landsberg has recently used the *Lee v. Macon* case to demonstrate how the three branches of the federal government cooperated to enforce the *Brown* standard and, in a broader sense, overcome limitations placed upon the Supreme Court as an arbiter of social change. He and others have argued that the *Brown* decision not only eliminated de jure segregation in education but also was subsequently applied by the courts to other forms of segregation and was therefore a legal watershed. Some also point to its symbolic and inspirational value and argue that it was even a cultural watershed. These scholars would admit, though, that equal educational opportunity remains elusive over half a century after *Brown*, and that the irony of the decision is that it resulted in the effective integration of almost everything *but* schools.[22]

One long-influential thesis insists that the Supreme Court offers little hope for effecting social change, in general. Reflecting this, some scholars have taken a dim view of *Brown*, arguing that the decision has failed to live up to its promise. The most influential interpretation of the last fifteen years holds that the direct impact of *Brown* was minimal, incidental, and unintended and that the violent segregationist reaction against it was ultimately more consequential. In this analysis, *Brown* only mattered insofar as it inspired direct action protests, which in turn sparked a violent white backlash, which then accelerated the sort of reforms sought by the protest movement, as Americans recoiled at the violence broadcast from places like Birmingham and Selma. The Civil Rights Act of 1964 is said, then, to be the true catalyst for school desegregation. A number of scholars have problematized this thesis, and a closer look at *Brown*'s implementation in Alabama should do the same.[23]

Black activists placed a tremendous amount of faith in litigation at a time when direct action often required associated legal challenges to see results. When *Brown* was handed down and the NAACP began its implementation campaign, activists developed a framework for a sustained litigious assault upon segregated schools. Breakthrough came in 1963 because enough federal judges in the U.S. Fifth Judicial Circuit had become fed up with obstructionism and delay on the part of state and local officials. The Sixteenth Street Baptist Church bombing was a direct response to that breakthrough. The quickening development of law-and-order-style resistance to integration grew apace with the litigious assault against segregation, which itself culminated in the statewide desegregation order in *Lee v. Macon* in 1967. That order allowed a federal trial court to administer the restructuring of Alabama's entire public education system, with federal administrative bureaucracies like the Department of Health, Education, and Welfare (HEW) playing only a tertiary role. Alabama does not fit, then, the mold of litigious failure followed by the growth of direct action inspired by *Brown* and a violent response to those protests, followed by enforcement of the Civil Rights Act.[24]

More importantly, focusing on the violent segregationist reaction to direct action, and the national disgust with that violence, blinds us to the more durable and consequential law-and-order movement. White resistance in Alabama did not flare and fade with the protest campaigns of the 1950s and 1960s, as the backlash narrative suggests. The disciples of law and order simply rejected the counterproductive resistance perpetrated by a violent minority, in order to allow a nonviolent white majority to take command. This ultimately undermined the direct action movement and helped preserve white privilege by protecting white money, white property, and the white rights to freedom of choice and freedom of association. White flight substantially diluted *Brown*'s impact directly, and the Lid Bills and more recent legislation have frustrated the quest for social justice and equal educational opportunity more broadly.

Finally, much of the focus in the *Brown* debate has been on the justices of the Supreme Court. Some have suggested a more sustained look at the trial courts, where the battles played out on a daily basis, and where judges like Alabama's Frank Johnson shepherded desegregation law for years while the high court remained silent. These judges were not judicial activists or crusaders. They were motivated by a commitment to the role of courts as guarantors of constitutional rights for the disadvantaged. While Johnson and a few others became lightning rods for segregationist vitriol, they also sustained a faith in the ability of federal courts to act as agents of meaningful social change within the law. One of the premises underlying the backlash thesis is that judges generally reflect the society that produces them and are not, therefore, well placed to effect social change. But trial and appellate court judges who facilitated the implementation of *Brown* were often working against the will of white society. They led the way in holding officials accountable, and when the Supreme Court finally spoke again on desegregation implementation, it was following these judges and the plaintiffs and lawyers in whose favor they ruled—the practitioners of genuine color-blindness.[25]

The imperatives of litigation in those federal courts shaped the way that whites battled the civil rights movement. Scholars have demonstrated that the New Right was molded from much more than just racism and civil rights backlash. But they rightly appreciate that the effort to preserve white privilege was nonetheless at the heart of a maturing conservative movement in the late 1960s and early 1970s. By that time, the most prescient segregationists had a model for effective resistance. As school desegregation cases dragged on, whites perfected their defense by learning to satisfy the courts. A last stand against federal government threats to individual white rights then nurtured a libertarian defensiveness that would become the nexus to other political concerns. But segregationists first learned how to mask their massive resistance by combating black activist-litigants who were themselves seeking access to equal educational opportunity. What follows is the story of both efforts.

CHAPTER 1

"The NAACP Organized— Why Not You," 1954–1960

As the morning sun began to shine upon Montgomery, Alabama, on September 2, 1954, the sidewalks filled with people heading toward the State Capitol and other offices of the state government on Goat Hill. At the foot of the hill were the banks of the meandering Alabama River, the thoroughfare that had made the city suitable for settlement and fostered its development as a cotton port before the Civil War. Gone, of course, were the steamboats, cotton bales, and horse-drawn wagons of those days. But even the cars and busses that ferried people to their Thursday morning affairs in 1954 seemed to abide by a time-honored code of sauntering. Little moved quickly in the self-proclaimed Cradle of the Confederacy.[1]

The tranquility of early morning was, as ever, fleeting, and the city quickly sank into the kind of deep, suffocating heat that all southerners knew well but seemed to shrug off, one of those unfortunate facts of life to which one grew accustomed. That heat seemed to saturate everything. The air would become so thick with moisture that just walking down Commerce Street—the wide boulevard leading from the old slave market down to the river—would give one the sensation of swimming. Or drowning. That was life in the long, hot Alabama summer.[2]

As temperatures began to approach the ninety-five-degree heat of midday, a group of black schoolchildren and their parents gathered in the Abraham's Vineyard neighborhood on the south side of town, where they met with leaders from the local branch of the NAACP. They were apprehensive but hopeful. The branch had coordinated a direct action protest with the local Parent-Teacher Association, and the group was poised to become the first in state history to attempt to enroll black students in all-white public schools. Parents and children walked from their respective homes to meet at the Vineyard School, the neighborhood's all-black elementary school. From there they marched together to all-white Harrison Elementary School. The march itself was mercifully short—Harrison sat at the other end of the same block as Vineyard—but its origins were buried deep in Alabama's dark and tortured past, and its implications would be felt for decades.³

Harrison was a brand-new school. The twenty-classroom facility had been built to accommodate 650 white students from a rapidly growing neighborhood on the edge of town. As white Montgomery spread south, Harrison faced the middle-class sprawl to the north and invited students to begin the education that would transform them into the state's leaders of the future. Vineyard School faced south toward Abraham's Vineyard, a black working-class community on what had once been considered the outskirts of town. Recent renovations to the tiny schoolhouse revealed much about segregated education in Alabama. At the behest of the PTA, Montgomery's all-white school board had agreed to paint the dilapidated building, add a third classroom, and install running water and indoor toilets to replace outhouses. Even after that, Vineyard still lacked gas, electricity, and a lunchroom. If Harrison beckoned white students to move up and out, Vineyard loomed over its namesake and reminded black students that they were meant to stay put.⁴

Similarly, the principal at Harrison reminded the Vineyard students and parents of their place when they arrived that September day. After the white students had all registered and gone home, he invited the party, led by the NAACP's E. D. Nixon and Horace Bell, into his office. There he politely told them that they could not enroll the children at Harrison: they lived outside of the attendance zone. And this was true, after all. The school board had recently drawn up gerrymandered attendance zones to reflect residential segregation patterns. Segregated education had been constitutionally mandated in Alabama since 1901, so this had not been necessary in the past. Local officials had decided to shield themselves from any potential impact from what were then being called the "school segregation cases" before the U.S. Supreme Court.⁵

Few whites in Alabama believed that the *Brown v. Board of Education* decision would have any meaningful impact there. The court had declared legally mandated segregation in education unconstitutional, but this ruling was the "law of the case," most reasoned, not the "law of the land." It therefore only applied to the several school districts directly involved in the litigation, not the entire South. The NAACP disagreed, so there at Harrison Elementary that day sat Nixon, Bell, and a handful of families waiting to enroll. But local school officials understood, even then, that if Alabama law was threatened, they could draw lines around segregated neighborhoods and claim that the process had been color-blind.⁶

The Vineyard parents braced for angry reprisals from the city's segregationist whites. Everyone understood that challenging the status quo in Alabama had dire consequences. And they knew that breaking through the smothering shroud of white supremacy would require tearing the very fabric of southern society. Racial hierarchy was, from birth, woven so deeply into the consciousness of every southern child that unraveling it had long seemed impossible. For most whites, *Brown* was an alarming sign of the times that nonetheless could be contained. But for many blacks *Brown* was a tear in the seam that let in a faint enough glimmer of light to expose a way out. No one understood this better than Alabama's NAACP field secretary, W. C. Patton. After Harrison turned down admission of black children, Patton announced that the NAACP would not back down. Those who risked their lives to pay NAACP dues demanded as much. The attempted enrollment, he explained, was but the beginning of his organization's effort to force the implementation of *Brown* upon a recalcitrant South and a reluctant nation.[7]

"Operation Implementation" and the Citizens' Council Response

Five days after the Supreme Court handed down its decision in *Brown*, seventeen southern state NAACP presidents met in Atlanta to formulate a "program of action." All five cases decided under *Brown* were NAACP sponsored, and litigation was the forte of organization. Many assumed that the association would simply follow up by filing more cases. But when the NAACP national office announced what it called the "Atlanta Declaration," it indicated that it would first undertake a "community action program." Local branches would petition state governments and local school boards, asking them to comply with *Brown* and to present plans to desegregate. If those were rejected or ignored, then they would move forward with litigation. W. C. Patton carried the details of the plan to two hundred of the association's leaders at a meeting in Montgomery days later. Ruby Hurley, in charge of the Southeast Regional Office, began contacting local branches, encouraging action in order to quickly capitalize on what she called "our greatest victory."[8]

No one expected immediate success. *Brown* itself had taken too long. The goal was that the "the Negro [would be] Free in 1963." Nonetheless, Hurley and Patton acted with an assurance that victory was imminent. Hurley told branch leaders to work with their state conferences in getting petitions formulated and signed and in securing legal counsel to represent them in discussions with local school boards. She explained on a radio broadcast that she and others were "fully cognizant of [white] resistance." The efforts to "circumvent" the decision, Hurley predicted, "[would] be lost—the law is binding." Branch leaders ought to try to convince whites, she urged in a memo, to "resign themselves to the fact that state laws notwithstanding, segregation in public education is legally dead. When it will be buried is up to the people in our communities." It was the local NAACP's role to do the "real work" and to "hasten the day of the funeral."[9]

What was soon dubbed Operation Implementation slowly got rolling that fall. In Alabama, in addition to the Harrison Elementary enrollment attempt, groups of twenty to thirty parents signed petitions in the northeastern city of Anniston; the city of Fairfield, an industrial suburb of the state's largest city, Birmingham; and the small town of Brewton in Escambia County. The petitioners asked school boards to take "immediate steps" to end segregated education in accordance with *Brown*. While the boards publicly ignored the petitions, the behind-the-scenes strategy employed by school officials was both more sinister and more effective. Upon receiving the Brewton petition, for example, the board turned it over to the local newspaper, which then published the list of signatories. Twelve parents then recanted, and another three disavowed any association with the NAACP.[10]

Later that year, speaking to the NAACP's Southeast Regional Advisory Board, the association's director of branches, Gloster Current, declared that the organization would persist in its effort to force implementation, despite the beginnings of what appeared to be an economic reprisal campaign. Current told the state conference presidents, field secretaries, and other officers that the NAACP would "not be deterred" by those who would "frighten and intimidate the Negro leaders throughout the South." Ruby Hurley echoed those sentiments in announcing her region's annual conference of branches. "We will continue to work as we have in the past forty-six years," she vowed, "and ultimately, after the tumult and din has died, we will win." When around two hundred delegates converged on Atlanta for the conference, they declared their intention to ensure that *Brown* would become "a second Emancipation Proclamation."[11]

The organization of white resistance to the NAACP's implementation activities began to rapidly accelerate that fall. On November 29, 1954, twelve hundred whites gathered at a rally in the city of Selma, in the West Alabama Black Belt. They came to hear a delegation from neighboring Mississippi speak about what were being called Citizens' Councils. The Black Belt was the old plantation zone once renowned for its rich black soil and fine white cotton, grown almost exclusively by slaves before the Civil War. Like whites in the Mississippi Delta, where the Citizens' Councils were born, white people in the Alabama Black Belt were outnumbered by blacks, in some counties by as much as two to one. And they clung to political and economic power— to white privilege—more tightly than whites anywhere else in the country.

They had experience in stamping out any threats to their power structure during and before World War II. The Citizens' Councils would give them the organizational structure to systematically counter the newly victorious and empowered NAACP.[12]

Mississippi state representative J. S. Williams told the white citizens of Selma that the councils could do this much more effectively than the existing institution that claimed to maintain "law and order" and to protect white supremacy—the Ku Klux Klan. The Klan, Williams argued, was a crass, violent assemblage of lower-class hooligans who had a penchant for self-defeating forms of extralegal resistance. The Citizens' Councils were smarter. White people controlled the money in the South, Williams observed, and this was "an advantage" that the councils could "use in a fight to legally maintain complete segregation of the races." Any NAACP "agitators" who disagreed could expect to receive "the pressure." Williams clarified, "We intend to make it difficult, if not impossible, for any Negro who advocates desegregation to find and hold a job, get credit, or renew a mortgage." The entire purpose of the Citizens' Councils was to "give a direct answer" to the NAACP. "The NAACP's motto is 'The Negro shall be free by 1963.' And shall we accept that," he asked? The assembled answered with a resounding "No!"[13]

One week later, four hundred white men of nearby Marengo County gathered. This time the featured speaker was Alabama state senator Walter Givhan, a man destined to become perhaps the state's most ardent segregationist. He suggested that the United States was a "white man's country" threatened by NAACP "outsiders" and Communists who were hell-bent on destroying it. According to Givhan, Alabama's "negroes" were "good" and understood that southern whites were their "friends." But they had been poisoned, Givhan explained, by NAACP "trouble makers," who ultimately wanted to "open the bedroom doors of our white women to the Negro men." Race "mixing" in schools was just a first step toward "mixing" in the bedroom. And miscegenation would lead to the "mongrelization" of the white race. Givhan's brother also spoke. He surmised that rallying opposition to the NAACP's campaign would be simple. Just ask white men everywhere the question, "Would they like to see their daughter marry a nigger?" Walter Givhan then concluded by assuaging these deepest of fears. "The whole of the U.S. Army is not strong enough to force that upon us," he swore. Councils were soon organized there in Marengo and nearby Perry and Hale Counties.[14]

Two months later, in February 1955, the newly organized Dallas County Citizens' Council held its first regular meeting. Five hundred white men showed up to hear Mississippi's Robert Patterson, a plantation owner from Indianola, the founder of the first Citizens' Council, and the executive secretary of his state's association of councils. Patterson, by then accustomed to speaking to civic groups and large gatherings to grow the council movement, chided the men of Dallas County for being "complacent and apathetic." Patterson warned, "If 50,000,000 of us can't keep our race white, then we aren't fit to be white, and we won't be white very long." He elicited a roar from the crowd when he defiantly declared, "I have three little children, and they are either going to a white school, or they are not going to a school at all." Local Presbyterian minister George Cheek also spoke, assuring the men that segregation was ordained by God. "I'm not a Negro hater," he cautioned. "I believe they should be treated in a humane, just, and fair way, but I believe the Negro has his place." Cheek concluded, "I would turn over in my grave if I knew my little grandchildren should pollute the Caucasian race through intermarriage." The council closed the meeting with a resolve to meet regularly to discuss which blacks should "receive the pressure."[15]

The NAACP was busy organizing a second round of petitions to present to local school boards that spring and summer. Branches in Mobile, Gadsden, Butler County, Phenix City, and Macon County presented petitions that read, "The [*Brown v. Board of Education*] decision, to us, means that the time for delay, evasion, or procrastination is past. Whatever the difficulties in according our children their constitutional rights, it is clear that the school board must meet and seek a solution to that question in accordance with the law of the land." A few of the school boards ignored the petitions or dismissed them as "harangues by radical groups of either race or their representatives." The response of Mobile school officials was typical. The Mobile board announced that "the traditions of two centuries" could be "altered by degrees only" and that "any integration now" would be "impossible without a disruption of our school system to such an extent to substantially impair its efficiency for an indefinite period." By the end of the month, ten more NAACP branches had filed similar petitions.[16]

Black parents quickly began to recant. Nine of thirty parents in Bullock County who had signed asked the school board to strike their names from the petition and swore in affidavits that they had been "misinformed" as to its purpose. They claimed to have thought they were petitioning simply for "better roads" or "better schools," not for integration. In Selma five petitioners asked that their names be withdrawn, and two of the five disavowed any association with the NAACP. In Greenville six people requested retraction of their names and supposedly claimed to have "signed the petition without knowing what was in it." In one instance, a man reportedly claimed, "I informed the man who brought me the petition that I wanted my community improved and I surely did want a water line run to my place."[17]

In announcing an investigation into the issue, W. C. Patton defended the state's NAACP branches. The petitions were, as a matter of course, thoroughly explained to all who signed. The real reason for the repudiations was fear. In Selma, when news of their participation was published by the *Selma Times-Journal*, sixteen of the twenty-nine signatories were fired, and others suffered various other means of economic reprisal. Ethel Griffin was dismissed from her job as a maid but told by the woman who employed her that she could return if she withdrew her name. Interior decorator Ernest Doyle had his credit withdrawn and his debts called in by his white creditors. Local farmer Richard Winston was unable to secure his annual spring loan from the bank. Barber H. W. Shannon was evicted. All of the victims were members of the local NAACP. The situation was the same in the Black Belt's Butler and Bullock Counties and in Houston County in the southeastern Wiregrass region.[18]

The chairman of the Dallas County Citizens' Council, Alston Keith, the unofficial spokesman for all of Alabama's Councils, insisted that the firings in Selma had been "spontaneous." The council, he claimed, deserved neither "credit nor censure." Despite his initial disavowal, Keith ultimately could not resist taking the credit that he and his cohort deserved. "I don't believe," Keith mused, "there would have been unity of action that there was without the educational work of the Citizens' Council." He surmised that "probably all of [the petitioners] who had jobs were fired." To clear up any ambiguity, he added that those who had done the firing, withheld the credit, called in the debts, and kicked people out of their homes and businesses all "did just what we have been advocating right along."[19]

The NAACP was startled but unmoved. The Southeast Regional Advisory Board issued a report calling Operation Implementation the "number one objective of the NAACP in this region." Ruby Hurley sought to reassure local branches in an end-of-the-year assessment. "White citizens' councils and their counterparts" had been gaining strength, but the regional office was "investigating every case of intimidation" and "working out plans of action to protect [its] people and counter-attack" the councils. Hurley wrote, "Any thoughts that the Deep South would accept with grace and dignity the fact that the bonds of slavery were being loosened for and shaken off by its Negro citizens were dispelled completely before six months of 1955 had passed." She urged the branches to "keep the faith and continue to hold fast to our ideal of full freedom so that we can carry on with the fight until we win—and win we must."[20]

The council movement continued to grow. As the Montgomery bus boycott grabbed headlines in the spring of 1956, and as Autherine Lucy sought admission to the University of Alabama, the councils' numbers swelled beyond just the Black Belt. Leading Birmingham businessmen and attorneys began appearing at Citizens' Council rallies around the state. Sydney Smyer told a Selma rally, "If we are forced to accept the dictates of those who want to force integration upon us, it will destroy all the peace and tranquility we've enjoyed in the Southland." He concluded, "We must preserve the integrity of our race and the freedom that God has given us." Black Belt council pioneers were also coming north. Walter Givhan spoke to organizers in Birmingham and Tuscaloosa, telling newly minted members that "legal resistance" could bog down the NAACP's campaign for years. Givhan argued, "The Communists know that if they can mongrelize the Anglo-Saxon southern white, then they can destroy us." He importuned them, "We're going to keep these little white boys and these little white girls pure, and we're going to do it legally." Three weeks later, Givhan spoke at a council rally in South Alabama. "The law is on our side," he assured his listeners. "I don't think you will convict a man for white supremacy when he is within the law."[21]

The state soon boasted twenty-six Citizens' Councils, including one in every Black Belt county, and as many as forty thousand members, among them doctors, lawyers, city and county officials, judges, and state legislators. Leaders formed four regional councils and an Alabama Association of Citizens' Councils. For executive secretary they tapped Macon County's Sam Engelhardt, a Black Belt planter and state senator who claimed to have entered politics solely to keep poor black tenant farmers from "taking his property." Engelhardt made no secret of his views on race, once publicly haranguing, "Desegregating the schools will lead to rape! Damn niggers stink. They're unwashed. They have no morals; they're just animals. The nigger is depraved! Give him the opportunity to be near a white woman, and he goes berserk!" The conclusion: "The nigger isn't just a dark-skinned white man. He's a separate individual altogether." Such an impassioned belief in biological racism was not uncommon among Alabama's whites, even if most leaders were not so candid in their public remarks.[22]

Whether delivered by an Engelhardt or Givhan or by more measured leaders, the councils' core recruiting pitch remained the same: "The NAACP organized—Why not you?" Journalist David Halberstam, soon to win the Pulitzer Prize, went undercover into a small South Alabama town and observed the dynamics of council growth based on this rhetorical question, which he described in a piece for *Commentary* magazine.[23] The mayor of the town called an urgent meeting to determine a response to local "agitation." After tossing around possible solutions, like throwing the leader of the local NAACP into the river, they turned to a state legislator and local attorney named Reid Walles. Walles suggested, "What we need here is a Citizens' Council." The councils were "doing fine work" and had been effective in "forming boycotts and other pressures against niggers, nigger-lovers, and a few politicians that won't go along with us." He warned his audience to look five years down the road. "If your kids are playing and going to school with burr-headed niggers and the niggers are taking over the town and molesting your women, well, don't blame Reid Walles." If they wanted to avoid "white girls going off to dances with some big black buck and dancing to jungle music," then they ought to organize.[24]

A leaflet passed out to white miners in the industrial Birmingham suburb of Bessemer represented a more creative effort. The sheet purported to feature a speech made by a "Professor Roosevelt Williams of Howard University" to an NAACP meeting in Jackson, Mississippi. Williams had supposedly told those at the meeting, "The negro is the white man's superior." The NAACP ought to demand "the abolition of all state laws which forbid intermarriage of the different races ... the white woman is dissatisfied with the white man, and they along with us demand the right to win and love the negro man of their choice, so they can proudly tell the world he is my man, a man in every respect." It was an enunciation of the white man's greatest nightmare, and every word of it was fabricated by the Citizens' Council. It was later revealed that Roosevelt Williams did not exist, but the white miners of Jefferson County did not know that. The bottom of the pamphlet carried the message: "If you wish to help prevent this aim of NAACP contact Citizens' Council, P.O. Box 6221, Tarrant, Alabama."[25]

As the council movement continued to grow, the ranks began to include a wider variety of segregationists. The respectable old "Bourbon" leadership of the Black Belt councils, the pseudo-aristocrat types who traced their lineage to the scions of the antebellum South, soon found themselves having to marginalize more plebian and less restrained elements that did not fully embrace the concept of a lawful and orderly defense of segregation. The most influential leader of the latter cadre was a one-time filling station operator and would-be radio personality named Asa Carter. Carter was the president of the Birmingham Regional Council, which drew members mostly from the city's working-class suburbs. Carter was simultaneously affiliated with the Ku Klux Klan, and he and his Klan cronies were responsible for a number of violent acts, including attacks on the entertainer Nat King Cole, on stage at a concert in Birmingham, and Autherine Lucy, as she attempted to enroll at the University of Alabama.[26]

"Ace" Carter shared with Sam Engelhardt and others deep fears of "mongrelization, degradation, atheism, and communistic dictatorship." But he accused the council leadership of engaging in "compromise," "evasion," and "political chicanery." He broke away from Engelhardt's state organization and formed his own Alabama Citizens' Council. Carter's group quickly came under fire for its violence and anti-Semitism. Engelhardt's Citizens' Councils of Alabama issued a statement calling Carter a "grassroots, demagogic rabble rouser," a "prisoner of hate," and a "spreader of poison for [his] own political gain." His influence in organization and agitation remained, for a time, confined to the Birmingham area, and his extremist wing of the council movement was gradually marginalized.[27]

In February 1956, Engelhardt's organization made a public showing of its newfound strength, at a rally in Montgomery's agricultural coliseum. An estimated twelve thousand "shouting, cheering, flag-waving" segregationists from all walks of life filled the arena with repeated rebel yells, as a band played the old southern anthem "Dixie" over and over. They gathered to hear what reporters afterward described as "blood curdling . . . tirades" against the NAACP. They wanted to wrest control of events from the Klan, whose violence was bad for the city's image, and Governor Jim Folsom, whom many considered hopelessly weak on racial matters and unfit to lead a segregationist retaliation. The immediate impetus for what was billed as the largest segregationist rally of the century was the violence unleashed by the Montgomery bus boycott, but the featured speaker, Mississippi's U.S. senator James Eastland, knew what would strike the loudest chord. The "good people of Alabama," he knew, did "not intend for the NAACP to run [their] schools" for them. They needed to join with the councils and strengthen the cause of lawful resistance.[28]

The following day, a group of black and white liberals gathered at the state's black teachers' college, Alabama State, for what they called a symposium on "resolving community conflicts" using biracial committees. They were members of the Alabama Council on Human Relations (ACHR), an affiliate of the Southern Regional Council. Noted activist and longtime ACHR member Virginia Durr reflected that the ACHR was "composed of extremely conservative liberal people." They were "a very fine group of middle class people who did believe in all the right things." The black members were educators and attorneys; the whites were often clergy from the Episcopal or Methodist churches. They sought to provide a counterweight to segregationist reactionaries. As one member described it, joining the ACHR was an opportunity to demonstrate that "white people . . . could sit down to a table, for God's sake, with somebody of the opposite color and eat . . . without any obvious, immediate ill-effects."[29]

The ACHR's gathering of three hundred in the immediate wake of the councils' massive rally underscored the futility of biracial liberalism in the face of the surging campaign of "lawful" reprisal. The ACHR played a noted role in resolving conflicts around the state throughout the 1950s and 1960s. But its milquetoast approach spoke neither to more motivated black activists in the movement nor to the thousands of average white supremacists, who were unmoved by the ACHR's mission to promote "greater unity in ... racial development" and to reduce "race tension." By championing law and order, the Citizens' Councils won over many whites who might otherwise have been repulsed enough by the violence of the Klan to consider biracial cooperation.[30]

Two months after the Montgomery rally, council members from across the state gathered in Birmingham, this time to hear Georgia white supremacist Charles Bloch, of Macon. Speaking of the Klan assault on Nat King Cole orchestrated by Ace Carter a week prior, Bloch asserted that such "incidents" did "nothing to help the South in trying to solve [its] problems." They only gave "extremists all over the nation" more "excuses for agitation." Bloch was Jewish, so it was perhaps no surprise to hear him single out the anti-Semitic Ace Carter for reproach. But as a legal scholar dedicated to showcasing the "respectability" of the new segregationist movement, Bloch also understood the damage that extralegal violence could do to the cause of white supremacy. He reminded the council members that they must use "all *lawful* means to bring about a reversal" of the unconstitutional *Brown* decision and that they must "prevent the use of force in their implementation" of that reversal. This was the only way to eliminate "festering sores on the body of the nation such as the NAACP," which feared "lawful" and "counter-attacking, opposing organizations" like the Citizens' Council most of all. Someone passed out membership cards which read, "I _____ do hereby pledge" to "REGISTER and VOTE for officials supporting segregation" and to "help defeat the NAACP."[31]

"Pupil Placement" and the Legislative Response

The Alabama state legislature had been readying the state's defense of segregated education since before *Brown* was decided. Legislators understood that continually passing segregation laws would tie up the NAACP in a never-ending litigious battle. And as race became the driving force in politics, they knew they could score points with constituents by proposing as many "nigger bills"—as they would soon come to be known in the legislative chambers—as possible. As the Supreme Court was preparing to hear the *Brown* cases in the late summer of 1953, the legislature passed a resolution decrying a potentially adverse ruling. The legislators argued, "The employment, seniority and tenure of teachers, the location and design of schools, the number and routing of school busses, the content and arrangement of the curriculum in every school, the standards of instruction, and practically every other aspect of the educational system of the state are based upon the present [racial] separation and would have to be drastically revised if the principal of separation should be invalidated." The white supremacist 1901 state constitution plainly provided for this "separation," reading, "Separate schools shall be provided for white and colored children, and no child of either race shall be permitted to attend a school for the other race."[32]

When *Brown* came down, some state officials, including the State Board of Education, insisted it was simply the "law of the case" and did not apply to Alabama, as the state was neither a party in the lawsuit nor had its own constitution been challenged. Incoming state superintendent of education Austin Meadows, a died-in-the-wool segregationist, revealed the insecurity of this position when he pledged to "find a *legal* way to maintain segregation in schools." Fearing a more direct legal challenge, Sam Engelhardt proposed removing the segregation language from the constitution and even suggested eliminating compulsory school attendance altogether and establishing private schools.[33]

Engelhardt's proposals seemed drastic at the time, but many in the legislature understood that something had to be done. A committee was tasked with proposing some course of legislative action. Chairing it would be state senator Albert Boutwell, a staunchly conservative attorney from Birmingham. He was the biggest of the so-called Big Mules—the elite industrialists and businessmen of the Birmingham area and the politicians who represented them. Boutwell also served on the Interim Committee, a collection of civic-minded segregationists who had begun to articulate the businessmen's defense of segregation: integration was a threat to "law and order" since it would generate violence and civil unrest, and it was therefore bad for the city's image and bad for business. The Interim Committee was philosophically like the Citizens' Council. Indeed, Boutwell had attended early council rallies alongside attorney Sydney Smyer to gather information and offer Birmingham's support.[34]

In one sense, Boutwell and Sam Engelhardt were unlikely bedfellows. Engelhardt's Bourbon planters benefited from a disproportionate share of the state's legislative power. Urban and suburban growth without legislative reapportionment had left Big Mules like Boutwell at a disadvantage. Reapportionment would undoubtedly cause the Black Belt bloc to lose seats to metropolitan areas. But the Big Mules and the Bourbon planters knew they could count on each other when it came to defending segregation, as both had much to lose if it were to fall. Thus did Boutwell and Engelhardt find themselves working together closely on what was being called the Boutwell Committee. When the committee released its report in October 1954, it revealed incorporation of much of what Engelhardt had proposed and the basic tenets of the Big Mule businessman's rationale.[35]

The committee argued that "forced integration" would create an "intolerable situation" and would lead to "violence, disorder, and tension" and economic reprisal too. "White employers," the report read, "would be strongly induced to withhold employment from Negro parents who would take advantage of the intended compulsion, leases would likewise be terminated, and trade and commercial relations, now in satisfactory progress, would be affected." The committee also concluded that "Negro children would be harmed, and warped by belligerent resentment of their forced acceptance, by innumerable daily incidents emphasizing it, and by the sharp disclosure of a generally lower scholastic aptitude."[36]

The committee recommended adopting an omnibus constitutional amendment eliminating the mandate for segregated education and adding these words: "Nothing in the constitution shall be construed as creating or recognizing any right to education or training at public expense, nor as limiting the authority or duty of the legislature to require or impose conditions or procedures deemed necessary to the preservation of peace and order." Boutwell had rejected statewide school closure, chiefly because that might also be bad for industrial recruitment. The new amendment would instead allow local officials to close schools threatened with desegregation and provide parents with grants-in-aid to send their children to private schools "provided by their own race."[37]

Boutwell and Engelhardt pleaded with the lame duck governor, Gordon Persons, to call a special session of the legislature to consider the proposal, but Persons refused. The issue thus fell into the lap of incoming governor Jim Folsom in January 1955. The six-foot-eight, 275-pound former insurance salesman known as "Big Jim" had served as governor once already, prior to Persons. His folksy style and appeals were widely popular, and he probably would have defeated Persons in 1950 had state law not prevented him from serving consecutive terms as governor. The "little man's big friend" from the Wiregrass would have preferred to avoid the issue of segregation. He talked of uniting the state's working-class whites, politically at least, with their "colored brothers." He publicly scoffed at the Citizens' Council. He even reached out to the Council on Human Relations at one point. His administration's more or less open approach to corruption and his own fondness for alcohol would quickly cause him trouble. But it was his refusal to take a firm stand on segregation that bothered lawmakers the most.[38]

During the winter and spring of 1955, Folsom called three special sessions of the state legislature. He wanted a bond issue for a farm-to-market road program and a legislative reapportionment bill. Legislators used the sessions to instead launch a barrage of resolutions condemning *Brown* and lauding the "great economic, cultural and social benefits" of segregation. Meanwhile, the U.S. Supreme Court handed down its long-awaited implementation decree, which came to be known as *Brown II*. In order to present a unified front, Chief

Justice Earl Warren had compromised. The unanimous court shot down the "law of the case" interpretation and made clear that *Brown* applied to the entire South, but it essentially remanded the issue to the region's federal trial courts for further proceedings. And in lieu of concrete details and instructions—to school districts or the lower courts—the justices provided ambiguous language like "prompt and reasonable start," "good faith," and, most infamously, "all deliberate speed."[39]

Warren and the other justices believed that, if nothing else, *Brown II* would give the white South time to absorb the impact of the decision. It might have had the effect of encouraging moderates like Folsom to take the initiative away from more radical segregationists, but that was not to be. Legislators in Alabama understood the decision to be an affirmation that no actual desegregation would ever take place in their state, provided they took the necessary measures to safeguard themselves. Walter Givhan called it "a decided victory for the South" and a recognition that "integration wasn't feasible and never would have worked, and that the southern people under no condition would have stood for it." Sam Engelhardt was assured that "no brick [would] ever be removed from [the state's] segregation walls." The two men then set about ensuring that some sort of protective legislation passed in the 1955 regular session.[40]

In lieu of the official Boutwell Committee plan, the legislature approved an alternative version, cosponsored by Engelhardt and Boutwell. Attorneys working with the Boutwell Committee had drafted the bill with the assistance of a special committee on constitutional law appointed by the president of the state bar, segregationist state circuit judge Walter Jones. The language was entirely color masked, insofar as it avoided words like "race," in order to make it more legally defensible. Lawmakers contended that "any general or arbitrary reallocation of pupils" based on any one "rigid rule" would be "disruptive." So this new law would provide a new "procedure for the analysis of the qualification, motivations, aptitudes, and characteristics of . . . pupils for the purpose of placement" in schools. This was essential in order "to assure the maintenance of [the] order and good will" necessary to maintain a public education system.[41]

What became known as the Pupil Placement Law gave local school boards new tools with which to thwart desegregation. In determining "placements," school officials would be able to consider practical matters, like available classroom space, transportation, and students' distance from a particular school. More tellingly, boards could also consider "the adequacy of the pupil's academic preparation," one's "scholastic aptitude and relative intelligence," and one's "psychological qualification." A board could even consider pupils' "interests," their "home environment," and their "morals, conduct, health, and personal standards." Finally, officials could contemplate whether or not a pupil's enrollment in a particular school would negatively affect "established or proposed academic programs" and whether it might create the "possibility or threat of friction or disorder" or "breaches of the peace or ill will or economic retaliation within the community."[42]

The placement law was supposedly intended to guarantee that "the less advanced pupil" would not be "penalized by being placed in the class with pupils who [were] more advanced or capable of learning at a more rapid rate," while also ensuring that "exceptionally bright and able pupils" would not be "held back to a level below their ability to learn." No one doubted what "less advanced pupil" and "exceptionally bright and able pupils" really meant. And if black students seeking transfer to white schools had somehow risen above the socioeconomic disadvantages and structural inequality engendered by the very segregation they were trying to overcome and passed aptitude tests, then local boards could take their pick from the remaining criteria: perhaps the student could be shown to be of impeachable health, morals, or standards. Maybe they had a disruptive "home environment," or maybe they simply lived closer to a black school. Officials could certainly rest assured that any placement of a black child in a white school would result in "friction, disorder, breaches of the peace, ill will, and economic retaliation within the community."[43]

Birmingham's African American daily newspaper, the *World*, called the plan "legally worthless and morally defective." Folsom called it redundant and unnecessary. Most white political observers applauded the law, assuming it was a legally foolproof defense of the status quo. Over the course of the spring and summer, other southern states began passing pupil placement laws of their own. In addition to giving school boards broad authority for assignment, the laws forced black students seeking transfer to navigate a byzantine application and appeals process designed to either intimidate or frustrate them with technicalities. And they made for a more scattered target for the NAACP, by ostensibly removing legal liability from the state and handing it to local officials. One legal scholar observed, "Pupil placement laws are by far the best device segregationists have yet discovered to keep Negroes out of federal courts and to make civil rights litigation expensive, time-consuming, and frustrating. And it can all be done with the veneer of legality."[44]

State superintendent of education Austin Meadows was convinced that more was needed. Before the end of the legislative session that spring of 1955, Meadows proposed a $150-million bond issue to fund a school equalization program. He believed that "separate but [actually] equal" might satisfy both activist blacks and the courts. The governor supported the proposal, arguing that blacks deserved more than "shotgun shacks" and that the efforts of Boutwell and Engelhardt were simply a lot of "noise . . . guided by prejudice and bigotry." Folsom also endorsed Meadows's call for a $36-million increase in overall school expenditures. The legislature agreed to present the issues to the people of Alabama via a referendum, to be held that December.[45]

That summer a three-judge appellate panel issued a ruling in one of the remanded *Brown* cases that assured lawmakers in Alabama that they were on the right path. North Carolina judge John Parker wrote for the court in *Briggs v. Elliot*, arguing that the Supreme Court had not, in *Brown II*, "decided that the states must mix persons of different races in the schools or must require them to attend schools or must deprive them of the right of choosing the schools they attend." All the court had determined, according to Parker, was that "the Constitution . . . does not require integration. It merely forbids discrimination." Parker reiterated, the Constitution did not "forbid such segregation as occurs as the result of voluntary action." It simply forbade "the use of governmental power to enforce segregation." This "*Briggs* dictum," as it would later be called, would be the preferred judicial interpretation of *Brown* for years to come. It immediately assured state legislatures that pupil placement laws, and any such laws that avoided outright defiance of *Brown*, stood a very good chance of passing legal muster.[46]

The people of Alabama rejected Meadows's equalization plan in December, in what was widely interpreted as a rejection of Folsom's pragmatism and a well-founded vote of confidence in the placement law. When the NAACP and local activist-litigants began to challenge such laws, some of the more egregious ones were struck down, but the carefully crafted were upheld. Judge Parker himself wrote the order upholding North Carolina's placement law, which was similar to Alabama's. Parker wrote, "Somebody must enroll the pupils in the schools. They cannot enroll themselves; and we can think of no one better qualified to undertake the task than the officials of the schools and the school boards."[47]

Folsom called the legislature into its fourth special session the following month in an effort to secure a convention to rewrite the state's 1901 constitution. He instead got what the *Atlanta Journal* called "the loudest Rebel cry from Virginia to Mississippi." Legislators used the session to introduce a nullification, or "interposition," resolution. The idea of nullification had been resurrected from its antebellum grave by Virginia's U.S. senator Harry Byrd and the influential Richmond newspaper editor James Kilpatrick. It was Byrd and Kilpatrick who first called for "massive resistance" to *Brown*. Along with Charles Bloch, Kilpatrick led the way in offering a defense of segregation apart from the plainly racist appeals that had theretofore dominated the discourse. Kilpatrick suggested that, in order to stop "encroachments by the federal judiciary upon the reserved powers of the states," state governments could "interpose" their authority between their citizens, especially local school officials, and the federal government and declare *Brown* null and void in their state. Kilpatrick reasoned that this might generate a federal retreat, not unlike the retreat from Reconstruction in 1877. In jettisoning race in favor of a language of federal encroachment upon individual and states' rights, Kilpatrick provided an early lesson in color masking that was destined to cast a very long shadow.[48]

Freshman representative and Engelhardt crony Charles McKay drafted Alabama's interposition resolution, which directly channeled Kilpatrick by insisting that the *Brown* decisions were unconstitutional and thereby "null, void, and of no effect" in the state. Lawmakers pledged to "take all appropriate measures honorably and constitutionally available . . . to void this illegal encroachment upon [their] rights" and upon the rights reserved by the states via the Tenth Amendment. Folsom called it a "a bunch of hogwash" and "claptrap" from the "descendants of the landed gentry . . . trying to maintain the antebellum way of life." The governor likened it to "a hound dog baying at the moon" and added that it was "simply a piece of paper." It passed nearly unanimously on February 2, 1956, and became official without his signature.[49]

The following day, Autherine Lucy's enrollment at the University of Alabama sparked three days of rioting, which the university used as an excuse to suspend her "for her own safety." Folsom sat binge drinking and fishing in Florida, having relinquished control of the special session to the hard-line segregationists. Already under intense public scrutiny for entertaining New York congressman Adam Clayton Powell—a black man and an activist "Yankee" to boot—at the governor's mansion to discuss the ongoing Montgomery bus boycott, Folsom had agreed to a deal with his foes in the legislature. He would end his resistance to a new Boutwell Committee proposal if they would agree to support a constitutional amendment for senate expansion. Folsom then repaired to Florida to distance himself from all of the racial "claptrap."[50]

On February 8, the legislature approved the Boutwell Freedom of Choice Plan by a combined vote of 132–1. As a companion piece to the placement law, and similar to the Boutwell Committee's original proposal, the freedom of choice plan disestablished compulsory public education by removing any pertinent language from the state's constitution, and it gave the legislature the authority to abolish public schools. It made school officials judicial officers, in order to make them, in Boutwell's words, "immune from personal liability lawsuits and harassment from radical agitators." Finally, it gave the legislature the authority to require the state's attorney general to defend suits brought against any boards of education. Boutwell frankly admitted that the plan was intended to "give the legislature the authority to prevent the forced mixing of the races in our elementary and high schools." It was presented in the form of a constitutional amendment, which would go before the people in August. When Folsom returned from Florida to finally address the Lucy situation, he called it "a down to earth proposition we can all work with."[51]

In March 1956, 101 of 128 southern members of the U.S. Congress, including every member of Alabama's congressional delegation, endorsed interposition, encouraged their states to "resist forced integration by any lawful means," and signed a "Declaration of Constitutional Principles" that came to be known as the Southern Manifesto. An increasingly isolated Folsom continued to try to chart some sort of middle course. At the behest of the ACHR, he called a special conference of 150 of the state's newspaper editors and publishers and tapped a handful of those attending to serve on a committee that would draft a bill to present to the legislature. The bill would call for the creation of a biracial commission to advise the governor on how to handle racial crises. The conference included only one black reporter, while the committee included known Citizens' Council members, inviting sharp criticism from liberals. The state association of Citizens' Councils also condemned the efforts, insisting that the NAACP did not really want a settlement.[52]

That spring Folsom and a slate of allied candidates had to sit for the election of state delegates to the Democratic National Convention. Folsom had been there before. During his first term as governor, he had been defeated in his bid to be a delegate to the 1948 national convention, due in large part to his speaking out against the Dixiecrats—those who briefly split from the Democratic Party in 1948, opposing the nomination of Harry Truman in an attempt to harden the party line on race, unwittingly providing a model for a great shift in the politics of Dixie. Folsom in 1956 insisted that the Citizens' Councils were composed of the "same faces, rank and serial number, and issues that led to the Dixiecrats in 1948." He refused to answer a candidate questionnaire the Citizens' Councils were circulating and declined to "swear allegiance to the leadership of any group that's trying to tear up the Democratic party in Alabama." All but one of Folsom's candidates were defeated in the delegate election, and the governor himself was annihilated by none other than Charles McKay—Citizens' Council member, Engelhardt ally, and interposition resolution author.[53]

Folsom still had two more years in the governor's office, but the politics of race had forced him into the margins. He continued chasing the windmill of political reapportionment by way of a constitutional convention, while state legislators submitted segregation bills at such a tremendous rate that a "super-segregation committee" had to be appointed to weed out the more bizarre and unfeasible proposals. With Folsom marginalized, the way was open for the emergence of a new leader, fully committed to the segregationist cause, to take the state on the offensive. It turned out to be not one of the state's most prominent segregationist lawmakers but rather the state's highest law enforcement official—Attorney General John Patterson.

Patterson's political star was rising at the perfect hour. As Folsom was fading away, Patterson was emerging in stark contrast. He was a veteran of both World War II and the Korean War, with a distinguished career as an enlisted man and as an officer. He held a law degree from the University of Alabama, and by 1956, though young, he was already a household name. Patterson had returned from military service to join his father's law practice in Phenix City— Alabama's notorious "Sin City." Sitting just across the Chattahoochee River from Columbus, Georgia, and the U.S. Army's Fort Benning, Phenix City had become a playground for rowdy soldiers and a hotbed of organized crime. Patterson's father, Albert, had used his position as a state senator to combat the city's organized criminal elements, which included corrupt city and county officials. In 1954 Albert Patterson had secured the Democratic nomination for state attorney general. But he was assassinated less than a month later by elements of the criminal network he had pledged to stamp out.[54]

John Patterson vowed to avenge his father's death and soon found himself thrust into his father's place in the election. He rode Albert's martyrdom to the attorney general's office, then quickly established his own credentials by helping eliminate organized crime in Phenix City and by targeting the rampant graft and general malfeasance in the Folsom administration. But the young attorney general realized that fighting crime and battling corruption could only carry him so far. He would later recall that, "like everyone in politics at that time," he knew exactly "what was on the minds of the people." Nothing, he understood, would capture the gaze of Alabama's white voters quite like issues of race.[55]

In the summer of 1956, Patterson and Albert Boutwell cohosted a secret gathering of southern state officials and constitutional lawyers in Birmingham. The group intended to devise a common strategy for massive resistance. Patterson later admitted that most of those present could agree that "school integration was inevitable." But, he argued, there was a consensus among the attendees that the South should fight it in order to delay it as long as possible. Patterson had been encouraged to help spearhead the effort by Lindsey Almond, the attorney general (soon to be governor) of Virginia. Almond, who would lead his state in a futile effort to close its public schools, convinced Patterson that in massive resistance lay massive political rewards, and that attacking the NAACP was the way to do it. Almond had already assailed the organization using dusty old laws designed to prevent the solicitation of litigants and the profiting therefrom. The NAACP had been able to parry those thrusts, however, so Patterson would have to find another way.[56]

He found it in Louisiana, where the state had recently revived an old statute once intended to curb the violent activities of the Klan. Alabama had adopted a similar statute decades before. The law required that "foreign corporations"—those with headquarters outside of the state—register with the state and pay a licensing fee in order to "conduct business." On June 1, 1956, Patterson began his offensive by asking circuit judge Walter Jones for a permanent injunction, restraining the NAACP from conducting any business whatsoever in Alabama on the grounds that it had not registered as a "foreign corporation" and paid the fee. "Disruptive outside forces, such as the NAACP," he argued in the complaint, were trying to create "a breach of the peace" and destroy the "good relations" that had "traditionally existed between the White and Negro races" in the state. It was surely with some sense of irony that Patterson argued that the NAACP was simply "trying to capitalize upon racial factors for private gain and advancement."[57]

Walter Jones's ruling was never in doubt. He was a widely respected veteran on the bench and the president of the Alabama Bar Association. His white southern pedigree was unrivaled. His father had served under Stonewall Jackson in the Civil War, had been present with Robert E. Lee at the Confederate surrender at Appomattox, and had returned to state politics, serving as governor in the 1890s and as a federal judge thereafter. The elder Jones was also a delegate to the 1901 convention that produced the state's white supremacist constitution. Walter Jones had himself served as a state representative and had been a state judge since 1920. He was an outspoken promoter of the Confederate Lost Cause—the mythological idea that the antebellum way of life had been idyllic for everyone, black and white, until it was destroyed by greedy "Yankee" opportunists, who nearly ruined the South during Reconstruction. The Klan and the Democratic Party had saved what they could of the Old South, so it went. And it was up to every good white man to do his best to protect what had been "redeemed."[58]

Walter Jones also wrote a regular column titled "Off the Bench," which appeared in the *Montgomery Advertiser* and other southern newspapers. In it he praised the achievements of the white race, extolled the virtues of segregation, condemned the U.S. Supreme Court, and argued for states' rights. He insisted that whites were being "unjustly assailed all over the world" and subjected to attacks by "radical newspapers and magazines, communists and the federal judiciary," all of whom were engaged in a "massive campaign of super-brainwashing propaganda." According to Jones, the "real and final goal" was "intermarriage and [the] mongrelization of the American people" or "an impure, mixed breed that would destroy the white race." The "integrationists and mongrelizers," the judge argued, did not "deceive any person of common sense with their pious talk of wanting equal rights and opportunities."[59]

In 1954 a prominent Mobile attorney asked Jones to denounce the council movement in the name of the state bar, arguing that the policy of economic reprisal was immoral and un-Christian. Jones declined, arguing instead that if the opponents of segregation were using "all legal means within their power," including "forces of such social, political, and economic pressures as they can mobilize," then segregationists ought to be able to do the same. But while in 1954 Jones saw both the NAACP and the Citizens' Council as operating within their constitutional rights, by 1956 he had evidently changed his opinion about the NAACP. During the ensuing legal proceedings he would make it publicly clear that he intended to "deal the NAACP . . . a blow from which [it would] never recover."[60]

The blow took the form of an order restraining the NAACP from "conducting any further business of any description," including organizing chapters, soliciting contributions, collecting dues, and importantly, "filing . . . any application, paper or document for the purpose of qualifying to do business" in Alabama. Sam Engelhardt called it "a step forward towards our goal of race harmony in the South" and observed snarkily that the NAACP was finally "against the law." The NAACP's board of directors understood this to be a response to its implementation campaign and called Jones's ruling a "direct violation of the . . . constitutional principle of freedom of association," adding that the organization would "not be intimidated" and would fight the claim. Unfortunately for the NAACP, the injunction appeared to prevent the very actions—applying for a license and paying a fee—that would enable the association to resume activities.[61]

Days later, a three-judge panel of the U.S. District Court in Montgomery issued its ruling in the civil case arising from the Montgomery bus boycott, *Browder v. Gayle*. On June 13, 1956, the court, citing *Brown*, found that segregated busing laws in Montgomery violated the equal protection clause of the Fourteenth Amendment and ordered the city to cease operation of segregated busses. An appeal by the city ensured that the case would drag on, but the landmark ruling announced the arrival in the public consciousness of two individuals who would remain major players in the long battle over segregated education and in the immediate struggle over the fate of the NAACP—Fred Gray and Frank Johnson.[62]

Fred Gray was a tall, lanky, and bright twenty-six-year-old attorney from Montgomery. He had recently graduated from Case Western Reserve University in Cleveland, Ohio. Like each of the few black attorneys in Alabama at the time, he had been compelled to attend law school out of state. None of Alabama's three state-supported black colleges offered a law degree, but thanks to the NAACP, the state was forced to pay for black students to attend law school elsewhere. In his own words, Gray returned to Alabama in 1954 to "destroy everything segregated I could find." After establishing a practice in Montgomery, he began attending local NAACP meetings, where he connected with local chapter president E. D. Nixon and youth director Rosa Parks. Nixon asked Gray to serve as counsel for the plaintiffs in the civil suit that accompanied the bus boycott and as counsel for the organization itself in the "foreign corporation" suit. Gray thus found himself in the summer of 1956 preparing to fight to save the NAACP in the overtly hostile state court system at the same time he was preparing to handle the *Browder* appeal in the sometimes more equitable federal court system.[63]

In the *Browder* case, the presence of Judge Frank Johnson on the three-judge panel was crucial. The thirty-eight-year-old Johnson was the lone trial court judge in Alabama's Middle District at the time. Federal judges often harbored the same racist beliefs and commitments as their white neighbors, among whom they had to live and work, but Johnson had begun to prove that he was different. He had little tolerance for civil disobedience, but he was firmly committed to the legal struggle to secure constitutional rights. Johnson had also been imbued with a staunchly independent, mountain-grown Republicanism at an early age. His father had been a probate judge in North Alabama's Winston County and, at one point, was the sole Republican sitting in the state legislature. Frank attended law school at the University of Alabama, then served as an officer in the infantry during World War II and later as an attorney in the Judge Advocate General's Corps. After the war, he managed a veterans' campaign for Dwight Eisenhower, for which he was rewarded with appointments, first as U.S. Attorney for the Northern District of Alabama, then as U.S. district judge in 1955.[64]

Johnson was joined in the *Browder* majority by circuit judge Richard Rives, a sixty-one-year-old native of Montgomery and a veteran of World War I whom Harry Truman had appointed in 1951 and whose view of segregation was becoming increasingly dim. The NAACP was compelled to fight its legal battles, when it could help it, in federal court, in the hope of landing on the docket of a Rives or a Johnson, judges who were willing to deliver justice, even if it meant being ostracized by the white community. Fred Gray knew he faced an uphill battle in Walter Jones's state court. He partnered with prominent Birmingham attorney Arthur Shores and Robert Carter, the assistant director of the NAACP Legal Defense and Education Fund (LDF), the NAACP's independent litigating arm. Gray answered Patterson's complaint by arguing that this was a clear attempt to keep the NAACP from "help[ing] secure federal statutory and constitutional rights and due process of law for Negroes." The state had never asked the association to register or pay this fee before, and prior to the filing of the complaint it had never notified it that it was in violation of any state statute. Furthermore, the injunction violated the association's First and Fourteenth Amendment rights.[65]

Patterson asked the court to order the NAACP to produce a mountain of records, including branch charters, membership lists, bank records, and any correspondence relevant to the bus boycott or to Autherine Lucy's enrollment. Jones granted the motion. W. C. Patton immediately hid the membership rolls in a nondescript Birmingham office space, a move that later appeared shrewd when Patterson raided the office of the activist Tuskegee Civic Association. NAACP executive secretary Roy Wilkins stood behind his field secretary, explaining, "In too many instances the officers of state and local governments are, to all intents and purposes, one and the same with the leadership of the white Citizens' Council." NAACP members in Alabama, like those who signed petitions during Operation Implementation, had already been "subjected to economic pressure and personal threats and acts of violence," and the organization could not "risk exposing [its] loyal members to such reprisals."[66]

The NAACP offered to produce all of the records except the membership rolls. Jones held the association in contempt, writing that the court could not "permit a party, however wealthy and influential, to take the law into his own hands, set himself up above the law, and contumaciously decline to obey the orders of a duly constituted court" lest there be "no government of law." Jones fined the NAACP $10,000. Contrary to his assertion, the NAACP was not wealthy. There was no way it could afford to pay the fine, which increased to $100,000 on July 31. Two weeks later, the state supreme court denied the association's petition for appeal, as a blackface effigy hung in a Montgomery street, just a few blocks away, bearing the name "NAACP." Gray, Patton, and Nixon would have to try to find relief in federal court, otherwise the NAACP was indeed finished in Alabama.[67]

Shuttlesworth and Armstrong

The seven-story Masonic Temple dominated the western skyline of Birmingham's Northside—a thriving black business district that ran along Fourth Avenue North just west of downtown. It housed professional offices and a large ballroom that hosted popular black entertainers like Duke Ellington and Count Basie. On June 1, 1956, it hosted a small meeting of NAACP officers that was interrupted by a Jefferson County sheriff's deputy. The deputy marched into the meeting to inform the officers that their organization was officially "outlawed." As the deputy began to list all of the things that the NAACP could no longer do, one man asked, "Then what *can* we do?" The deputy smugly replied, "You can't do nothing." As that prospect began to sink in, during a brief moment of tense silence, another man spoke up. "That isn't so," he said flatly, with as much confidence as if he had invoked the word of God. "There's never a time when a man can't do anything. You aren't going to stop people from trying to be free." It was Fred Shuttlesworth, the pastor of Bethel Baptist Church and the local membership chairman. He was prepared to carry the fight forward, NAACP or not.[68]

Arthur Shores confirmed the information regarding the injunction the next day, whereupon Shuttlesworth and a small group of others agreed to the formation of the Alabama Christian Movement for Human Rights (ACMHR). Shuttlesworth denied that the group was a successor to the NAACP, which was partly true. Shuttlesworth would direct ACMHR with a sense of urgency, maybe even reckless abandon, that would have been out of place in many NAACP chapters. The ACMHR was founded on the values of the working-class community that Shuttlesworth represented. It was fearless and uncompromising. And Shuttlesworth found himself immediately at odds with the leadership of a more cautious, middle-class black establishment in the city. While they urged patience, ACMHR included in its "Declaration of Principles" a commitment to "beginning Now!" It took out recruitment ads in the *Birmingham World*, insisting, "The action of the attorney general makes it *more* necessary that Negroes come together in their own interests and plan together for the furtherance of their cause."[69]

Shuttlesworth focused his immediate attention on Birmingham's schools. It was too late to mount any effective challenge for the 1956–57 school year, but ACMHR began to prepare for the fall of 1957. The organization gathered signatures that summer and presented the Birmingham school board with a petition. The 1954–55 NAACP petitions had been vague requests for overall compliance with *Brown*. This one specifically targeted the Pupil Placement Law. The petitioners asked that thirteen black schoolchildren, from nine families, be assigned to the schools nearest their homes, since proximity was, after all, one of the factors that school boards could consider.[70]

The Birmingham board received the petition on August 20, 1957, but it refused to act on it until it met on September 6, two days after the official start of the school year. By September 2, families had already begun to bend to pressure and intimidation and withdraw their children's names. That day Klansmen from Ace Carter's local outfit kidnapped a randomly chosen black man—J. Edward "Judge" Aaron—from a rural Jefferson County road, just outside the city. They took Aaron to their Klan "lair," where they beat him and taunted him by asking if he thought his children were good enough to go to school with their children. They told him to deliver a message to Shuttlesworth: tell him to stop trying to send "nigger children and white children to school together, or we're gonna do them like we're gonna do you." The "Cyclops" then ordered one of the men to get "nigger blood on his hands." The man asked Aaron if he preferred to die or be castrated. The Klansmen proceeded to pistol-whip him, sever his scrotum, and pour turpentine into the wound. They threw Aaron in the back of a truck, drove him out of the city, and dumped him on the side of the road, where he was picked up by passing motorists, covered in blood from waist to ankles. Three Klansmen attended the school board meeting four days later, wearing buttons emblazoned with the image of a lynched black man.[71]

The school board set the wheels of the pupil placement law in motion. Shuttlesworth issued a statement, observing that the board wanted to "continue ... through 'routine' channels, [with] interviews, studies, tests, social factors, reports to the board, etc." In reality, he argued, this meant "*never* without actually saying it." He noted the hypocrisy in the segregationist officials' talk of preventing "breaches of the peace" and "disturbances." "In their failure to recognize the law of the land and to make at least some steps towards eventual compliance," he explained, "the stage is [set] for tension, confusion, and violence, which they claim to fear. Hence these threats and intimidations of Negroes and these brutally vicious attacks upon innocent Negroes at night by robed white Klansmen. ... But neither official[s] nor blood thirsty riders can stop our quest for first class citizenship. This we seek by good will if possible; by law if necessary." Shuttlesworth concluded that parents had no alternative to "presenting [their children] for immediate enrollment" at the schools to which they had petitioned for transfer. And so, rather than take his daughters Pat and Ricky to all-black Parker High on September 9, he drove them to all-white Phillips High instead.[72]

When the Shuttlesworth family arrived that morning, they found that an enraged mob had gathered in front of the school. To the disbelief of his family, Shuttlesworth stepped out of the vehicle. He was immediately set upon by a gang of fifteen to twenty men, who beat him with fists, brass knuckles, and a bicycle chain. His wife, Ruby, got out in an attempt to rescue him, followed by Ricky, who subsequently had the door slammed on her ankle. As the mob began breaking out the car's windows, police on the scene finally stopped the mayhem long enough for Shuttlesworth to break loose, return to the car, and speed away. He arrived at the hospital with what were, miraculously, only minor injuries, but the family discovered that Ruby had been stabbed. Shuttlesworth vowed to return to Phillips "whether they kill us or not." But he knew the real battle had to take place in the courtroom. A deep rage seethed in the black community in the following days, and disorder reigned in Birmingham schools. There were impromptu demonstrations with Confederate flags, bomb threats, boycotted classes, attacks on black school buses, and random cars. But for once Shuttlesworth waited.[73]

By October, incessant harassment had driven most of the petitioning families to withdraw their names. Only Shuttlesworth's daughter Ricky and three other children pressed on. They were subjected to intelligence, comprehension, and psychology tests by school officials, who also conducted a survey of white parents at the potentially affected schools. Parents were asked to answer yes or no or to "write any opinion you may have" to a litany of questions that Shuttlesworth described as "suggestions of the answers the board wanted to receive." If these students were admitted to white schools, the board asked, would parents allow their children to stay or pull them out of school? Would they allow them to "take part in classes?" What about "athletics, play, recreation . . . social affairs . . . music groups, clubs, and similar organizations?" Did they believe that there would be "serious disorders" or "tension or controversy" in the schools or in the community?[74]

The ACMHR filed suit in federal district court against the Birmingham school board on December 18, 1957, on behalf of the four remaining children and their parents. *Shuttlesworth v. Birmingham Board of Education* was Alabama's first school desegregation case. The plaintiffs sought an injunction against the board's use of the placement law and a ruling that the law was unconstitutional, per the equal protection clause of the Fourteenth Amendment. Since the plaintiffs were challenging the constitutionality of a state statute, a three-judge trial court was designated to hear the case. In addition to circuit judge Richard Rives, it included federal district judges Hobart Grooms and Seybourn Lynne. Grooms was an Eisenhower appointee and, at least up to that point, a strong advocate for segregation. Lynne was a paternalistic white supremacist who identified with the Citizens' Council movement. He had opposed judges Rives and Johnson in *Browder v. Gayle*. He was, in fact, openly hostile to plaintiffs' causes in civil rights cases and became known for letting such actions linger on his docket.[75]

The court's ruling was surprisingly unanimous. The judges chose to follow the lead of judge John Parker—the author of the *Briggs* dictum. Parker had made a distinction between the North Carolina pupil placement law "on its face" and in its application. On May 9, 1958, the *Shuttlesworth* court held that a plain reading of Alabama's placement law showed that it "furnish[ed] the legal machinery for an orderly administration of the public schools in a constitutional manner." Rives admitted that "no intellectually honest person would deny" that placement laws had been "passed to meet and solve problems presented by [*Brown*]." But he added, "We must assume that it will be so administered." If not, then it was possible that the law could, "in some future proceeding," be "deemed unconstitutional in its application." The judges were giving school authorities the opportunity to avoid court-ordered desegregation by using the placement law to enroll a token number of black children in white schools.[76]

Shuttlesworth was able to appeal the decision directly to the U.S. Supreme Court, since it was the decision of a three-judge trial court. The court agreed to hear the appeal. As the ACMHR awaited a ruling, the opening of schools in September in Birmingham was met with renewed violence and intimidation. The Klan burned crosses at fourteen white schools in Jefferson County. A crowd of 150 white men and teenagers gathered outside Phillips High to ensure that no blacks entered. Shuttlesworth's church was bombed for the second time in two years. And three white men threw dynamite bombs at black homes in the formerly all-white Fountain Heights neighborhood. Meanwhile, Albert Boutwell spoke to a Citizens' Council rally in Selma, saying, "We are winning the segregation battle, [but] now is the time for us to take the offensive," because people were "disgusted by the advocates of change."[77]

In November the Supreme Court issued a brief opinion affirming the trial court's decision in *Shuttlesworth*, although it carefully added that this was based on "the limited ground on which the district court rested its decision." Earlier in the year, with its decision in the Little Rock case of *Cooper v. Aaron*, the court had reaffirmed the principles in *Brown* and firmly established its role as final arbiter of the constitutionality of state and local education laws. But with *Shuttlesworth* it indicated its willingness, at least temporarily, to embrace tokenism and ignore evasive maneuvers by the states, provided they were color masked. In endorsing carefully crafted pupil placement laws, the court also allowed the onus for effecting desegregation to be placed back on black schoolchildren and their families. One court observer called *Shuttlesworth* "the most important pro-segregation victory since *Plessy v. Ferguson*," the ruling that sanctioned Jim Crow during Redemption. Another called it the "end of the legal phase of massive resistance," a decision with which a "constitutional crisis ... passed into history." So it must have seemed at the time.[78]

State leaders were relieved. John Patterson had just ridden his segregationist message into the governor's office. Walter Jones had administered the oath of office, Albert Boutwell became lieutenant governor, and other archsegregationists, like Sam Engelhardt, had taken positions in the administration. All of them praised the *Shuttlesworth* ruling. Austin Meadows sent out a memo to local boards suggesting ways in which they could use the law to avoid even token desegregation. "By careful assignment of pupils," Meadows wrote, "school officials can avoid maladjustments which will hinder the education of our young people." For instance, "a child who is angry or emotionally upset in his school assignment," he offered, "certainly is not in a suitable frame of mind to profit from his teacher's instruction or carry out his school work efficiently." Shuttlesworth himself was unmoved, announcing, "If the court can rule that [the placement law] can be applied without discrimination then it is up to the Birmingham school board to apply it without discrimination."[79]

The court's warning about the future application of the law did not go unnoticed. Many whites were apprehensive that if the state did not initiate token desegregation, an adverse ruling would soon follow. They became keenly interested in the course being charted in Virginia by John Patterson's close friend, then-governor Lindsey Almond, whose administration had been closing public school systems threatened with desegregation and supporting the establishment of segregated private schools in their stead. In January 1959, a three-judge federal court shot down the possibility of such state-initiated closures, arguing that a state could not order some schools closed and continue to operate others. But statewide abolition of public education was still an option, as was locally initiated school closure, and the latter had already been encouraged in Alabama by the Boutwell freedom of choice bill.[80]

Efforts to capitalize on *Shuttlesworth* soon accelerated, though not in Birmingham. Martin Luther King Jr. had announced in late 1958 that his Montgomery Improvement Association intended to encourage black students to apply to white schools, using the placement law, the following spring. King expressed hope that the law would be administered faithfully but admitted that he was "realistic enough to know . . . this will have to end up in court." The "grand dragon" of the Ku Klux Klan, Tuscaloosa's Robert Shelton, promised "bloodshed" if such litigation was filed, and Governor Patterson—to whom Shelton was an unofficial advisor—warned blacks in his inaugural address, "Speak out now against the agitators of your own race whose aim is to destroy our school system. If you do not do so," he declared, "we will have no public education at all."[81]

Patterson knew that the placement law was doomed to eventual invalidation. But the governor remained resolute about school closure, insisting that "if any school in Alabama [were] integrated," it would be "over [his] dead body." He twice sent representatives to Prince Edward County, Virginia, to study the efforts of local officials there who had closed schools and established a private school for the county's whites. Patterson's attorney general, MacDonald

Gallion, argued that whites could afford to establish private schools, whereas blacks could not, so the mere threat of closure ought to "place the Negro in the position of sticking the dagger in his own throat." Gallion and Patterson also reasoned that black teachers—among the most influential leaders in the black community—would strongly oppose desegregation, if they were convinced it would lead to school closure and job loss. Gallion established an Alabama Education Fund Foundation to coordinate fund-raising for local private school corporations.[82]

In February, a group of prominent whites in Montgomery organized just such a corporation. Jolted by King's call to desegregate schools but encouraged by correspondence with planners in Virginia, the committee announced plans for a school dedicated solely to "students of white parentage" and began receiving tuition commitments immediately. It established the state's first segregation academy that fall—the Montgomery Academy. The Montgomery Citizens' Council, meanwhile, announced that "no person who [enjoyed] success, leadership, or acceptance" in the city would continue to enjoy those things "should he aid in making things more difficult for our mission of maintaining segregation." Anyone who threatened to "to alter or modify our segregated pattern in the schools" would be "marked" as an "enemy of the white people" and a "traitor." Klan activity also increased, as Klansmen erected "welcome signs" outside the city—fiery crosses painted crudely on circular saws with red teeth—and cross burnings and floggings increased in frequency. Worse, perhaps, than those activities themselves was a pervasive atmosphere of acceptance and approval of them. Pressure on King began to take a toll. There would be no school suit in Montgomery in 1959, nor would there be one for the next five years. King himself left the city to return to Atlanta the following year.[83]

The banner of school desegregation fell once again to Fred Shuttlesworth, who had already begun to organize plaintiffs for a new lawsuit. Eleven students had applied for transfer to white schools that spring, but after administering "achievement" tests, the Birmingham school board denied the applications. The next step would have been filing the suit, but this was impossible thanks to a roadblock erected almost single-handedly by judge Seybourn Lynne. After the *Shuttlesworth* case, Lynne had started enforcing a procedural rule that required out-of-state attorneys to "associate" with a local attorney before bringing any action in his court. He knew that Shuttlesworth's attorney, Ernest Jackson, was from Florida. And he knew that the city's black attorneys were in negotiations with white moderates, trying to obtain better facilities for parks in black neighborhoods, a path Lynne himself had encouraged by reminding black leaders that the city could simply close the parks in the event of litigation. Shuttlesworth had rejected these negotiations, and in retaliation the city's black attorneys refused to associate with Ernest Jackson. What the black press took to calling the "Birmingham Stalemate" would not be broken until that fall, when Willie Williams became the city's eighth black attorney and agreed to help Shuttlesworth.[84]

Williams, Jackson, and Shuttlesworth orchestrated a new lawsuit, *Armstrong v. Birmingham Board of Education*, and Shuttlesworth presented a new petition to the city school board in November 1959. Eighty-one parents had signed the document, which audaciously asked that the board formulate a plan by December 1 for the desegregation of the entire school system. The board dismissed the petition, and the suit was filed. Instead of alleging that the board had unconstitutionally applied the placement law, the complaint charged the school board with maintaining a racially "dual school system," with a "dual set up of zone lines ... predicated on the theory that Negroes are inherently inferior to white persons and, consequently may not attend [or teach at] the same public schools." The plaintiffs asked for an injunction against operating such a system or for the court to require the school board to submit a plan to replace it.[85]

James Armstrong was the father of four of the children on the list. He had also been involved in the initial *Shuttlesworth* suit. Originally from the Black Belt, Armstrong was a veteran of the Normandy invasion who had moved to the city after the war and become a barber. As a self-employed man in an all-black neighborhood, he was shielded from economic reprisal, making him a well-placed plaintiff. But he was not immune to other forms of intimidation. City commissioner Eugene "Bull" Connor instructed his personnel to harass the Armstrong home continually. Plumbers came to the home at one o'clock in the morning with a backhoe to "fix" the septic tank, which was not in need of repair. The fire department came in response to bogus fire calls. There were calls about a car for sale that Armstrong had never listed and an unpaid hotel bill from a city he had never visited. And there were always the anonymous calls with heavy breathing and threats to the family. Armstrong lost business too because Klansmen watched his barbershop, and his customers were afraid of what might happen there. He chose, however, to stay the course, which would be a long one.[86]

The *Armstrong* case landed on the docket of Judge Lynne, who was content to let it lie there, unadjudicated, for nearly three years. Shuttlesworth had provided the model for initiating the dismantling of the state's dual school system. But the prospects for success must have seemed bleak at the time. Moderates and liberals had been marginalized. Jim Folsom had disappeared. An arch-segregationist bloc was in command of state politics, warning white voters that school desegregation would result in miscegenation and the destruction of white civilization as they knew it. Walter Jones had banished the NAACP, and the Patterson administration was preparing for school closures and the creation of segregated private schools. The Klan was active and violent. And the Citizens' Councils were engaged in both economic reprisal and spearheading legislative action.

Black activism continued to spread, though. The first three years of the 1960s saw a flurry of civil rights agitation in the state—most notably the integrated interstate bus journeys known as the Freedom Rides, which resulted in a series of violent segregationist outbursts, the exposure of Patterson's intransigence to the nation, and a ruling from Frank Johnson mandating the riders' protection. As the Citizens' Councils initiated a program of "Reverse Freedom Rides," paying desperate black families' bus fares to leave the state, the *Armstrong* complaint withered away on Judge Lynne's docket. By 1962 Alabama remained one of only three states in the South to maintain absolute segregation in education. But the Kennedy Justice Department had begun to take an increasingly active role in enforcing *Brown*, and a group of judges on the Fifth Circuit Court of Appeals had become impatient with southern officials' defiance. The stage was set for a showdown.[87]

In retrospect, the most ominous development of all—which ensured that the school desegregation struggle would be milked for every ounce of its political value—was the rise in state politics of a former state circuit judge from the Black Belt's Barbour County. He was a onetime close friend of Frank Johnson at the University of Alabama, a boxer, and a Folsom protégé who had cut his political teeth as a liberal. This was the man who had promised, after his defeat at the hands of Patterson in the 1958 gubernatorial election, to never be "out-niggered" again—George C. Wallace.

CHAPTER 2

"Our Most Historical Moment," 1962-1963

On January 14, 1963, George Wallace was inaugurated as governor of Alabama. Like John Patterson before him, Wallace reminded his inauguration speech audience that he stood atop the same Confederate star upon which Jefferson Davis had sworn his oath as the president of the Confederacy. True to the segregationist one-upmanship of his campaign, Wallace also invoked Confederate general Robert E. Lee, the quintessential southern hero, who had fought valiantly to the bitterest of ends against insurmountable odds. Wallace's address that day was the magnum opus of Klansman, Citizens' Council leader, and top Wallace aide Asa Carter. In a pithy encapsulation of southern white defiance, like a forlorn battle cry before a hopeless siege, Wallace declared, "In the name of the greatest people who ever trod this earth, I draw the line in the dust and toss the gauntlet before the feet of tyranny, and I say segregation *today*, segregation *tomorrow*, segregation *forever*!" And the roar came.¹

Wallace had promised segregationists that he would defy the federal government, especially the judiciary, and black activists, especially the NAACP, just as Confederate rebels had resisted Yankee aggression and "carpetbagger" invasion one hundred years prior. Segregationists had elected him for it, and he wanted to reassure them, so the rest of the speech read like a Citizens' Council broadsheet. Wallace wanted to exploit fears, even if it meant making promises he could not keep. Before delivering the "segregation forever" line, he spoke passionately about "freedom-loving blood" and called on Alabama's whites to "send an answer to the tyranny that clanks its chains upon the South." These were the stakes: enslavement by the federal government, dilution of the white race, and the upturning of southern society. It was whites' duty to "sound the drum" and go to battle to prevent this.²

Wallace quickly turned to the most terrifying threat. The reports of violence in desegregated schools in Washington, D.C., he opined, were "disgusting and revealing." The federal troops deployed during the recent crisis at the University of Mississippi would have been better served, he suggested, guarding the white schoolchildren of the nation's capital. To avoid the fate of Washington or Ole Miss, Wallace insisted that they must put the federal government on notice: "We give the word of a race of honor that we will tolerate their boot in our face no longer." He then reminded them who the nearest representatives of that government were: "Let those certain judges put *that* in their opium pipes of power and smoke it for all it's worth." Many listeners understood that Wallace referred especially to his old friend from law school, Frank Johnson, who was known to enjoy a tobacco pipe in his chambers down the street.[3]

After comparing southern whites to the Jews of Nazi Germany, and black activists to communist revolutionaries, Wallace reminded his audience of the threat of miscegenation and mongrelization. Ace Carter allowed Wallace to bring this in at the conclusion of the speech, just as he returned to the language of the Civil War, Reconstruction, and Redemption: the great Lost Cause. The governor warned anyone "who would follow the false doctrine of communistic amalgamation" that the white people of Alabama would not "surrender [their] system of government, [their] freedom of race and religion." When the South was "set upon by the vulturous carpetbagger and federal troops, all loyal Southerners were denied the vote at the point of a bayonet, so that the infamous, illegal 14th Amendment might be passed." But southerners fought, Wallace demanded, "and they won." He concluded by calling out the business moderates, the liberals, and anyone else not behind the line of defiant resistance. "I stand ashamed," he said with as much disgust as he could muster, "of the fat, well-fed whimperers who say that it is inevitable, that our cause is lost. They do not represent the deport of the majority of the people of Alabama or the people of the Southland," who, he promised, would soon "grasp the hand of destiny and walk out of the shadow of fear and fill [their] divine destination. Let us not simply defend," he urged, "but let us assume leadership of the fight." Wallace concluded, "God has placed us here in this crisis. Let us not fail in this, our most historical moment."[4]

The "Year of Grace" Begins

In the year prior to Wallace's inauguration, the wheels of desegregation had finally begun to turn, so by the time he entered office he would be immediately forced to make good on his campaign promises. In Birmingham, Huntsville, and Mobile, activists pressed the issue. The Justice Department escalated its involvement. And if segregationist judges like Seybourn Lynne refused to act, the Fifth Circuit Court of Appeals signaled its intention to accelerate matters on its own accord. As the appellate court ordered desegregation to proceed in other parts of the South, some Alabamians began to see the writing on the wall. The rest listened to George Wallace.[5]

In the summer of 1962, civil rights activists in Birmingham attempted to bypass Judge Lynne, who continued to ignore the *Armstrong* case. They filed a separate suit, hoping that it would land on the docket of Judge Hobart Grooms instead. Local attorney Orzell Billingsley filed the action in June on behalf of Reverend Theodore Nelson and his children, Agnes and Oswald, all of whom were soon disappointed. The case did fall to Judge Grooms, but Grooms refused to consider the complaint on account of the almost identical pending claim in *Armstrong*. There would be no hearing on a preliminary injunction in *Nelson v. Birmingham Board of Education* until there was a hearing on the merits in *Armstrong*, which Lynne had been delaying for over two years. Billingsley asked the Fifth Circuit appellate court to issue a writ of mandamus—an order that would force Grooms to adjudicate *Nelson*.[6]

An appellate panel composed of circuit judges Richard Rives, John Minor Wisdom, and John Brown unanimously approved Grooms's decision to wait. But Brown issued a separate opinion in which he lambasted Lynne for his "impermissible delay." He considered it "simply beyond belief" that *Armstrong* had sat undecided since 1960, especially given that the "old and ancient" issue was "the very, very simple one of a federal court order to put an end to a segregated school system," about which he figured there was "no real dispute." Brown continued, "We have now made plain by cases which are an affectation to cite that a plan of desegregation must be offered or the district court must fashion its own plan. Here it is 1962 . . . eight years after the warning to commence with deliberate speed." And local officials had until October to offer "non-existent defenses" so Birmingham could "put off the 'evil' day" and deny the plaintiffs a "matter of clear right."[7]

Judge Brown's concurrence was among a number of rulings that signaled an ideological shift in the appellate court. Prior to *Brown*, the court had comprised mostly New Deal Democrats who defended the racial status quo. After *Brown*, not only did President Eisenhower appoint several pro-integration Republicans to the court—Brown, Wisdom, and Elbert Tuttle—but also the liberal Democrat Rives was elevated to the court's chief judgeship. Many segregationist federal jurists, like Lynne, frustrated civil rights actions. Some even made racist remarks from the bench, openly lamented *Brown*, and publicly voiced their support for segregation. But Brown, Wisdom, Tuttle, Rives, and a small number of district judges like Frank Johnson began to fill the void in school desegregation jurisprudence left by the Supreme Court, which had become increasingly quiet in the wake of *Cooper v. Aaron* and *Shuttlesworth*.[8]

That summer the appellate court issued rulings in several school desegregation appeals, underscoring the hard line it was beginning to take. In one case the court held that pupil placement laws were unconstitutionally applied when they were administered "in a manner to maintain complete segregation in fact." This was the opportunity provided by *Shuttlesworth*, in which the court had found Alabama's placement law constitutional "on its face" only. The court also ruled that Louisiana's placement law clearly fulfilled a "behind-the-face function of preserving segregation." The law had been "hailed as the instrument for carrying out a desegregation plan," while "all the time the entire public [knew] that in fact it [was] being used to maintain segregation." Anyone attuned to the activity of the federal courts could have drawn the reasonable conclusion that Alabama might well be next. The *Birmingham News* argued that it was "folly for city officials, school people, or [the] public to refuse to face the record." The *News* concluded, "*Birmingham probably has one year of grace between next month and the following September.*"[9]

That September, as riots erupted on the campus of the University of Mississippi following the attempted enrollment of James Meredith, activists in two Alabama cities attempted to enroll in white schools. Less than an hour's drive northeast of Birmingham, six black students tried to enroll at all-white Gadsden High. Flustered staff summoned the superintendent, who told the students that the school system had tried "to give the Negro schools the type of instruction that [would] best train them in courses that they both need and want." By this he meant cosmetology, industrial arts, and "diversified occupations," not chemistry and physics. He told them the registration period had ended the week before, sent them away, and dismissed their effort as a "publicity stunt." The students could at least rest assured that the city's black activists had already filed an omnibus desegregation suit in federal court that May seeking the desegregation of every public facility in the city. Meanwhile, a much more ominous threat for segregationists loomed to the northwest in the city of Huntsville.[10]

The same day as the Gadsden enrollment attempt, Ladonna Burnett's mother brought her to Huntsville's all-white Madison Pike Elementary in an attempt to register. The superintendent, Raymond Christian, blithely told her that her child had been assigned to Cavalry Hills School for Negroes and dismissed her with a vague promise for a hearing. Mrs. Burnett's husband was a sergeant in the U.S. Army, stationed at nearby Redstone Arsenal. The children of black personnel at Redstone, along with the children of NASA personnel from the Marshall Space Flight Center, were forced to attend local black schools. The Huntsville NAACP had alerted the Justice Department (DOJ) to this situation in 1959, adding that the school board was prepared to use thirty-one acres of land donated by the federal government, and federal funds, to build a new segregated elementary school for whites. When the DOJ's Civil Rights Division began to investigate in 1961, the Madison Pike school was found to be among a handful of off-base schools whose segregated student bodies were entirely composed of the dependents of federal personnel.[11]

The Civil Rights Division (CRD) was established via the Civil Rights Act of 1957. In its earliest years, it focused on voting rights, operating under a mandate to enforce federal statutes prohibiting discrimination. But during the Kennedy administration it began to play a bigger role in school desegregation, often joining litigation by filing *amicus curiae*, or "friend of the court," briefs. By 1962 the division was exploring ways to assist the Department of Health, Education, and Welfare (HEW) in withholding federal funding from school districts with segregated schools in "impacted areas." These were school districts, like Huntsville, that received federal subsidies for enrolling and educating large numbers of children of federal personnel. That summer CRD chief Burke Marshall and his deputy, St. John Barrett, began to reach out to those districts.[12]

Marshall flew to Huntsville to assess the situation and negotiate with local officials. He met with Superintendent Christian and several of the city's leading white business moderates, most of whom had participated in biracial negotiations and were responsible for what had been a comparatively reasonable approach to voluntary desegregation. Racial tension in Huntsville had been mitigated over the years by the presence of a progressive, upper-middle-class white community associated with the federal facilities and by the fact that the city had fewer blacks than any other major city in the state. White leaders were willing to accept the unfortunate inevitability of desegregation, but they insisted to Marshall that white backlash would necessitate a court order forcing the issue. Barrett began drafting a complaint for Huntsville and for surrounding Madison County.[13]

That fall the *Armstrong* and *Nelson* cases came before the trial court for a combined trial. The attorneys for the plaintiffs—Orzell Billingsley, Willie Williams, and Ernest Jackson—had to establish the well-known fact that the city of Birmingham operated a racially dual school system. Birmingham school superintendent Theo Wright admitted that a black child showing up to register at a white school would not be registered. But he called this a "matter of custom" and argued that schools were simply designated "white" or "black" on account of their location in white or black neighborhoods. The school board's attorneys called Birmingham's head guidance counselor to testify to black students' supposed deficit in acumen and performance, then called Superintendent Wright, who argued that introducing such inferior pupils into classes with superior white ones would create "educational chaos." Billingsley tried to remind the court of the findings in *Brown*: segregation itself produced this apparent scholastic lag in black pupils, not only through discrimination in funding but also by creating a "psychological inferiority complex in the black student." The defense stuck with biological racism.[14]

The defendant officials' coup de grâce was a study, commissioned by John Patterson several years prior, presented by its author, Dr. Wesley Critz, a former anatomy professor at the University of North Carolina. Critz testified that humans were "not born equal in the biological sense" and that blacks were two hundred thousand years behind whites, anthropologically speaking. Integration was "evil" and "not Christian" and would lead inevitably to intermarriage between whites and blacks, which itself would result in the "invariable deterioration" of the white race's genetic pool. It was Citizens' Council creed cloaked in discredited science, and not only did Seybourn Lynne allow it, probably most whites in Alabama believed it. Lynne gave the parties until December 31 to file summary briefs and reply briefs, thereby delaying a ruling until midwinter of 1963–64 or later. When the plaintiffs' attorneys protested, Lynne insisted, "School doesn't open here until September, [and] nobody's in any hurry here."[15]

The following month, as the country celebrated the passing threat of the Cuban Missile Crisis, a group of black activists in the port city of Mobile asked the city-county school board to finally provide an answer to the Mobile NAACP's petition of 1955. The group tried to appeal to business moderates by calling on "citizens of good will and all who have respect for law and order [to] defend with their moral support a course of action which will bring to our city and county another instance of a high standard in race relations." Behind the effort was John L. LeFlore, a longtime black community leader whose activism could be traced back to his resurrection of the local NAACP chapter in the 1920s. LeFlore worked for the U.S. Post Office and had used that shield from economic reprisal to defend aggrieved black stevedores during World War II and, in the wake of the NAACP's banishment, to act as director of casework for the Non-Partisan Voters League. LeFlore knew the answer he would receive from the school board, so he had already secured local attorney Vernon Crawford to file a desegregation suit at some point that winter.[16]

As Crawford and LeFlore prepared for litigation, Wallace was elected governor. He had built his campaign on a promise to "stand up to those lousy, no-account judges that are trying to take over our school system." Voters knew he meant judges like Frank Johnson, with whom Wallace had sparred before.

As a state circuit judge, Wallace had once orchestrated a controversy over releasing voter rolls to the U.S. Civil Rights Commission so that he could claim to be protecting them from the federal government. He backed down when Johnson threatened to jail him for contempt, but the judge still rebuked Wallace for using "devious methods," "politically-generated whirlwinds," and "means of subterfuge" in an "attempt to give the impression that he was defying [the] court's order." Wallace dramatized the showdown as one in which he had "risked his freedom" in order to prevent "a second Sherman's March to the Sea." He publicly called Johnson an "integratin, scalawagin, carpetbaggin, no-good, bald-faced liar" and privately called him a "no-good, goddamn, lying, son-of-a-bitching, race-mixing bastard." He knew his old classmate would prove to be the perfect nemesis in the political drama he intended to direct.[17]

Facing the immediate threats of not only desegregation suits in Mobile and Birmingham but also Vivian Malone's court-ordered desegregation of the University of Alabama, Wallace realized that many segregationists were beginning to adopt a message of "law and order." This signaled, at that point, a reluctant commitment to abide distasteful changes in the law, largely because violence and disorder were bad for business. State Democratic Party chairman Roy Mayhall told Birmingham's Young Men's Business Club, "If integration comes to Alabama—by court order or what—I favor enforcing the law." He laid out the core of the law-and-order ethos when he added, "We may dislike some of our laws," but the "ugly, moronic violence of mob hysteria" would only make matters worse. The Alabama Council on Human Relations endorsed this line, counting among its goals a "dedication to the maintenance of law and order in the implementation of the decisions of the courts." One ACHR member explained, "Reasonable people know that violence hurts everybody, and also hurts the pocketbook, scares off payrolls, and chokes economic growth." Even a group of the state's white clergy issued an "Appeal for Law and Order and Commonsense" that winter.[18]

At the same time, the proliferation of school desegregation cases would give Wallace a chance to capitalize on white fear and anger and to support outright defiance of any desegregation at all. The day he took office, the Mobile school board formally responded to John LeFlore's request that it present a desegregation plan. The board told LeFlore that such action would be "ill-advised," noting a building program it had recently approved that included a $7 million commitment to modernize and expand black schools. "This program," the board surmised, "is far better for your people, as a whole, than the enforcement of any rights of a few to go to white public schools." An incredulous LeFlore concluded that the board had left him and Vernon Crawford "no choice" but to immediately file a suit. The two then realized that they could bypass the state's ban on the NAACP by enlisting the assistance of the Legal Defense and Education Fund. They called NAACP attorney Constance Baker Motley and asked her to "associate" with Crawford. Motley then brought in the LDF's Jack Greenberg, and the group began drafting a complaint to file as soon as possible, hopeful that it might lead to results that fall.[19]

Meanwhile, the CRD filed "impacted areas" suits in Alabama, targeting not just Huntsville and Madison County but also Mobile, which was home to the U.S. Air Force's Brookley Field and nearby Dauphin Island Air Warning Station. The CRD sought to desegregate schools serving the children of federal personnel or to block millions of dollars in federal funds. Wallace called it "blackmail" and insisted that the litigation would be "resisted in every way." The state legislature fell in line, arguing defiantly, "At no time will we in Alabama voluntarily submit to integration of our schools." The governor then announced the creation of the Committee on Constitutional Law and State Sovereignty—a group of attorneys that would advise him on combating any such litigation. The U.S. Attorney in Mobile, V. R. Jansen, said he was "embarrassed" to be associated with the filing of the Mobile suit, which required his signature as a matter of formality. Jansen complained to the press, "Two days after LeFlore announces he's going to take the segregation issue to court, the Justice Department files suit," thereby giving the impression that it was "reacting to the will of the NAACP."[20]

LeFlore and the CRD were not actually working together, though LeFlore did move forward at the same time. Crawford and the LDF's Greenberg filed a complaint on behalf of four black students in the Hillsdale Heights neighborhood in West Mobile. The four attended St. Elmo High School for Negroes and had to travel thirty-four miles round trip to school each day, passing all-white Baker High, four miles away, along the way. They had previously attempted to enroll in Baker and had been rebuffed. At the top of the list of plaintiffs was Birdie Mae Davis, thus the case was styled *Birdie Mae Davis, et al. v. Board of School Commissioners of Mobile County*. Like *Armstrong*, the class-action suit avoided the issue of the placement law and sought instead a permanent injunction against the school board, prohibiting it from engaging in initial assignment of students to racially identifiable schools and prohibiting assignment of teachers, administrators, and staff on the basis of race, or any other action that would perpetuate a racially dual school system.[21]

At the same time, on the opposite end of the state, activists were filing a suit in Huntsville. Sonnie Hereford III, a general practitioner, and John Cashin, a dentist, had met at medical school in Tennessee and had been drawn to activism by the Student Nonviolent Coordinating Committee. SNCC had come to Huntsville in early 1962 to organize sit-ins. By the spring of 1963, Hereford and Cashin had forced the desegregation of the city's lunch counters and had even traveled north to picket the New York Stock Exchange with signs reading, "Don't Invest in Huntsville—It's Bad for Business." They enlisted Billingsley and Greenberg to file *Hereford v. Huntsville Board of Education* on behalf of five parents and their children, including Sonnie Hereford IV, and the case landed before Judge Grooms on March 11, 1963. Unlike in *Armstrong* and *Davis*, the *Hereford* plaintiffs sought to exploit *Shuttlesworth* by citing the unconstitutional application of the placement law. That spring there were eight school desegregation cases pending in the state—three impacted areas cases, *Armstrong* and *Nelson* in Birmingham, *Davis* in Mobile, *Hereford* in Huntsville, and finally, in Tuskegee, *Lee v. Macon County Board of Education*, one of the most significant school desegregation actions ever filed.[22]

Fred Gray, Solomon Seay, and the LDF's Motley prepared the complaint, which Gray filed on January 28, on behalf of sixteen black students in Tuskegee and their parents. The plaintiffs sought either a permanent injunction against the Macon County school board or its submission of a desegregation plan, which the court and plaintiffs could vet and monitor. Local activist Detroit Lee, a clerk at the local Veterans Administration hospital, had urged Gray to file the complaint years before. Lee was one of the organizers of the city's NAACP chapter and also a member of the Tuskegee Civic Association (TCA). In the late 1950s he had been a plaintiff in *Gomillion v. Lightfoot*, the landmark voting rights case resulting from Sam Engelhardt's efforts to gerrymander blacks out of the city limits. Even then, as TCA was prioritizing voting rights, Lee was pushing hard for school desegregation. Fred Gray promised him that if he could wait until the time was right, Gray would make one of his five children the lead plaintiff. Anthony Lee thus found his name attached to the case in the winter of 1963–64. Attorney General Richmond Flowers called *Lee v. Macon* the "most deadly" of the suits his office was forced to defend. As the lone case filed in the Black Belt, not only did it strike "at the very heart" of segregation in the state, it would be adjudicated by Frank Johnson.[23]

The "Stand" to the Fall

In March Fred Shuttlesworth finally convinced Martin Luther King Jr. and other leaders in the Southern Christian Leadership Conference to initiate a direct action campaign in Birmingham. Albert Boutwell had been elected mayor, but incumbent mayor Albert "Art" Hanes and police commissioner Bull Connor had refused to step aside. Litigation forced them to do so but not before Connor infamously ordered the fire and police departments to use clubs, high-powered water cannons, and the canine squad to disperse peaceful protestors in and around the city's Kelly Ingram Park. As marchers and picketers were hauled off to jail in an excessive crackdown that garnered international condemnation, the city's white business moderates fell in behind chamber of commerce president Sydney Smyer, who explained, "I'm no integrationist, but I'm not a goddamn fool, either." Smyer negotiated a settlement that called for the gradual desegregation of downtown businesses and a promise to work toward hiring black clerks. Klansmen responded by attempting to assassinate King via two separate bombings, prompting enraged blacks to initiate the first full-scale urban riot of the 1960s. Shuttlesworth, who had been in the hospital, expressed betrayal at what he considered a watered-down settlement. The ACMHR had been asking for much more, including a robust start to desegregating schools.[24]

As Birmingham smoldered, judge Hobart Grooms reluctantly ordered the University of Alabama to process Vivian Malone's application for summer admission. Grooms professed, "I don't see that I have any alternative." The court, he insisted, was "not a free agent in the matter of school segregation or integration." The university board of trustees also expressed resignation, arguing that "outright disobedience of the order of the federal court with consequent prison sentences and other severe penalties for the dean of admissions and any successor appointed for him" would still "not prevent the admission." Wallace declared his intention to engage in "legal resistance and legal defiance" and began orchestrating the charade commonly referred to as the "stand in the schoolhouse door."[25]

The CRD filed for a restraining order against the governor, which Judge Lynne granted. In an impassioned opinion, the first one in nearly thirty years as a judge that he had written in the first person, Lynne acknowledged that, "like Jonah of old," people were "angry even unto death." He revealed that it was his personal prayer that all Alabamians would "join in this resolution that law and order will be maintained." Lynne argued, "The concept of law and order, the very essence of republican government, embraces the notion that when the judicial process of a state or federal court . . . has been exhausted and has resulted in a final judgment, all persons affected thereby are obliged to obey it." Lynne then arranged a deal with Justice Department officials to ensure that Malone and fellow applicant James Hood would be enrolled, while at the same time allowing Wallace to make his "stand."[26]

On June 11, 1963, the governor stood poised in front of Foster Auditorium, the University of Alabama admissions building, ostensibly blocking the path of Malone and Hood. He was confronted by Assistant U.S. Attorney General Nicholas Katzenbach, who had made sure that the two students were officially enrolled in advance of the spectacle, allowing U.S. marshals to avoid arresting

Wallace for contempt of court. Flanked by the shortest state troopers that could be found—so the governor would appear taller for the sea of gathered reporters—Wallace read a prepared statement decrying the "illegal act" of ordering the two students' admission. President Kennedy federalized the Alabama National Guard, and the general in charge thereof told Wallace that it was his "sad duty" to ask the governor to step aside. Wallace finally did so, calling it a "bitter pill" to swallow. Attorney General Richmond Flowers later described the ordeal as "the greatest production since Cleopatra."[27]

The civil rights movement had finally pushed the Kennedy administration into a firmer commitment on civil rights, and events in Birmingham and Tuscaloosa provided the opportunity to make that public. That evening, after the "stand," Kennedy revealed a new civil rights bill that would outlaw discrimination in public accommodations and give the CRD and HEW more tools to begin enforcing *Brown*. He had once appealed to business moderates, arguing that racial discrimination was detrimental to economic growth and to America's international image, but in his partly ad-libbed national television address that night Kennedy instead called on citizens to "examine [their] conscience." Those who chose to stand by were inviting not only violence but also "shame." But those who chose to "act boldly" were "recognizing right." He argued that "law alone" could not "make men see right." Americans needed to realize that the nation was "confronted primarily with a moral issue" that was "as old as the scriptures and as clear as the Constitution." The assassination of NAACP field secretary Medgar Evers the following night in Mississippi demonstrated that violent segregationists refused to hear the president's plea. More ominously, those who began to resign themselves to the inevitability of token desegregation chose to ignore Kennedy's appeals to conscience and morality and to focus instead on the increasingly frequent calls for law and order.[28]

Two weeks later Wallace turned his attention back to the bigger threat—and, for him, the greater opportunity—K-12 desegregation. On June 28 he announced, "At the moment there is no court order telling us to admit Negroes to our high schools," but he vowed to make a "forceful" stand in order to maintain the "dignity of [the] state" and to "prevent tampering" if there ever were. The orders were coming soon enough. In *Armstrong*, Judge Lynne had refused to order the Birmingham school board to formulate a desegregation plan, as requested by the plaintiffs, having agreed instead with the defense's notion that "indiscriminate mixing" would produce "chaotic" or "catastrophic" results. And he had dismissed *Nelson* altogether on a technicality. By the summer, though, even he had to acknowledge that Birmingham was witnessing what the *Birmingham News* described as "the trickling of the last grain of sand from the legal hour glass." The city would soon have to brace for what Lynne called "discreet desegregation," by which he meant the token admission of the plaintiff children to white schools.[29]

Willie Williams and Ernest Jackson had appealed Lynne's refusal to enjoin the Birmingham school board, knowing there was a good chance for a reversal. Lynne had argued that the plaintiff children had not exhausted their administrative remedies by applying for transfer under the pupil placement law. But the Fifth Circuit had recently struck down the use of a placement law in a Savannah school case. And the Supreme Court had acknowledged that placement laws were "one-way ticket[s] leading to but one destination . . . continued segregation." It had also recently ruled that "deliberate speed" could not "countenance indefinite delay." Williams and Jackson were further encouraged when the appeal landed before a panel consisting of judges Richard Rives, Elbert Tuttle, and Walter Gewin. Recently appointed by Kennedy, Gewin was a former trial lawyer and legislator from Tuscaloosa who was understood to be a strident segregationist. But Rives and Tuttle were almost certain to side with the plaintiffs.[30]

As *Armstrong* awaited appellate review that summer, so too did most of the state's other school cases, all but one of which had produced defeat for the plaintiffs at the trial court level. Judge Grooms had dismissed the CRD's impacted areas suits against Huntsville and Madison County. As the CRD had feared, Grooms noted that Congress had "deliberately refused" to give the attorney general the authority to bring suits in any area other than voting rights. He also insisted that no students of federal personnel had applied for transfer under the placement law, though he dismissively mentioned the *Hereford* complaint in a brief footnote. Grooms suggested that the CRD should seek administrative relief with HEW.[31]

The plaintiffs in *Birdie Mae Davis v. Mobile* had been similarly frustrated. The lone federal judge in Alabama's Southern District at the time was Daniel Thomas. A one-time state solicitor and Truman appointee, Thomas had built a reputation as a personable and likeable judge and as a strong opponent of civil rights litigation. As he would illustrate vividly in the *Davis* case, he routinely frustrated plaintiffs' claims in civil rights cases if he perceived that things were "moving too fast." Justice Department attorneys who litigated before Thomas variously described him as "weak," "reluctant," and "unable to act as a neutral judge." One CRD attorney recalled that Thomas "found civil rights cases distasteful" and that he believed delay in such cases was "a legitimate judicial technique."[32]

Thomas was forced to issue a ruling in *Davis* that summer, however, after being admonished by the appellate court for taking his time. Constance Motley and Vernon Crawford had asked for a one-grade-a-year, "stair-step" plan. But Thomas agreed with the Mobile school board that such "wholesale reshuffling" on a "hurried or 'crash' basis" would result in "chaotic conditions jeopardizing the education of all the pupils." The judge also argued that Mobile was "perhaps the most desegregated city in the South, with no unfortunate incidents," and he insisted that if the appellate court would "be mindful" of the discretion afforded the trial courts by *Brown II*, then he was certain that there would continue to be no "unfortunate incidents." Like Lynne in *Armstrong*, he instructed the plaintiff students to apply for transfer under the placement law."[33]

Motley and Crawford appealed again, and a panel flatly rejected Thomas's assertion that, in their words, if "action [was] not too hastily taken, the problem [would] work itself out with no strife." The school board, they argued, had wasted a decade during which it should have been formulating a desegregation plan. The court directed Thomas to enter an order for a preliminary injunction, pending the trial of the case on its merits in November, and to order the school board to begin desegregation immediately using a grade-a-year plan. A separate appellate panel also reversed Judge Lynne in *Armstrong*, with Judge Rives calling Lynne's ruling "directly contrary" to recent decisions of the appellate court. The court ordered Lynne to enjoin the Birmingham school board from failing to begin desegregation that fall, though in this case using the placement law. This prompted Wisdom and Brown to quickly modify their order in *Davis*, rejecting the grade-a-year approach, with Wisdom writing, "There should not be one law for Birmingham and another for Mobile."[34]

Judge Gewin issued a sharply worded and lengthy dissent to the *Armstrong* decision that marked the beginning of a brief period of unusual judicial infighting. It revealed the sharp division between Rives, Tuttle, Wisdom, and Brown on one side of the circuit court, and Griffin Bell, Gewin, and Ben Cameron on the other. Gewin accused Rives and Tuttle of speaking in "inaccurate and disapproving terms" of a "distinguished" trial judge. According to Gewin, Lynne had preemptively "destroy[ed] every reason" they had put forth to reverse him. Meanwhile, Judge Bell, a Kennedy appointee from south Georgia, just as vehemently dissented from Wisdom and Brown's hasty modification of their panel's order in *Davis*. While he admitted that less desegregation was preferable, he argued that the appellate court should not "mold and enter an equitable decree affecting an entire school system . . . without hearing from the parties on the nature of the decree."[35]

Gewin then called for an en banc rehearing of the *Armstrong* appeal—a hearing before all of the judges of the appellate court. The request was denied by a 5–4 vote. Judge Cameron, a strident segregationist from Mississippi, entered a blistering dissent to that denial in which he quoted, with displeasure, a recent newspaper article focusing on Tuttle, Rives, Wisdom, and Brown. The piece referred to the judges as "The Four," described them as "hard core," and explained that they had "blazed new trails for nearly a decade in the deep south in the civil rights struggle" and had "moved at every opportunity" to implement *Brown*. Cameron lamented their "crusading spirit" and suggested that they had damaged the court's "stature." Finally he accused Tuttle of gross impropriety—insinuating that, among other things, the chief judge had purposefully designated two of "The Four" on each panel assigned to civil rights cases.[36]

The judges eventually came to a settlement, and the "Fifth Circuit Four" were able to remain in the vanguard of civil rights jurisprudence because the law was increasingly on their side. The Supreme Court was finally beginning to favor immediate implementation, at least in token fashion. The Kennedy administration was empowering the CRD and HEW, and the civil rights movement itself continued to press the pace of change. Segregationist judges faced increasingly difficult jurisprudential gymnastics in deferring the initiation of desegregation. Accordingly, on July 19, Judge Lynne was resigned to enjoin the Birmingham school board and order it to begin desegregation using the placement law. Judge Thomas did the same with Mobile a week later, followed by Judge Grooms vis-à-vis Huntsville in the *Hereford* case. Each system was to submit a plan for abiding by the rulings later that summer. In these three districts then, the "last grain of sand" was trickling from the hourglass. But there was one more case and one more district. And the hourglass there was about to be shattered.[37]

Lee v. Macon County was set to come before judge Frank Johnson that August for a hearing. Johnson was one of only a few southern trial court judges whose adjudication of civil rights cases fell in line with that of the Fifth Circuit Four. His neatly pressed black suit, rigid posture, severe gaze, dangling wire-rim glasses, and deadly serious attitude on the bench intimidated many young attorneys before him. CRD attorney Brian Landsberg later recalled that Johnson was a judge who "held attorneys to high expectations, who tolerated no nonsense from either side, and who imparted a sense of dignity and control." Solomon Seay remembered similarly, "If you had a case before Judge Johnson, at the very first hearing, you'd better know everything there is to know about your case, because if you don't, then he's going to know more about it than you. And you're going to be embarrassed." Johnson's adjudication of *Lee v. Macon* would demonstrate that when the law was clear and the injustice was profound, he was willing to use the fullest power of the court to grant meaningful relief as quickly and as wholly as possible.[38]

Johnson had made the United States a party to the *Lee* case *sua sponte*, or without a request from either party, that summer. It was highly unusual, though not entirely unprecedented. He ordered the Justice Department to represent the United States, not as a friend of the court but as a "litigating *amicus*." In Johnson's own words, this would not only "accord [the] court the benefit of [the CRD's] views and recommendations" but would also give the CRD the "right to submit pleadings, evidence, arguments and briefs, and to participate actively as a party in every phase of said proceedings." This meant that the CRD could ask for injunctions or contempt of court citations if it felt these were necessary to "maintain and preserve the due administration of justice and the integrity of the judicial authority" of the government. Johnson respected the work the CRD had already done in Alabama in voting rights cases, and he particularly respected John Doar, the assistant attorney general for civil rights. He also knew that adding the United States as a litigating amicus would give the court the additional resources of HEW and the FBI. More than anything, he understood that resistance was coming.[39]

At an August 13 hearing, after Fred Gray demonstrated the inequities in the segregated Macon County school system—including black schools that still had outhouses and lacked central heating—Johnson ruled from the bench, granting the plaintiffs' request for a preliminary injunction. Though Gray was asking for much more, Johnson was compelled to limit relief to what had been ordered in *Armstrong*, *Davis*, and *Hereford*. The board was to begin non-discriminatorily assigning pupils using the placement law and to present a plan for systematic desegregation by December. But Johnson cautioned, "Needless to say, the failure on the part of the Board to administer the Alabama Placement Law without regard to race or color will result in the law's being struck down on the basis of unconstitutionality." He also granted a request from the CRD to require local school officials to report to the court on all transfer requests it received and processed. This would allow the court, via the CRD, to monitor ongoing compliance efforts.[40]

Days later the Macon County school board received nearly fifty transfer applications from black students. With a court order to blame, local officials had accepted the inevitability of token desegregation and were prepared to sell it to the community with a message of law and order and begrudged acquiescence. Superintendent C. A. Pruitt, known to locals as "Hardboy," announced that he and the board were going to bring "mature thinking into the community." Meanwhile, they brought in the applicant students and, under the watchful eye of CRD representatives, administered a battery of standardized tests. They whittled the number of students down to a number they felt the county's whites would accept. Anthony Lee's evaluation indicated that he had "an ability to adjust with a normal degree of ease" and suggested that "with the proper motivation [he] would succeed." Twelve others would join him on the accepted list, all of whom were set to transfer from all-black Tuskegee Institute High to all-white Tuskegee Public High.[41]

Schools in Macon were scheduled to open on Monday, September 2, earlier than anywhere else under a desegregation order. Four days before that date, the TCA held a meeting for the accepted students and their parents at the Butler Street Methodist Church, where local NAACP chief K. L. Buford was pastor. Buford, Fred Gray, and Detroit Lee all spoke about what the children could expect—to be spat upon, called names, and threatened with violence. They were told not to respond in kind. When Buford opened the meeting up to questions, the first hand raised came from the back, and it was white. The Justice Department's John Doar was there, flanked by U.S. marshals and attorneys from the CRD. The Wisconsin Republican had been a key figure in steering the division toward more active enforcement of civil rights law, and he had come to Alabama, as Frank Johnson had intended, to ensure that the court's orders in *Lee v. Macon* were carried out without interference. Doar rose to assure everyone that federal officials would remain in Tuskegee as long as necessary to ensure the children's safety.[42]

That night the white Parent-Teacher Association held an informational meeting in the Tuskegee Public High auditorium. PTA president and Methodist minister Ennis Sellers chaired the meeting. Sellers was among a group of prominent moderates, including sheriff Preston Hornsby and chamber of commerce president Allan Parker, who were quietly working with black leaders to try to shepherd desegregation through with as little disruption as possible. Those three joined school officials and a handful of teachers and tried to make the case for law and order for around four hundred anxious white parents. Sellers argued that desegregation might be "a dose we don't like," but he added, "Let's go ahead and make the most of it." Most were unconvinced. There were calls from the crowd to reach out to Governor Wallace for help. Allan Parker asked whether Governor Orval Faubus hadn't failed to prevent desegregation in Arkansas. Likewise hadn't Governor Ross Barnett failed in Mississippi, and hadn't Wallace himself recently failed at Tuscaloosa?[43]

Immediately after Parker sat down, a local postal worker rose to demand defiance of desegregation, even if the result was bloodshed. Someone suggested that Wallace could close schools, maybe even provide transportation for white students to attend other schools. Finally, a man in the back stood. He was Hugh Adams—the assistant director of the Alabama Building Commission and a member of the Montgomery Private School Commission. Wallace had planted Adams at the meeting to drum up support for defiance. Adams dutifully explained that Wallace was indeed planning to close any school threatened with desegregation and to assist in the establishment of private schools.

Adams also knew, though he did not let on, that undercover state troopers were at the meeting to collect intelligence for Wallace. Wallace planned to use disorder as proof that it was necessary to close schools. He wanted another showdown, and he was about to get it.[44]

A similar process was simultaneously unfolding in Birmingham. Law-and-order moderates and city officials attempted to ensure peaceful compliance, while more defiant segregationists responded to Wallace's encouragement by redoubling their own efforts. Mayor Boutwell and the city council authorized the creation of a biracial advisory group called the Community Affairs Committee. Robert Shelton and a band of Klansmen picketed the committee's inaugural meeting. Klansmen also bombed the home of black attorney Arthur Shores. Boutwell himself received so many threats that city police began an around-the-clock watch of his home. Former mayor Art Hanes made daily public statements urging whites to form a "human wall" in front of the schools scheduled to be desegregated on the morning schools opened. The *Birmingham News* bemoaned those who continued to "flout law and order" and the "loud mouths," like Hanes, who continued "whipping [those] people up," by shouting, "Resist, resist, resist!" If folks continued to listen to these "misguided zealots," then they ought to "expect more trouble" when schools opened in two weeks.[45]

The *News* reflected on the mood of the city. "Almost no whites" saw the "painful school order imposed . . . by the federal courts" as anything other than "harmful to both races." But rather than close schools, the *News* reasoned, it was time to "face fact." The Community Affairs Committee was charting the proper course, with its "intent to uphold law and order" and its understanding that, "however regrettable" desegregation was, "compliant action [was] unavoidable." Many disagreed. One woman argued that accepting desegregation because it was inevitable was wrongheaded: "'Inevitability' states that we know it isn't desirable, but wrong is going to prevail anyway, so let's just make the best of it." Nothing "as wrong as integration"—which would force "amalgamation" on the next generation—was inevitable. Another reader agreed, arguing that the potential "destruction of the white race" demanded action. History had proven that "racial integration destroys civilization." Therefore, "When a white man fails to stand for segregation, he is destroying his own children and grandchildren."[46]

Edward Fields was among those who decided to stand. Fields was the leader of the local Christian Knights of the Ku Klux Klan and the information director for the National States' Rights Party (NSRP)—a local neo-Nazi organization headed by one J. B. Stoner, an attorney known to be responsible for numerous racially motivated bombings. Fields was the publisher of the

NSRP's official organ, the *Thunderbolt*, in which he called for the execution of the justices of the U.S. Supreme Court and the "repopulation" of blacks and Jews to Africa. Late that summer, Fields organized a series of rallies and began encouraging white students to boycott schools if they were desegregated. He hand-delivered a petition with thirty thousand signatures to the governor's office, calling on Wallace to close the schools, and spoke from the steps of the capitol, eliciting much applause upon deriding "Martin Luther Koon" and echoing Wallace's inaugural address, insisting it was time to "draw the line." Top Wallace advisor Seymore Trammell privately assured Fields that the governor was planning something even bigger than his "stand" in Tuscaloosa. Colonel Al Lingo of the state troopers had told Fields as much the week before. Lingo told Fields that if he made a show of protesting, that would give Wallace the excuse he needed to close the schools.[47]

Many whites were beginning to face the sad reality of failure. Even Judge Gewin, in denying a last-ditch petition to stay the court's order in *Armstrong*, wrote, "The issues here have long been settled by decisions of the U.S. Supreme Court." Referring especially to *Cooper v. Aaron*, he insisted, "Law and order cannot be preserved by yielding to violence and disorder, nor by depriving individuals of constitutional rights decreed to be vested in them by the Supreme Court." Wallace continued to rile everyone else. He told a crowd of white parents in the working-class west side of town that he "had a few secrets for Birmingham" and that he had plans for other places too, by which he meant Tuskegee, Huntsville, and Mobile.[48]

Mobile school officials had accepted that token desegregation was imminent, though they had worked with Judge Thomas to ensure that it would be as limited as possible. The school board accepted only two applications for transfer via the placement law—those of Dorothy Davis and Henry Hobdy, who had applied to all-white Murphy High. A small cadre of law-and-order moderates began to prepare the city for peaceful compliance. City Commissioner Joe Langan led this group, which included a few local clergymen and the newly organized Alabamians Behind Local Education (ABLE). ABLE affiliated itself with the Council on Human Relations and began disseminating pamphlets and organizing community meetings. It even produced a short television spot, calling for "open schools instead of no schools and a peaceful community instead of racial violence." ABLE's president, a local pediatrician's wife, succinctly described the organization's commitment. "We don't want to argue the relative merits of segregation or desegregation," she dismissively asserted, "but we believe that each of us has an individual responsibility to let official local leadership and our fellow citizens know that we stand on the side of law, order, and public schools."[49]

Defiant segregationists were more active. Fields sent thousands of petition forms to Mobile NSRP members, while locals organized the port city's first Citizens' Council. On August 30, nearly one thousand whites gathered at a National Guard armory to hear newly appointed state Citizens' Council executive director (and organizer of the student wing of the Lucy riots) Leonard Wilson encourage them to initiate a boycott of schools and to intimidate Hobdy and Davis into backing down. Art Hanes came down from Birmingham to speak too. He attacked the Kennedy administration and black "agitators," and he called the South the "the last bastion of race pride" and "the stronghold of true nationalistic feeling." The former mayor finished with the most resonant chord of all: "They say the Civil War was fought one hundred years ago, but I tell you that the Civil War is just starting."[50]

"Bitter Fruit"

At one in the morning on Monday, September 2, Reverend Ennis Sellers drove to a secluded dirt road on the outskirts of Tuskegee. There, in the pitch black of night, amid the thick pine forest and a chorus of chirping cicadas, the nervous PTA leader and Methodist minister found a nondescript black car waiting for him. Agents from the FBI had arranged the cloak-and-dagger meeting two weeks prior, when they secured Sellers's cooperation in assisting their investigation. The reverend had agreed to pick up an agent and take him back to his parsonage. Sellers greeted the agents in sober tones and followed through. On the way back into town, he offered to let the agent have his daughter's bedroom for the short remainder of the night. Neither man was certain what would happen when dawn came. At 5:00 a.m. the agent moved into the attic and set up his equipment to monitor whatever spectacle was to unfold below. Through one of the house's two dormer windows, he had a clear view of the building directly across the street—Tuskegee Public High School.[51]

Burke Marshall, the assistant attorney general for civil rights, had asked FBI director J. Edgar Hoover to dispatch local agents to Tuskegee to obtain and transmit to the CRD "any information regarding the existence, activities, and plans of any racist or segregationist groups in the vicinity . . . insofar as such plans or activities may bear upon possible interference with the carrying out of the court's order" in *Lee v. Macon*. Judge Johnson and the CRD's John Doar understood that monitoring enforcement was one of the division's roles as a "litigating *amicus*." This meant that the CRD would need to, in Doar's words, "anticipate and take such steps as [might] be necessary both through legal proceedings and direct action to prevent obstruction." It was in this capacity that Doar had come to Tuskegee and shown up at the TCA meeting at K. L. Buford's church the previous week. On Monday morning Doar was back in Tuskegee, and the FBI was in Ennis Sellers's attic.⁵²

Thirty minutes after the agent climbed into his perch at Sellers's parsonage, an Alabama state trooper made his way over to Superintendent Pruitt's house and knocked on the door. He handed Pruitt a copy of Executive Order Number Nine of the governor of Alabama, which Pruitt began to read in dismay. The "threat of forced and unwarranted integration of the public schools" had created "conditions calculated to result in a disruption of the peace and tranquility of this state and to occasion peril to the lives and property of the citizens thereof." Wallace ordered the Macon school board to postpone the opening of Tuskegee Public High School until the following Monday. He had simultaneously issued Executive Order Number Ten, which insisted that the Tuskegee police and Macon County sheriffs would be "organized as a unified force under the control and direction of the governor acting through the Director of the Department of Public Safety," Colonel Al Lingo. As Pruitt shut the door, just over one hundred of Lingo's heavily armed state troopers began setting up a cordon around Tuskegee Public.⁵³

Ennis Sellers and his wife grabbed their two sons and accompanied them across the street and into the gathering storm. Sellers, who was not a small man, boldly attempted to push through the trooper line, but he and his family were blocked and restrained. Two large troopers grabbed the minister by both arms and began carting him off. He was delivered through a smaller inner circle of troopers and presented to the commanding colonel. Lingo, who according to one bystander appeared to be drunk, barked something incoherent at the minister through the butt of a dead cigar as he toyed with the grip of the revolver at his waist. At that moment, Macon County sheriff Preston Hornsby, outraged at the usurpation of his authority, was demanding to be let through. In uniform with badge and gun, he told the troopers in the line, "I'm the chief law enforcement officer of this county. We're going to get in." The troopers relented, and a number of teachers fell in line behind the sheriff and his daughter Jane. As word spread about town that morning, other white moderates began to express incredulity. The county solicitor called it the "invasion of Macon County." Banker Allan Parker observed that Wallace had "alienated his own supporters."⁵⁴

The Macon school board was unsure what to do and summoned the advice of the state attorney general, Richmond Flowers. Flowers was an established opponent of Wallace's direct defiance policy, but he was nonetheless a devoted segregationist. He counseled the board that Wallace lacked the authority to close the school and that their following such an order would put them in danger of contempt-of-court citations. Wallace sent advisors to Tuskegee to counter Flowers's advice, which Wallace publicly stated was based on an "erroneous interpretation" of the facts and was therefore "unfortunate" and "a pity." The governor reaffirmed that, in order to "maintain peace and order," Tuskegee Public absolutely would not open before the following Monday, September 9. And that night he successfully pressured the Huntsville school board to postpone the next day's scheduled opening of schools there. He was digging in.[55]

On Tuesday morning, Wallace directed Lingo to move some of the troopers in Tuskegee to Birmingham, where schools were set to open the following day. Per the court's order in *Armstrong*, the Birmingham school board had accepted a token number of applications to transfer to white schools. Dwight and Floyd Armstrong would attend Graymont Elementary; Richard Walker would attend Ramsay High; and Patricia Marcus and Josephine Powell would attend West End High. Albert Boutwell had been encouraging reluctant compliance, and he stridently opposed school closure or any interference from the state. But defiant segregationists were all too ready to heed the governor's call to resist. Grand Dragon Shelton and the KKK held a rally that day at the Graymont National Guard Armory, where Edward Fields and the NSRP had set up a command center to direct their own efforts the following morning. Fields planned to lead white supremacist flying columns through police lines, in order to destroy the schools rather than let black students enter.[56]

The Birmingham school board initially resisted Wallace, while Boutwell and the city council insisted that the city's police could maintain law and order just fine on their own. They intended to mitigate any disruptions by postponing desegregation at Ramsay and West End, allowing only the Armstrong boys to enroll at Graymont on Wednesday morning. Burke Marshall flew to Birmingham Tuesday night, accessed the situation, and flew back to confer with the attorney general. The FBI had been in the city for several days and had made preparations, in conjunction with the CRD, similar to those made in Tuskegee. The Justice Department released a statement: "Gov. Wallace knows [that] the schools will be opened and the Negro students will attend them in accord with the orders of the courts. We hope it will be accomplished swiftly by the people of Alabama and their officials."[57]

On Wednesday morning, Dwight and Floyd Armstrong became the first black schoolchildren to successfully enroll in a formerly all-white public grade school in Alabama. Fields and his recruits had begun their morning at West End and had been sorely disappointed when no black students showed up. Upon learning of the enrollment of the Armstrong boys, Fields led his posse—sixty-five or so strong—via motorcade uptown to Graymont, where they recruited a number of onlookers and attempted to rush the line of Birmingham police ringing the school. The police repulsed the attack, at which point the NSRP's parade was literally rained on. Newly drenched, they moved on to Ramsay, where there were, again, no black students. Several frustrated protestors were arrested for taunting and threatening police. Fields retreated to his hotel room to plan his next move, accompanied by Shelton and infamous local Klansman Robert "Dynamite Bob" Chambliss, who had a plan of his own.[58]

Fred Shuttlesworth telegrammed Bobby Kennedy and requested around-the-clock U.S. marshal or FBI protection for all five of the desegregating students and their parents. Hours later, as night fell, Klansmen bombed the home of Arthur Shores for the second time in three weeks. Nearby blacks took to the streets in anger and frustration, assaulting arriving first responders, including police, all of whom were of course white. Before dawn broke on Thursday, four policemen, six additional whites, and eleven blacks had been injured. An unarmed black onlooker, John Coley, had been shot dead by police. Just after four in the morning, Wallace announced, "The Birmingham Board of Education has acceded my request to close temporarily the three schools scheduled to integrate."[59]

Mobile schools opened that morning. Wallace had been able to strong-arm the school board into postponing the enrollment of Henry Hobdy and Dorothy Davis at Murphy High. In Huntsville, however, authorities were refusing the governor's demand for a second delay in opening schools, then slated for the following day. Wallace ordered Lingo to send a contingent of 150 state troopers from Birmingham to Huntsville and issued another executive order insisting that no student be allowed to integrate Huntsville's schools. On Friday morning troopers blocked Sonnie Hereford IV, John Brewton, Terrell Pearson, and David Piggie and their parents and federal escorts from entering four separate schools. The troopers failed to stop an angry mob of white mothers and their children from breaching the line at Fifth Avenue Elementary. They jeered the heavily armed patrolmen, shouting, "You should be ashamed of yourself!" and "Go home where you belong!" One woman wondered aloud, in a German accent, whether this was happening in the United States, observing incredulously, "It reminds me of East Berlin."[60]

That afternoon Orzell Billingsley and Constance Motley filed a motion asking the court to add Wallace as a defendant party in the *Hereford* case. Ernest Jackson filed a similar motion in *Armstrong*, asking the court to enjoin Wallace from further interference and to order the Birmingham school board to open the closed schools. Public criticism came at Wallace from both familiar and strange directions. The Justice Department issued a statement acknowledging that the governor was "trying to provoke" the federal government into using force and that DOJ "would rather not accommodate him if it can be avoided." The *Anniston Star* concluded that an already "touchy situation" had been "made far worse" by Wallace's "ranting and raving," most of which was "entirely uncalled for." Even the staunchly pro-Wallace editor of the *Montgomery Advertiser* argued that the governor was behaving as if Alabama were "a banana republic" and as if he had "gone wild."[61]

On Sunday Wallace appeared on a podium with Edward Fields, Bull Connor, and Art Hanes at a rally for the segregationist United Americans for Conservative Government. He declared that he would "take any risk . . . within the law" to prevent desegregation, echoing a promise he had made at a Citizens' Council rally just days before, when he had promised to "work to resegregate any desegregated schools." That night the governor appeared alongside a cadre of attorneys in a statewide televised "report to the people," in which he argued that his actions the previous week had been "legal and lawful" and justified. He admonished viewers to "observe law and order" in their own continuing resistance. "We cannot win this fight if we resort to violence," Wallace told them. But if they stood with him in this fight, he swore, they could and would win. As Wallace spoke to his acolytes, someone firebombed the home of Birmingham's most prominent black businessman, A. G. Gaston, while Gaston and his wife sat quietly reading.[62]

In the early morning hours of Monday, September 9, the governor signed three more executive orders. Each read, "Integration of the public schools will totally disrupt and effectively destroy the educational process," constituting "an abridgement of civil rights of other children." It would deprive those "other children" of their rights to equal protection and "their rights, liberty, and property without due process of law." The orders insisted, "No student shall be permitted to integrate the public schools" of Birmingham, Tuskegee, and Mobile. Wallace had conceded Huntsville, where white moderate sentiment was strongest. As the governor doubled down on the other three locations that morning, Sonnie Hereford took his son to Fifth Avenue Elementary, where the latter became the first black child to attend class in a desegregated public grade school in Alabama (the Armstrong boys having only enrolled before Birmingham closed its schools). Sonnie Hereford IV was followed shortly by the other three *Hereford* plaintiff students.[63]

At the other end of the state, a convoy of 125 state troopers and other deputized law enforcement officials crossed the Mobile Bay causeway into downtown Mobile and headed west toward Murphy High School. Mobile police, who had already barricaded the area, were forced to abdicate control of the situation, allowing the troopers to blockade the school, as they had done in Tuskegee. When Hobdy and Davis arrived—accompanied by John LeFlore and attorneys Vernon Crawford and Clarence Moses—the trooper in charge handed them a copy of Wallace's executive order and turned them away. John LeFlore walked over to a crowd of reporters and told them, "We must bring a stop to this sort of thing that we [just] saw," adding, "Our only alternative is to go into the federal district court here in Mobile and seek compliance with the federal order and to restrain Governor Wallace from further interference." As LeFlore spoke, Crawford was on his way to draft a motion in *Davis* seeking exactly that.[64]

Mobile mayor Charles Trimmier was on hand to witness the confrontation and issued a brief statement thereafter. Mobile, he argued, had made "progress [in] basic race relationships without violence, hatred, or fear." It was "unfortunate," he lamented, that the federal courts had threatened that progress through the "forced integration of the schools," which was "disapproved by a majority of [Mobile's] citizens." Mobilians, though, were "respectors of the law" and would "discipline themselves without resorting to violence." Trimmier added that his city did not need "interference" from "Governor Wallace or anyone else."[65]

Two hundred miles northeast, state troopers again formed a wall around Tuskegee Public. The troopers had let white students and faculty into the building for the first time, but they were still poised to block the entry of Anthony Lee and his twelve companions. As soon as their bus drove onto the grounds, the commanding trooper, Claude Prier, boarded the bus and announced, "It is my duty to inform you that by order of the governor of the state of Alabama, you will be prohibited from entering the school." He then read the text of the executive order, handing a copy to each of the students and one to Superintendent Pruitt, who had begun to approach the bus from his trailing car. Prier rode the bus back to the superintendent's office, where the students disembarked and made arrangements to go home. Within hours, Fred Gray was phoning plaintiff families. He let them know that John Doar was on his way to the federal courthouse in Montgomery to file a motion in *Lee v. Macon* for a temporary restraining order against the governor.[66]

In Birmingham, attorneys Ernest Jackson and Oscar Adams escorted Patricia Marcus and Josephine Powell to West End High School, where state troopers had forced the removal of the police. As Jackson and his group approached, Colonel Lingo himself stepped in their way, held up his hands, and ordered, "You will not be allowed to enter; leave the campus." As Jackson turned to Adams to debate the next move, an irritated Lingo raised his voice, "You will leave immediately; leave the premises!" Jackson asked calmly, "Do I understand that you are asking me to leave?" Lingo replied, through teeth clenching his trademark cigar, "I am *telling* you to leave immediately!" As the group finally retreated, white students jeered from the windows of the school. Richard Walker suffered a similar fate at Ramsay High School, where he was met with cries of "Nigger, go home!" Lingo moved to Graymont Elementary so he could again confront Jackson and Adams, who were then accompanying the Armstrong boys with Fred Shuttlesworth. Lingo told them, "Governor Wallace's orders are that you will not be allowed to enter." Jackson pressed again. Would the colonel not, he asked, be willing to obey the federal court order that said the students should be admitted? "No, I will not," Lingo said flatly. At that point, Lingo noticed the Justice Department's Joe Dolan in the group and asked him snarkily, "Have you called the White House?" Dolan smiled wryly and answered no. Everyone knew that the real answer was "not yet."[67]

Dolan phoned Washington later that morning. President Kennedy issued a statement lamenting Wallace's refusal to respect "either the law or the authority of local officials." He understood that Wallace was "desperately anxious to have the Federal Government intervene" for "personal and political reasons." Wallace issued his own statement arguing that he was "completely willing to leave it to local communities" if only the president and the CRD would "do likewise." Meanwhile, John Doar spoke with the U.S. attorney general, Robert Kennedy, just prior to filing a motion for a restraining order against the governor in *Lee v. Macon*. The two decided that Doar should instead initiate a separate action altogether—against Wallace, Lingo, and each commanding state trooper who had denied students' admission. Doar filed the complaint, and Judge Johnson immediately called all federal trial court judges in the state—Grooms, Lynne, Thomas, and Clarence Allgood. All five judges had presided over at least one of the state's active school desegregation cases. They agreed to convene a rare five-judge court and to quickly issue a temporary restraining order in what was styled *United States v. Wallace*.[68]

Johnson drafted the order, which he signed on behalf of the other four judges for expediency. He described how Wallace had, within the previous week, "purported to order and direct" local school officials to disobey court orders and to prevent desegregation. The court enjoined Wallace, Lingo, and each of the named troopers from "implementing or giving force or effect to the executive order[s] of September 9, 1963"; from "physically preventing or interfering with students, teachers, or other persons" entering or leaving the affected schools; from "interfering with or obstructing" the Mobile, Tuskegee, Birmingham, and Huntsville boards of education; and from "failing to maintain peace and order within and around" the various affected schools. U.S. marshals set out that evening to serve the enjoined parties. Lingo and the troopers were duly served, but Lingo phoned to warn Wallace, setting the scene for an evening of Alabama-style theater of the absurd.[69]

No sooner did Wallace assemble a team at the state capital than the White House accidentally phoned Wallace's office while trying to reach John Doar, who at the time was thought to be in Richmond Flowers's office, in the same building. Apparently, the call had been misdirected. Wallace resolved to barricade himself in his office, determined to avoid being served, by Doar or anyone else, until he could mobilize the National Guard to replace the troopers at the various schools. When two U.S. marshals arrived at the capitol, they were told to wait in the hall. Over the course of the next three hours, the marshals knocked on the door of the office six times, only to be told by Wallace's bodyguards and cabinet members to wait, or that the governor was not there, and to have the door closed in their faces. When more than twenty brawny state troopers arrived and were let into the office lobby, the marshals called for assistance and joined four colleagues in positions covering the front and back doors to the building, lest Wallace try to sneak out.[70]

By 11:00 p.m., local press had begun assembling outside. Wallace aide Seymore Trammell emerged to read a statement. The governor, he announced dismissively, was working from the office, which had been "besieged" by U.S. marshals. Trammell added, "[Governor Wallace] wants peace, and you cannot have it in this type of condition. . . . This is intimidation." Trammell asked "unauthorized persons" to leave and claimed that if they did not, the National Guard would soon be on hand to "make them." Guardsmen arrived not long thereafter and physically barred the marshals from reentering the building, as state troopers began searching the capitol grounds for marshals thought to be hiding in the bushes. Wallace did not emerge until 1:30 a.m., by which time the marshals had left. He had issued yet another executive order, sending the National Guard to replace troopers in Mobile, Tuskegee, and Birmingham to "cope with circumstances and actions reasonably calculated to result in a breach of the peace and in public disorder."[71]

Word of the mobilization soon reached the Pentagon, which informed Attorney General Kennedy, who then woke his brother in the middle of the night. From his bedroom, President Kennedy signed a proclamation commanding "all persons engaged in . . . unlawful obstructions of justice, assemblies, combinations, and conspiracies" to "cease and desist therefrom and to retire peaceably forthwith." Kennedy also signed an executive order giving Secretary of Defense Robert McNamara the authority to take "all appropriate steps" to "remove obstructions of justice in the State of Alabama." Just after dawn on September 10, McNamara took command of the Alabama National Guard and ordered the guardsmen to return to their respective armories and to restore control of the various situations to the local police.[72]

That morning, nearly three thousand white students at Murphy High in Mobile sat in their classrooms awaiting the start of the school day, when they heard the voice of principal Bruce Taylor over the public address system. Taylor announced that two black students would be entering the school shortly. He beseeched students to go about their day as they normally would. He urged, "Don't do anything to embarrass our school." Taylor then went to greet Henry Hobdy and Dorothy Davis, who were flanked by over twenty local law enforcement officers, drawn from the hundreds of sheriff's deputies and police stationed on and around the campus. Taylor escorted the two students to their homeroom and to their first class. At the urging of the local Citizens' Council, white students began coordinating a boycott. A small group of demonstrators on the following day would become a throng of three hundred by the end of the week, as protests moved from the campus itself into the streets of downtown Mobile.[73]

In Birmingham, the Armstrong boys returned to Graymont, and Richard Walker desegregated Ramsay High. When Patricia Marcus and Josephine Powell arrived at West End High, they were hurried through a side door to avoid the growing crowd at the front of the school. When white students encountered them inside the building, some began to cry. Others walked out. By midmorning, over one thousand students were gathered on the front lawn of the campus and chanting toward the building, loud enough for Powell and Marcus to hear: "Two, four, six, eight, we don't want to integrate!" "We hate niggers!" "Get the niggers out!" "We hate Kennedy!" "We want Wallace!" Students who remained in the building were admonished with cries of "Nigger lover!" Many of the remaining teachers and students eventually came outside, to the delight of the horde. As one student began to play "Dixie" on his trumpet, others began to march about the grounds waving Confederate battle flags.[74]

Across the street from West End stood a crowd of two hundred or so white adults, including Edward Fields and NSRP head J. B. Stoner. They began cheering the white students on, as a small group of apprehensive blacks coalesced down the street. Police eventually attempted to disperse both the students and the adults. Some of the white adults resisted, obliging the police to make ten arrests, as the students simply reconvened on the football field behind the school. By midday a busload of police in riot gear finally removed both crowds. Meanwhile, in Montgomery, the governor empowered his executive secretary to accept service of the restraining order that he had so doggedly eluded the previous night. Wallace complained to the press, "I don't know what anyone can do but observe the orders. I can't fight bayonets with my bare hands."[75]

In Tuskegee the white reaction was just as swift. What it lacked in pompous protests, it more than made up for in exodus. When the thirteen desegregating black students entered Tuskegee Public, only 170 or so white students out of

600 were in attendance, and over 125 of those were in the elementary wing of the campus. The high school was nearly deserted. A tenth grader named Andy Sharpe was one of the few who remained in attendance. He later recalled the experience of witnessing the actual moment at which desegregation became a reality: "Mrs. Varner . . . was standing in front of the class reading from the textbook as if things were normal. They were not. She was wearing sunglasses. . . . About half-way through the class, there was a knock at the door. A young black girl was ushered in and took a seat at a desk. Not a word was spoken, and Mrs. Varner never missed a beat. She continued to read as if nothing had happened. At a moment like this, you really can't comprehend the historical significance of what you just witnessed. It was surreal."[76]

Toward the end of that class, Sharpe was called into the principal's office, where he was told that his father had just called. He was to come home immediately. "I knew that was it," Sharpe remembered. "I walked out and cried all the way home. I knew I would never set foot in that school again," he lamented, "And I never did." The following morning, only twenty white high school students came to school, and all of them left by the end of the day. Tuskegee Public High School was again segregated.[77]

On Thursday, September 12, a crowd of seven hundred whites gathered at the local VFW post to hear from representatives of the newly created Macon County Private School Foundation, set up in the wake of the PTA meeting the previous week. The foundation's newly tapped president, John Fletcher Segrest, insisted that the county's whites had "the forces to win" the coming "battle" and that they had the full backing of Governor Wallace. Wallace saw Macon as a potential model for the rest of the state to follow and began steering donors to the new foundation. He even solicited donations from state employees and pledged $100 himself. Before it even had a facility in which to hold classes, students registered for Macon Academy by the dozens.[78]

The new school's headmaster, Mrs. W. T. Wadsworth, telegrammed Wallace asking if the foundation could really get grants-in-aid for students to pay tuition. Wallace ensured her that it could and that the state would soon make the grants available, ignoring a recent decision of the Supreme Court striking such arrangements. Wadsworth carried that assurance to apprehensive white parents in a public announcement. She observed, "The picture has been painted . . . that Macon County is ready and willing to accept integration in [its] schools," but she insisted that this was not the case. "We have no hatred," she maintained, "we just believe [segregation] is right." She approached Ennis Sellers with the same pitch, asking if the foundation could use his church's education building as the school's campus until a new facility could be built. Sellers refused, having concluded that segregation contravened the teachings of the Methodist Church. He was rewarded with ostracizing, harassment, and threats of violence. By the end of the week, the foundation had acquired an antebellum mansion located directly across the street from Tuskegee Public.[79]

News of Macon Academy's establishment spread quickly. A Tuscaloosa man wrote to the *Birmingham News* to express his approval. "Hats off to the brave people of Tuskegee and Macon County," he wrote, for not "bowing to the tyrannical race-mixers of Washington or heeding the advice of Alabama's big city scalawag newspapers, which have tried for so long to brainwash us into acceptance." This was "the fighting South at its very best." Macon would be "an inspiration and a guidepost to all who [were] inclined and willing to follow the example." Indeed it was. A group of parents led by William Hoover, of the segregationist American States' Rights Association, established West End Parents for Private Schools, which, with Wallace's encouragement, initiated plans to open two private schools in Birmingham—Jefferson Academy and Hoover Academy.[80]

Protests in Birmingham had spread citywide by the end of the week. Fields and the NSRP, Shelton and the Klan, and boycotting students all rode in raucous motorcades from school to school encouraging students to leave and join them. At one point the roving mob comprised upward of one hundred cars, horns honking, with people leaning out of windows waving Confederate flags. There were crude signs and bumper stickers: "Keep your children out of integrated schools." "Kan the Kennedy Klan." "We want private schools." "Close mixed schools." One pickup truck carried two caskets in its bed and dragged a black-faced effigy from a rope attached to the trailer hitch. On one campus, a fight erupted when teachers and student-leaders asked the protestors to leave. The police intervened to prevent a similar episode at Phillips High downtown, only to watch students storm the football stadium, chanting, "Eight, seven, six, two, we don't want a jigaboo!"[81]

Five hundred students then staged a protest at Birmingham City Hall. Students picketing outside the building chanted, "Eight, six, four, two, Albert Boutwell is a Jew," while the mayor, who was not Jewish, was at lunch. He returned to find that some of the students had stormed his office and were climbing atop his desk, putting out cigarette butts on his furniture, waving battle flags, and generally raising hell. Flabbergasted, he importuned them to observe law and order, saying that only in this way could they stifle the forces of integration. Woodlawn High senior David Littleton heeded that advice, resolving to circulate a petition the next week in which he would challenge desegregation in "the only legal way." Littleton reminded his fellow students that God had given them the "duty to choose between . . . right and wrong." Integration was wrong, and no "governing body" could "infringe a wrong on the majority just because a minority demand[ed] such." So Littleton vowed to support George Wallace. The governor, he told them, would "protect and defend our age-old traditions for the right of life, liberty, and the pursuit of Alabama's happiness." He would stand up, in other words, for white rights.[82]

Two days later, on the morning of Sunday, September 15, as the sun rose over Ruffner Mountain and began to pour into Jones Valley, most folks were getting ready for church. Boutwell was among them. The mayor had been stunned by the protests, but he was confident that he could convince the city's whites that law and order and begrudged compliance would ultimately win the day. Edward Fields and J. B. Stoner were preparing to host a large NSRP rally that day in the industrial western suburb of Midfield, after which they intended to lead another motorcade. West End Parents for Private Schools planned to be there too, drumming up support for the city's two newly proposed segregation academies.[83]

Bob Chambliss had already prepared. He was just awaiting the wicked harvest. Under cover of darkness the night before, "Dynamite Bob" and his Klan brethren had planted a bomb beneath the steps leading to the side entrance of Sixteenth Street Baptist Church on the city's Northside. Chambliss would later claim that the unsophisticated device was supposed to detonate when the building was unoccupied. It did not. The bomb exploded at 10:22 a.m., while two hundred people filled the church for worship. In the chaotic aftermath of the explosion, first responders and volunteers discovered the bodies of fourteen-year-olds Cynthia Wesley, Addie Mae Collins, and Carole Robertson, and eleven-year-old Denise McNair. The four children had been in a basement bathroom, preparing for Sunday school, when the structure above them collapsed. Violence begat more violence. Within hours two major fires burned, and roving black crowds began to assault passing whites—most of whom had descended on the area to gawk, many even to celebrate and taunt. At one point a police officer ordered Johnnie Robinson, an unarmed black teenager, to stop in his tracks. When Robinson instead turned to run, officer Jack Parker shot him in the back, killing him.[84]

The Jefferson County Sheriff's Department and the Birmingham police convinced Edward Fields to cancel the NSRP motorcade, though this did not stop some members of the West End Parents for Private Schools from hosting a rally behind City Hall, where someone burned an effigy of Bobby Kennedy. Nor did it stop Phillips High seniors Michael Farley and Larry Joe Sims. The two disappointed youths left the NSRP headquarters on a motor scooter and resolved to lead their own personal parade through a nearby black neighborhood. When friends warned them that two black children were throwing rocks around the corner, Farley assured them that he would "get them."

Brothers James and Virgil Ware were indeed around the corner, harmlessly riding their bike back from a junkyard, where they had searched for parts for a second bike to use on their paper route. As the scooter approached the brothers' bike, Farley handed a .22 pistol to Sims, who then shot Virgil Ware twice, killing him.[85]

By nightfall the Alabama state troopers and the National Guard again patrolled the streets of Birmingham. Mayor Boutwell gave a televised address, calling the bombing "inconceivable" and "shocking." He urged people to avoid creating "more senseless trouble" that night and to instead stay home and "pray and think." Boutwell implored, "I urge as strongly as I know how for the children of Birmingham to get about the business of their education and leave this fearful task to the School Board and their attorneys, and to our law enforcement officers."[86]

Citizens' Council pioneer Walter Givhan blamed black "agitators." Givhan suggested that they had planted the bomb in order to blame whites for it and that they had simply botched the operation and mistimed the blast. It was a story that fit nicely into established stereotypes and council doctrine, and probably a majority of whites in Alabama genuinely believed it to be true. The *Alabama Baptist*, for example, wondered if the "deplorable" act was the work of "radical Negroes who seek to stir up trouble." Even those who would acknowledge that blacks did not plant the bomb seemed to suggest that they were still somehow to blame. The Talladega *Daily Home* singled out "agitators who have cried for trouble even as they have pretended to counsel for love and peace." Some, including the governor, blamed the president. The *Cullman Times* argued that "the Kennedys, Martin Luther King, and numerous others," who had pushed for desegregation "for their own personal gain," had "blood on [their] hands."[87]

Some insisted that Wallace himself ought to shoulder some of the blame. The *Daily Home* pleaded, "May God forgive the politicians who have wittingly or unwittingly set man against man and race against race." The *Huntsville Times* condemned "leaders who made political hay of promises they knew they couldn't keep." And the Tuscaloosa *Graphic* suggested that Wallace ought to "face the facts and settle down to being governor" because his "charade of meaningless defiance" and "political demagoguery" were "costing Alabama support every day." *Time* magazine put Wallace on its cover the following week—his defiant face superimposed on an image of the bombed-out facade of the church.[88]

Most white Alabamians doubled down on law and order. Judge Clarence Allgood called for a special grand jury to indict anyone who had obstructed desegregation or who might have been responsible for the bombing. In his charge, Allgood said that he was "sickened" by the bombing, and he insisted that no one could "murder, or intimidate, or mock the judgment of the law, no matter how distasteful or unpopular that law may be." He described the bombers as "traitors to their cause" of preserving segregation and said they were "doing the South a disservice." A group of Birmingham lawyers issued a similar statement, admitting, "Each of us has on occasion felt that a particular case should have been decided differently, but whether we agree or disagree with the result in any case, the court's decision is the law and must be obeyed."[89]

The state's newspaper editors almost unanimously called for law and order. The *Alabama Baptist* had "never endorsed integration," but it was "certainly for law and order." The *Tuscaloosa News* hoped that "pleas for law and order" would be "backed up by more than empty words." The *Northwest Alabamian* argued, "We must return to law and order, for only then will we have an atmosphere conducive to reasonable solutions of the problems which will be with us for a long time." The *Selma Times-Journal* assured segregationists, "Nobody has to abandon principle to take and maintain a stand for law and order." The *Union Springs Herald* admitted that there were "moral overtones" to the movement in Alabama that "[could] not be denied." But the "means . . . being employed" to achieve the movement's goals were disturbing. More "senseless slaughter" ought to be avoided, but if leaders continued to act "irresponsibly," then the "tree of civil rights" would "bear a bitter fruit indeed."[90]

Even amid the rubble of Sixteenth Street Baptist, there was no moral awakening. Precious few advocated compliance for the sake of anything more than image and economic viability. Those few that did, did so passionately, however. A Birmingham woman wrote to the *News* and wondered why "the great majority of Birmingham's white citizens were quick to admit that they found the bombing of a church and the willful murder of children appalling," but were "even quicker to attempt to excuse those acts with accusations hurled at the Supreme Court, the NAACP, the Kennedy brothers, etc." She asked, "How can responsible, clear-thinking white people possibly believe that there is any excusing such acts?"[91]

A young Birmingham attorney named Charles Morgan, among those who had recently sued to force reapportionment of the state legislature, had the audacity to ask the same question before a meeting of the city's Young Men's Business Club. He began by bluntly demanding, "Who did it? Who threw that bomb? The answer should be, 'We all did it.'" Morgan argued that anyone who had "in any way contributed . . . to the popularity of hatred" and "intolerance and bigotry" was "at least as guilty as the demented fool who threw the bomb." He excoriated everyone from the "crude oaf" who told racist jokes at parties to businessmen who only decried violence for its damage to the city's image. He criticized ministers who were "too late" in condemning violence and who still refused to condemn segregation. He blasted the city's all-white police force, which had, for obvious lack of trying, failed to solve any racially motivated bombings. He pointed the finger at white newspapers that "timorously defend[ed] the law," white southern liberals who sat "in fearful silence," and Albert Boutwell, mayor of a "leaderless city in which everyone wants to blame someone else." He concluded, "Birmingham is not a dying city; it is dead." A few applauded as Morgan left the podium and sat down. But when one person suggested that the club add a black member, there was silence. The death threats to Morgan and his family began at five the next morning and continued, by letter and phone, for weeks.[92]

Birmingham businessmen James Head and Charles Zukoski issued an indictment similar to Morgan's, if less scathing. Their cowritten open letter accused the city's whites of failing to face certain "basic truths," the first being that "the Negro [was] a human being, with all of the feelings, the hopes, the aspirations of his white fellow man." Next, they knew "in their hearts" that segregation was white society's way of "keeping the Negro in his place." Also, there was "no rational hope" that the *Brown* decision would be overturned. So why, they wondered, would anyone listen to "misguided prophets" who counseled "bitter-end resistance"? Describing the realization that token desegregation was unavoidable, they wrote, "Even when, as the pressure grew, some few wise citizens were bold enough to face the inevitable and come out with a plea for law and order, there was no heart in their voices and their words were unaccompanied by any moral conviction." They concluded, "Unless Birmingham begins to face up to the great moral issue involved, and to recognize the rightness as well as the inevitability of change, it will indeed be dead."[93]

As everyone wrestled with the implications of the tragedy, the FBI pegged Bob Chambliss as the lead perpetrator in the bombing. Al Lingo quickly arrested him, however, to ensure that his case would be tried in state court. Chambliss, along with Sims and Farley, pled guilty to reduced charges and served no jail time. Chuck Morgan, after crosses were burned on his lawn and his wife and child were followed around town, elected to move to Atlanta. The motorcades and school-front demonstrations died down that fall. But all of the state's active school desegregation cases were still awaiting trials, and new litigation in other districts seemed inevitable. George Wallace continued to search for a way to capitalize on whites' fears by encouraging and facilitating defiance, particularly via the establishment of private schools. Most whites seemed to support law and order—some favoring continuing defiance, others reluctantly advocating compliance, while at the same time searching for ways to limit desegregation just the same. Almost no one questioned the righteousness of white supremacy and the value of segregation.⁹⁴

One man displayed an acute understanding of the struggle that lay ahead. In a letter to the *Birmingham News*, H. H. Perritt wondered whether the murders might shock whites "into speaking out for freedom of the oppressed, opportunity for the deprived, and love for the despised among us," especially those "who by accident of birth have darker skin." He predicted, "Hatred will continue, [and] murder will continue, unless we admit our mistakes and undertake positive action to eliminate from our laws and customs the wrongs we have committed against our fellow Americans for generations." He determined, "We cannot have respect for 'law and order' while at the same time using every available means short of violence to circumvent or defy the law of the land as interpreted by the courts. Only by positive steps [and] admission of our sins," he concluded, "can we begin to purge our society of the sickness in its soul."⁹⁵

CHAPTER 3

"Now a Single Shot Can Do It," 1964–1966

One year to the day after George Wallace's inauguration—on the morning of January 14, 1964—Macon County superintendent Hardboy Pruitt found himself in Frank Johnson's courtroom in Montgomery, answering questions posed by attorney Fred Gray. Gray had asked the court to subpoena Pruitt in the *Lee v. Macon County* case. He wanted to know what progress the Macon County school board had made in formulating its comprehensive desegregation plan, due to the court in March. The answer was "none." Pruitt told the court, "I can conceive of no plan at this time that would be submitted that would be accepted by the white people." Blacks in Macon County, in the heart of the Black Belt, outnumbered whites. Therefore, even limited desegregation would, Pruitt concluded, "end the public school system in the county as far as white people are concerned." Circumstances seemed to support this conclusion. Every one of Tuskegee Public High School's white students had withdrawn, and most had enrolled in the public white high schools in nearby Shorter and Notasulga or Macon Academy.[1]

Under cross-examination by the state's assistant attorney general, Gordon Madison, Pruitt argued that he and the school board had been "placed in the position of complying with a court order and being charged with defying a very popular governor." But they had complied, he confirmed, despite harassment from the white community. Pruitt revealed intimidation from the state as well. State school superintendent Austin Meadows had ordered the school board to provide bus transportation for the white students who had fled to Shorter and Notasulga. The plaintiffs and Judge Johnson were already aware of this, and Johnson had already ordered the board to stop. According to Pruitt, Wallace had pressured the board to defy the court's order too, which Pruitt insisted it had refused to do, despite more pressure and threats. The governor subsequently arranged to have the students transported in state trooper cars and state trade school busses.²

By the conclusion of the hearing, Fred Gray had begun to wonder who was really running the school system in Macon County. Wallace loved to demonize the federal government in Washington for usurping local authority. But the state government appeared to be doing the very same thing. That summer Wallace's actions began to sweep everyone involved in *Lee v. Macon* into a gathering storm. The case became the vortex around which local attorneys and plaintiffs, the NAACP Legal Defense Fund, the state NAACP, the Justice Department, HEW, and the Wallace administration all swirled, struggling to determine the fate of public education in Alabama and beyond. Local officials like Pruitt fought to remain grounded, as whites across the state looked to Tuskegee as the example of defiant resistance and escape. The case that initially involved thirteen black students in Macon County was about to become the most far-reaching school desegregation suit in the nation.³

Moses and the Burning Bush

The southern Black Belt stretches from South Carolina to the Mississippi River, and African Americans historically have constituted the majority of the population in many counties throughout the region. As a general rule, the higher the percentage of blacks to whites in a given area, the greater the perceived threat to white rule, and thus the more desperate the defense of segregation and white supremacy. Accordingly, the Alabama Black Belt, like the Mississippi Delta, saw some of the most virulent efforts to preserve white supremacy in America. Each of the Deep South states also has a northern piedmont, though, in which whites have enjoyed heavy majorities, not unlike those in the states of the Peripheral South. Whites there have been less fearful and therefore less reactionary. This was true of northern Alabama. Alabama also has a southeastern Wiregrass region, below the Black Belt, where whites are in the majority but have often been just as dogged in their defense of the status quo; a central section, including the city of Birmingham, whose demographics shifted dramatically, first from influxes of black farmers during the Great Migration and after World War II and later with the winds of white flight; and finally a southern panhandle surrounding Mobile Bay, where race relations have been, like the region's history, perhaps the most complex.⁴

Of Alabama's 114 public school districts, from Huntsville to Mobile, six were facing desegregation litigation in the winter of 1964, including the Black Belt's Macon County. About 1 percent of the South's schoolchildren were attending desegregated schools. In Alabama, it was .004 percent. There were small signs of progress in North Alabama. In Huntsville, ten children of federal personnel had joined Sonnie Hereford IV and the three others in desegregated assignments. And school boards in nearby Florence and Sheffield had voluntarily initiated token desegregation. But there were also innumerable signs of stagnation. For example, when the plaintiffs in *Birdie Mae Davis v. Mobile* proposed a plan that would have fully integrated schools in three years, defendant local officials called to the witness stand the same racist pseudoscientist, Wesley Critz, who had testified in Birmingham's *Armstrong* case. It must have seemed inconceivable that developments in the state would begin to steer the country toward more efficient desegregation litigation, even more so that the paradigm shift would begin with a Black Belt case.[5]

In Tuskegee, though, what initially appeared to be regression soon pointed the way forward. On January 30, 1964, the State Board of Education ordered the Macon County school board to close Tuskegee Public High School, where only Anthony Lee and the other *Lee v. Macon* plaintiff students, then numbering eleven, were attending. State officials cited a law that mandated school closure "where the teacher load is insufficient to justify paying teachers." They ordered the county to not only transport the boycotting white students to the white high schools in Shorter and Notasulga but also to transfer the *Lee v. Macon* plaintiff students to "other schools in the Tuskegee area," meaning all-black Tuskegee Institute High, their old school. After conferring with state attorney general Richmond Flowers that night, the Macon board acceded.[6]

Fred Gray later recalled that the realization hit him "like the burning bush speaking to Moses." Since *Brown*, the Alabama state legislature had gone to great lengths to give the impression that public school systems in the state were autonomous. This was the motivation behind the local control mechanism in the pupil placement law and the removal of the compulsory segregation language from the state constitution. Yet the governor had issued multiple executive orders the previous fall mandating school closures. And here was the state school board ordering another closure and dictating the terms of transfers and transportation. If Gray could prove that the state controlled local school systems, the court could perhaps force the state to use that authority to desegregate not just Tuskegee but also every system in Alabama. This possibility soon became apparent to some within the Wallace administration. Flowers called it a potential "catastrophe." Another official admitted that state authorities had made "a tactical error." Since *Brown*, he explained, the strategy had been "to spread this out as much as possible, so any court action taken is a scattergun action. Now," he predicted, "a single shot can do it."[7]

When Anthony Lee and company arrived on the morning of Monday, January 3 to find that Tuskegee Public had been padlocked, Gray drafted an amended complaint in which he argued that the governor and the state board were attempting to "circumvent and evade" the orders of the court. He asked the court to add the board, its individual members, and its president (the governor) as defendant parties in the case and enjoin them from any further interference. Gray offered two possible avenues for the court to proceed—order the reopening of Tuskegee Public or order the transfer of the twelve plaintiff students to Shorter and Notasulga. Then he took the single shot. Since it had become clear that the state was able to order local school systems to remain segregated, Gray proposed that the court order the state to use that power to *de*segregate every school system not already under a court order.[8]

Judge Johnson granted a temporary restraining order against Wallace and the state board that afternoon, enjoining them from further interference in Macon County. Rather than order the reopening of Tuskegee Public, Johnson ordered the Macon board to transfer the twelve black students to Shorter and Notasulga. Gray had already arranged to have six students attend each of the two schools. Johnson set a hearing for February 13 to consider enlarging the temporary restraining order into a preliminary injunction, but he noted that this hearing would be limited to the issues involving Macon County itself. While the issue of interference with the court's order in Macon was plain and simple, a statewide desegregation order would have been unprecedented and would have required more careful consideration.[9]

Wallace called Johnson "rash" and "vindictive" and denounced the ruling as a "judicial tantrum" and an "order of spite." He lamented that Johnson "aimed to sow discord" based solely upon the "affidavit of a Negro attorney," which was "the same as the NAACP." He convened an emergency meeting of the State Board of Education, at which the board adopted a condemnatory resolution. It vowed to maintain what it called "our way of life" and declared, "The State Board of Education deplores the Order of Judge Johnson and pledges every resource at our command to defend the people of our State against said Order and will defend the people of our state against every Order of the Federal courts in attempting to integrate the public schools of this State and will use every legal means at our command to defeat said integration Orders and pledges our full support to the local boards of education." At Wallace's behest, the state board also called on Macon County officials to begin providing tuition grants to parents "forthwith."[10]

The county prepared for the scheduled transfer and enrollment of the twelve *Lee* students later that week. Less trouble was expected at Shorter, in the southwestern corner of the county, where the planter gentry might counsel against violence. Notasulga was another matter. Located in the hill country on the county's northeastern edge, it was a community of poor farmers and textile mill workers. The town's mayor, a self-proclaimed "country lawyer" named James "Kayo" Rea, had described whites' attitudes toward desegregation by observing, "We believe in law and order, but it may be touch and go at times." Rea asked Wallace to send in the Alabama state troopers in advance of an anticipated Wednesday enrollment. Al Lingo prepared, calling the town a "powder keg" and "worse" than Tuscaloosa or Birmingham. Richmond Flowers described it as "the most explosive situation" he ever saw.[11]

Rea was ready to emulate the governor. On Monday night, he and the town's council passed two hastily drafted ordinances. The "Civil Disturbance Ordinance" gave the mayor the authority to "close any public facility" in order to prevent "riots, violence or physical injury to persons or property." And the "Safety Ordinance" created the office of safety and fire prevention inspector, to which Rea himself was quickly appointed. The mayor's first official act as inspector was to call the principal at Macon County High School at Notasulga and ascertain the number of people currently enrolled and employed there—174. Rea then set the official capacity of the facility at 175. When Klansmen began burning crosses on the lawns of school board members—and two barns and a farmhouse on one board member's farm—the new fire inspector seemed less concerned.[12]

Students and parents, meanwhile, began talking about boycotting Shorter High and Macon County High, despite appeals from a few seniors. With public school options in the county exhausted, inquiries began to pour into Macon Academy on Tuesday morning. Academy leaders assured parents that the fledgling school could accommodate all comers. Some parents took their children out of the public schools on Tuesday. Gathering crowds of reporters observed one man sobbing uncontrollably in his car while his son went into the facility at Shorter to gather his books. Another man sitting in his car outside the Notasulga facility told reporters, "This all could have ended at [Ole Miss], if it had just been bloody enough." As he fingered the end of a switchblade knife, he told them that he doubted if the black students would even make it out of Tuskegee the next morning. And if they did, he sure hoped that the state troopers were not there to protect them.[13]

That morning, Macon County awoke to a cold, steady rain. Lingo and the state troopers arrived before dawn, wearing their yellow raincoats and plastic hat covers. Sixty-five of them headed for Shorter, and seventy-five went to Notasulga. With the latter group was Dallas County sheriff Jim Clark. As Dallas County was over ninety miles away, Clark had no business being there. But he had a horse-mounted posse of deputies and a tendency to show up anywhere there was racial trouble afoot. At Shorter, troopers and their cruisers lined the circular driveway leading up the hill to the school. A little over half of the 125-member white student body showed up. Heloise Billes, Carmen Judkins, Janice Carter, Ellen Henderson, Harvey Jackson, and Wilmer Jones then arrived, accompanied by U.S. marshals and attorneys from the CRD, and successfully entered and enrolled.[14]

Anthony Lee, Willie Wyatt, Robert Judkins, Patricia Jones, Martha Sullins, and Shirley Chambliss sat silently as their bus began the nine-mile drive from Tuskegee to Notasulga, with marshals and attorneys not far behind. As their caravan approached the center of the town, a man drew a shotgun from the window of his store and displayed it for the passing bus, putting a temporary shock into both the students and the federal personnel. They turned onto Main Street and away from the town square and immediately saw the gathering mass a mile down the narrow two-lane road. Troopers' vehicles lined the street in every direction and filled the spaces along the short driveway leading up to the facility—a Spanish mission–style building that looked out of place in the Alabama countryside. Journalists and about thirty angry whites gathered across the street. As soon as the bus turned into the school's driveway and passed the flagpole—bearing only the state and Confederate flags—it was stopped by Notasulga policeman E. A. Harris.[15]

Someone had informed Lingo that there was a journalist on board. The journalist was Vernon Merritt, a twenty-three-year-old student at the University of Alabama who was working for the Black Star Agency of Birmingham. Most segregationists considered a white journalist who supported civil rights a traitor to the race and the ultimate persona non grata. And so it was with great gusto that E. A. Harris and Jim Clark boarded the bus and found Merritt hiding. They smashed his camera, flushed him out of the bus, and beat him as he lay helpless on the curb. Clark landed repeated blows with his electric cattle prod, all the while screaming at Merritt, "Don't you strike me!"—to give the impression of self-defense.[16]

The journalists on the lawn across the street tried to move in to document the affair, but they were held back by troopers, who ordered them not to take pictures. The troopers were then put in the position of having to protect the journalists from assault by the crowd of angry white spectators, who evidently took inspiration from the beating of Merritt. Federal officials remained in their vehicles and kept their eyes on the bus, where the students sat horrified. Clark, in trench coat and Confederate cavalry hat, lit a cigarette. Merritt tried to get up and walk away toward town, but this diverted the attention of the mob, which began to jeer "Nigger lover!" and "Come over here and we'll fix you!" Lingo ordered troopers to follow Merritt and shield his escape.[17]

The bus pulled down the U-shaped driveway toward the school. There stood Kayo Rae defiantly. "I have determined," he bellowed, "that the maximum safe capacity of Notasulga High School is the present enrollment." The town's new fire safety ordinance, he explained, prevented their entrance and enrollment. White students watching from the doors and windows of the school cheered in approval. After ensuring the black students' safe exodus, attorneys from the CRD called John Doar, who contacted Burke Marshall. The attorneys in the field were told to draft a complaint against James Rea, seeking an injunction against the enforcement of the bogus town ordinances and against any further interference in general. Fred Gray began preparing an amendment to his already amended complaint in *Lee v. Macon*, seeking the same. Gray added a request that the court enjoin any application of the state's tuition grant-in-aid statute.[18]

The following week, a suspicious fire destroyed part of a water treatment facility in town. Rea ordered all schools in Notasulga closed due to a water shortage, which he deemed to be a fire hazard. A bomb threat provided the opportunity to close Shorter High too. Both schools were back open by the end of the week, but the white exodus was by then underway. Some fled to white schools in other counties. Most prepared to enroll at Macon Academy. The president of the academy's foundation admitted that the court orders forcing the admission of the twelve black students at Shorter and Notasulga had "given [them] Macon County." The academy had already received nearly two hundred applications and was poised to double its enrollment. The state hastily approved its accreditation request, and administrators began preparing to hire additional teachers, many from local public schools, and to organize double-shift days, with half the student body attending in the morning, the other half in the afternoon.[19]

Wallace seemed to finally realize the potentially catastrophic consequences of his actions. His administration began backtracking clumsily. He made a show of requesting an advisory opinion of the state supreme court, asking whether the State Board of Education had the authority to assign and transfer pupils and teachers, close schools, direct local boards to provide transportation, and require local boards to provide grants-in-aid—all of the things the board had already done. The justices dutifully answered no. The court wrote, "We think it clear that the authority to exercise general control and supervision over the county and city boards of education does not include the authority to exercise powers and authority which the Legislature has specifically conferred upon such local boards." Wallace called an emergency meeting of the state board, which then resolved to "repeal and rescind" all of its previous orders directed at Macon and other systems. Richmond Flowers asserted that this would "possibly enable" Wallace to "save them from the [their] blunder." Fred Gray and John Doar were, at that moment, at the state board's offices inspecting records they hoped would help them prevent such rescue.[20]

Judge Johnson had requested the designation of a three-judge court for *Lee v. Macon*. While Wallace was stumbling to cover his tracks, Fifth Circuit chief judge Elbert Tuttle granted the request and designated Judge Rives and Judge Grooms to sit with Johnson. The court set a hearing for February 21. At the same time, Johnson granted an injunction in *United States v. Rea*, preventing Kayo Rea from engaging in any further interference. Johnson had determined that the town ordinances were clearly a "subterfuge" and a "devious means" of preventing the admission of the six students at Macon County High. All twelve plaintiff students were soon back in school. There were, however, no white students left. Wallace had pledged to "spend whatever money" to help Macon's white students enroll in other schools. He called on whites across the state to support Macon Academy and suggested that Shorter and Notasulga might need to be closed in light of the boycott. The court was listening.[21]

At the February 21 hearing, Fred Gray's team, which included the LDF's Jack Greenberg, focused on state superintendent Austin Meadows. Gray forced Meadows to read all of the various resolutions instructing Macon officials on how to proceed with school closures, transportation, and tuition grants. This clearly irritated Meadows, who revealed his displeasure at one point by beginning to read rapidly and monotonously through the documents. The no-nonsense Johnson admonished him to "read it right." Gray was also able to demonstrate that state employees had contributed nearly seven thousand dollars to Macon Academy, at Wallace's urging. The most damning evidence developed by the plaintiffs, however, was a long list of public pledges of defiance that various state officials had made to the press. They had made no secret of their intentions.[22]

The Justice Department was also focused on state control of local systems, but it began to take a different tack. The CRD's St. John Barrett argued that there were behind-the-scenes developments that revealed, even more clearly, the state board's control. Barrett called state senator George Yarbrough to the stand. Yarbrough had recently worked for the State Department of Education and was forced to acknowledge a memorandum that he had sent to local systems the previous fall. When HEW had contacted impacted areas' school districts regarding their obligations to desegregate, Yarbrough had instructed those districts, "Refer [HEW] to the Alabama State Board of Education since there are at present no independent school districts operating in the state of Alabama." On cross examination, Yarborough tried to equivocate on the meaning of "independent school districts." But it appeared that the state had assumed control of what should have been bilateral communications.[23]

Richmond Flowers represented the Macon County school board. He tried to demonstrate that local officials were simply trying to follow the directives of the state. At the same time, Flowers tried to protect the state from a statewide desegregation order by arguing that the state board and the governor did not understand the limits of their own authority. In lieu of the outcast Flowers, Wallace and the state board had retained their own private counsel. Wallace's team entered motions to dissolve the temporary restraining order and to dismiss the complaint altogether, contending that the state board had only exercised its constitutional "general control" in "a consolatory and advisory capacity and not administratively." What seemed like directives or orders, they argued, were merely recommendations.[24]

At the conclusion of the hearing, the court gave each party fifty days to file briefs on six issues: Should the temporary restraining order be enlarged into a preliminary injunction? Should the governor, state superintendent, and the State Board of Education be enjoined from interfering in desegregation, not just in Macon, but throughout the state? Should the court declare the Alabama Pupil Placement Law unconstitutional in its statewide application? Should the state's latest tuition grant statute also be declared unconstitutional? Was Macon Academy a public institution based on the state support it had received, and should it be added as a defendant party? And finally, should the court enter an order forcing the state board to desegregate all the school systems in the state, "based upon the assumption or usurpation of [local] authority" by the defendant state officials?[25]

The plaintiffs and the CRD submitted their briefs in March. It was obvious that the state had interfered in Macon County and was assisting in the establishment of Macon Academy, using an unconstitutional tuition grant law. An injunction seemed inevitable. A statewide desegregation order was another matter. Barrett and his team noted the defendants' numerous statements in which they had pledged, for example, to "stand against every order of the federal courts in attempting to integrate the public schools." In doing so, they had "asserted plenary authority over the Macon County School Board," which "demonstrated their plenary authority over all local school boards." Gray argued these same points. The CRD noted, though, that beyond the high-profile interference and bold public statements lay a vast record of everyday involvement. The State Board of Education seemed to exercise authority "in practically every aspect of local public school education." And it was "that power," not "some lesser power involving only Macon County," that the state should use to desegregate the its schools.[26]

The CRD enumerated the ways that the state controlled local systems. The state school board approved all local construction contracts and local transportation procedures. It approved and purchased textbooks, and it even mandated the reading of the Bible, despite a recent Supreme Court decision striking such a mandate. The state board exercised its greatest measure of control, though, via the "purse strings." State funding accounted for the overwhelming majority of most local systems' budgets, and the state controlled the amount they received by allocating "teacher units" based on a system's size and needs. The CRD team had even uncovered a memorandum from state superintendent Meadows, in which he told local superintendents, point blank, "This Board of Education has control of the elementary and high schools of this state" through its power over state funding.[27]

Wallace assured white Alabamians, "It is just a brief that they filed," adding, "We are going to continue to have segregation in the public schools of Alabama just as they do in most states of the union." The defendant officials argued that the plaintiffs were "obviously seeking forced integration and not simply cessation of state activities which may be discriminatory on account of race." And they reasoned that if state actions had been unlawful, why would the plaintiffs want the court to compel the state to continue exercising the unlawful authority? The CRD attorneys replied bluntly, "The answering briefs of the defendants have failed to present any reason, either in fact or in law, why the conclusions urged by the United States and by the plaintiffs in their opening briefs should not be adopted by the court." None of the cases state officials had cited were relevant, and the court surely could not "remain ignorant of what every other person in Alabama must know." After all, in the State Department of Education's own official enrollment records, for the school year 1961–62, all 527,075 white students in the state attended "white" schools, while all 280,012 black students were in "Negro" schools.[28]

As the court took the briefs under consideration, Tuskegee simmered. One morning that April, the city awoke to find two life-sized effigies hanging downtown. One was in blackface and bore the name "Lee." The other sported a toy gun and had "Preston" scrolled across its chest. Detroit Lee and moderate county sheriff Preston Hornsby were running against one another for probate judge. Days later Detroit's son Anthony and the other five students at Macon County High at Notasulga were greeted with graffiti on the school's facade—"Nigger," in three-foot-tall letters, along with "Judge Johnson's and Bobby Kennedy's School," "Detroit Lee S.O.B.," "Go Home, Damn Nigger, Damn Nigger, Damn Nigger," and "You Have Been Told Once—and That's All." These had been painted on a layer of white paint used to cover up similar messages from a month earlier. The following night arsonists set fire to the high school, destroying a substantial portion of the facility. A few days after that, two white teenagers looted thousands of dollars of science, music, and athletic equipment that they intended to give to Macon Academy.[29]

After the fire, the county school board, acting on the advice of Richmond Flowers, transferred the six students back to Tuskegee Institute High. Fred Gray filed a motion asking the court to order the board to enroll the six "in some other school . . . other than those restricted to attendance for Negro children." The court issued the motion four days later, and the board elected to make room for the students among the remaining facilities at Notasulga. There Anthony Lee, Willie Wyatt, and Robert Judkins completed their senior year of high school, in Wyatt's words "brown-bagging it" every day, since the lunchroom had been destroyed in the fire. During the final week of classes, the principal called them into his office and presented them with their diplomas. A scheduled ceremony at the school was canceled. The Tuskegee Civic Association held its own ceremony, though. The keynote speaker was Margaret Anderson, a teacher from Clinton, Tennessee, one of the South's first desegregated school systems. She told them, "Boys and girls, there are many roads to the top of the mountain, but once you reach the top, the view is the same."[30]

Macon Academy held a graduation ceremony for its fifty-three seniors. The school took out a full-page ad in the local newspaper, proclaiming, "The entire county hails you, first graduates of a splendid new school that symbolizes the characteristics of the spirit that gave this nation its beginnings." The ad concluded, "We know that the problems that you have overcome at Macon Academy will be a vital factor in molding you into the leaders of tomorrow." Richmond, Virginia, newspaper editor and massive resistance pioneer James Kilpatrick gave the commencement address. Kilpatrick was in the process of softening his rhetoric for a column in William F. Buckley's *National Review*, but he was still a staunch defender of white privilege. He asked the graduates to imagine a "strangely different world" and alluded to George Orwell's dystopian novel *1984*. They might one day find themselves shaping public policy in a world in which people lived crammed into "high-rise hives" in overcrowded cities, and in which old boundaries no longer had the same meaning. He asked them, "Can individual freedom survive in such a world?" Alabama's forward-thinking segregationists had begun framing the question just that way.[31]

"An Awakening to Reality"

In May and June 1964, the Supreme Court and the Fifth Circuit Court of Appeals transformed the legal context in which the trial court would consider *Lee v. Macon*. In May the Supreme Court handed down opinions in *Griffin v. County School Board of Prince Edward County* and *Calhoun v. Lattimer*. Prince Edward had pioneered the process of locally initiated public school closure when the Supreme Court struck down state-initiated closures in Virginia. The court in *Griffin* deemed locally initiated closures, where public funds were used to maintain segregated private schools, to be unconstitutional. And in *Calhoun v. Lattimer*, the court insisted that the context for desegregation litigation had been "significantly altered" by the passage of a decade since *Brown*. It determined that Atlanta's one-grade-a-year, reverse stair-step plan (token desegregating a grade a year, starting with twelfth) was too limited.[32]

The fallout hit the Fifth Circuit the following month. On June 18 the appellate court issued rulings in four school cases, including *Davis v. Mobile* and *Armstrong v. Birmingham*. The court determined that each city's plan was too limited and instructed the respective trial courts to order the school systems to desegregate four grades that fall and to begin assigning first-year students without regard to race. District judges Daniel Thomas and Seybourn Lynne subsequently ordered the Mobile and Birmingham school boards to submit revised plans. Judge Hobart Grooms then interpreted the appellate court decisions as a call for uniformity within the circuit and ordered similar relief in the Huntsville, Madison County, and Gadsden cases. Judge Johnson then did the same in cases recently filed by Fred Gray and the LDF against the Black Belt system of Bullock County and the combined Montgomery city-county system.[33]

Just under a month later, the three-judge trial court rendered its opinion on the six issues under consideration in *Lee v. Macon*. Judge Johnson wrote for the court. He acknowledged that the superintendent and school board had "fully and completely attempted to discharge their obligations as public officials," but they were not "blameless." And the plan they had submitted—which called for desegregation of only the twelfth grade—was "completely unacceptable." They would have to submit another. The court determined that the state's tuition grant law was constitutional on its face but insisted that it would be deemed unconstitutional, as applied, if grants were awarded in places where public schools had become "unavailable" and private schools existed only for white students. As for Macon Academy, Johnson argued that it had clearly benefited from "public interference and public support and services." Academy officials would have to come before the court and explain why theirs should not be considered a de facto public institution.[34]

On the pupil placement law, the judges essentially maintained the position taken by the court in *Shuttlesworth*. Johnson argued that the law ought not to "be stricken down because of its application in Macon County . . . since its illegal use [there] was brought about through intense pressure" from state officials. The law might still be applied constitutionally under "somewhat more normal circumstances." Accordingly, the court enjoined the State Board of Education, its individual members, Meadows, and Wallace from any further such intervention "anywhere in Alabama."[35]

Finally Johnson turned to the one issue that had given the court "considerable concern"—a potential statewide desegregation order. The State Board of Education clearly exercised "general control and supervision" of the state's obviously segregated public schools. And the recent meddling in Macon County had left "no question" as to the state's "considerable authority and power over the actual operation of local school systems." This was true "irrespective of any supposed limitations on that power as set out in the Alabama law" or any backtracking attempts. Despite all of this, Johnson wrote, "Through the exercise of considerable judicial restraint," and "*at this particular time*, this Court will not order desegregation in all the public schools of the State of Alabama." The court would instead "proceed upon the assumption" that state officials would "comply in good faith" with the injunction prohibiting their interference.[36]

Johnson noted the day-to-day state controls established by the CRD at trial, especially "[rigid] control of the finances" of local systems, and suggested that the state might be forced to use these to desegregate, if it or local systems did not comply. He instructed the defendant state officials to begin formulating and implementing "plans designed to make the distribution of public funds . . . only to those school systems that have proceeded with deliberate speed" to desegregate. "Needless to say," Johnson wrote, "it is only a matter of time until [the state's] illegal and unconstitutional support [for segregated systems] must cease." Had Johnson been the only judge hearing the case, he might have entered the statewide order at that point. But Judge Rives and especially Judge Grooms were more deliberate and more willing to afford segregationists time to adjust. All three judges understood that issuing such an order would have been unprecedented. But each believed that local school boards could carry out token desegregation on their own if they were free of state interference and intimidation.[37]

Despite the lack of a statewide order, Jack Greenberg called the ruling "the most sweeping decree in the history of the Legal Defense Fund's school integration campaign." Richmond Flowers called it "momentous" and "the most far-reaching [decision] since *Brown*." Not only had the court proposed a "new concept in school desegregation cases," Flowers observed with alarm, it had all but issued the edict already. "The order is coming," he told reporters. "I'm afraid we'll not even be able to get by this year, [because] time requests don't work anymore." The *Montgomery Advertiser* agreed, concluding that the court had "ordered virtual statewide school desegregation" for "all practical purposes." The *Birmingham News* determined that the "landmark" decision, which state officials had "brought upon themselves," was a "predicate for more drastic action" and was therefore "very disturbing."[38] The editors at the *News* tried to encourage reluctant Alabamians to get behind law and order and begrudged compliance, while they still had the chance. "Obviously Alabamians do not want desegregation," they wrote. "There is no argument as to the vast majority feeling. But the fact of the law as it stands, and of court insistence on positive action as against continued resistance, must be understood. A time of grave decision is all but upon us. It is, we think, a matter of months. And it most comes to rest on officials. Will enough Alabamians see this and demand an awakening to reality?"[39]

Whites across the state were already on edge, thanks to the enactment, two weeks prior, of the Civil Rights Act, despite southern members of Congress mounting the longest filibuster in congressional history. Initially white anxiety was focused on the law's provisions for desegregating public accommodations—especially parks, motels, and restaurants. The Citizens' Council proposed a legal challenge to the law, prompting Birmingham restaurateur Ollie McClung, owner of the popular Ollie's Barbeque, to file such a challenge in federal court. This resulted in one of two landmark rulings by the Supreme Court upholding the law in its entirety.[40]

Lost in the furor over public accommodations were two sections of the act that dealt with schools. Title VI prohibited discrimination in any program that received federal funding and authorized HEW's Office of Education (USOE) to initiate administrative proceedings to cut off those funds. Burke Marshall and John Doar at the CRD had helped draft the legislation, hoping that the threat of losing federal funding might force school districts to begin to desegregate. This had been the CRD's approach in impacted areas litigation. It was also the federal version of the enforcement mechanism the CRD was suggesting in *Lee v. Macon* and had been suggested by the NAACP as early as 1955. Title IV gave the U.S. attorney general the authority to initiate school desegregation suits on behalf of the Justice Department, which up to that point had been limited to participating as an amicus in suits initiated by private plaintiffs. The editors at the official organ of the Citizens' Council, the *Citizen*, described it as a "death sentence" for southern school systems.[41]

If segregated education was on death row, that was not reflected by the modest increase in desegregation in Alabama that fall. Huntsville became the school system with the largest number of black students desegregating, with thirty-one. Neighboring Madison County schools desegregated by admitting four black students to a white high school. Twenty black students enrolled in Gadsden's two white high schools. Three black students enrolled at Bullock County High. The Macon County school board elected to close Shorter High and Macon County High at Notasulga and reopen Tuskegee Public High School, which enrolled fourteen black students that fall. They were joined by

133 white students who returned to Tuskegee Public over the course of the semester. Across the street, Macon Academy enrolled 322 white students. The state's flagship universities quietly increased their desegregated enrollment—the University of Alabama admitted ten black students, and Auburn University admitted its first two black undergraduates, none other than *Lee v. Macon* plaintiffs Anthony Lee and Willie Wyatt.[42]

The number of black students in white schools in Mobile increased from two to seven. John LeFlore observed that, in a school system enrolling twenty-eight thousand students, this was "a rather poor reflection of compliance with the federal court order that the pace of desegregation should be accelerated." Montgomery admitted three black students at each of its two white high schools and two at Harrison Elementary. Lead plaintiff Arlam Carr was not among them, as the ninth grade was not one of the four grades desegregated. Birmingham admitted seven new black students to white schools, and the Mobile-Birmingham Catholic diocese approved the admission of four black students at John Carroll High School in suburban Birmingham. Edward Fields and J. B. Stoner led small demonstrations in Birmingham and Montgomery, but beyond that, the opening of schools in the fall of 1964 was relatively uneventful—insofar as it was unmarred by interference from state officials, mass demonstrations, or violence.[43]

Segregationist leaders praised whites for their commitment to law and order in the face of repugnant change. Superintendent Meadows told reporters that he was "extremely well pleased" that Alabamians had "demonstrated their belief in law and order, even though they, and I along with them, disagree with the principle involved." Attorney General Flowers similarly announced that "law and order" was "the only sane and sensible attitude, and the only attitude, that we in the South can take and survive." State chamber of commerce chairman Winton Blount observed, "We believe in law and order," meaning, "When legislation is enacted through the normal constitutional process we will abide by this legislation even though we believe the law to be unwise and even though it is abhorrent to us in every way."[44]

Wallace, meanwhile, called the legislature into special session in order to adopt a resolution calling for an amendment to the U.S. Constitution that would guarantee state control of public education. He described it as the "first shot in a battle" for "states' rights" and "home rule." Meadows supported the resolution and displayed his penchant for increasingly ridiculous bloviation by insisting that "dictatorship nations" had traditionally used the education system to "capture the minds and souls of their youth," and that this was what the federal government really had in mind. Condemning the federal government at that point meant condemning the national Democratic Party. The

Democrats had controlled the "solid" white South for one hundred years, though southern unease with some of the party's positions and flirtations with those of the opposition stretched back at least as far as the New Deal. The passage of the Civil Rights Act and the breaching of the wall of segregated education began to accelerate what would eventually become an exodus from the party.[45]

That fall Arizona Republican Barry Goldwater—who voted against the civil rights bill—carried sixty-two of Alabama's sixty-seven counties. Incumbent Democratic congressmen had urged voters to split their tickets, suggesting that they vote Republican for president only. But many of them were swept out of office on the rising tide. Only one Democrat with Republican opposition retained his seat, and Alabama sent Republicans to Washington for the first time since the nineteenth century. State Democratic Party chairman Roy Mayhall reflected, "Persons who call themselves Alabama Democrats try to put political views on the basis of liberal and conservative, but the basic issue in the state is segregation. The race issue is the cause of the whole march of people from the Democratic Party." It was time, he argued, "for Alabama to rejoin the Union," to "furl the Confederate flag," and to "unfurl the American flag."[46]

The march would neither soon be stopped nor the battle flag furled. In early 1965, the Civil Rights Act's school desegregation provisions came to bear. The Justice Department had developed a two-pronged strategy under the terms of the new law. The attorney general would initiate select suits. The CRD would litigate those suits while also supporting the program being initiated by the Office of Education. The USOE was preparing to call on school systems in the South to sign "assurances of compliance" with a set of nondiscrimination regulations attached. The innocuously named "Form 441" was a pledge to end discrimination and to submit a comprehensive desegregation plan to the USOE for approval. Systems that refused to submit signed assurance forms and then plans would have their federal funding deferred or cut entirely.[47]

As soon as Form 441 went out, Austin Meadows called a meeting of the state's superintendents and fumed to the press that the proposed sanctions would have a "crippling effect on education in Alabama." The state was set to receive over $30 million in federal funds the following fiscal year. Meadows lamented, "We are damned if we do sign, and twice damned if we don't." He accurately explained the second prong of DOJ's strategy, "If a school board refuses to sign this assurance, this will only advertise the fact that it does not plan to abide by the Civil Rights Act, and this in turn would provoke a desegregation suit under Title IV of the same act." Meadows nonetheless instructed the superintendents at the meeting not to sign the forms. At a meeting of the state's white teachers' association days later, he wondered why the federal government could not simply "let Alabama continue its progress, nurture its fine culture, and further its goal of peaceful existence in the only way it knows to exist?" After all, he observed spuriously, "Every type of educational facility available to the majority group in Alabama has been made available to the minority group."[48]

Local officials indeed found themselves with a conundrum. They could refuse to sign what the Citizens' Council of Alabama called a "destructive and diabolical agreement" and "a bribe." But some frankly admitted that their systems were so reliant on federal dollars that they "wouldn't have money to keep the boilers hot" without them. One superintendent tellingly evoked the sale of slaves as he beseeched reporters, "The public needs to understand [that] we don't have any choice when you come down to it. They think we are selling them down the river for a little money if we sign." He explained further, "If I could assure us of keeping our schools white by not taking the money, I'd do it. But we'll come nearer having Negroes in our schools next year if we don't sign. We would be foolish to turn the money down and maybe next year take Negroes anyway."[49]

Scrutiny of local school officials was temporarily mitigated that March, as the eyes of the world turned to events in Selma. The attack on peaceful protestors preparing to march for voting rights and in memory of yet another murdered activist once again brought international attention to Alabama. An injunction from Judge Johnson allowed the Selma-to-Montgomery march to proceed, but the outcry over "Bloody Sunday" and two more murders that followed it, led to renewed calls for law and order. Business moderates, frantic to spare what was left of the state's image, took out a full-page ad in the major newspapers, announcing, "We believe in obedience to law, even though some may question the wisdom of particular laws." This created an environment in which school officials could quietly sign Form 441, and by the end of the month, all but eleven of the state's local school boards had signed. The Bessemer city board of education announced not only its refusal to sign the document but also its intent to file a suit challenging HEW policy.[50]

Wallace praised the Bessemer board, calling Form 441 "repugnant to the American system," and the State Board of Education voted unanimously to refuse signing, pending the outcome of Bessemer's suit. Wallace and Meadows encouraged local systems not to sign or to rescind any forms already signed. The U.S. commissioner of education, Francis Keppel, in a letter to Meadows, expressed "grave concern" over the state's actions. Keppel also wondered if Alabama's local systems realized that simply signing the assurance forms was not enough. They had to submit desegregation plans by May. Keppel wrote,

"We can only conclude that they did not realize that they were committing themselves to full and immediate compliance or they did not understand what full compliance means." Meadows relayed the commissioner's message to local superintendents but told them to continue using the pupil placement law and to retain counsel as soon as possible.[51]

The federal government then raised the stakes considerably. In April, Congress passed the Elementary and Secondary Education Act (ESEA), allocating $1.3 billion in federal funds for states to distribute to local school systems, the largest such commitment in American history. Title I of the act provided for aid to school districts with "high concentrations of low-income families." According to HEW, this was a recognition of "the long-standing relationship between educational achievement and the cycle of poverty." The majority of school systems in Alabama could apply to the state for a share of millions of federal dollars. They could then use that money on supplementary and remedial instruction programs, guidance and counseling services, health and welfare services, equipment, and facilities. Unless, of course, they refused to sign Form 441 or to submit a desegregation plan to HEW.[52]

Days after the ESEA was enacted, HEW issued its "General Statement of Policies under Title VI of the Civil Rights Act of 1964 Respecting Desegregation of Elementary and Secondary Schools." This document, soon known simply as "the guidelines," outlined the requirements for systems that wanted to maintain federal funding. The USOE, relying heavily on the latest jurisprudence, indicated that it would accept either geographic zone plans or what were being called freedom of choice plans. Geographic zone plans would include the elimination of "racially separate attendance zones" and the creation of a "single, non-racial zone," the boundaries of which were drawn "to follow the natural boundaries or perimeters of compact areas surrounding schools." Freedom of choice plans would give all students in a system a choice of which school they wanted to attend and ideally would include safeguards against discriminatory application of such policy. Acceptable plans would also include provisions for desegregating faculty, transportation, and all services, facilities, activities, and programs. Systems were to show a "good faith start" that fall—by desegregating at least four grades, making initial assignments without regard to race, and initiating faculty desegregation—and to achieve full desegregation by 1967.[53]

Wallace described the guidelines as "vicious procedure[s] heretofore unknown in a society of free people, but universally employed in totalitarian nations" and implied that the "left-wing liberals" at HEW were communist sympathizers. He insisted, "We will resist as long as we can within the law," and he announced support for a resolution of the state board instructing local boards not to sign Form 441. A small group of legislators branded the resolution another "so-called 'nigger resolution'" and suggested that it could "rise up and haunt us," by inviting a statewide desegregation order. Over the course of a long filibuster in the state senate, the resolution's opponents asked Wallace to quit "rubbing the sores" with "bluff and blunder." One senator referenced Wallace's inaugural address, suggesting that he had "laid the gauntlet before the feet of tyranny" and that Martin Luther King Jr. had "picked up that gauntlet and beat our people over the head with it." Others simply kept their distance. When the state congressional delegation endorsed the resolution, Senators Lister Hill and John Sparkman and North Alabama congressman Bob Jones refused to sign.[54]

Despite Wallace's posturing, an almost certain loss of federal funding was more than most school boards were willing to risk. By June, 108 out of 111 had at least signed Form 441, while 53 had actually submitted desegregation plans for the fall. Upon initial review, HEW approved only thirteen of the plans, but that number steadily increased as local officials negotiated with the USOE. All of the plans were freedom of choice plans. A few, from North Alabama districts with comparatively few black students, called for the application of freedom of choice to all grades that fall. The governor's office sent telegrams to these systems arguing that any plan that called for "so-called non-descrimination [sic] in all grades" was "beyond even the minimum requirements." Therefore, it continued, "We think it would be advisable for your school board to reconsider your action in the submission of your compliance plan." Officials in Washington took note. HEW's director of compliance described Alabama state officials as "playing Russian roulette" with $30 million in federal aid.[55]

As the threat of desegregation became more real for more systems, new private schools emerged, especially in the Black Belt. With the assistance of local Citizens' Councils, foundations were set up in Selma, Demopolis, Greensboro, and Lowndesboro. At the same time, state legislators, including Walter Givhan, pushed through a new tuition grant law to replace the 1957 law, which had been ruled unconstitutional in *Lee v. Macon*. Lawmakers erased any mention of race and earmarked $2 million per year for grants of $185 to any family that removed their child from a public school because they believed it had become "detrimental" to the well-being of the student. The state Citizens' Council set up a hotline to inform parents of the new law via a recorded message from Wallace himself. The governor told callers that the new grant law was "our best example of intelligent resistance."[56]

In Birmingham, parents soon accepted grants for their children to attend Hoover Academy instead of desegregated Graymont Elementary. More parents were taking advantage of another option, though. The city began to see an increase in white flight to its burgeoning suburbs. Early suburban development around the city had been concentrated in industrial, working-class cities like Bessemer and Tarrant to the west and north. By the 1920s, affluent whites had begun to slip out of the city and "over the mountain"—that is, over Red Mountain, which ran along Birmingham's long southern underbelly—to newly incorporated Homewood. Southern suburban growth increased significantly after World War II, as blacks began moving into white neighborhoods and as violent segregationist resistance earned the city the nickname "Bombingham." The incorporation of Mountain Brook in 1942 and Vestavia Hills in 1950 gave wealthy whites two new enclaves to which to escape. With Birmingham under a desegregation order in *Armstrong*, and with HEW now knocking at the door, the trickle to those three cities was turning into a stream.[57]

Of the over-the-mountain suburbs at that time, only Mountain Brook had its own school system, independent of the Jefferson County system. Mountain Brook, however, had no black residents. So when the LDF and its associated counsel in Birmingham looked to expand desegregation in the metropolitan area that summer, they filed new suits against Bessemer, its neighbor Fairfield, and Jefferson County. The CRD joined in each suit. Meanwhile, a decision of the Fifth Circuit Court of Appeals signaled strong judicial support for HEW's guidelines. In *Singleton v. Jackson*, the court acknowledged that HEW had modeled its guidelines on court-ordered plans and announced that the court, in turn, attached "great weight" to the guidelines. The court insisted that there ought to be a "close correlation" between HEW standards and the courts' standards. If the courts' standards dropped lower than HEW's at any point, that would place a "premium on recalcitrance" for reluctant school boards. As the fall of 1965 approached, it was a bad sign for Bessemer and for segregationists in general.[58]

"Whatever Means That Is Peaceable, Legal, and Honorable"

One afternoon in the summer of 1965, farmer Jordan Gully, a black man, answered a knock at the door of his Lowndes County home. He was surprised to find two white men standing on his porch. Before Gully had a chance to wonder why the two had driven to his house, one of them, Buddy Woodruff barked, "What kind of shit are you trying to run over me?" Taken aback, Gully replied, "I don't know what you're talking about." Woodruff began, "Ain't you got a girl named Pearlie Pate?" Realizing where this was going but feigning ignorance, Gully said yes and asked why they wanted to know. "When was the last time she's been here?" Woodruff demanded. She'd moved to South Alabama, to Geneva, Gully told them. Irritated, Woodruff persisted. Didn't Gully have another daughter named Wilma Jean? Where was she? She was in the house. "You're the head of this house, ain't you?" Woodruff said. "Yes," Gully allowed, trying to maintain his dignity while also avoiding escalation. Woodruff wanted to know: didn't Gully realize that his daughters had applied for transfer, under the county's desegregation plan, to attend all-white Hayneville High School? Gully replied simply that he did know that.[59]

Outraged, Woodruff snarled, "Don't come to me for any help no more." The other man, Brady Ryan, finally added that Gully could forget about coming to him for help too. These kinds of threats had become common where poor black farmers, most of them sharecropping tenants, were beholden to a small oligarchy of white landowners, bankers, and business owners. Falling out of favor with these people meant exposure to economic reprisal or worse — violence. Woodruff continued to grill Gully on the porch, accusing him of "paying attention to them folks running up and down the roads," referring to the recent Selma-to-Montgomery march. "We didn't bother about y'all registering [to vote]," he grumbled, "We didn't bother y'all about going to mass meetings." But schools were another thing entirely. Woodruff concluded his tirade: "I'll be goddamn if this shit is going over this time. . . . This shit ain't going to pass this time. We going to stop it. Don't you ask me for no goddamn help for nothing." Such was the impact of the mere threat of token desegregation in the Alabama Black Belt.[60]

Most of the forty-seven black families whose children had applied for transfer in Lowndes County were similarly harassed that summer. They were told they would "lose friendships" with whites. They were told "Mr. Bob" or "Mr. John" would not approve of their actions. They were warned of potential "trouble" that fall. They were threatened with job loss and eviction. They were told to ignore activists from SNCC and local civil rights organizations. Some were threatened directly with violence — which, after Selma, everyone understood was a real threat indeed. Despite the pressure, only one of the forty-seven families removed their child's name from the application list. However, the school board rejected all but five of the requests. This prompted local black leaders to petition the Justice Department to initiate a suit against the board.[61]

It happened that way across the Black Belt. When the mother of the lone girl accepted to Greene County's white high school objected to her being transported on a segregated and therefore otherwise empty bus, the local sheriff accosted her, screaming, "No one was on the bus, and no one will be riding with her; no one will sit with her; no one will have a damned thing to do with her!" The local Klan gathered to watch the girl enter school each day, until she finally withdrew. In Pickens County, the sheriff visited black parents and told them to withdraw their applications. Hale County school board members harassed black students themselves, denying all requests for transfer from those who admitted to attending mass meetings or participating in a local boycott of black schools. Klansmen burned the building of an activist black church in Marengo County, where local whites joked that they "hoped the church was full when they started the fire." And the desegregated white high school in Elba, in South Alabama's Coffee County, was dynamited.[62]

Local resistance was not confined to the Black Belt. That summer, the USOE convinced the Anniston school board to adopt a model desegregation plan, applying freedom of choice to all twelve grades. Klansmen organized a march though the city, and the NSRP hosted a rally featuring what the U.S. Civil Rights Commission called "some of the most widely known racists in the country." Local blacks told federal agents that they were reluctant to apply for transfer under the plan because "somebody might bomb the house" or because "I don't think my boss would like it." A racially motivated shooting that summer pushed tensions in the city even higher, prompting a group of white moderates to issue a statement prior to the opening of schools that fall. "Regardless of our personal feelings over the merit or lack of merit of [desegregation]," the group urged, "we feel that the Anniston Community must react to this new situation confronting us in a responsible, realistic, and thoughtful manner" and "within the framework of law and order."[63]

Nearly one thousand black students attended formerly all-white schools across the state that fall—a significant increase from the 101 who had done so the previous fall. The Alabama Council on Human Relations called it a "token of tokenism," though. HEW had approved eighty-four school systems' plans. But most of the approved plans were freedom of choice plans, meaning the burden for desegregation was on students like Pearlie and Wilma Jean Pate, not local school boards. Also, many systems that had submitted approved plans experienced no desegregation at all, either because no blacks dared to apply for transfer or because no transfers had been approved. Half of the state's 118 school districts remained entirely segregated. Ninety-nine percent of the state's three hundred thousand black pupils still attended all-black schools. No faculty desegregation whatsoever had occurred. Even districts that had immediately adopted freedom of choice in all twelve grades saw limited results: three black students in Morgan County, two in Cleburne County, two in Geneva, and so on. Some systems with only four-grade freedom of choice saw better results: thirty-four in Walker County and thirty-one in Selma. Others did not: two black students in Opelika and none in Dallas County.[64]

Despite the negligible results—and the injunction in *Lee v. Macon*—the governor, the state superintendent, and the State Board of Education embarked on a campaign of systematic, open harassment of local school officials, particularly those who had gone "beyond the requirements of the law." When HEW officials designated Lauderdale County's plan as a "model plan," Wallace, Lieutenant Governor Jim Allen, and Speaker of the House Albert Brewer sent a telegram to the Lauderdale officials: "Your statement to the governor's office . . . that you are satisfied with the public school situation in Lauderdale County, where more Negro pupils are enrolled in previously all-white schools [73] than there are in either of the large cities of Birmingham and Montgomery, and your further statement that you plan to eliminate eventually all Negro schools in the county and transfer the pupils to white schools, could do more to destroy the public education system in Alabama than any action since the infamous 1954 [*Brown*] decision. Those who have worked diligently to raise support of public education to a high level in our state resent and reject this attitude. We call upon you to align your policies with the minimum requirements of the law and of court orders." To generate pressure on the board from below, Wallace's office sent the telegram to the local newspaper in Florence and to the Associated Press."[65]

Wallace, Allen, and Brewer sent similar telegrams to each school system that had adopted a twelve-grade plan. Wallace then called every superintendent in the state to a mandatory, closed-door meeting in Montgomery, where he reminded them to use the placement law, as Meadows had said, "for all it's worth" and insisted that they await the outcome of the Bessemer suit against HEW before undertaking any further compliance measures. In case there was any confusion, Wallace said, "Our purpose here is to minimize the effect of integration." Lieutenant Governor Allen added, "We're in favor of maintaining the dual system in Alabama by whatever means that is peaceable, legal, and honorable."[66]

It became clear that fall that the voices of law and order were calling two different tunes. Some, like *Tuscaloosa News* editor Buford Boone, began to accuse Wallace of encouraging the "violent and the lawless" through "his frequent reference to resistance and his general antagonism to necessary change." Boone argued that a better leader would have told the people, "The honorable [and] correct way is unpleasant and undesirable, but it is a way that we must walk." Others defended Wallace, insisting that he abhorred violence and was simply standing up for their rights. Some, in other words, saw reluctant acquiescence to tokenism as the sensible way to comply with the law and avoid any further violence, while others denounced violence but still favored continuing defiance.[67]

The dissonance manifest itself when the state's sixteen noncompliant school districts were called before an HEW panel for "extensive negotiations," and three failed to show. Bibb County joined the City of Bessemer in its legal challenge. Tarrant acknowledged that it would rather forego federal funding than desegregate. And Barbour County decided not to embarrass its native son, George Wallace. A number of Black Belt county boards sent delegations. Their systems were among the poorest in the state and therefore stood to lose the most money—approximately half a million dollars each—by missing out on ESEA Title I funding. Even as Wilcox County officials were pleading their case with HEW, though, the Wilcox school board was busy firing seven teachers because of their association with an activist black preacher who had applied for his children to transfer to all-white schools.[68]

By the end of the year, the Justice Department was receiving numerous complaints about similar intimidation. The CRD filed suits against school boards in five Black Belt counties, and it filed amicus briefs in two other cases. This brought the number of school systems in Alabama facing litigation to seventeen. In February 1966, Judge Johnson entered an order, in the CRD's case against Lowndes County, which he intended to serve as a model for accelerating desegregation in recalcitrant systems. He ordered the county to open six grades to freedom of choice that fall, with the other six grades to follow the next year. The school board was to provide remedial educational opportunities to the system's four thousand black students in order to "eliminate the past effects of racial discrimination." It was also ordered to close twenty-four substandard black schools. Most of the schools had fewer teachers than grades. Many lacked plumbing, some were ramshackle, uninsulated wooden structures, and a few even lacked a source of fresh drinking water. Johnson subsequently entered similar orders in the Montgomery and Bullock County cases and in *Lee v. Macon*.[69]

The following month, the USOE issued a revised set of desegregation guidelines. More than seventeen hundred of around two thousand school districts under HEW scrutiny had agreed to open all twelve grades to freedom of choice by that fall. Federal court orders, though, like those handed down the previous month by Judge Johnson, had become more stringent than the original HEW guidelines. USOE officials determined that school systems that were not under court orders "could and should make more progress." Accordingly, the revised guidelines required a start to faculty desegregation, such that schools would no longer be "identifiable as intended for students of a particular race, color, or national origin" or such that teachers and staff of a particular race were not "concentrated in those schools where all, or the majority of, the students are of that race." The new standards also called for the immediate desegregation of all transportation programs and extracurricular activities and the closure of inadequate school facilities.[70]

In a second review of the *Singleton v. Jackson* case, which became known as *Singleton II*, the Fifth Circuit Court of Appeals reiterated that it attached "great weight" to the guidelines as a set of "minimum standards" and expressly endorsed the revised standards involving faculty desegregation. But it did not speak to the most controversial aspect of the new guidelines, as it had not been raised in the appeal. HEW had acknowledged that "longstanding community attitudes" tended to "preclude or inhibit the exercise of a truly free choice" for minority students. The USOE would therefore scrutinize freedom of choice plans "with special care." And the "single most substantial indication as to whether a free choice plan [was] actually working" would be the "extent to which Negro or other minority group students [had] in fact transferred from segregated schools." In other words, freedom of choice plans were going to be judged according to numerical benchmarks.[71]

HEW wanted to see "substantial increases" in desegregation, with a general standard of around 15 percent of black students in desegregated schools for the fall of 1966. In a given school system, "If a significant percentage of the students, such as 8 or 9 percent," had transferred the previous fall, then "total transfers on the order of at least twice that percentage would normally be accepted." But if the percentage for 1965–66 had been "closer to 4 or 5 percent," then a substantial increase "would likely mean triple that percentage in 1966–67." If the 1965–66 percentage was lower than 4, then the increase would need to be "proportionately greater." If freedom of choice failed to result in the desired increases that fall, then systems would be required to "take additional actions as a prerequisite to continued use of a free choice plan."[72]

The LDF and CRD adjusted their strategies to fall in line with the new guidelines. The LDF moved for further relief in its cases at the trial level, including the Birmingham, Huntsville, Madison County, and Gadsden cases, while the CRD petitioned the Fifth Circuit for the consolidation of all appeals in all of its cases, including Jefferson County, Bessemer, and Fairfield. As news of the new motions hit Alabama's headlines, HEW's revised compliance instrument, Form 441-B, went out to local school boards. The secretary of HEW insisted that the revised policy was not intended to provide "rigid means" for obtaining compliant status. It was merely supposed to help initiate a "reasonable beginning," followed by "reasonable progress," all with "considerable flexibility." Nonetheless, segregationists immediately branded the pupil benchmarks as quotas and resisted with renewed vigor.[73]

Savvy politicians began to attack the revised guidelines using language in the Civil Rights Act. One clause in the act read, "Desegregation shall not mean the assignment of students to public schools in order to overcome racial imbalance." It had been inserted to assuage the fears of northern, western, and midwestern senators and representatives whose school systems were arguably not segregated by law—de jure—but which were certainly segregated in fact—de facto. Another clause precluded the requirement of any action "with respect to any employment practice of any employer." Wallace and others insisted that these ought to shield school systems from pupil quotas and faculty desegregation requirements. The governor called another meeting of the state's local superintendents, at which he and Austin Meadows called for a "friendly suit" challenging the revised provisions. Wallace contended, "We must obey the laws, just and unjust, but we should not have to obey edicts of bureaucratic officials which go beyond the law." The superintendents adopted a resolution with that thesis.[74]

That summer the USOE sent teams of investigators into the South to hold statewide meetings with local school officials. At the inaugural Alabama meeting, locals echoed the complaints presented by the Wallace administration, while the HEW team relayed established departmental rebuttals. Frustrated, both sides began to express exasperation. At one point a superintendent asked, "What if I can't find a Negro teacher qualified to teach in a white school?" One of the HEW representatives replied, "If she isn't qualified, what is she doing in your system," adding, "The separate but equal ruling was made in 1894, [but] you aren't even willing to go that far!" Meadows telegrammed Commissioner of Education Harold Howe after the meeting to complain about HEW's deployment of a "horde of snoopers" to usurp the authority of local school boards. The guidelines were abhorred by "every board member and superintendent in Alabama," he explained, and would be "disastrous . . . if followed."[75]

The biracial Alabama Advisory Committee to the U.S. Civil Rights Commission protested the deployment of only a five-person team to monitor compliance. It issued a statement, arguing that there was "an increasing polarization between the attitude of the moderate white who intends to comply with federal law, but such compliance moving only as rapidly as white society permits," and the attitude of those who were seeking more than "simple compliance with law." The federal government ought to be working toward "far more than token compliance with existing laws." This was particularly true, the committee maintained, "in view of the enormity of the problem of school desegregation, the general intransigence of school administrators at the state and local levels, and the history of inadequate enforcement of last year's Guidelines."[76]

"General intransigence" was meanwhile giving way to uniform defiance again. Wallace set the tone by calling the new guidelines the "last straw" and claiming that Alabamians had gone "just as far" as they were "going to go." They would not eat the "political sop" cooked up by the "liberal, socialistic, beatnik crowd ... using school children as pawns." Wallace was joined by more than just the usual suspects. As the *Birmingham News* noted, the USOE's "do-it-now-or-else mandates" had alienated "many people besides those from whom criticism of federal actions [was] almost a reflex action." The list included Republican congressman and gubernatorial candidate Jim Martin and the generally aloof U.S. senators John Sparkman and Lister Hill. Hill announced that he would do "all in [his] power" to get the new guidelines rescinded because, "in addition to being illegal," they were "unreasonable and ... impractical" and threatened "to disrupt the orderly compliance with the law by [local] officials."[77]

For a moment, it looked like Martin might harness the unusually unified, defiant energy. Then Wallace's wife Lurleen handily won the Democratic nomination for governor. George had unsuccessfully tried to amend the state's constitution to allow himself to run for a second consecutive term. He had then resolved to run his wife in his stead, more or less openly admitting that he would continue to run the state as a regent. Wallace was prepared to leave mundane responsibilities to Lurleen while he indulged his dominating urge to seek the presidency by carrying his now racially coded message nationwide. As soon as Lurleen had secured the nomination, George arranged a meeting of the state's congressional delegation in Montgomery. The group adopted a resolution calling for defiance of the "illegal" guidelines and urging local school boards to "stand firmly upon their constitutional rights, power, and prerogatives" to refuse to sign Form 441-B or to rescind if they had already signed.[78]

Fewer systems had signed the new forms than had signed the original 441. The USOE reported that fifty-four systems in the state had made some effort to comply, while Meadows was reporting the number as twenty-four. The reason for the disparity was that some school boards had signed and submitted Form 441-B but had withheld the carbon copy from the State Department of Education, for fear of exposure and reprisal. Others had refused to sign the official form but had generated their own "Resolution of Compliance" instrument. Still others had signed the form but had inserted a caveat indicating that they would not take any actions that went beyond the requirements of the Civil Rights Act. Anniston superintendent Revis Hall even asked the USOE to accept a certified copy of his school board's meeting minutes in lieu of Form 441-B. Hall admitted that "certain factors" in the state had the board worried about "adverse publicity." Referring to a proposed construction plan, Hall also explained that state officials had the power "to not only determine who the architect will be, but also the extent to which local capital outlay millage ... can be extended for certain purposes"—factors already noted by CRD attorneys working on *Lee v. Macon*.[79]

The pressure mounted. The State Board of Education recommended that local boards withdraw any signed 441-B forms. According to the state, the USOE had "erroneously attempt[ed] to desegregate teachers and set up quota or percentage ratios of pupils in schools . . . in violation of the Civil Rights Act." Meadows sent a personal letter to each superintendent in the state, in which he reiterated his request to not sign or to withdraw and instructed them to report any action to his office. He told them that he was "completely certain" the USOE would not really cut off federal funds. The state legislature finally waded in too, adopting a resolution calling on local officials to "resist all illegal requirements imposed by the 1966 Guidelines."[80]

Wallace and Meadows again sought to place local elected officials in the difficult position of defying the public will in trying to comply with federal requirements. The two initiated a behind-the-scenes campaign of harassment and intimidation that included a wave of telegrams and phone calls. Meadows lied about the number of systems that had refused to sign or that had rescinded their agreements, trying to make other systems feel isolated. Superintendents began complaining to the USOE that they were under "considerable pressure" from both the state and the "lower, uneducated elements in their area." One superintendent told investigators that, with the "pressure from the people and the government," there was "absolutely no chance" that they could comply. Another told them plainly, "[We] won't sign until Governor Wallace says so."[81]

When HEW agents reported to Commissioner Howe on the intimidation campaign, Howe sent a public memo to Meadows in which he sought to "make it absolutely clear" that the USOE would defer funds for all noncompliant districts. At the same time, HEW tried to mollify local authorities' concerns by essentially adopting a version of the caveat clauses that some systems had unilaterally added to their compliance forms. The amended forms read, "This assurance does not commit this school system to comply with any requirement of [HEW] which is contrary to the Civil Rights Act of 1964." But Wallace began to directly threaten school boards, claiming that he would hold mass meetings in their communities so that they would be forced to explain themselves to angry white locals. The superintendent of the Florence system explained, "It seemed best not to go beyond our present position for fear that a certain party might cause an explosion in our otherwise peaceful and harmonious community," which had been "threatened with called mass meetings to oppose the signing of 441-B." Another superintendent told USOE investigators, "I don't want any fight with the governor; that's a fight you can't possibly win."[82]

Some local officials embraced Wallace's position and even undertook their own intimidation campaigns. Marengo County superintendent Fred Ramsey required all teachers to answer a questionnaire with questions like these:

"Would you be willing to teach children of the opposite race from you?" "Would you willingly resign, if it became necessary, to carry out full integrated faculties?" In Crenshaw, Wilcox, Greene, and Hale Counties, teachers were intimidated and in some cases fired for encouraging student activism or for communicating with civil rights volunteers. The Wilcox school board refused bus transportation to black transfer students. When the father of one of the students began transporting them himself, he was fired from his job with the school system, had his mailbox destroyed by shotgun blast, and had his car pelted by rocks. The family of a black transfer student in Wetumpka had its home burned to the ground. Another family was refused a burial plot in the local cemetery for their son, who was killed in Vietnam. Activists from Crenshaw County relayed their frustrations in a letter to the CRD. "We colored people . . . listen to Governor Wallace say the federal government is bluffing and can't do anything with Alabama, because he is boss here, and what he say goes. It seem to be working so well, we hardly know what to believe."[83]

As summer gave way to the third consecutive fall of expanded desegregation, the state legislature reentered the fray, further intensifying pressure on local officials. State lawmakers in September passed what became known as the "anti-guidelines act." The law was purportedly designed to "preserve peace and order" in the public schools and to "preserve the integrity of the local school systems against unlawful encroachment." According to lawmakers, the HEW guidelines were "unreasonable, arbitrary, capricious, and unconstitutional," and the threat of defunding was "immoral and repugnant." Accordingly, the legislators articulated what was quickly becoming the dominant ethos of maturing segregationist resistance: "The time has come when the citizens of Alabama are no longer willing to abide by such infringements of constitutionally guaranteed personal rights and freedoms."[84]

The coup de grâce of the anti-guidelines bill was nullification. Only this time it was nullification not of federal laws but of local school board actions. The legislature declared all signed Forms 441 or 441-B "null, void, and [of] no binding effect." The law read, "No local county or city board of education shall have the authority to give any assurance of compliance with the guidelines or to enter into any other agreement with any agency of the [federal] government" if that agreement or assurance would obligate them to adopt a desegregation plan designed to "overcome racial imbalance" in schools or to alter their "employment practices" in any way. The state sought to interpose itself between local boards and federal authorities by creating a 160-member "Governor's Commission" to deal with HEW in the local officials' stead. Of the 160 members, 141 "happened to be" members of the legislature. The fourteen-member executive committee of the commission was chaired by George Wallace.[85]

HEW had already announced that it was initiating administrative proceedings to defer federal funds to twenty-three Alabama public school systems. The Governor's Commission promised anxious local officials that the state could replace these funds, though it almost certainly could not. Wallace insisted that the "socialists" in the federal government could take their money and "[knew] what they [could] do with it." He characterized the anti-guidelines act as "freedom legislation" that would free school boards from "the threats, the intimidations, and the blackmail of quasi-secret agents." Within a week the governor had ordered those same local officials to renege on signed compliance agreements by reassigning teachers and students who had been transferred.[86]

Among those being pushed toward the brink was the Tuscaloosa board of education. The board had assigned two black teachers to formerly all-white schools as part of its HEW-approved plan. In response, two thousand white parents had signed a petition asking the board to remove them. Klansmen picketed schools, and white parents organized a march, at which some accused the school board of "selling out" by not following the governor's advice and waiting for the Bessemer suit to play out. Austin Meadows phoned three times urging the board to move the black teachers back. Wallace's legal advisor, Hugh Maddox, also called, promising that HEW could not really cut off federal funds. Finally Meadows offered to assign the school system two additional "teacher units," which would give it the state funds necessary to hire two new white teachers—who could then teach the white students originally placed in classrooms with the two transferred black teachers.[87]

Meanwhile, to further protect those fleeing desegregated schools, the legislature amended the current tuition grant law. Only two hundred grants had been paid out the previous year, prompting lawmakers to relax the standards for eligibility. Previously a student was eligible if his or her application to transfer to another school within the school system had been denied. Under the amended law, students could apply to any public school in the state and would become eligible when their application was denied. The legislature also added an additional $2 million allotment on top of the $1.7 million remaining from the previous year. Wallace continued soliciting donations from the public. In a televised address, the governor asked viewers to help people in the state who were "being forced to conduct private schools because of the destruction of their public schools." These people, he suggested, "are fighting for their freedom too, a freedom that affects all of us."[88]

The nearly $4 million allotted by the legislature was sufficient to pay the tuition of all eleven thousand white students in seven Black Belt counties facing desegregation where segregation academies were already up and running. In the preceding year, academies had been opened in Dallas, Hale, Perry, Greene, and Marengo Counties, in addition to those already opened in Tuskegee, Montgomery, Birmingham, and Tuscaloosa. Some academy administrations were wary of accepting the grants, lest that open them up to litigation, though that did not deter them from operating the schools on what funds they could get otherwise. As Lowndes County arch-segregationist and local engineer Ray Bass explained regarding the soon-to-be-opened Lowndes Academy, "We're prepared to carry the load ourselves."[89]

That fall HEW estimated that there were around twelve thousand black students attending formerly all-white schools in Alabama. This was a significant increase from the previous year but still just over 4 percent of the state's black pupil total. More than one thousand teachers had been given desegregated assignments, though the vast majority of these were white teachers assigned to all-black schools. Of the 118 school systems in the state, 17 were under court orders, and 49 others were found to be in compliance with HEW's guidelines. Of the 52 noncompliers, 47 were involved in administrative proceedings with HEW; 3 had already had their federal funds deferred; and 2 had seen their federal dollars completely cut off.[90]

Local authorities remained in a tight spot vis-à-vis HEW. Some lashed out. The attorney for the Crenshaw County school board—Dallas County Citizens' Council founder Alston Keith—wrote HEW's general counsel, calling the 441 forms "asinine" and explaining that folks in Crenshaw were "fed to the teeth with [HEW's] unlawful attempt at social reform." Others hid behind the anti-guidelines law. One superintendent told investigators that his board was not "defying or resisting," it was just that "the action of [the] legislature [had] made it very difficult" to comply. He and several others insisted that they had stopped implementing approved plans because they felt like they would be in violation of state law or that they would incur the wrath of the Wallace administration. Butler County superintendent H. L. Terrell explained, "In Alabama, local boards of education and superintendents of education [exist] solely at the disgression [sic] of the Governor and State Legislature." "As you can see," he concluded, "our Board of Education is sort of caught between 'the devil and the deep.'"[91]

A litigious counterattack came swiftly. The CRD asked to be added as a full-fledged plaintiff in *Lee v. Macon* and filed a supplemental complaint against the amended tuition grant law. Birmingham's Orzell Billingsley and Oscar Adams, on behalf of the NAACP, filed a separate lawsuit against Wallace, Meadows, and the Governor's Commission, asking the court to enjoin the application of the anti-guidelines act. A three-judge panel of Judges Johnson, Rives, and Virgil Pittman was appointed to hear the case—styled *NAACP v. Wallace*—

and ordered the United States to appear as amicus curiae. Finally, Fred Gray filed a motion in *Lee v. Macon* seeking either a contempt citation against the governor or an injunction against the enforcement of the anti-guidelines law. Gray also asked the court to revisit the issue of a potential statewide desegregation order.[92]

Even some of Wallace's supporters began to question his reckless defiance. The *Birmingham News* determined that the governor had "led Alabama up a blind alley" by creating "the type of political-legal circus in which he thrives." He was "flirt[ing] with a jail term to promote his own political future." The *Montgomery Advertiser*'s editors wrote, "As the suit snowballs to federalize Alabama schools, accommodating the death wish of Gov. Wallace and the Legislature ... grief has replaced anger that the state would be so foolish." With the injunction in *Lee v. Macon*, the state had already been "put on clear notice that a statewide school desegregation [order] would follow if the Governor and state school officials did not stop interfering with local schools." They concluded dryly, "It seems impossible to unscramble that egg now." Alabama's whites might not like the "arrogant" way in which HEW was dangling the "carrot" of federal funding before them. But they ought to remember that the "court stick" to that carrot was "Paul Bunyan size."[93]

CHAPTER 4

"More Than a Mere Word of Promise," 1966–1968

Fred Gray had been pacing the courtroom floor, questioning his witness, for what must have been an hour. It was a balmy day for late November in Montgomery. A warm breeze blew through the open windows. It carried the smells of the changing seasons through the tall limestone arches, standing like sentries along the walls of the Depression-era chamber, reaching up to the high, stenciled ceiling, with its semi-ornate beams and lights hanging down like dismal stalactites. The second floor of the federal courthouse was packed to capacity. Nervously shifting reporters and school officials filled the few rows of wooden benches behind the attorneys' tables, and they jammed the gallery in the back.[1]

At the front of the room stretched a long bench. There sat judges Frank Johnson, Richard Rives, Hobart Grooms, and Virgil Pittman. Behind the judges, another high limestone arch receded into an antechamber and a blue wall adorned with gold stars. At the top of that wall, a clock was steadily ticking its way through the decorous silence. Before the panel of judges sat attorneys for the defendant state and local officials, the plaintiffs, and the United States. And in the middle of it all—at a simple wooden witness stand below the center of the judges' bench—sat Austin Meadows, facing the attorneys, the gallery, the press, his colleagues, and, in a sense, the entire state of Alabama. Fred Gray decided that it was time.[2]

"'Segregation,'" Gray began reading, slowly, "is a perfectly good word. It has been practiced throughout the ages for good results [and] used by the people of the civilized world for man's greatest advancement." Austin Meadows began to laugh. "Segregation," Gray continued reading, "is the basic principle of culture, [whereby the] good join to separate themselves from the bad." Did not the Lord set aside "segregated fruit for Adam and Eve," and did Eve not disregard the Lord's wish, forcing "honest men and women" to "work for their living ever since"? Meadows stopped chuckling long enough to interject, "That's right." Gray paused briefly to look up, then resumed. Marriage, he read, "was the highest type of segregation," without which "there would be no family unit," and segregation was "one of the principles of survival throughout the animal kingdom," for animals joined "their own kind to defend themselves by numbers against other animals that would destroy them without such segregated bond." Gray again paused, this time for effect. "Birds of a feather," he read, "truly flock together."[3]

The usually stern and reserved federal judges began to grin. Gray finished reading, "Wild geese fly across this continent in V formation but they never join any other flock of birds. . . . The wild eagle mates with another eagle and not with any other bird. Red birds mate with red birds, the beautiful blue birds mate with other blue birds and so on through bird life. There can be segregation without immoral discrimination against anyone. Integration of all human life and integration of all animal life would destroy humanity and would destroy the animal kingdom." Gray was reading from a memorandum that Meadows had written and sent to every local school superintendent in the state that summer. It was now autumn 1966, and the four-judge panel had been convened to hear witness testimony and oral arguments in both *Lee v. Macon County* and the recently filed *NAACP v. Wallace* case. Gray, as lead attorney for the plaintiffs in *Lee*, had set up the moment perfectly.[4]

Meadows had been uncooperative and equivocal earlier as Gray began to ask him about his affirmative duty under the 1964 *Lee v. Macon* court order. "Have [you] recommended or encouraged any superintendent of education to abolish segregation in his particular school system," he asked. Meadows replied incoherently, "No, I don't remember it, because I approach it from discrimination; nondiscrimination if that is necessary; I have told Superintendents if this is necessary to not discriminate, to integrate pupils, and then you must follow that and abide by that in your opinion, you should do it." Gray asked if there were any records in his office that would indicate that he had taken any action to encourage desegregation. Meadows insisted, "Whatever they are, I have already furnished them to you." Gray was more specific: were there any releases to local superintendents in which he had "promoted the elimination of racially dual school systems"? "No," Meadows allowed, "I approach it from nondiscrimination." Gray then offered the "segregation" memorandum into evidence and asked Meadows pointedly, "Is it your understanding that by circulating that release to the City and County Boards of Education, it would encourage them to segregate rather than to integrate?" No, Meadows snapped, it was simply "an editorial statement on the word *segregation*."

He was squirming uncomfortably in the witness chair. As Gray began again, Judge Rives instructed, "You might read the statement to us . . . if you will, Mr. Gray."[5]

Just below the surface of the supposedly innocuous statement—which the court would later call a "racist parable"—lay the same white fears that had animated segregationist resistance since the Citizens' Council had organized. Desegregation was abhorrent to God because it would lead to miscegenation, which would itself emasculate white men and ultimately lead to the destruction of Western civilization. If whites did not band together, they would be overrun by blacks. It was their moral obligation to defend segregation, provided they observed law and order in doing so. Meadows argued in his memo that a "time of reckoning" was coming on the "fundamental principles of segregation and non-discrimination." The latter could be maintained, he argued, without destroying the former "in its truest sense." By that November day in the courtroom in Montgomery, he would have to convince four federal judges that this was true. And they were laughing at him.[6]

The judges had decided that "common questions of law and fact" warranted the combined hearing of the two cases. The plaintiffs in both *Lee v. Macon* and *NAACP v. Wallace* were targeting the defiance campaign orchestrated by George Wallace. The court had declined to issue a contempt citation for the governor, but the stakes were still high. In *Lee*, Gray had reintroduced the prospect of an order forcing the state school board to use its authority over local boards to carry out desegregation on a statewide basis. Meanwhile, the Justice Department and the NAACP Legal Defense Fund were awaiting the adjudication of a consolidated set of appeals, including *U.S. v. Jefferson County Board of Education* and several other Alabama cases. They had asked the appellate court to explicitly order the adoption of the more stringent, revised HEW guidelines in cases throughout the Fifth Judicial Circuit. As the new year approached, a decade of tectonically slow movement in school desegregation litigation seemed ready to finally rupture the segregated southern education system. And Alabama looked to be the epicenter.[7]

"Means to an End"

As all parties were preparing for the hearing in *Lee v. Macon* and *NAACP v. Wallace* that fall, many students, families, teachers, and administrators were dealing with the reality of token desegregation for the first time. Developments in the courtroom and in the halls of bureaucracy informed their daily lives, but their daily lives gave meaning to those battles at the same time. The seven thousand or so black students in desegregated, formerly all-white schools, young men and women, boys and girls, experienced everything from cautious friendship to outright hostility, from inspiration, hope, and reward to disillusionment, despair, and regret.[8]

Many white teachers went out of their way to be kind to black students, sometimes even shielding them from the behavior of white students. But just as often white teachers antagonized black students. Some teachers exploited the fact that some black children were unaccustomed to saying "yes, ma'am" and "no, ma'am." As one student recalled, "[The teacher] got fed up because I got tired of her trying to make me say 'yes, ma'am,' and I started saying, 'I think so.'" Other students reported teachers repeatedly using the word "nigger," segregating their classrooms by race, allowing white students to avoid sitting next to or behind black students, and assigning black students older books and lab equipment. One girl revealed that her teacher told the class when discussing desegregation, "In a little time, our freedom will be gone."[9]

Another student reflected that white students, who "knew nothing about black folks," had been told, again and again, "to expect the worst of us." Still, many black students insisted that white students were "not entirely hostile." Some mused about family and peer pressure, saying, "You can tell some of them want to say something [friendly] to you, but they are scared that if they [do], then the other one is going to call them 'Nigger lover' and all that kind of junk." Some explained that the pain of being ignored could be the worst, though there were, of course, a litany of abuses. By far the most common harassment was being called "nigger." Beyond that, there was always the violence. "I'm tired of getting hit," one student admitted, especially since "nothin' [was] ever done about any of it." One student in Choctaw County received a typewritten message that read, "YOU AND YOURS SISTER ARE GOING TO GET THE HELL BEAT OUT OF YOU AND YOURS SISTER UNLESS YOU AND YOUR SISTER STOP COMMING TO SCHOOL. Go to your on negere schools."[10]

For a lot of students, desegregation meant disillusionment. "Some people think that white people are higher class than Negroes," one girl reported, "but from the way the children behave, they are lower class." Many black students excelled in the classroom at their new schools, and one recalled that going to a white school "removed this mystique about white students being better." Desegregation also meant sacrifice—of extracurricular activities, accolades, or student-voted designations. One student had been the president of his student council and president of his class. This would not be possible at the formerly all-white school to which he had transferred, and his family wondered if this would affect his scholarship prospects. His mother beseeched the school board to allow him to cancel his transfer request, saying he "really did not realize what he was doing." The board denied the request.[11]

Disillusionment also came in the form of reproach from members of the black community. One girl remembered, "We had to deal with a lot of criticism, because [some people] just didn't feel like this was something that needed to have been done." She was called "stuck up" and accused of being aloof. One girl's friend assumed that because she went to the white school that she and her family were "big Niggers" and "had a lot of money." Others were accused of endangering their neighbors. "They said that our house was going to be burned and the Ku Klux Klan was going to get us and lots of people was going to get killed," a girl said. Then "our house did get burned, and when it did people said, 'That's what I told you was going to happen.'"[12]

Finally there were the textbooks. Black students had traditionally been given hand-me-down books that were tattered and out-of-date—if they had been given any textbooks at all. But as transferring black students and their parents explored the newer history texts at white schools, they found something even more disturbing—a narrative that served as an apology for segregation and white supremacy. Though there were several such books, none was more controversial than *Know Alabama*, the official, state-approved history text for the fourth grade. It was written by Dr. Frank Owsley, a historian who once described former slaves as "half-savage blacks" who could "still remember the taste of human flesh." He had also professed that the "purpose of [his] life," was undermining the great "Northern myth" of the Old South by influencing fellow historians, who would then "teach history classes and write textbooks and . . . gradually and without their knowledge be forced into our position."[13]

Know Alabama presented an idyllic, paternalistic portrait of slavery and plantation life in the antebellum period—"one of the happiest ways of life in Alabama before the War Between the States." It featured the loving "Mammy," who had dutifully earned the white children's love by raising them with care. There were the field hands, with "rows of bright white teeth," who happily "helped grow the cotton." Most of them were "treated kindly," because "the first thing any good master thought about was the care of his slaves." There was the mistress, who was "the best friend the Negroes [had], and they [knew] it." And there were the slave children who liked to play "cowboys and Indians" with the white children and who "gladly went off to be the Indian, to hide and to get [themselves] captured."[14]

Then there was "Black Reconstruction," when Republican "carpetbaggers" from the North "came to steal and cheat people," and "scalawags" in the South "turned against their own people." Fortunately, a group of men decided that they ought to "do something to bring back law and order." Many a fourth-grade child read, "It happened that at this time a band of white-robed figures appeared [and] rode through the towns like ghosts and disappeared." The Ku Klux Klan "did not ride often, only when it had to." Whenever people did "bad, lawless things," the Klan "would appear on the streets," then "go to the person who had done the wrong and leave a warning," or, if necessary, hold "court" in the "dark forest at night," then pass "sentence" on "the criminals." Eventually the Klan scared the carpetbaggers into going back north, upon which Negroes "decided to get themselves jobs and settle down to make an honest living." When the last of the Republicans was run out of office by good, loyal Democrats, "law and order were restored," and "there was no more need for the Ku Klux Klan." Thus were the white children of the South indoctrinated.[15]

The problem was widespread enough that the U.S. House Subcommittee on Education began looking into the "problem of racially distorted textbooks" that fall. The USOE and the Council on Human Relations tried asking school boards to replace the books. In early November, George Wallace broached the subject in an interview with the *Citizen*. Wallace argued that HEW's Harold Howe was "going to be in complete charge" of the content taught to children in the South and warned that "HEW bureaucrats" were going to "completely capture your child." But there was hope. "We passed this law in Alabama," he explained, speaking of the anti-guidelines law. "It's now being attacked by the NAACP, but we felt that we could bring [the conspiracy] out into the open [to] prevent a complete takeover of the school system before the people knew about it."[16]

That November, Lurleen Wallace crushed Jim Martin in the gubernatorial general election—538,000 votes to 250,000, and sixty-five counties to two. Martin had campaigned on a cautious, intelligent defense of segregation, accusing George Wallace—his real opponent—of reckless defeatism. But voters had been mesmerized by Wallace's racial demagoguery. Martin might have ridden a Republican surge, but his stance on segregation looked weak when up against Wallace's brazen defiance. The incumbent governor's powers of hypnosis allowed him to become the governor by proxy, but not before he and his administration had to stand trial in *Lee v. Macon* and *NAACP v. Wallace*.[17]

By the time the four-judge court convened to hear testimony later that month, pretrial motions had complicated the posture of the litigation. The defendant state officials in *Lee* had attempted to file a cross-claim against the United States, alleging that the revised HEW guidelines were unconstitutional. The attorneys for the state did not realize that the U.S. government was protected by sovereign immunity in this case. The Justice Department actually wanted to litigate the issue, however, so it acquiesced to the naming of Commissioner Howe and newly installed HEW secretary John Gardner as defendant parties. When all parties gathered at the federal courthouse in Montgomery, the issues before the court included the constitutionality of the anti-guidelines law and the latest tuition grant law, the constitutionality of the revised HEW guidelines themselves, the question of whether state officials had violated the injunction in *Lee v. Macon*, and whether or not state interference warranted some sort of statewide desegregation order.[18]

St. John Barrett led the CRD team that had, over the six weeks leading up to the trial, deposed seven state officials, thirty-eight local superintendents, HEW's Howe, and the USOE's lead investigator, Gene Crowder. The CRD wanted to establish that the state board had a prominent role in operating and perpetuating a statewide dual school system. Two things were of particular interest—the harassment campaign undertaken by Wallace and Meadows and a system of annual surveying conducted by the State Department of Education. State surveyors examined facilities in each school system every year and, in addition to labeling each school as either "Negro" or "white," made recommendations as to whether each facility was in satisfactory condition, in need of repair, in need of consolidation with another school, or in need of closure.[19]

The depositions added some unexpected value for the CRD. Most superintendents were cautiously cooperative and revealed limited efforts at compliance amid obvious intimidation from the state. Others were standoffish or recklessly racist and combative. J. R. Snellgrove candidly described the demographics of his Enterprise city school system with apparent disregard for the formality of the proceedings. "We have three sections of the nigger race in Enterprise," he began. "Holly Hill doesn't have anything except white people. There is not a nigger that lives over in that section of the community. I believe we have at this time," he said, "ten niggers in the Hillcrest Elementary there." The CRD attorneys tried to maintain stoic expressions as Snellgrove carried on, "College Street Elementary, 565 whites and 26 niggers. . . . Enterprise High School is 912 whites and ten niggers. Coppinville High School, 389 niggers, that's seven through twelve." Also at Coppinville, he said, "We have full time one white teacher, eighteen full time niggers and one part time white teacher." He almost forgot, "Plus we have a guidance counselor over there. Of course, she is nigger."[20]

When the trial itself finally began, Fred Gray called Austin Meadows to the witness stand. The tense and lengthy exchange between the lanky, young, bespectacled black attorney and the obdurate, old, and annoyed segregationist administrator was the centerpiece of the two-day affair. At one point, Gray asked Meadows about the state's program to provide out-of-state tuition for black college students when the state's black colleges did not offer a particular program. Meadows said, "I approved a grant for out-of-state aid for you to study law." Gray acknowledged that Meadows had indeed approved Gray's grant to attend Case Western Reserve School of Law when he was just out of Alabama State College for Negroes. And now there sat Meadows in the witness chair, forced to recount his interference before a packed courtroom, at Gray's insistence.[21]

Meadows was visibly annoyed by Gray's pointed and persistent questioning. He frequently put his feet up on the railing of the witness stand, wiped his nose with his tie, stared at the ceiling, and answered "yep" and "yeah" to the attorney's questions. But he found it impossible to explain away the telegrams, letters, and memorandums uncovered by Gray's team and the CRD. In addition to the "'segregation' is a perfectly good word" memo, there were numerous telegrams to local school boards threatening to withhold state funds if they did not report on the status of their Form 441. There was also the telegram to the Lauderdale school board condemning its plan as "beyond the law," as well as the letter to the Tuscaloosa officials offering more teacher units. Gray revealed that Meadows had offered to create more budget room for any system seeking to avoid black teachers in white classrooms.[22]

The attorneys for the defendant state officials called a number of local superintendents to the stand. They were attempting to show that Gene Crowder and the USOE had made "ridiculous demands" and that state officials had done nothing more than advise not going "beyond the law." Opening up the local officials to cross examination, however, allowed Barrett and Gray to further expose the nature of the segregated state system and the extent of state control and harassment. Several superintendents reluctantly revealed that county school systems routinely accepted black students from autonomous city systems in order to keep the city schools all-white. Others admitted that, although their systems had reportedly been in compliance with the original guidelines, they never really were. Most damningly, multiple officials agreed that it "would take a court order" for them to ever desegregate at all, as that was the only way they could face the white community.[23]

The boldest move of the trial was undertaken by the man *Time* magazine described as "the most prominent segregationist lawyer in the country." Mississippi's John Satterfield had been brought in to bolster the state's defense. Over the robust objection of both Barrett and Gray, Satterfield called Alabama's senior U.S. senator, Lister Hill, to testify as to congressional debates on the HEW guidelines. Hill explained that Virginia senator Harry Byrd had argued in committee that the guidelines exceeded the statutory authority of the Civil Rights Act. The committee had, Hill recounted, subsequently issued instructions to HEW to avoid drafting "onerous guidelines that [contravened] legislative intent." During cross-examination, Gray forced Hill to admit that, in his many years in the Senate, he had not once voted for a civil rights bill. When the defense rested its case, the court gave all parties thirty days to condense the mountain of evidence before it into briefs and deposition summaries, after the submission of which a hearing would be held. Then the court would finally decide the two cases.[24]

As the trial in Montgomery was wrapping up, the Fifth Circuit appellate court handed down its decision in a consolidated set of appeals from school cases, initiated by the CRD and including *U.S. v. Jefferson County*, under which the opinion was rendered. John Minor Wisdom wrote for the majority: "*The only school desegregation plan that meets constitutional standards is one that works.*" The revised HEW guidelines, he argued, were the "best system available for uniform application, and the best aid to the courts in evaluating the validity of a school desegregation plan and the progress made under that plan." To put an end to all of the "beyond the law" talk, Wisdom described the guidelines as "based on decisions of this and other courts, within the scope of the Civil Rights Act of 1964, prepared in detail by experts in school administration, and intended by Congress and the executive to be part of a national program."[25]

Those who argued that the guidelines went "beyond the law" often pointed toward the 1955 holding of district judge John Parker in *Briggs v. Elliott*, one of the remanded *Brown v. Board* cases. Parker had contended, "The constitution does not require integration; it merely forbids discrimination." In *Jefferson*, Wisdom described that portion of the opinion as "pure dictum"—it was tertiary to the issues before the court and was therefore not binding. This "*Briggs* dictum" had become a legal "cliché" that had drained *Brown* of its "significance." Wisdom went even further, writing, "*The only adequate redress for a previously overt system-wide policy of segregation directed against Negroes as a collective entity is a system-wide policy of integration.*" The immediate goal had to be conversion to "a unitary, non-racial system—lock, stock, and barrel."[26]

It was the first significant judicial indictment of freedom of choice. Wisdom contended that freedom of choice plans served to "preserve the status quo" and offered "little prospect of . . . ever undoing past discrimination or of coming close to the goal of equal educational opportunities." While the court did not find freedom of choice itself to be unconstitutional, it held that it must only be allowed within a "*bona fide* unitary system," in which there were "not white schools or Negro schools—just schools." To get to that point, school boards under court order would have to adopt plans that met a new set of judicial standards, including facilities and program equalization and immediate desegregation of faculty and staff. The hope, Wisdom explained, was to make freedom of choice "more than a mere word of promise to the ear." District judge Harold Cox, a committed segregationist, dissented and called for an en banc rehearing of the appeals. The entire appellate court would get to weigh in.[27]

Two weeks after *Jefferson* was handed down, Lurleen Wallace was sworn in as the state's first female governor, and her husband became its first governor-regent. The Wallaces would have a new partner in resistance, though. Austin Meadows had seen enough. Convinced the country was headed for a "tragic era," he opted to retire. His replacement was Ernest Stone, whose introduction to George Wallace had come via a letter he wrote in 1965, when Stone was a local superintendent. He told Wallace, "I will match my segregation philosophy and beliefs with any man in Alabama." His credentials, he explained, included being raised in a "sundown town" on Sand Mountain, where blacks were not allowed to travel after dark. His Jacksonville school board had registered compliance with HEW, but he insisted that the board did "*only* what [it] had to do in order to keep our schools open." Stone maintained that his State Department of Education would operate on the same principle. "Laws and court orders [had] to be obeyed," but he promised, "we will volunteer no more."[28]

Stone asked the court to discharge him as a defendant in *Lee v. Macon*, arguing that it was Meadows, not he, who had behaved badly. But, the court explained, the injunction followed the office, not the man. So Stone was forced to prepare for the upcoming joint hearing in *Lee* and *NAACP v. Wallace*. When the court convened in February, attention turned quickly to the guidelines. Judge Rives revealed reservations, in light of the recent decision in *Jefferson*. "It worries me," he admitted, "whether there is any requirement of integration beyond true freedom of choice. I think there are some Negro children," he continued, "who prefer to go to purely Negro schools and some white children who prefer to go to purely white schools." He asked the CRD's St. John Barrett, "If you classify students by race for the purpose of forced integration, aren't you coming close to depriving people of their rights under the equal protection provision of the Constitution?" And when the LDF's Henry Aronson suggested that freedom of choice was not working, Rives replied, "If the goal is to mix, I will concede that freedom of choice will not work, but if the goal is to abolish discrimination, then . . . it might work."[29]

After the hearing, the judges had to address a thorny issue of timing. The trial courts' decisions in *Lee v. Macon* and *NAACP v. Wallace* would be appealable directly to the Supreme Court, as they were decisions of a three-judge court. They might also contradict the coming ruling of the entire Fifth Circuit appellate court in the en banc *Jefferson* decision, insofar as the guidelines were concerned. This could create unnecessary confusion. The guidelines were a secondary issue in *Lee v. Macon*, but the state had put them front and center in

NAACP v. Wallace. Rives polled his fellow circuit judges, who decided that the court ought to wait for the *Jefferson* ruling before issuing its ruling in *Wallace*. In *Lee v. Macon*, the judges had decided that they should issue some sort of statewide order, but the guidelines issue had put forth the question of exactly who would be effected by it. By March Judge Johnson had convinced Judges Rives and Grooms that the court should bind every school system in the state that was not already under a court order, ignoring their HEW compliance status. This would allow the court to go ahead and hand down its ruling in that case.[30]

It came on March 22, 1967. Judge Johnson wrote the opinion, in which he blasted the defendant state officials. They had, "through their control and influence over the local school boards," clearly "flouted every effort to make the Fourteenth Amendment a meaningful reality to Negro school children in Alabama." Johnson meticulously recounted the myriad ways in which state officials had, since the reprieve in 1964, not only continued to neglect their constitutional duty to desegregate but also actively fought to thwart others' efforts to do the same. "*One* of the most illegal ways" in which they had done this was in lying to local school systems and telling them not to go "beyond the law." Additionally, there were the numerous incidents of "dramatic interference"—from Meadows's ludicrous "racist parable" to the chastising telegrams, phone calls, and threats to call mass meetings. More importantly, the plaintiffs had presented "absolutely overwhelming" evidence that the state exercised "general supervision and operation" of local systems—through control over construction, teacher assignments, transportation, and, most importantly, funding.[31]

Johnson condemned the tuition grant law with equal force. It was "unmistakably clear," he wrote, when analyzing the law "in the historical context which gave rise to its enactment," that it was "but another attempt" to "circumvent the principles of *Brown* by helping to promote and finance a private school system for white students not wishing to attend public schools also attended by Negroes." The state had failed to provide any sort of rational basis for the law that trumped the plaintiffs' assertion that it was an attempt to "fill the vacuum" left by the enjoined 1957 tuition grant law. The court warned that if the "concerted effort to establish and support a separate and private school system for white students" did not cease, then it would be forced to declare the "private" system a state actor, which could bring the segregation academies under the statewide order then being issued.[32]

The court decided that the relief awarded in *Lee v. Macon* had to "reach the limits of the defendants' activities." Accordingly, the defendant state officials would be required to oversee the implementation of a "uniform state-wide plan for school desegregation." Local school boards would not themselves be parties to the suit, but the court warned that they might be added as such in the future if they resisted the state's directives. The "state's plan" would be provided by the court and would therefore, to a certain extent, be the plaintiffs' and the CRD's plan. "For the time being," the court decided that this would mean statewide freedom of choice. Johnson issued another word of warning, though. If "choice influencing factors," like segregated faculties and inferior facilities and curricula at black schools, were not "eliminated," then freedom of choice itself was a "fantasy," and "some other method of desegregation" would become necessary. Echoing Judge Wisdom's reasoning in *Jefferson*, Johnson explained that freedom of choice was "not an end in itself" but merely "a means to an end."[33]

Ernest Stone effectively became an agent of the court. He was ordered to compel the ninety-nine school systems in the state that were not already under court order to adopt a model desegregation plan and to begin implementing it that fall. The model plan included provisions for the desegregation of pupils, faculty, staff, activities, and transportation. It required the publication of choice periods and explained when those periods should run and what choice forms should look like. It even included a sample letter to parents. School boards had twenty days to adopt plans and report to Stone, who was required to then report to the court. Stone was also required to develop a statewide plan for equalization, whereby the "physical facilities, equipment, services, courses of instruction, and instructional materials" in black schools would be brought up to par with those at formerly all-white schools.[34]

Johnson had very closely followed the "proposed decree" submitted by the CRD. While it was not unheard of for a federal court to maintain a close relationship with the Justice Department or for a judge to adopt a proposed decree wholesale, this was a special relationship. The legal scholar and former CRD attorney Owen Fiss called it the "truest sense of *amicus* ever in American law." Johnson respected and trusted the CRD attorneys, especially John Doar. Doar understood this and always approached cases in Johnson's court with the expectation that the judge was counting on CRD attorneys to demonstrate not only a commanding understanding of the issues at law but also a willingness to act as the court's investigative arm. More than anything, both Johnson and Doar understood that the CRD had manpower, funding, and time, which the court did not. All that Johnson, Rives, and Grooms had were a few clerks and the already overburdened U.S. marshals.[35]

The symbiotic relationship between the court and the CRD would be pivotal moving forward through implementation, which itself would be unprecedented. The court had issued the first statewide "structural injunction" in U.S.

legal history. As Wisdom had suggested in *Jefferson*, the judges insisted that a desegregation injunction ought to be remedial, in order to eradicate the effects of past discrimination. As CRD attorney Brian Landsberg later explained, "Because the racial segregation was systemic, the violation could be cured only by systemic relief." What made the *Lee v. Macon* decision unique, though, was the concept of enjoining state officials to provide *statewide* remedial relief. A federal court initiated the restructuring of a state institution, a process in which the court itself was, in effect if not in principle, the administrator, acting with the assistance of the plaintiffs' attorneys and the CRD and using the State Department of Education as the conduit.[36]

Not only was this kind of structural injunctive arrangement unprecedented, it also proved to be influential. Johnson himself would soon use an almost identical relief structure in cases aimed at reforming Alabama's prison system and mental health facilities in the 1970s. *Lee v. Macon* would also later serve as the inspiration for Alabama's landmark voting rights case, *Dillard v. Crenshaw County*, in which the state legislature was found to have systematically blunted the effect of the black vote.[37]

More immediately, *Lee* began to significantly alter the relationship between the federal courts and HEW. It resulted in a complete role reversal between the court and the USOE. The vision of Title VI of the Civil Rights Act had been that courts would establish desegregation standards, and the USOE would enforce those standards. But as the *Yale Law Journal* correctly predicted in reviewing the *Lee v. Macon* decision, the USOE in Alabama would soon be "at best ... serving in an advisory role, helping the courts determine the applicable standards and then helping, in tandem with the Justice Department, to advise the courts on the adequacy of the desegregation plans submitted to school districts." The court had already embodied standards in its model plan, and it would now be in charge of enforcing compliance. As events would soon demonstrate, not everyone at HEW accepted this arrangement.[38]

Perhaps the most significant impact of the March 1967 decision was its redefining the potential of a single desegregation case. It had eliminated the need for ninety-nine more cases, ninety-nine more sets of plaintiff families, or ninety-nine more actions brought by the CRD—and all of the time and costs associated therewith. The *Christian Science Monitor* called it "the most sweeping implementation of [*Brown*] yet rendered by a lower federal court." The *Birmingham News* predicted "historic implications," which seemed prescient when Jack Greenberg indicated that the LDF would seek "similar orders in other hard core states." Both the LDF and the CRD soon did just that, resulting in omnibus desegregation orders in cases in Georgia, Mississippi, Texas, Arkansas, and South Carolina. Owen Fiss would later claim that he saw in Johnson's adjudication "something as ingenious, as path-breaking, as innovative as *Marbury v. Madison*."[39]

One week after the landmark decision, the full Fifth Circuit appellate court issued an 8–4 decision in the en banc rehearing of *U.S. v. Jefferson*, upholding the majority ruling and adopting Wisdom's uniform decree, with minor changes, as the standard for the entire circuit. Greenberg observed that *Jefferson* and *Lee* together had finally put the LDF "in a position to bring about substantial school desegregation in the Deep South for the first time." The Southern Regional Council called the decisions "the most significant school desegregation actions of the 1960s." The *Yale Law Journal* concluded that the two were "judicial acknowledgments" that the "administrative process," via HEW, was inadequate to the task of fulfilling the promise of *Brown*.[40]

Some of the arguments raised in dissent of *Jefferson* would prove to be highly influential themselves. Drawing on Judge Cox's dissent to the trial court ruling, judges John Godbold and Griffin Bell argued that *Jefferson* constituted an "unclear and unfair" infringement on personal liberty. Godbold argued that freedom of choice was ultimately a choice "of associates." In past litigation, this had meant the right to organize, but Godbold here meant "associational rights" that were "personal in nature." By threatening an individual's right to associate with one of his or her choosing, the court was sending "paternalistic authoritarianism" colliding "head-on" with "individual freedom." While he couched this critique in terms of black schoolchildren and their families, who might choose to continue attending all-black schools, the implications were clear. White individuals might also chose to associate with those of their own race by attending private schools or moving to the suburbs.[41]

A few weeks after the rulings, Frank Johnson made the cover of *Time* magazine. The piece was titled "Interpreter in the Front Line," with the issue dedicated to "The Law and Dissent." The cover featured an oil portrait of the judge, with his characteristic courtroom glare—a stern, thoughtful gaze directed right at the reader. Inside he described his legal philosophy in civil rights cases. "I'm not a segregationist, but I'm not a crusader either. I don't make the law," Johnson explained. "I don't create the facts. I interpret the law." He added, "I don't see how a judge who approaches these cases with any other philosophy, particularly if he was born and reared in the South, can discharge his oath and the responsibility of his office." The writer illustrated the beginning of a hearing in Johnson's courtroom: "Through a door in the starry wall strides the judge, lean and tanned in his unvarying crisp black suit, white shirt and black tie. He usually shuns robes: 'If a judge needs a robe and a gavel, he hasn't established control.'"[42]

"Now Let Them Enforce It"

The day after the en banc Fifth Circuit ruling in *U.S. v. Jefferson* was announced, the governor of Alabama went before the legislature, and on television, to address the state. Lieutenant Governor Albert Brewer accidentally introduced George Wallace. Considering the nature of the former governor's new regency, Brewer might have been excused for the gaffe. The legally elected governor—Lurleen Wallace—was not flustered. While the former governor Wallace was holding closed-door meetings with local school officials and drafting a resolution of opposition to the *Lee v. Macon* ruling, the new Governor Wallace had been preparing to deliver this speech in opposition to the same. Twenty television stations and forty-three radio stations had descended on the capital, which, according to the governor's office, made it the most widely covered political event in Alabama history. Frank Johnson had already telegrammed the Justice Department and advised John Doar, "You might make arrangements, as you see fit, to have the address taped."[43]

Governor Wallace began by forcefully invoking the state's motto, declaring, "Alabama and its elected officials dare defend our rights!" This was met with thunderous applause. The recent decisions were, she explained, "calculated to destroy the school system of Alabama." The governor called it "the last step toward a complete takeover of children's hearts and minds," which was "exactly what Hitler did in Germany." *Lee*, in particular, "destroy[ed] the authority" of state and local officials by giving control over "every single aspect of the operation of every school system" in the state to "agents of the district court, who must execute the commands of three judges." The judges would now demand "massive reassignment[s]" and "force white children to go to all-Negro schools, and Negro students to go to predominantly white schools." They would throw dissenting parents in jail and forbid anyone to even discuss the order in a negative light. Worst of all, Lurleen Wallace bemoaned, the court was threatening "to have your elected public officials coerce local school boards and cut off state funds to any of our public schools and state colleges which fail to abide by their interpretation." The average Alabamian probably did not appreciate the mind-boggling irony of such a statement.[44]

The governor articulated the southern segregationist's distorted understanding of federalism, which federal courts had been trying desperately to dispel. She argued that the state's police power was the "highest law" and stood "above the individual and above the three judge Federal district court." She therefore issued a call to arms. The *Lee v. Macon* decision was "impossible" to implement and ought to be resisted "in every way possible." The state was appealing and seeking a stay of the order, but Wallace also called on the legislature to "resolve itself into a committee of the whole," which could then issue a "cease and desist" order to the court and place all authority over education in her hands. She concluded by attempting to channel Andrew Jackson (whose concern was Indian removal), announcing defiantly, "They have made their decree; now let them enforce it." State Senator Alton Turner called it "the greatest speech [he] ever heard in eight years of service in the legislature."[45]

Down the street, Frank Johnson began drafting a list of statements made by the governor that did "not appear to have any basis in fact." At the same time, Fred Gray was preparing a memorandum in opposition to the state officials' request for a stay. Gray included the full text of Wallace's address as an attachment, which allowed Johnson to fashion his "list of statements" into a rebuttal in his order denying the stay request. Johnson explained that the recent order in *Lee* "did not involve any new or novel constitutional or legal principles and did not add to the defendants' obligations to eliminate discrimination in Alabama's public schools." He wrote, "Interpretations of [the order] to the contrary are erroneous and not factually sound, particularly public statements, now a part of the record in this case, made by one of the defendants in this case to the following effect," at which point he paraphrased only some of the governor's more egregious claims—that the three judges would determine pupil and teacher assignments, that the court would require busing to achieve racial balance, that no one could criticize the order, and that it was "rendered in malice and animosity." Wallace's speech, Johnson recognized, was an attempt to mislead parents and school officials who were "not personally familiar with the decree."[46]

George Wallace went on record decrying the rulings too. His eye was increasingly trained on the presidency, and he would use every opportunity to denounce the federal government in ways that might resonate throughout the country. He called the *Lee v. Macon* decree an attempt at "intellectually moronic control of our children." The federal government would try to "cram [the] decree down our throats," he predicted, just as they had tried to tell southerners who to "let use our restrooms" and who they could "take a showerbath with." Wallace insisted defiantly, "You know what we goin' to tell them when they ask us to give 'em more in the schools of Alabama this fall? I'll tell you what we'll tell 'em," he said, "Goddamnit, we jus' ain't." Lieutenant Governor Albert Brewer, Wallace's former point man in the legislature, insisted, "People are not going to sit still for someone to come and tell them that their children must be transferred to a school of another race." He predicted, "You are going to have riots; you are going to have knifings and stabbings in every school in this state."[47]

Defiant rhetoric continued to encourage defiant action. And not everyone was committed to resistance within the bounds of law and order. Hate mail and death threats began to pour into the district court in Montgomery. Many thought Johnson was the only judge hearing the case, so he received the lion's share of harassment. He had a cross burned on his lawn. He received a letter from a group of self-described Vietnam veterans of dubious credentials calling themselves "FIVE VOLUNTEERS," who demanded that he "withdraw, rescind, cancel, void" the *Lee v. Macon* order. If Johnson chose to ignore the demand, they wrote, "Your son, an innocent person will pay the penalty first, then your mother who is also innocent, then will be your time." They assured him that his bodyguards would not be able to save him. The "volunteers" had "plenty of practice killing Viet Congs off by the dozens," and they would soon be "getting rid of some of the bastards" who were destroying "freedom in the U.S."[48]

Rives and Grooms were not immune. Another letter addressed to all three judges was probably penned by the same "volunteers." These "armed service men," who had spent "two years in Vietnam killing, sniping, and going through hell," insisted that the recent order of the court "MUST be rescinded—reversed—done away with altogether" or else the judges and their families would "not live to see the end of the year." The group called out each judge individually. "Judge Grooms," they warned, "that fine daughter of your [sic] will pay the penalty with you." "Judge Johnson," they continued, "If your son should survive he will have to enroll in a public school—not a private school this year." Finally, they addressed Judge Rives: "YOU OLD SOB had better get ready also ... the sooner we get rid of you the better it will be. ALL THREE OF YOU GET READY TO GO OUT LIKE A LIGHT." Some went beyond threats. Someone bombed Johnson's mother's Montgomery home, blowing out windows and creating a two-foot hole beneath the house's foundation, while the elderly Mrs. Johnson was in an upstairs bedroom watching television.[49]

At the same time, the state legislature was meeting as a "committee of the whole," as Lurleen Wallace had suggested. It heard testimony from local school officials, some of whom revealed a sense of relief. School boards could now tell people that they had resisted as long as they could. When George Wallace and Ernest Stone called a meeting of state superintendents in the midst of the legislative hearings and Wallace called on the local officials to issue some sort of defiant resolution, they refused. Many local leaders seemed prepared to finally accept the inevitability of token desegregation. State leaders in other states evidently were as well. Wallace attempted to arrange a summit to chart a unified defiant course. Lurleen was dispatched to meet with other southern governors, but only four attended, issuing a statement condemning *Lee* and *Jefferson* but nothing more.[50]

On May 3, the three-judge court hearing *NAACP v. Wallace* finally rendered its opinion. The court held that the en banc decision in *U.S. v. Jefferson* was "entitled to such great deference and respect" that the court was "unwilling to depart from it." The judges also determined that it was "too clear for extended discussion" that the Alabama anti-guidelines law was unconstitutional. A state could not simply nullify the effort of a federal agency to implement a federal statute. The court added several "ancillary findings," mostly to help facilitate the implementation of the *Lee v. Macon* decree and assuage anxieties created by the misinformation pouring out of Montgomery. The court insisted that any school systems facing funds deferral would have the opportunity for judicial review of that process and that compliance with HEW guidelines would not necessarily mean "compulsory mixing of the races," only the elimination of the racially dual system. Finally, the court tried to underscore the primacy of the *Lee v. Macon* court vis-à-vis HEW. "As courts attempt to cooperate with executive and legislative policies," they wrote, "so too [HEW] must respect a court order for the desegregation of a school system."[51]

The four judges involved in *Wallace* and *Lee v. Macon* were prepared to leave the administration of the statewide decree in *Lee* to Judge Johnson alone. Judge Rives acknowledged in a letter to a fellow circuit judge who had admired the *Lee* opinion, "The glory belongs entirely to Judge Frank Johnson." Rives added that Johnson had also agreed to take on "the vast amount of administrative work" to come. Johnson knew he would have the CRD and Fred Gray and Solomon Seay to assist him. John Doar had already stationed a team of attorneys in Montgomery to monitor state government and local school board activity. Johnson told Doar that he assumed any further state action would be predicated "upon the theory that it is incumbent upon the governor, in the exercise of her police power, to maintain 'law and order.'" If so the CRD and Gray and Seay stood ready to enter the necessary motions for further relief.[52]

In mid-April, Ernest Stone delivered his first court-ordered report on local school systems' desegregation plans. All but one system—Bibb County—had made some attempt to comply. The CRD found that half of the submissions were inadequate, however, and the court agreed. Most of the unacceptable plans included no specific provisions for faculty desegregation. Some systems had simply submitted press releases indicating that they were in compliance with the original HEW guidelines. Others had sent in signed Form 441-B agreements. A few had submitted plans that were completely inadequate even in providing for token pupil desegregation. The court ordered Stone to notify the most recalcitrant systems that more was needed. When four of those systems failed to respond satisfactorily, the CRD moved to have them added as defendant parties, and the court ordered the Autauga, Cullman, Pickens, and Bibb County school boards to show cause why they should not be individually enjoined.[53]

At a hearing in early May, the CRD informed the court that three of the four had agreed to adopt the court's model plan. In direct correspondence with Johnson, they had also agreed to certain localized provisions. For example, Cullman County had agreed that black students from a closed all-black school would no longer be bused out of the county. Bibb County came to the hearing prepared to fight the show cause order. The Bibb school board's attorney, Reid Barnes, made a bumbling argument, which St. John Barrett quickly discredited. The court then made Barnes's client the first local board to be individually enjoined in the litigation. The CRD then submitted an analysis of forty-eight revised desegregation plans it had previously deemed inadequate. Five of the plans remained unsatisfactory, so Johnson issued another show cause order. Three of those five boards subsequently decided to cooperate and were discharged as defendant parties. But by the end of June, Marion and Thomasville had become the second and third systems to be individually enjoined. Bibb County appealed its injunction.[54]

That summer Ernest Stone's office worked tirelessly compiling the required reports for the court. The state superintendent not only had to submit regular reports on individual systems' progress in implementing their pupil desegregation plans, he also had to formulate statewide plans for equalization of facilities, for the elimination of racially dual transportation systems, and for encouraging faculty desegregation. When Stone submitted these to the court, Johnson forwarded them to the CRD and to Gray and Seay for review. The CRD quickly determined that they were too vague and asked the court to order Stone to submit more specific plans. It then detailed what such plans might look like, including an itemized inventory of inequalities in the ninety-nine local school systems. The CRD also asked the court to have Stone work with the each local system in submitting individual equalization and transportation plans, which it could then scrutinize. The court granted the motions, with Johnson essentially copying the CRD's language verbatim.[55]

Where Stone had failed to fully take the initiative, the CRD had stepped in and gained a measure of direct control over the desegregation process. Johnson told John Doar, "This Court expects, and requires, your office to 'follow through' on these matters by consultation" with Stone and local school boards, "and, if necessary, as a final resort, by appropriate petition or petitions presented to the Court." This was the blueprint for the next year of implementation of the *Lee v. Macon* statewide decree. School boards would submit plans and reports to Stone, who would report to the court, which would farm out review to the CRD and Gray and Seay, who would then make recommendations to the court. Complicating this arrangement was HEW.[56]

The court and HEW disagreed as to whether or not the ninety-nine *Lee v. Macon* systems were subject to the "final order" of a federal court. Per the revised HEW guidelines, this would automatically mean that they were "in compliance." However, HEW officials insisted that, with the exception of Bibb, Marion, and Thomasville, these systems were not direct parties to the litigation and were therefore still subject to HEW scrutiny. This meant that school systems previously deemed noncompliant by HEW were still facing deferral of federal funding for the upcoming school year. But that prevented those systems from hiring and placing teachers, among other things, and therefore prevented them from implementing their court-approved desegregation plans. Judge Johnson conferred with Judges Rives and Grooms and advised Doar that HEW was "thwarting the implementation of our order." He asked Doar to arrange a "high level conference" with HEW leaders and "work out some policy" that would guarantee continuing funds for the ninety-nine *Lee* systems.[57]

In the meantime, HEW investigators continued to pressure local officials. Johnson had assumed that HEW would bring motions before the court before it moved to defer or terminate funds, in the same way the CRD had been bringing motions before the court any time it found plans to be inadequate. But HEW was acting unilaterally. Doar insisted to the increasingly irritated judge that this was probably being directed by "some low level bureaucrat" who lacked the proper authorization. In fact, the new head of HEW's Office of Civil Rights, Peter Libassi, had instructed investigators to proceed with the deferral process for noncompliant systems, regardless of their status in the *Lee* litigation. Upon learning this, the court considered enjoining HEW itself in some way, but Johnson decided that would be counterproductive. The court would soon need HEW to assist the CRD in monitoring compliance with court-approved plans, once "paper compliance" had given way to actual implementation.[58]

Matters came to a head in July, when HEW moved to terminate funds to the Lanett city school system. Lanett had adopted a satisfactory desegregation plan, as determined by the CRD and the *Lee* court. But HEW investigators cited the continuing use of an all-black high school and limited pupil desegregation, which the school board had promised the court it would address in the near future, as reasons to move for termination. HEW then moved to defer funds to the Talladega County system, whose efforts to comply had been described at one point by Judge Johnson as "magnificent." Johnson told his fellow judges on the *Lee* panel that the "ridiculous situation" now warranted an injunction against HEW leadership. He drafted and entered an order adding Peter Libassi,

HEW secretary John Gardner, and HEW attorney James Dunn as defendant parties in *Lee v. Macon* and temporarily restrained them from terminating funds to any of the ninety-nine systems.⁵⁹

At a hearing in late July, Johnson was compelled to comment from the bench on the bizarre circumstances, saying, "The court observes—and I guess it is permissible for me to say this—that there are several ironies in this case." He admitted, "At this posture it has reached the point, almost, of being ridiculous." The Justice Department attorneys already on the case were obligated to defend the HEW officials, while counsel for the defendant state officials found themselves in complete agreement with the court for once. St. John Barrett lobbied for HEW's ability to continue with its regular program, calling Libassi to the stand, only to see the testimony frequently sidelined by arguments with Judge Rives, who at one point announced angrily, "We've gone about our limit in trying to work with HEW." The three judges agreed that HEW could continue to monitor compliance and even develop a factual record via administrative hearings. But it could not defer or terminate funds to the *Lee v. Macon* school systems without first bringing a motion before the *Lee* court.⁶⁰

At the end of the hearing Johnson argued that, in filing their desegregation plans and submitting to the authority of the court, the ninety-nine *Lee* systems had become de facto parties to the litigation. To allow HEW to unilaterally terminate funds to those systems would be "an abdication on the part of the Court of its authority to require compliance with a court order." There could be "no administrative supervision or review," Johnson explained, "of a judicial decree." He concluded, "The Court is the only authority to do it." The court then ordered HEW to rescind its termination of funds to Lanett and enjoined the department from any further terminations without its approval. HEW's Derrick Bell called it a "pseudo-legal" interpretation and lamented, "In Alabama, the decision certainly means that our basic tool for bringing about compliance—if not taken away—is at least placed in the background."⁶¹

The opening of schools that fall saw another incremental increase in desegregation in Alabama and throughout the South, almost all of it through some form of freedom of choice. In the ninety-nine *Lee v. Macon* systems, there were 7,441 black students and 541 black teachers in formerly all-white schools, and there were 346 white teachers in formerly all-black schools. Desegregation via the nineteen independent school cases in the state brought the number of students in desegregated assignments up to nearly sixteen thousand. But this remained a fraction of the state's black pupil population. And desegregated faculty assignments rarely exceeded more than one teacher of the minority race at a given school. The upshot was that almost all of the state's schools remained racially identifiable—schools for mostly whites, or schools for just blacks. Until there were, in judge Wisdom's words, "just schools," freedom of choice looked to produce only a "token of tokenism."[62]

Further complicating matters were the ongoing efforts of state leaders to thwart the *Lee v. Macon* order. Judge Rives expressed confidence, writing in a letter to Judge Johnson, "I would doubt whether any intelligent person can hope to defeat our decree legally." But he cautioned, ominously, "It is the actually but covertly illegal moves which will probably trouble us most—the attempts to work some people up into a frenzy and practically to substitute mob rule for a rule of law." The Wallace administration and its legislative allies were planning both types of resistance. The governor's office had instructed school boards that summer to send out forms to parents, asking them to indicate whether they would prefer that their child was taught by a teacher of their own race, or by a teacher of the opposite race. Some school boards added the sensible option, "I prefer that the board of education assign qualified teachers, regardless of race," and a few refused to circulate the forms. Wallace's demagoguery was still holding local officials hostage nonetheless. One superintendent who called the district court to complain suggested that "someone ought to go to jail," then abruptly told Johnson's law clerk to "forget he had called."[63]

Lurleen Wallace announced in August that the vast majority of the state's parents wanted a teacher of their own race for their children. This, she argued, was grounds for the *Lee v. Macon* court to admit that its March order was "erroneous" and to rescind it. It was also the purported basis for the passage on September 1, 1967, of the Teacher Choice Act. It declared that "all students, acting through their parent or guardian, shall be required to exercise a choice . . . of the race of [their] teacher." It continued, "No child shall be required to have a teacher of a race different from the one preferred by his or her parent or guardian except where the preference made does not reflect the majority will of parents or guardians similarly situated." The law threatened uncooperative school boards with termination of state funding, and it gave the governor the authority of enforcement through "such administrative action as is deemed necessary."[64]

The legislature also passed yet another tuition grant act, the third since *Brown*. This incarnation called for the creation of a "Financial Assistance Commission," appointed by the governor, that would administer funds for students attending private, nonsectarian schools across the state. The law was color masked, but no one misunderstood the purpose—to facilitate the growing white exodus from desegregating public schools. Fred Gray filed a motion for further relief in *Lee v. Macon*, asking the court to issue "the third—and hopefully last—strike" on tuition grant laws. Gray also asked the *Lee* court to enjoin enforcement of the teacher choice law. Gray argued, quoting from the March 22 order, "It constitutes the most recent—and reckless—form of 'dramatic interference with local efforts to desegregate public schools.'" The CRD filed a supplemental complaint of its own in *Lee v. Macon*, while the state NAACP filed a similar motion in the *Brown v. Board of Education of City of Bessemer* case. George Wallace acknowledged that it was then "up to the judges," but he added that an invalidation of the law would simply prove that the Constitution had "been raped" and that the courts had "taken over completely."[65]

At the hearing on the motions in *Lee* in September, state officials' attorneys introduced the results of the recent poll, which the judges found to have no value, even as an indication of what parents wanted. The defense also argued that the tuition grant law was a "freedom of choice plan" and that it could be used to help all students looking at private schools, regardless of race. Gray countered that, under the previous tuition grant law, "every dollar" was given "to students enrolled in all-white private schools established when the public schools desegregated." And the stakes had since increased—prior to the March 22 ruling, only nineteen school systems were threatened with desegregation; now all of them were. The state was determined, Gray insisted, to ensure that the "magnitude of the refuge from desegregated education in Alabama" kept pace "with the implementation of *Brown*." Judge Johnson tried repeatedly, to no avail, to get the state's attorneys to admit to the law's real purpose, asking why the state needed to "establish a school system in addition to the public school system already established."[66]

The hearing had become an omnibus affair, reflecting the increasing complexity of the *Lee* case. In addition to the teacher choice and tuition grant acts, the court also had to consider a request to intervene and a motion to add more school boards as defendant parties. The CRD wanted the court to enjoin seven school systems for their failure to adequately address faculty desegregation. These systems had not only failed to place an adequate number of teachers in desegregated assignments, they had also assigned white teachers to black schools on a part-time basis and assigned black teachers to white schools only in roles like physical education instructor, vocational education instructor, study hall monitor, and librarian. The school boards argued that there were not enough teachers willing to take desegregated assignments. The court understood this to be evasive and sympathized with the CRD, but it was so late in the summer that the judges denied the motion.[67]

The request to intervene had been made by the Alabama State Teachers Association (ASTA), the state's black educators' organization. Sol Seay represented ASTA and told the court at the hearing that, when *Lee v. Macon* systems were forced to close substandard all-black schools, black teachers and administrators were summarily dismissed or demoted, in blatant disregard of the March decree. Seay also revealed that school boards were assigning uncertified white teachers to black schools or otherwise allowing young white teachers to use black schools as a "back door" to better assignments. Local systems were, at the same time, Seay explained, insisting that black teachers in white schools be "light, bright, or damned-near white." The court allowed ASTA to intervene as a plaintiff to help the court, through Seay, monitor this aspect of compliance.[68]

Two months after the hearing, in early November, the *Lee v. Macon* court declared both the teacher choice and tuition grant acts unconstitutional. Judge Rives wrote the opinions this time. The new grant law was "clearly" an "evasive scheme to circumvent *Brown*" by encouraging "private persons to engage in the kind of racial discrimination which would be condemned if attempted by the state." In striking the teacher choice law, Rives cited the Supreme Court's decision in *Loving v. Virginia*, in which the court overturned that state's antimiscegenation law and held that state laws using racial classification had to be "necessary to the accomplishment of some permissible state objective, independent of . . . racial discrimination." Rives observed that race was, in fact, "the only factor upon which" the teacher choice law operated.[69]

The following month the Supreme Court affirmed all recent decisions in *Lee v. Macon*, including the March 22 order. At the same time it declined to review the Fifth Circuit's decisions in *U.S. v. Jefferson County*. This was a strategic move. Agreeing to hear *U.S. v. Jefferson* would have had the effect of delaying the implementation of the many plans that were based on the Fifth Circuit's model decree outlined in that decision. The model desegregation plan in *Lee v. Macon* was almost identical to the one in *Jefferson*. In affirming *Lee v. Macon*, the court indirectly placed its stamp of approval on the en banc Fifth Circuit's decision in *Jefferson*, while ostensibly avoiding any further delay. School systems across the South would have to begin eliminating choice-influencing factors and start implementing system-wide, freedom-of-choice pupil desegregation.[70]

After passing on *Jefferson*, the Supreme Court agreed to hear the plaintiffs' appeal in *Green v. County School Board of New Kent County*. Jack Greenberg and the LDF had appealed a recent decision of the en banc Fourth Circuit appellate court, which had upheld a Virginia federal trial court's approval of New Kent's desegregation plan. The plan applied freedom of choice to all grades, but it had resulted, as most others had, in only token desegregation. The LDF's position was that freedom of choice did not appear to be bringing about the elimination of the dual racial system in the county and ought to be jettisoned. John Doar suggested that the CRD support the LDF's appeal, and Derrick Bell at HEW's Office for Civil Rights asked the CRD to include a statement of HEW policy in its amicus brief—freedom of choice plans were only acceptable under the HEW guidelines if they worked. This was the standard the court had just tacitly approved in affirming *Lee v. Macon*. Everyone expected a more forceful and direct ruling on the principle in *Green*.[71]

The CRD's Stephen Pollack and others at the Justice Department thought that the court ought to bring the other judicial circuits in line with the Fifth Circuit and *Jefferson*, which Pollack called the "present high water mark" for school cases. Others, including the solicitor general, Ralph Spritzer, wanted the court to go even farther. Spritzer suggested asking the justices to declare freedom of choice per se unconstitutional and therefore overturn *Jefferson* and essentially every other desegregation decree then in effect. Pollack felt that this would threaten the progress that had recently been made. It would also mean asking the court to go significantly farther than the other two branches of government had been willing to go. Pollack prevailed, but the CRD, HEW, and LDF were still asking a lot. If the Supreme Court declared freedom of choice unacceptable where it did not "work," then many school systems across the South—still reeling from initial token desegregation—would soon have to confront a new reality.[72]

"Beyond Freedom of Choice"?

Sol Seay first met Fred Ramsey, the superintendent of the Marengo County school system, in a narrow hallway in the federal courthouse in Montgomery. Ramsey was a large man at around six foot seven and 250 pounds. He approached Seay, introduced himself, and attempted to loom over the black attorney—who was not small, short, or passive himself. Ramsey proceeded to lecture Seay on the constitutionality of segregated schools. "Now, I'm not a racist, Seay," he began. When he had finished, the Howard-educated Seay, who was representing ASTA at a hearing to be held in Judge Johnson's chambers, suggested that perhaps Ramsey might just advocate for the return of slavery itself. The Black Belt educator quickly replied that, in that case, he would like to own Seay. The headstrong Seay insisted that Ramsey would not want that, because he would undoubtedly have to "make a house nigger" out of Seay, and surely he couldn't have "this big black buck anywhere around the big house."[73]

Not long after that, Seay had an encounter with Ramsey at the county courthouse in Linden, where the superintendent was scheduled to be deposed. Ramsey had made an unusual overture to Seay and the attorneys from the CRD, asking them to meet him in a separate boardroom prior to the deposition to confer. The CRD attorneys ignored the request, but Seay was curious to see what Ramsey was up to. When Seay opened the door to the room, he found it full of black teachers and administrators, all staring at him as he stood, frozen, holding the door ajar. Ramsey boisterously announced that he had invited his "good friends" to meet with Seay, so that the attorney could tell them what he planned to do "to help them feed their families" when he and the Justice Department succeeded in "shutting down the school system and leaving them with no jobs." Stunned and livid, Seay turned and walked out the door.[74]

The episodes between Seay and Ramsey illustrated the evolution of both the mechanics of *Lee v. Macon* enforcement and segregationist resistance. As the attorney for ASTA, Seay drove all over the state to meet with school boards and craft faculty desegregation plans with protections for black educators. Like the CRD attorneys, Seay reported to the court and submitted such motions for further relief as he deemed appropriate. White resistance to black teachers was obdurate. Administrators like Ramsey believed it was their duty to frustrate faculty desegregation at every turn. Most of them accepted as a fait accompli that whites in majority black systems—like Marengo County—would flee the system en masse rather than accept integration. In their steadfast defiance of the *Lee v. Macon* court, which often brought political rewards, they facilitated the very exodus that they claimed to be trying to prevent.

While Seay barnstormed the state, boards of education began writing Ernest Stone and Judge Johnson complaining. Joe Payne, the superintendent of the Dale County system, told Stone, "It is getting to the point that we all dread to see someone come in or dread to hear the phone ring." According to Payne, the black teachers were "not capable" of teaching in white schools. "They give tests and write words on the chalkboard with incorrectly spelled words," he wrote, "They are using verbs in the wrong place, using plural words in the wrong place, their sentences are incorrect, they are using words in places they do not fit, and none of them have any discipline." Of black students in white schools, Payne added, "It is disgusting for me to have to say, that 86 percent of them are failing." He concluded, "These incapable Negro teachers is why these students are failing today in our white schools. If we have to lower our educational standards," he insisted, "we might as well close the schools down and return to the jungles of prehistoric time."[75]

Of course, any black teachers who struggled were no more incompetent than the white teachers who did so. Furthermore, if a few black teachers were at a disadvantage, it was because they had been educated in, and forced to teach in, the same segregated and inherently inequitable school system that was then being dismantled. White administrators simply did not care about the efficacy of black teachers until they began teaching white pupils. Regardless, the courts had repeatedly asserted that the dual school system would not be abolished (and especially freedom of choice could not work to abolish it) if choice-influencing factors were not eliminated so that systems could approach the status of "just schools." Segregated faculties, along with grossly inferior black school facilities and curricula, were at the top of the list of such factors and would thus remain the focus of the *Lee v. Macon* litigation throughout the spring and summer of 1968.

Judges Rives and Grooms agreed that this "most important and difficult" administrative phase of the case would be "necessarily left" to Judge Johnson's "capable hands alone." And Johnson's plan for navigating it relied heavily on the CRD. John Doar had stepped down, making way for Stephen Pollack to head the division. Johnson told Pollack that winter that he had already scrutinized the CRD's analysis of the ninety-nine school systems' current desegregation plans. He indicated which systems he felt ought to be required to make changes. Generally, if a system had more than the statewide average of 6 percent of black students in desegregated schools, then they should expect leniency. Otherwise they should be required to further eliminate choice-influencing factors. Johnson told Pollack that he expected the CRD to "speak for the court" on these matters and even admonished the attorney for the division's recent lag in response time to his communications.[76]

The changing posture of *Lee* and the beginning of Pollack's tenure brought a change in the CRD's role. Initially the CRD had been defending the "process of the court" against official interference, as a litigating amicus. Since the proceedings leading up to the statewide order, though, the CRD had been operating as plaintiff-intervenor or as a fully active litigant in the case. Pollack maintained that an active litigant should not speak for the court. He recommended that HEW's Office of Civil Rights be solely responsible for contacting local school systems. He suggested that the CRD continue only in an analytical capacity, submitting analyses of systems' plans to Stone and motions for further relief to the court as necessary. The CRD could still maintain an office in Montgomery, with attorneys available to consult with local school officials at their own discretion. After some initial resistance, Johnson called this arrangement "entirely satisfactory."[77]

Reintegrating HEW proved to be more difficult. The court had curtailed HEW's ability to defer or cut off funding to *Lee v. Macon* systems, but it still needed the department's assistance. Meanwhile, Ernest Stone was trying to keep HEW investigators away from local school boards entirely. Stone wrote to Peter Libassi at the Office for Civil Rights and argued that HEW was making demands in excess of what was laid out in the March 1967 *Lee v. Macon* decree. Stone at one point despaired, "Our school boards, Mr. Libassi, are near the breaking point!" Judge Johnson had to inform Stone that local systems were still required to cooperate with HEW field visits and requests for reports. This was, he explained, an integral part of how implementation of the statewide decree would proceed. HEW agents would work directly with local officials in crafting acceptable plans that comported with the expectations of the court. Stone and HEW would in turn report to the court on those plans. Finally, the CRD, Gray, and Seay would analyze all plans and advise the court.[78]

The arrangement got messier that spring, when it became clear that additional proceedings would be necessary to desegregate the state's athletics systems. Alabama still operated with two athletics associations—the Alabama High School Athletic Association (AHSAA), for white and formerly all-white schools, and the Alabama Interscholastic Athletic Association (AIAA), for black schools. Only AHSAA was recognized nationally, meaning, among other things, that AHSAA state champions and record holders were given credit, regardless of what anyone in AIAA might have done. AHSAA was token desegregated, as a few black students attending formerly all-white schools had chosen to play sports. Indeed, many of them had been recruited by white coaches for this specific purpose. But this led to more serious problems, namely the harassment of integrated teams, most often by opposing teams' fans but sometimes by the other teams themselves and at least once by state and local police. By early 1968, Judge Johnson had forwarded enough complaints to the CRD that it filed a motion with the court to force Stone to merge the two associations.[79]

After hearing testimony, the court in April entered an order directing the merger. The two associations would work together on a plan. Much to his dismay, Ernest Stone would be in charge of mediating the discussions. The court enjoined the ninety-nine systems from perpetuating the racially dual athletics system and informed them that if they chose to belong to any statewide association at all, it would have to be the one produced by the court-ordered merger. Johnson subsequently entered a similar order in the *Carr v. Montgomery County Board of Education* case, serving notice on the eighteen other non-*Lee* systems that they should assume that conformity would be required of them as well.[80]

The resulting negotiations between AHSAA and AIAA were unsurprisingly contentious. AIAA president Allen Frazier wanted compulsory scheduling between formerly all-white schools and all-black schools, but Stone and AHSAA president Herman Scott argued that it would "kill" high school athletics, because formerly all-white schools would eliminate their athletics programs rather than play black schools. Stone also predicted that "blood [would] flow" if any of these "clashes of the races" ever took place, especially if black teams started running roughshod over white teams. Frazier also wanted some sort of organizational oversight on "recruiting" because, he told the court, he had received in the previous year numerous complaints about white schools "raiding" black schools and "taking away their best athletes." In one case, black basketball players had tried unsuccessfully to transfer back to an all-black school after they were accused of "beating their own people."[81]

The completed merger plan and new association, approved by the court in May, called for the creation of a biracial legislative council and central board. AHSAA's Scott would become the executive secretary, with AIAA's Frazier serving as associate executive secretary. There would be no compulsory interracial scheduling, but the use of geographical districts guaranteed that there would be games between formerly all-white schools and black schools. The plan allowed for investigations into the "raiding" of black players, but Scott would have full discretion in such cases. Sol Seay, whose offer to represent AIAA had been rejected, criticized the plan for this and other reasons. As long as there were racially identifiable schools, he argued, there would be a need for a black executive with substantive authority, and Frazier did not have that in the new regime.[82]

Faculty desegregation, meanwhile, became an even more encompassing concern that spring, not just in *Lee v. Macon* but also in *Carr v. Montgomery*. It had become clear that Montgomery officials were trying to work around a fall 1967 order. The school system's desegregated faculty consisted of seven white teachers in all-black schools, and the school board had in the previous six months hired seventy-five new teachers and placed them all in schools in which their race was the majority. The board was also in the process of building three new schools in an affluent white neighborhood, tailored to the number of white students therein, and was openly marketing them as alternatives to token desegregated schools. The board had begun hiring an all-white faculty and staff, including a head football coach, who had been distributing a spring practice schedule to potential white players who wanted to come play at Jefferson Davis High. The board publicly announced that the school would not have bus transportation, since white families in the area had automobiles.[83]

Johnson was livid. In February 1968 he entered an order citing the board's blatant disregard for the court's orders and explaining that further delays in implementation would "not be tolerated." Unless freedom of choice was used "more effectively and less dilatorily," he wrote, then the court would "have no alternative except to order some other plan used." He added a supplement to the board's existing desegregation plan that brought it in line with the model plan in *Lee v. Macon* and addressed the existence of the three new schools. Johnson ordered the board to provide transportation to the schools, to inform all student-athletes of their eligibility to play at them, and to send out form letters, drafted by the CRD, informing parents that their children were eligible to attend them. Finally, he instructed the board to send representatives to each black school in the system to explain to students directly that the school board would honor "the choice of each Negro student who chooses to attend Jefferson Davis High School during the 1968–69 school year, in the absence of compelling circumstances."[84]

The school board was horrified. The order created the possibility of substantially black schools in the dead center of the city's wealthiest white neighborhood. But the most controversial and influential aspect of Johnson's February order turned out to be the provisions for accelerating faculty desegregation. Johnson gave the board until the fall of 1970 to ensure that "in each school the ratio of white to Negro faculty members is substantially the same as it is throughout the system [roughly 3 to 2]." The system would need to have approximately one-sixth minority teachers in each school for the upcoming fall, then one-fifth the following fall, in 1969. Officials across the state, fearing application of this standard in *Lee* and other cases, lashed out at the use of "strict rules" and "set quotas for race mixing." The Montgomery board applied for a stay, pending appeal.[85]

Johnson then issued a surprising amendment to the February order. He first defended himself, arguing, "We have reached the point where we must pass 'tokenism,'" and calling the board's charge that his order was unprecedented "incorrect—in both law and fact." He explained that the 3:2 ratio for faculty desegregation was to be gradually achieved, noting that the Fifth Circuit had approved such benchmarks in *U.S. v. Jefferson*. He compared the transportation requirements to those already ordered in *Lee v. Macon*. He described the board's opening the three new all-white schools as an "aggravated type of discrimination" that "fairness and justice" would "simply not permit." And he characterized the court's insistence that the board honor black students' requests to attend Jefferson Davis High as a temporary measure intended to counteract that discrimination, which, he added, affected poor whites as well as blacks.[86]

Johnson then agreed, however, to stay "certain features of the order" to which the Montgomery board had "most strenuously" objected. This included the faculty desegregation guidelines and the transportation requirements. Johnson also agreed to change the language of the letter of notice to students, from "You are eligible to attend Jefferson Davis" to "You are eligible to choose to attend Jefferson Davis." The *Montgomery Advertiser* tried to assuage white fears, arguing that the order, as amended, was "short of anything revolutionary." Most reassuring of all, "Jeff Davis" High would "not be required to take *all* Negro applicants" as previously suspected. Reassuring or not, all of this was pending the review of the Fifth Circuit that summer.[87]

The appellate court had just heard an appeal in the *Davis v. Mobile* case. The LDF had, for the second time, appealed the trial court's approval of the Mobile school board's desegregation plan. The unified Mobile city-county system was the largest in the state, with ninety-three schools and seventy-five thousand pupils—thirty-one thousand of whom were black. The school board had adopted a hybrid geographic zone and freedom of choice plan for the city of Mobile and the suburbs of Prichard and Chickasaw, while maintaining just freedom of choice for the more sparsely populated rural areas of the county. In the metropolitan area, students new to the system, new to a zone, or moving from one school to another could elect to attend a school outside of their zone. But the board could boast a 100 percent increase in pupil desegregation from 1966–67 to 1967–68, with 29,031 black students, or 38 percent of total enrollment, in 33 desegregated schools. This was enough for district judge Daniel Thomas. It was not enough for the Fifth Circuit.[88]

Judge Homer Thornberry wrote the opinion of the unanimous three-judge panel. He called the pupil desegregation numbers in Mobile "superficially acceptable," but he observed that "beneath the surface" the picture was "not so good," especially when applying the qualitative standard of *U.S. v. Jefferson*. Not only were two-thirds of the system's schools still completely segregated, the number of pupils in desegregated assignments had been skewed by the fact that four white students were attending formerly all-black schools, thus adding all of those black students to the tally. There were only 692 black students attending formerly white schools. While this was a 200 percent increase over the previous year, it was still only 2 percent of the system's black student population. There were also twenty-seven hundred teachers in the system, of whom only fifteen (twelve black and three white) had chosen to work in desegregated assignments. Thornberry argued that this "hardly scratched the surface" of the problem.[89]

Again citing *U.S. v. Jefferson*, the court demanded that Mobile adopt a "pattern of teacher assignment" that did not perpetuate the racial identifiability of the county's schools. To begin with, the board was to assign at least one teacher of the minority race to each school, and, "wherever possible," it was to assign more. As for pupils, not only did the court find that the city's geographic attendance zones had been drawn to limit desegregation, it also found that "superimposing" freedom of choice options upon the attendance area plan had significantly reduced what effectiveness it might have otherwise had. Thornberry paraphrased Judges Johnson and Wisdom, insisting that freedom of choice was "not a goal in itself" and was "but one of many approaches" toward eliminating the dual system. "If it does not work," Thornberry wrote, "another method must be tried." The court ordered the board to redraw the attendance zones and insisted that students assigned to a particular zone could not transfer out "absent some compelling nonracial reason." It was the first time a court explicitly ruled that freedom of choice was not working and had to be abandoned. And it was a harbinger of things to come.[90]

Three weeks later, James Earl Ray shot and killed Martin Luther King Jr. in Memphis. The shocking murder outraged blacks across the country. The ensuing rioting might have served as an indication of the frustration and dismay felt by many blacks in the nation's cities, where ghettoization, unemployment, police brutality, and racism in general continued to stifle opportunity. But it mostly served to reinforce whites' preconceived notions about the volatile and violent nature of black communities. This was particularly troubling in the urban South, where segregationists stood ready to marshal these events as evidence that school desegregation was a threat to the well-being of their children. In Mobile newly organized white protest groups seized the opportunity to say, "We told you so." And the segregationist narrative of resistance began to shift toward highlighting a lack of respect for law and order on the part of blacks—a shift that was shepherded by state leaders like George Wallace.[91]

Meanwhile, Lurleen Wallace's physical condition rapidly deteriorated. She had been quietly battling cancer since the previous summer. By that April it had spread to her colon, liver, and lungs, and she weighed less than eighty pounds. When she died on May 6, Alabamians mourned the passing of the state's first female governor, who had earned the adoration of her husband's supporters while avoiding the ire of many of his enemies. George Wallace quickly returned to the national campaign trail, where he had spent the majority of his wife's short term in office. Lieutenant Governor Brewer assumed the state's top office. Brewer was keen to shore up his credentials as an ardent opponent of integration and an avid advocate for law and order. The escalating crisis in Mobile gave him an immediate opportunity to demonstrate both.[92]

Just over a week after Governor Wallace's death, the Mobile school board began to release the names of schools affected by the March decree in *Davis*, prompting protests from white parents. When white residents of a middle-class neighborhood on the west side of the city learned that their children would be reassigned from Murphy High and its feeder schools to formerly all-black Williamson High and its feeders, they besieged a school board meeting. One indignant mother argued that sending her daughter through the all-black Maysville section to attend Williamson would endanger the child's life. "I wouldn't let my dog walk down some of those streets," she claimed, "and yet you're telling me I must send my 15-year-old daughter through one of the roughest sections of Mobile to go to school." Another parent asserted that Maysville was "known to police as a jungle, the worst colored area in Mobile."

A third stood and declared furiously, "I'll tell you now, my child is not going to that school, and that's final. And I think that goes 100 percent for all of us who live in these neighborhoods that are affected."⁹³

Whites were realizing that the shield of tokenism was being pried away, and Albert Brewer seized upon their fear. He announced that Alabamians were "satisfied with the operation of the freedom of choice plan" and lamented that federal courts were using "innovation by judicial decree" to "[declare] that a person in this republic can no longer exercise a choice." Meanwhile, as more and more details of the Mobile desegregation plan were released that spring and summer, white parents mobilized. They formed organizations like Operation Snowball, Whites Organized for Rights Keeping (WORK), and simply Whites Rights. They planned to stage protests to pressure the district court, the Justice Department, and the school board. WORK leaders even suggested that school board members ought to defy the court and accept contempt citations and jail time.⁹⁴

The most successful of the new segregationist groups was STAND—or Stand Together and Never Divide. The group's founder, local tree surgeon Lamar Payne, modeled his organization after the Citizens' Council and prided himself on its air of respectability and commitment to law and order. One of the group's rallies drew nearly ten thousand people to a local National Guard armory, after which its attorney—Harvard-educated state senator and local Citizens' Council leader Pierre Pelham—filed a motion to intervene in *Davis v. Mobile*. Pelham argued that increasingly violent and hostile black neighborhoods were a threat to white children. Judge Thomas granted the motion, and STAND entered the case.⁹⁵

Blacks Mobilians also organized. One group resurrected was the once influential but long moribund Neighborhood Organized Workers (NOW). NOW began to hold mass meetings and stage protest marches on city hall and student pickets at black high schools. Not only did its leaders insist that city officials were not doing enough to end racial discrimination and inequality, they also brought a militant edge to their activism and rejected longtime leader John LeFlore's strategy of patient accommodation. Many of NOW's members had been influenced by former Student Nonviolent Coordinating Committee leader Stokely Carmichael, who was scheduled to speak at a NOW rally that summer. They were more receptive to "black power" than increasingly hollow promises of rewards in biracial cooperation.⁹⁶

Leaders from NOW, STAND, and other groups all converged on Mobile's Municipal Auditorium in late May when the school board held a community hearing. The meeting devolved into a circus when nearly one thousand angry whites stormed in and demanded to be heard. White parents yelled at board members, shouted down speakers, snapped back and forth with black parents and NOW members, and vowed to disrupt the current plan at any cost. When the wife of NOW president David Jacobs assumed the podium, three hundred whites staged a walkout. An incensed Jacqueline Jacobs shouted, "Run, run! You can't run forever!" The spectacle flirted with complete chaos as Jacobs continued screaming and gesturing, and remaining whites responded in kind.[97]

When the police and the school board chairman finally restored order, Jacobs conceded that Maysville was a rough neighborhood. But her children, she said, had been forced to walk through it to go to Williamson. Why was it that no one cared until white children were faced with the same problem? The aging John LeFlore followed Jacobs, calling for calm and understanding. He was followed by local Catholic priest Leon Hill, whose parish was located in a predominantly black section of the city. Hill called for cooperation, arguing, "Changes are coming, whether we like it or not, so why delay, delay, delay?" The priest was mercilessly jeered and departed the podium upon receiving a particularly salient barb from one white parent: "How many kids do you have, father?"[98]

Several white parents spoke of gunfire, sirens, and screams coming from Maysville and of a "burden" that was "too great" for their children to bear. One parent argued, "We have begged, but we beg no longer. We have petitioned, but we petition no longer. We will stand together 100,000 strong—and more if necessary, [and] God being our helper, we will succeed in saving our children and our schools." The applause that greeted those remarks was surpassed only by applause in response to the next white parent. "I don't care how many plans you sit here and make, or how many court orders you get," he said flatly, "My children are not going to Williamson or any other Negro school." The sense of urgency was soon underscored by events in Washington.[99]

One week later, on May 27, the Supreme Court handed down its decision in *Green v. County School Board of New Kent County*. The school board had argued that its freedom of choice plan was adequate and that requiring it to do anything more—"compulsory integration"—would violate the Fourteenth Amendment. The court disagreed. As Justice William Brennan prepared to deliver the opinion of the unanimous court, Chief Justice Earl Warren slipped him a note that read, "When this opinion is handed down, the traffic light will have changed from *Brown* to *Green*. Amen!" Brennan read, "What is involved here is the question whether the Board has achieved the 'racially nondiscriminatory school system' *Brown II* held must be effectuated in order to remedy the established unconstitutional deficiencies of its segregated system." Token desegregation would not meet the measure. Brennan continued, "The fact that, in 1965, the Board opened the doors of the former 'white' school to Negro children and of the 'Negro' school to white children merely begins, not ends, our inquiry."[100]

Like the trial court in *Lee v. Macon* and the appellate court in *U.S. v. Jefferson*, the Supreme Court did not go so far as to declare freedom of choice plans unconstitutional. If such a plan "offer[ed] real promise" of disestablishing the dual system, then it could be acceptable, though Brennan acknowledged that the "general experience" with freedom of choice had shown it to be ineffective, particularly in New Kent, where fewer than 15 percent of black children had chosen to attend formerly all-white schools and no white children had chosen to attend black schools. If school systems could not prove that freedom of choice was working to eliminate the racial identifiability of schools, and if trial courts determined that "other more promising courses of action" were reasonably available, then those systems, Brennan read emphatically, would have to "*come forward with a plan that promises realistically to work, and promises realistically to work now.*" The justices had embraced the thrust of *Jefferson*, *Davis*, and *Lee* and had heralded the beginning of the end of the era of tokenism.[101]

Green was fuel for Alabama politicians to add to the fire of defiance, which seemed to burn hottest in Mobile. Former lieutenant governor Jim Allen took to the port city in his campaign to replace the long-serving Lister Hill in the U.S. Senate. Referring to both *Green* and *Davis*, Allen told supporters at a rally, "These two decisions show the length to which the Washington crowd is going to take over our schools, our children, and the daily lives of our young people." But "even the federal judiciary" would eventually "move in the face of aroused public opinion." As an example, Allen offered Johnson's recent modification of his order in the *Carr v. Montgomery* case. The court had backed off, according to Allen, when "public opinion was aroused and the people acted." Such "action" would "do wonders" in Mobile too if the people would only resolve to make sure the courts knew that they were "not going to submit." He added, "I stand with STAND . . . 100 percent."[102]

Albert Brewer also poured it on. He applauded the efforts of STAND, asked the state's congressional delegation to propose legislation that might somehow overturn *Davis*, *Carr*, and *Green*, and praised the Alabama Education Association for condemning the decisions. "There is a serious question," he surmised, "as to how long we can continue to operate our public schools if the federal courts abandon all restraint and continue to encroach upon local control." "Logically extended," Brewer argued, "this rule can be applied to determine where a person lives and how he can make a living." Most people in Alabama, he explained, were perfectly happy with freedom of choice. He implicated the familiar enemy, the NAACP, claiming that a "very small, but vocal and suit-conscious minority" was responsible for frustrating the will of "people of all races." Freedom of choice had to be salvaged, or individual rights and freedoms—not just states' rights and local control—were at risk of being violated, perhaps even lost. Segregationist leaders had taken to defending that which the state had just fought for fifteen years to avoid.[103]

On June 9, 1968, STAND held another rally at the National Guard armory in Mobile. Anxiety was high on both sides of the color line, with some fearing widespread violence. Outside the armory Pierre Pelham told assembled media, "When you had token integration there was resistance, but now you're way beyond that. You're getting home. It's a more personal thing." Inside the building he assured the crowd that Brewer was prepared to commit "the full resources of the governor's office" to "protect the public school system of [the] state." He was convinced of the righteousness of their cause. "It is not you who are tearing down buildings and burning up cities," he observed. Neighborhoods like Maysville were unsafe, in other words, because black people were violent. Pelham concluded, "No man, nowhere, would tell me to send my child to an unsafe school."[104]

STAND's William Westbrook took the podium next. Westbrook described STAND's plans to coordinate marches on courthouses, assuming, as Jim Allen had suggested, that this would force the courts to demonstrate some sort of retreat. This would almost assuredly not work as described, but Westbrook and Pelham knew the crowd of white parents wanted a call to arms. Westbrook gave them one predicated on racist assumptions whose roots stretched down nearly three hundred years into the Alabama clay. He told them to show federal judges that they would not let their children "go into an environment that will make bums, loafers, hoodlums, and criminals out of them." He asked them to "consider the impact" of "50,000 people heading to the courthouse . . . clean shaven and neatly dressed, to attend court in behalf of our children." And if the school board felt like anything was inevitable, then board members ought to "get ready to go to jail in defiance of the open court orders."[105]

Segregationists had fought token desegregation head-on and lost. Violent resistance, economic reprisal, and even lawmaking had all failed. It appeared to some that it was time to learn from the enemy. They had already begun to mold the civil rights movement's strategic focus on constitutional individual rights into a rationale for continuing massive resistance—moving beyond freedom of choice meant deprivation of the individual freedoms of white parents and students. And they had begun arming themselves with the tactics of the nonviolent movement for black equality—protest marches and jail-ins. All that remained was to steal the rhetorical flourish. That night, Westbrook obliged. He closed his remarks at the armory, to the delight of the gathered, by evoking the recently murdered Martin Luther King. "We have had a dream too," he declared. "Our dream," he explained, "is we are not going to surrender our schools and our homes to the social-minded reformers and Constitution wrecking judges." He concluded, defiantly, "We are not going to send our children to Negro schools, and that is a fact and not a fantasy."[106]

CHAPTER 5

"Depths of Disillusionment," 1968–1970

"We teach our children, all children, that the United States of America is dedicated to law and order. We lie." Thus began a Southern Regional Council (SRC) report on the state of school desegregation in the South. The council had monitored schools throughout the 1967–68 school year and had concluded that the promise of *U.S. v. Jefferson, Carr v. Montgomery, Davis v. Mobile,* and *Lee v. Macon* had not been fulfilled. *Jefferson* and *Lee,* in particular, had seemed to portend the dawn of a "new judicial era." When the U.S. Supreme Court sanctioned these decisions in *Green v. County School Board of New Kent,* it put the entire region on notice that freedom of choice was an acceptable desegregation strategy *only* if it actually worked to eliminate the racial identifiability of schools and therefore the racial duality of school systems. But something had gone wrong. The SRC lamented, "After a generation has beheld successful evasion, rationalized vacillation, [and] outright flaunting of the law, only a country absolutely wedded to the totalitarian concept of order without law could turn on the victims of lawlessness and accuse them of destroying the fabric of society."[1]

When *Green* came down in May 1968, segregationists had just begun to accept the inevitability of token desegregation. The prospect of moving beyond that put them in the position of defending an institution that they had spent the better part of two decades trying to avoid. Having begrudgingly accepted freedom of choice by deferring to law and order, most continued to seek solutions within the law. Instead of states' rights and local control, they began to decry the usurpation of their individual rights, especially to associate with those of their own choosing. Freedom of choice had threatened that right of association. But freedom of choice seemed to at least preserve tokenism and was, therefore, preferable to genuine integration. Whites' newfound claims that freedom of choice was working for everyone revealed a fundamental misunderstanding of the goals of black activist-litigants and the Justice Department, as well as the law as most federal courts then understood it. Freedom of choice was not a permanent compromise. It was a means to a legal end. Its fate was to be determined by the results it wrought. And in the spring of 1969, those results were far from promising.[2]

By that time, the grassroots movement to salvage tokenism had begun to affect Washington. Mississippi congressman Jamie Whitten introduced a proposed amendment to the annual appropriations bill for HEW, which his colleagues described as a "congressional sanction to freedom of choice." It read, "No part of the funds contained in this Act may be used to force busing of students, abolishment of any school, or to force any student attending any school to attend a particular school against the choice of his or her parent." Whitten had characterized *Green* as a call for "racial balance" in schools, a concept that would threaten school systems in other parts of the country, in which de facto segregation was common. Whitten shrewdly argued that what had been "visited upon" the South was about to "spread throughout the nation." Along with Mississippi senator John Stennis, South Carolina's Strom Thurmond, and George Wallace, Whitten was deploying what has been called a "northern strategy": force "Yankees" to face the threat of integration, and they will lay off the South. Maybe they would even see a Thurmond or a Wallace as a defender of white rights everywhere.[3]

Whitten's scare tactics garnered his amendment significant support but not enough to alter the appropriations bill. Nevertheless, the debate underscored growing concern over the vulnerability of white privilege and a desperate need to embrace tokenism as tightly as possible. Many southern leaders in Congress who had hovered above the racial fray since the doomed filibuster against the 1964 Civil Rights Act dove back in. The threat was greater. And it required a strategy born of the decades-old litigious battle that had dragged segregationists, kicking and screaming, to that point. The Southern Regional Council concluded, "We have shown a generation of American children, in the public institution closest to their lives, the schools, that this nation's fundamental law need not be obeyed; we have clearly demonstrated to them that what we expect is their conformity to lipservice to the shibboleth," or what the courts would call "paper compliance" with freedom of choice. The council wondered, "What will be the awful effects of this lie upon children, black and white alike? What depths of disillusionment when they hear us say 'law' and observe only 'order.'"[4]

"White Americans Have Their Rights under the Constitution, Too"

As the head of the Civil Rights Division, Stephen Pollack realized that *Green v. New Kent County* gave the Justice Department the chance to press forward in its school cases across the South. The Supreme Court had affirmed *U.S. v. Jefferson* and *Lee v. Macon* and declared New Kent's freedom of choice plan deficient based on the low percentage of students in desegregated assignments and the lingering racial identifiability of schools. Given these criteria, Pollack determined that in nearly all of its 190 school cases, the freedom of choice plans being implemented would fail to meet the standard for "working" plans. In June 1968, as many at the Justice Department reeled from the shocking assassination of former attorney general Bobby Kennedy, Pollack advised Attorney General Ramsey Clark that the department had a "responsibility" to file motions for further relief in those cases, seeking some other, more effective method of desegregation. He predicted that there would be "threats of forcible interference" from segregationists, including "a concerted effort ... directed towards undermining the public school system." And he acknowledged that private litigants would probably file similar motions of their own.[5]

Fred Gray indeed filed a motion in *Lee v. Macon* on June 7, 1968. The *Lee* court had granted the state an "interim period of tolerance" for the use of freedom of choice plans. Gray argued that, with *Green*, that period had passed. He asked the court to require state superintendent Ernest Stone to prove that each school board was "employing the method of pupil assignment which promises the speediest and most effective conversion to a unitary, nonracial school system." The CRD filed its own motion in *Lee* a week later, in which it painted a grim picture of the most limited tokenism in seventy-six school systems that fell under the *Green* criteria for further relief. All-black schools still operated blocks away from token-desegregated white schools. No white children had chosen to attend black schools. Faculty desegregation was minimal. In a massive appendix, CRD attorneys recommended specific school or grade closures and student reassignments for each system. In some cases, they recommended "pairing" schools—a formerly black school would take all students from grades 9–10, for example, and a formerly white school would take those same pupils for grades 11–12.[6]

Judge Johnson set a hearing on the motions for August 1968, and the court ordered the CRD to begin contacting school boards to gauge their willingness to voluntarily move beyond freedom of choice. The response of the Autauga County board of education was typical. The Autauga superintendent argued, "If this board were forced to have a compulsory attendance district, the [schools] that you mentioned ... would become ... totally Negro school[s]," which would be "repugnant to the purpose as set forth" by the CRD. School officials assumed that a white exodus would follow any sort of compulsory pupil assignment plan. They might have considered ways to mitigate this, of course, but that would have carried the potential for community pressure and political backlash. Most officials chose instead to use the threat of white flight as an excuse to avoid doing anything more, despite the fact that the Supreme Court had quashed this as legal strategy.[7]

Local resistance was again encouraged by state officials, including Governor Brewer. Brewer considered himself a progressive reformer, since he wanted to improve education for all by increasing spending and bringing teachers' salaries up to competitive levels. He figured he represented a new class of business booster leaders, poised to move the South beyond the racist demagoguery of the past and into the vanguard of a Sunbelt rising. He was certainly not above racial politics, however. Brewer had simply rejected George Wallace's strategy of high-profile, outright defiance and instead adopted the more effective, fully developed law-and-order style: reluctantly accept freedom of choice tokenism, under the threat of sanction, while condemning it and federal judges loudly and frequently; criticize and demonize black plaintiffs; accept white flight as an inevitable outcome of further desegregation; doggedly contest all desegregation litigation; convince whites to defend their right to freedom of association; begin adopting a color-masked rhetoric; and begin looking at meaningful and durable legal protections for white privilege.[8]

In response to the motions for further relief in *Lee v. Macon*, Brewer offered his support for a defiant resolution issued by the State Board of Education, which he said would put the state "on the offensive rather than the defensive." He called the upcoming hearing in *Lee* "gravely" concerning and the recent order in *Davis v. Mobile* "arbitrary," and he ensured local school boards that they had the support of his office in their fight to preserve freedom of choice. The state board, in turn, announced its own commitment "to defend the right of each local school board to determine for itself the question of whether the freedom of choice plan will be retained." Such plans had been "involuntarily accepted" by each local school system, but, the board claimed, they had then been implemented in good faith. If no students had been denied their right to choose—and this was a dubious claim in itself—then freedom of choice must be "working."[9]

The numbers told a different story, and they were on display at the August hearing in *Lee v. Macon*. According to HEW reports compiled that summer, only 5.4 percent of the state's 233,000 black pupils were in formerly all-white schools. And in the seventy-six systems named in the CRD's recent motion, 91 percent of black students were set to attend all-black schools that fall. State officials nonetheless stood by their argument at the hearing. Brewer took the stand to accuse the Justice Department of "emphasizing statistics and social objectives" and to reiterate the claim that any substantive increase in integration would force whites to flee for private schools and then turn their backs on needed increases to public education funding. Ernest Stone echoed the governor's testimony, suggesting that if the percentage of black students in white schools increased beyond 15 percent—the yardstick for *Green* compliance—then whites would surely leave. Forty local superintendents testified to the same.[10]

As the court considered the testimony, Johnson indicated that he did not believe the "interim period of tolerance" for freedom of choice had passed but rather that the court and local officials must continue to focus on eliminating choice-influencing factors. In cases involving Crenshaw, Autauga, and Barbour Counties, Johnson acknowledged, "It is one of the facts of life that white students will not elect to attend and will not, if any other choice is available, attend a predominantly Negro school." And he called it "naïve to the point of ridiculousness" to believe that improvements at black facilities were going to attract white students, as Brewer and other officials claimed. He ordered each system to close certain black schools, or certain grades, and to reassign their students to white schools. He also granted an injunction against the Ku Klux Klan, to "dispel the fears of Negro parents" of schoolchildren, because the Klan had been engaging in a campaign of violence, intimidation, and economic reprisal where school systems had come under court order and HEW scrutiny.[11]

On August 28, 1968, as Chicago police attacked protestors outside the Democratic National Convention, the *Lee v. Macon* court issued a ruling partially denying the motions for further relief, reflecting Johnson's recent decisions. The court determined that freedom of choice remained "the most feasible method to pursue" as long as choice-influencing factors could be mitigated or eliminated. Johnson had carefully reviewed the CRD's analysis of each school system's plan, and he used that to establish specific requirements for the seventy-six school boards named in the CRD's motion. Each was to make an effort to achieve a faculty desegregation ratio of one black teacher for each six white teachers, and most had to close or partially close substandard black schools and move those students to desegregated schools. Johnson emphatically stressed that this was only the court's ruling "*at this time.*"[12]

The CRD and Fred Gray saw it is a partial victory. Albert Brewer saw it differently. The governor chided the judges for using "devious and roundabout means to effect social aims" and for paying "lip service" to freedom of choice. He complained, "These people want to come along and want to tear down all we have done and all we want to do for public education." Brewer and Stone petitioned the court to modify the order, arguing that carrying out the faculty desegregation requirements that fall would be "*an impossible task.*" They had legitimate administrative concerns, given the eleventh-hour nature of the order. But they also hyperbolically predicted "mass teacher resignation," and they lamented the contravention of the state's teacher tenure law, which had been designed to thwart desegregation in the first place. They also insisted that school closures would lead to overcrowding, which they blamed for the organization of new private schools. Brewer began publicly showcasing the case of Chambers County, where a $1-million black school had been temporarily closed. The governor stressed that the facility had a brand-new swimming pool. His white audience understood the unspoken message—local officials had begun installing pools at black schools in an effort to keep blacks from trying to desegregate white community pools.[13]

At a statewide school board conference the following month, Brewer told local officials that they were not "under any obligation to obey any orders ... from the Justice Department." Anticipating such an argument, the CRD had already filed a motion for "clarification" of the August 28 order in *Lee v. Macon*, asking the court to stress to school boards that its requirements were not "the sum total of their constitutional and legal obligations for the coming year." The structural injunction from the original March 1967 order still applied to all of the ninety-nine systems involved in the *Lee* litigation. They were required to report regularly to Stone, who was to report to the court, which would submit reports to the CRD for analysis and determine whether or not systems were making good-faith efforts to comply. Brewer could play the politics of law and order, but most local officials by then understood their legal responsibilities.[14]

That summer, as the *Lee v. Macon* court was grappling with the implications of *Green*, segregationists in Mobile were fighting desperately to preserve freedom of choice in *Davis*. The word "busing" entered the Mobilian lexicon and quickly took on the connotation of the racial apocalypse. "Busing" had become a way for whites to describe any sort of compulsory pupil assignment program that required theretofore unnecessary transportation. The Fifth Circuit had ordered the Mobile school board to adopt a city-wide zoning plan, which the board submitted to the trial court in July. The CRD and the LDF submitted their own more stringent plans, which the board condemned as "busing plans" involving "obvious gerrymandering ... to achieve some sort of racial balance." Judge Thomas set a hearing to consider the three plans.[15]

STAND leader William Westbrook called for demonstrations outside the courthouse, paradoxically urging a crowd of six thousand "law-abiding" whites to tell the court, "We are not going to abide by any boundary lines that take away freedom of choice plans," and "We will not allow our children to attend a predominantly Negro school, whether the Justice Department, [HEW], or the NAACP believe it or not." Westbrook delighted the crowd by again mocking the late Martin Luther King Jr. "I have not seen a mountaintop," he bellowed, "but

I have seen the light." STAND attorney Pierre Pelham tried to back away from Westbrook's call for a mass protest, arguing that instigating a circus outside the courthouse, a potential violation of federal law, was not the way to positively influence Judge Thomas, who was almost certain to employ some sort of delaying tactic anyway. Nonetheless, six hundred or so STAND supporters showed up at the courthouse, which was lined with U.S. marshals, FBI agents, and local police in riot gear.[16]

Inside the courtroom, parents expressed support for freedom of choice and denounced "outsiders telling us where our children must go to school." Pelham called Mobile's chief of police in an attempt to paint black schools like Williamson High and Blount High as hubs of criminal activity. Pelham even encouraged the chief to describe black neighborhoods, in general, as festering with violent animosity toward whites. The CRD and LDF argued that the school board had plainly designed the attendance zones in its plan to limit desegregation and called educationists to testify in support of their own respective plans. On cross-examination, Pelham was able to establish that the education scholars had not been very thorough in their studies or very well acquainted with the Mobile school system. His attack went awry, however, when he returned to STAND's fundamental issue. He asked Dr. Myron Lieberman, "Do you believe white children should be forced to go to an unsafe school?" Lieberman provided a poignant lesson in genuinely color-blind policy, replying, "If the school is unsafe, no children, including Negroes, should be allowed to attend it."[17]

After the hearing, Judge Thomas ordered the implementation of his own plan. It pleased no one. Thomas established his own attendance zones for the metropolitan area's elementary and junior high schools, estimating that this would place around three thousand black students in formerly all-white schools that fall. While that was more than four times the roughly seven hundred blacks in white schools the previous year, it was only 10 percent of black students in the system. Thomas retained freedom of choice for the metro area's high schools. He noted that the Fifth Circuit had allowed for the consideration of "compelling, non-racial" reasons in limiting zoning, and he wrote, "This court is compelled to find under the evidence that such reasons exist for deferring the attempt to devise rigid attendance zones for Mobile's high schools for the time being." Thomas argued that adopting zones for the high schools "would result in locked-in segregation to a substantially greater degree than will be the case under the freedom of choice system."[18]

Vernon Crawford and the LDF appealed, as did the CRD, the school board, and STAND. About the only people encouraged by Thomas's ruling seemed to be the media. The *Mobile Press* praised the judge's "solid, practical approach," chastised the NAACP and the Justice Department for "applying dictatorial means to achieve school desegregation more rapidly," and accused the Fifth Circuit and the Supreme Court of "judicial despotism." The *Birmingham News* reproached the CRD for using Mobile as a "guinea pig" and for attempting to "abolish all semblance of freedom of choice" through "judicial fiat." Thomas himself understood that, whatever the reaction, it was far too late in the summer to effectively challenge his plan before the start of fall classes. His self-made compromise would stand for at least a year.[19]

Violence marred the opening of schools in September. Most of it was associated with faculty desegregation or freedom of choice in the high schools, though, not with newly imposed compulsory assignment in the elementary or junior high schools. Interracial fights were common. White parents assaulted the vehicles of two black teachers arriving for work at a formerly all-white school in rural Mobile County. One incident at Vigor High in Prichard resulted in the suspension of a white student, which itself prompted a demonstration involving over one hundred white students and parents. Police dispersed the protestors, who subsequently complained to the school board that white teachers were showing favoritism to black students and that certain of the hundred or so black students were intimidating their 1,550 white classmates.[20]

STAND founder Lamar Payne offered white Mobilians' rationale for resistance. He noted that whites had reluctantly accepted freedom of choice. "But now," he complained, "the government says that's not enough." For STAND's thirty thousand followers, any form of compulsory assignment was unacceptable. "I'm not anti-anything except Communists," Payne explained, "I don't hate Negroes, and STAND will not tolerate haters in the organization." But he and his supporters were prepared to "build [their] own private school system throughout the nation" to avoid integration via compulsory assignment. He concluded, "I realize Negroes and other minorities have their rights, but white Americans have their rights under the Constitution, too."[21]

Just as in *Davis* and *Lee*, *Green* resulted in motions for further relief that summer in each of the Birmingham area's desegregation suits. Local attorneys Oscar Adams and Harvey Burg filed motions to move beyond freedom of choice and accelerate faculty desegregation in *Armstrong v. Birmingham*, *Brown v. Bessemer*, *U.S. v. Fairfield*, and *U.S. and Stout v. Jefferson County*. The CRD followed with motions of its own. Judge Seybourn Lynne acknowledged that these school systems could "not pretend" to be in "full compliance" with their desegregation plans, but he maintained that "substantial progress [was] being made." He denied the motions to accelerate faculty desegregation, except in Birmingham, where he ordered a modest increase. And he postponed until the following year a ruling on freedom of choice. As with Thomas's ruling in Mobile, it was not enough for some segregationists, who in this case chose to simply get out.[22]

Whites had been fleeing Birmingham for decades. The mere existence of the affluent, white suburban communities across Red Mountain, on the city's south side, was a testament to twenty years of flight, initially from black "encroachment" into white neighborhoods. Two of those cities—Mountain Brook and Homewood—had rejected a plan to merge with Birmingham in 1964, fearing the prospect of being drawn into the city's desegregation litigation. Hyper-affluent and all-white Mountain Brook had, in 1959, broken away from the county system and established its own independent city school system. And students in Homewood and all other suburban cities attended Jefferson County schools that in 1964 were still safely segregated. But by 1968, Jefferson County was under court order, and freedom of choice seemed to be in peril too. So that summer Homewood and others watched as the city of Hueytown, to the west of Birmingham, resolved to follow Mountain Brook's example.[23]

Hueytown's city limits had been drawn to exclude black neighborhoods. But as part of the county system, Hueytown's schools would be facing a potential influx of black students if freedom of choice were quashed. Hueytown was no Mountain Brook, and purchasing facilities and equipment from the county would be difficult for the working-class city. A group of Hueytown parents had organized a "Citizens Committee" earlier in the summer and had begun stumping for separation, convincing others that it would be worth it. The committee prepared a fifteen-page report to distribute to the community, along with letters, pamphlets, and candidate information for upcoming local elections. They promised "control of . . . local schools vested in local citizens" and assured "freedom from involvement in federal court cases concerning the Jefferson County Board of Education, and freedom from rulings resulting from such cases." Thus began a movement for educational secession.[24]

That fall the *Lee v. Macon* court denied Albert Brewer's and Ernest Stone's petitions for modification and granted the CRD's motion for clarification of the court's August order. Some school boards, encouraged by Brewer and Stone, had been arguing that certain requirements were either impossible or unreasonable. Judge Johnson explained that black school facilities were not meant to be closed forever—they simply could no longer be operated as all-black schools—and he acknowledged that there were administrative limitations on teacher hiring and assignment. He then identified nineteen school systems that had failed to demonstrate good faith or failed to make "effective efforts." The court then added those school boards and their individual members as defendant parties in the litigation. They were called to show cause why the injunction against HEW funds deferral should not be lifted for their systems.²⁵

Brewer mistakenly believed that the judges were testing him, attempting to gauge his relative weakness, as compared to Wallace. He and Stone filed another motion, this one arguing that the issues of teacher transfer and school closure had never been properly raised in the proceedings. The two claimed that they should have had the opportunity to present evidence to support their petition for modification. Judge Johnson responded with a blistering denial, in which he wrote, "This court is at a loss to understand the basis for these contestations." He accused Brewer and Stone of being "either unwilling or unable to grasp the nature of [the] lawsuit." Johnson noted numerous occasions when both issues had been raised, including in Stone's own deposition. Johnson even suggested that the court was doing the defendant officials a favor in formulating its own plans, as opposed to adopting the CRD's proposed plans wholesale. The state had not offered a plan of its own, he reminded them. Finally, Johnson called the assertion that state officials were entitled to an evidentiary hearing on their motion for modification "simply preposterous" and "border[ing] on the ridiculous."²⁶

Infuriated, Brewer called a press conference, at which he appeared visibly angry, calling Johnson, Rives, and Grooms "devious" and "callous" and describing the denial of his motion as a "shocking disregard for due process of law" and a "subterfuge." Days later, at a presidential campaign rally for George Wallace in Anniston, he lamented the "scapegoating" of the nineteen systems and assured them that state funds would continue to flow. Some wondered if that meant that the state would appropriate emergency funds to replace federal dollars lost by way of HEW deferrals. There was little Brewer could do at that point within the litigation. The addition of the nineteen systems as defendant parties put the rest of the ninety-nine on notice that, if they displayed similar recalcitrance, they might also be added to the suit, ordered to show cause, and threatened with HEW action or contempt citations.²⁷

The administrative process Johnson devised that fall would become the model moving forward in enforcing the existing *Lee v. Macon* orders. Local officials added as parties to the suit would come to the courthouse with their counsel, on what Johnson's clerks began to call "school board Saturdays." They would negotiate in chambers with Johnson as to what the court would require and when it had to be implemented. Fred Gray or Solomon Seay were usually in attendance, along with someone from the CRD and often Judge Rives. Judge Grooms came down from Birmingham only for important hearings. Johnson rewarded good-faith efforts with sympathy for legitimate administrative difficulties and often with a reprieve of a semester or more for certain obligations. As soon as those requirements were met, the school boards could be discharged as defendant parties. The court also continued to monitor the efficacy of freedom of choice in the rest of the ninety-nine school systems, whose boards were still obligated to report to Stone and HEW.[28]

That October, the appeal of Johnson's order in the *Carr v. Montgomery* case came before the Fifth Circuit. The school board had objected "strenuously" to the fixed ratios for faculty desegregation. Judge Walter Gewin joined district judge J. Robert Elliott in a 2–1 opinion upholding most of Johnson's order but overturning the faculty ratios. The court relied on recent rulings, including in the *Davis v. Mobile* and *Brown v. Bessemer* cases, in which the appellate court had "declined to enhance *Jefferson*'s demands" or to "tinker with the model decree." Standards, Gewin wrote, could not be "totally inflexible." The court therefore modified Johnson's order to include the words "substantially" and "approximately" and determined that the benchmark need not be the percentage of black pupils in the system. Judge Homer Thornberry dissented and called for an en banc rehearing of the appeal, which was denied by a 6–6 vote. Chief judge John Brown wrote a dissent of the rehearing denial, in which he argued, "It is not the spirit, but the bodies which count." Knowing that the dissension among the circuit judges would compel the Supreme Court to grant certiorari, the LDF appealed.[29]

As that appeal awaited its hearing, the federal executive office was changing hands, casting uncertainty over enforcement of school desegregation. With the quagmire of the Vietnam War dragging his administration down, Lyndon Johnson had declined to seek another term. Following the assassination of Bobby Kennedy over the summer, the mantle of the party had been given to Hubert Humphrey at the violence-tainted Democratic Convention in Chicago. Humphrey was subsequently defeated by Richard Nixon that fall, in a race in which ten million votes went to third-party candidate George Wallace. Nixon would have preferred to limit school desegregation, particularly as it was beginning to threaten supposedly de facto segregated systems outside the South with heavy Republican constituencies. But he inherited an office that had been advancing desegregation for two administrations, while the judiciary and legislature were committed to at least eradicating de jure segregation in southern schools. As one Justice Department official would later characterize it, Nixon was "left holding the remedial *Brown* bag."[30]

The Nixon administration very quietly committed itself to the Johnson administration's policy: end segregation in the South, but protect segregation elsewhere. Southern senators and representatives were even then rallying around a potential amendment of the Elementary and Secondary Education Act, proposed by Mississippi senator John Stennis, that might tear down that policy. The "Stennis Amendment" would make freedom of choice "an inviolate right" and would erase the de jure or de facto distinction protecting nonsouthern school districts. As with the failed Whitten Amendment to the HEW appropriations bills, the idea was that uniform national enforcement of desegregation would scare whites in the Northeast, Midwest, and West enough to cause them to back off of the South. For the time being, however, HEW continued in its Title VI enforcement program, and the CRD continued to support existing litigation.[31]

In its first major action of the Nixon era, the CRD backed the LDF's appeal in *Carr v. Montgomery*. In March the Supreme Court rendered its opinion. Alabama's own Hugo Black lauded Judge Johnson for his "patience and wisdom" and concluded that Johnson had never intended for the faculty ratios to be "absolutely rigid and inflexible." Johnson had, in fact, demonstrated an understanding that "the way must always be left open for experimentation." To reverse his order, Black argued, would unnecessarily delay "the day when a completely unified, unitary, nondiscriminatory school system becomes a reality, instead of a hope." The court affirmed Johnson's entire order as he had originally written it. Jack Greenberg immediately moved to incorporate the new guidelines into all of the LDF's other cases.[32]

Nixon and *Alexander*

During the spring of 1969, Frank Johnson's administration of *Lee v. Macon* occupied as much as half of the judge's time. Each system had its own problems and had to be dealt with individually, through both negotiations and additional proceedings. At the same time, the CRD and Fred Gray's office were preparing motions that would actually broaden *Lee v. Macon*'s scope. Sol Seay filed a motion in February on behalf of the Alabama State Teachers Association, the black teachers' organization that was in the process of a court-ordered merger with its white counterpart. Black teachers and administrators were supposed to be transferred to similar positions at other schools when black schools were ordered closed. Instead, school boards were still dismissing, demoting, or arbitrarily reassigning them.[33]

Black principals almost always became assistant principals at white schools, often with a reduced salary and sometimes with teaching duties. Black assistant principals became teachers. Black teachers were asked to teach vocational classes. Gray and Seay asked the court to order Ernest Stone to compile and submit a list of all black teachers and administrators who had been affected by the 1968 order. The court granted the motion and tasked the plaintiffs' attorneys with analyzing the information once Stone's office had produced it. Seay took the responsibility of working directly with very reluctant, often obdurate school boards, trying to prevent future discrimination and bringing motions for further relief before Judge Johnson and the court.[34]

Two months after Gray and Seay filed to protect ASTA, the CRD filed a motion for further relief, seeking the desegregation of the state's trade schools and junior colleges. The March 1967 statewide decree had called for this, but the state had done nothing to effect it. The State Board of Education operated twenty-seven trade schools (twenty-one white and six black) and fifteen junior colleges (thirteen white and two black). Each school had an attendance zone it served, and the white and black zones overlapped. There were also significant disparities in funding between the black and white institutions, and the white ones had much more diverse course offerings. The CRD asked the court to order the state to design and adopt a desegregation plan specific to these schools.[35]

The court was wary of proceeding in this area on the same basis as with elementary and secondary schools. Johnson himself had just served on a panel that had determined that *Green v. New Kent* did not apply to institutions of higher education. When the state had begun financing the four-year satellite of Auburn University in nearby Montgomery (AUM), Gray had filed suit to block the bond issue. Gray argued that the aim was to ensure that the city's four-year institution for African Americans, Alabama State, remained all-black, and that AUM would remain at least *mostly* white. The court decided that opening new colleges involved "a wide range of educational policy decisions in which courts should not become involved" and declined to interfere beyond ensuring that the new school did not discriminate in admission. Nondiscriminatory admission in higher education, the court determined, was "analogous" to freedom of choice in elementary and secondary schools, and that was as far as it would go in the former.[36]

Accordingly, when the court in *Lee v. Macon* granted the CRD's motion and ordered the state board to produce a plan for the trade schools and junior colleges, it limited the parameters to eliminating racial identifiability and opening each institution to freedom of choice. When the state submitted a plan that promised little change, Johnson was compelled to enumerate what the court considered choice-influencing factors in these schools: overlapping attendance and transportation zones, racially identifiable faculties, and overlapping programs and curricula in institutions in the same geographical area. When the state had submitted no such plan by the end of the summer, the court ordered the Office of Education to formulate one. The USOE subsequently undertook a survey of the system, ensuring that this phase of the litigation would drag on into 1970.[37]

Meanwhile, Ernest Stone filed his annual report with the court reflecting the results of the spring freedom of choice enrollment period in the *Lee v. Macon* systems. Johnson reviewed the report and determined that overall progress was excellent; over 30 percent of black students in the state would attend desegregated schools in the fall. He nonetheless advised Judges Rives and Grooms that the court should "take some further action." Progress was limited to a relatively small number of school systems. Others lagged woefully behind, with black student populations below 10 percent and in some cases as low as 1 percent. Johnson told Rives and Grooms, "I do not believe that we can sit by.... It is quite obvious that freedom of choice has not worked in these systems. I see no reasonable probability that it will work." He advised issuing show cause orders to over two dozen school boards, as with the first nineteen systems the previous fall, and giving them an opportunity to prove that they should not be required to use some other method of desegregation. Judge Rives "heartily" agreed that adding the "laggards" as parties to the suit should be the next step.[38]

Upon learning that the CRD was in the process of drafting motions of its own to address the same problem, the court agreed to have Johnson write letters to each of the "laggard" systems, "calling their attention" to *Green* and asking if they had planned for "any further desegregation," "without further Court action," before the fall. A few systems responded and developed, in conference with Johnson, further steps that would significantly increase their numbers. Most did not. So the CRD entered a motion in July to add those systems as defendant parties, ultimately a total of twenty-three. Each received very specific instructions. Some were to substantially increase faculty desegregation. Others were to stop busing black students past white schools, to close certain all-black schools, to grant choices previously denied, or to pair certain white and black schools. The court also ordered the USOE to formulate its own plans for each system, in case local officials refused to comply.[39]

As the court was preparing the order to add the twenty-three systems as direct parties to the suit, schools opened for the fall. Students across the state experienced substantial desegregation for the first time. Some systems had increased their desegregation rate by over 50 percent, and almost all of the *Lee v. Macon* systems had complied with specific requirements for faculty desegregation and school closure and reassignment. Johnson asked Rives and Grooms if the court ought to move to add those systems that had not met requirements as parties to the suit or just "let them ride." Rives argued that midyear teacher hires were difficult, and Grooms insisted that the systems that had failed to achieve the desired pupil desegregation rate needed time "to 'season'" or to acclimate themselves to desegregation. Johnson agreed to let them ride until the following year.[40]

Sol Seay, meanwhile, had used Ernest Stone's faculty report to identify thirty-three systems that continued to engage in a wide variety of discriminatory employment practices, which directly contravened the orders of the court. They paid black teachers less. They transferred the most experienced black teachers to white schools, while placing newly hired white teachers in black schools. They demoted black administrators in favor of white administrators with less experience and training, And they demoted or simply terminated black teachers and replaced them with white teachers where convenient. Seay asked that these systems be added as defendant parties, but the court denied the motion on a technicality. Since ASTA was about to merge with formerly all-white National Education Association, the judges felt that it ought to be the new integrated organization that brought the motion.[41]

By that point, the *Lee v. Macon* court had determined that twenty-eight of the ninety-nine school boards involved in the litigation had successfully disestablished their racially dual systems. Of the remaining seventy-one, thirty-five had been added as defendant parties and were under direct orders to fully desegregate by the beginning of the 1970–71 school year. Johnson felt that the remaining thirty-six should be added as parties and receive direct court orders "right away." These would be what the court called "terminal type" orders, those that set out the final requirements for a school system to have itself removed as a direct party to the litigation, after which the court would simply monitor implementation of its desegregation plan until the system had attained "unitary status." Adding the final thirty-six was, Johnson argued, not only for the sake of uniformity but also because many them had "not yet taken any realistic approach" to desegregating at all. Rives and Grooms agreed, and the court issued the order in October.[42]

Anticipating that at least some of these school boards would file grossly inadequate desegregation plans, the court also ordered the USOE to file its own plans for each. When the USOE's Division of Equal Educational Opportunity subsequently sent letters offering its "assistance," a furious Johnson immediately notified the local U.S. Attorney that such a "casual approach" would not "in any way comply" with the court's orders. Johnson insisted that HEW was under an obligation to work directly with these school systems in formulating terminal type orders for presentation to the court in January. The initiative, he noted, could "not be left up to the local school systems," and the court had neither the resources nor the expertise of the USOE. Ever flexible, the *Lee v. Macon* court was not only willing to extend leniency to local officials in certain circumstances but also willing to reprimand federal agents that frustrated the court's enforcement program.[43]

The reluctance of HEW to take a more proactive role in *Lee v. Macon* indicated a general retreat from strict enforcement under the Nixon administration. Those in the administration who favored a stronger commitment to rapid desegregation—like the head of HEW's Office of Civil Rights, Leon Panetta—found themselves marginalized or, as in Panetta's case, replaced. Those who remained were forced to balance the interests of white southerners, who expected a reversal on desegregation as a reward for their electoral support, with those of many in the Republican base, who expected a final push to fully desegregate the South. By that summer, the administration looked to be bending to pressure from southerners in Congress and developing a national desegregation policy like that proposed in the Stennis Amendment. While HEW secretary Robert Finch ultimately declined to rewrite the HEW desegregation guidelines to explicitly indicate a national enforcement policy, the department nonetheless began moving to cut off funds in certain segregated northern school districts.[44]

At the same time, the administration's handling of existing litigation, particularly a consolidated set of appeals in thirty-three Mississippi school cases under the styling *Alexander v. Holmes*, signaled a stand-down vis-à-vis the South. Early that summer, the Fifth Circuit, citing *Green*, overturned trial court orders and instructed the USOE to submit plans for the thirty-three systems to fully desegregate that fall of 1969. The USOE submitted the plans, but the White House pressured Finch, who wrote directly to Fifth Circuit chief judge John Brown, telling him that HEW was "gravely concerned that the time allowed for the development of these terminal plans has been much too short." Finch added that widespread application of *Green* in Mississippi that fall would result in "chaos, confusion, and a catastrophic educational setback." The CRD then formally petitioned the appellate court for a delay in the implementation of the plans until December 1, which ostensibly meant until the following school year.[45]

In August the appellate court granted the CRD's motion. It was the first time the division had opposed the LDF in a school case. In addition to stunning the attorneys at the LDF, it generated a backlash from veterans at the Justice Department. CRD attorneys openly questioned the administration, privately assisted local attorneys, and in one case resigned. The LDF ran a full page ad in the *New York Times* accusing the federal government of "breaking its promise to the children of Mississippi," and the Civil Rights Commission observed, "Those who have placed their faith in the processes of law cannot be encouraged." Jack Greenberg appealed directly to Justice Hugo Black, the Supreme Court's Fifth Circuit supervisor, to vacate the delaying order, while Nixon's solicitor general encouraged Black to allow it. Black wanted to vacate the order, writing, "There is no longer the slightest excuse, reason, or justification for further postponement." But he acknowledged that this would go beyond anything the court had theretofore ordered, and he reluctantly denied the LDF's request. Greenberg then petitioned for a writ of certiorari, which the court granted. It would hear the case that fall.[46]

The administration had adopted the rhetoric of law and order, yet it was arguing that the Supreme Court should abandon the thrust of *Green*. The *New York Times* called it "astonishing" and reflected that Nixon was "more responsive to the prejudices of Southern politicians than to the legitimate demands to put an end to the illegally maintained dual school systems." The irony, according to the *Times*, was that such a retreat would "reinforce Negro suspicions of separate justice for black and white, thus inviting resort to mass disruption as a substitute for the essential faith in justice under a government of law," or, as the administration liked to describe it, disorder. The *Baltimore Afro-American* argued that the administration had "exposed its own 'law and order' hypocrisy," through its "double-talk, pussy-footing delays, [and] appeals for court slowdowns." It was just the "type of encouragement for Dixiecrats to defy court rulings that one would expect from George Wallace and other segregationists from Deep South areas." The head of the CRD, Jerris Leonard, dismissed the criticism as folks "running off at the mouth" and suggested that the immediate enforcement of *Green* in the Mississippi cases would be a waste of time.[47]

Nixon's unofficial policy, echoing southern officials, was to "do what the law requires, nothing more." More desegregation was occurring under Nixon's leadership than any president preceding him, but he had to instruct his staff to "quit bragging" about it. He was compelled to continue advancing the policy to its logical conclusion, but he had to let southern white voters know that he was unhappy about it and that he was willing to mitigate it whenever possible. HEW and the CRD would thus continue to support the enforcement of existing litigation, while at the same time seizing opportunities, like the one presented in *Alexander v. Holmes*, to reward the white South with delay.[48]

This new Nixon policy soon manifest itself in the *Davis v. Mobile* case. The previous spring, judge Daniel Thomas had again rejected motions to expedite desegregation. Mobile was still implementing the plan designed by Thomas himself and initially implemented in the fall of 1968. The city of Mobile's elementary and junior high schools operated under an attendance zoning plan, while rural Mobile County and the metropolitan area's high schools continued to operate under freedom of choice. This had resulted in a superficially large increase in the number of black students in formerly all-white schools, but almost 90 percent of the system's 31,130 black students still attended either all-black schools or those that had been token desegregated by white students, almost all of them from poor families.[49]

That summer the Fifth Circuit reversed Thomas's decision to continue with his own plan. The court described his attendance zones as "constitutionally insufficient and unacceptable." Not only had Thomas "ignored the unequivocal directive to make a conscious effort in locating attendance zones to desegregate and eliminate past segregation," but also, in allowing minority-to-majority transfers, the judge had provided "an authorization to white students to resegregate." Maintaining freedom of choice in the metro area's high schools was furthermore a direct rejection of the appellate court's prior insistence that no distinction be drawn between the system's elementary and secondary schools. The freedom of choice plan for the county had also "singularly failed" to achieve its objective. The appellate panel ordered the USOE to begin working with the Mobile school board on a new plan and to develop its own in the likely event that none could be developed in concert.[50]

As expected, the school board chose not to work with HEW and submitted no plan of its own. HEW officials called for the complete elimination of freedom of choice and the use of noncontiguous zoning and pairing of schools. Their plan would require busing around two thousand of the system's eighty thousand students from the core of the city out to other parts of the metropolitan area. News of these details incited outrage among white Mobilians. The city's congressional representative, Jack Edwards, complained to Finch at HEW, calling the plan "the wild notion" of Finch's "stable of dreamers." Judge Thomas was prepared to again soften the blow. On August 1 he approved the HEW plan, as modified by himself. He maintained the attendance zones for rural Mobile County and the metro area west of Interstate 65 as drawn. But for the area east of I-65, which included much of Mobile itself and Prichard and Chickasaw, he reinstated his previous plan: token-integrated elementary and junior high schools and freedom of choice only for the high schools.[51]

Despite Thomas's modifications, STAND leaders once again attempted to browbeat the school board into defying the court altogether. William Westbrook argued that the freedom to choose was "what America was founded upon" and told the school board, "This is still America, we are still free, and we intend to remain free." He then enumerated a litany of white fears, declaring, "We want no pairing of schools, no closing of schools, no busing of children, no rigid boundary lines, no black history, no sex sensitivity courses, and no social welfare within our schools." Pierre Pelham introduced a resolution in the state legislature, at the behest of George Wallace, which passed easily. It called on parents across the state to "take their children to the school of their original choice and insist upon [their] enrollment," and it instructed local officials to "take whatever action is required to accommodate parents in their exercise of freedom of choice, including the opening of closed schools, elimination of busing to achieve racial balance, and prompt enrollment."⁵²

The week before classes were to begin, STAND took out an ad in the *Mobile Register*, calling for a white boycott of classes at formerly all-black or otherwise substantially integrated schools. Wallace made a public appearance in Prichard that same week and told parents, "Any [of you] whose child is not being allowed to go to the school of your choice, I hope you will carry that child to that school anyway—and let's see what they do about it." Thousands of parents and students heeded the call. On the first day of classes, many of them either stayed home or showed up at the school of their choice. STAND staged a march to the school board's central office the same day, to commemorate the "death of freedom of choice." The organization held a rally that night at which protestors burned an effigy of Robert Finch.⁵³

The LDF, meanwhile, appealed Thomas's latest ruling in *Davis*, giving the Nixon administration the opportunity to demonstrate that it believed, in Nixon's words, that there were "limits to the amount of coercion that can reasonably be used" in "a free society." Nixon considered himself to be charting a middle course between "two extreme groups"—one that wanted "instant integration" and the other that wanted "segregation forever." Accordingly, as they had done in *Alexander*, Jerris Leonard and the CRD opposed the LDF's appeal, instead supporting Thomas's watered-down plan. Mobile was not the only Alabama district in which freedom of choice was in serious jeopardy, though. The CRD had been forced to deal with similar developments in Birmingham, where the Jefferson County cases portended significant compulsory assignment.⁵⁴

The previous spring, judge Seybourn Lynne had approved for the Jefferson County system a county-wide freedom of choice plan that the Fifth Circuit soon rejected. The appellate court considered it "clear" that freedom of choice was not working and that the plan Lynne had approved would "not meet the test of *Green*." Lynne was compelled to order the county school board, along with the Bessemer city school board, to formulate plans for the fall that used some other method of desegregation. "All recent decisions of the federal courts," he wrote, "have declared that 'freedom of choice' is unacceptable, in that, according to these courts, it does not tend to end segregated schools." The county school board issued a statement to parents, explaining that it was the board's "unfortunate duty and responsibility" to carry out court orders. "Despite our personal feeling relative to the unfair interference and interruption of our educational program," they concluded, "our nation is based on a system of law and order."⁵⁵

As in Mobile, the Jefferson County school board declined to work with HEW, though unlike the Mobile board it did submit a plan of its own. It called for a three-year process, by which undercapacity white schools would be filled with nearby black students, and all-black schools would be "phased out." HEW proposed a plan that would fully desegregate the system in two years. Despite the gradualism inherent in each proposal, enraged white parents reacted swiftly. Jefferson County superintendent Revis Hall was besieged by parents who asserted that their children had been "kicked out of their school because of those niggers" and who advocated burning down schools rather than desegregating them. After a hearing on the proposed plans, a Pleasant Grove man told reporters, "I will not send my kids to a Negro neighborhood under any circumstances. I will go to a federal penitentiary before I do it." A Midfield woman added, "I don't think it's right for them to bus white children to Negro schools. That's something that white people aren't going to stand for."[56]

The plaintiffs in *Jefferson* also vigorously protested certain elements of the school board's plan. A number of schools that fall would remain all-black. The black schools slated for desegregation were in all cases to be renamed. Formerly all-white schools in affluent areas were only facing token desegregation. And the county school board was prioritizing construction projects that would tend to perpetuate segregation, like building a new high school in mostly white Midfield. District judge Clarence Allgood was sitting for the aging Judge Lynne by that point, and he decided to approve the county's plan, despite the objections. Like Lynne, Allgood would have preferred preserving freedom of choice wholesale, since it was "doing the job in a feasible manner" and had been "accepted by the general public in this area, both black and white." The Fifth Circuit had regrettably "changed its mind" on the matter, though, and Allgood lamented that the trial court was obliged to follow suit. As with *Davis*, the LDF appealed, bringing the number of school cases pending Fifth Circuit review that fall to thirteen. The appellate court ordered the thirteen cases consolidated for an expedited en banc review.[57]

Jefferson County's white parents became more organized and determined to resist. A group calling itself Concerned Parents for Public Education moved to intervene in *U.S. v. Jefferson*, took out an ad in the *Birmingham News* accusing the appellate court of "completely destroy[ing] the county school system," and began holding mass meetings to discuss options beyond litigation. At one meeting in late August, the county school board's attorney, Maurice Bishop, told the parents to support white teachers who refused to teach integrated classes and to remember that the ballot box was the "most powerful arsenal in the repertoire of war." Likening black activist litigants to the Nazis, Bishop argued that since a "well organized and well financed" 10 percent of the black population had been "calling the shots," the "fine white people" of Alabama ought to match their organizational fervor and fight back.[58]

Governor Brewer called for a conference of southern governors and the U.S. attorney general to discuss the "intolerable situation." Brewer blamed desegregation orders for a spate of recent dropouts in the state and wondered if "people at the federal level" would ever "be reasonable enough to see what they are doing to our schools." He then appealed to Alabamians' growing awareness of white rights, musing, "Maybe it's time Alabama went into court and asked for equal protection of the laws." Brewer's color-masked, law-and-order rhetoric left no room for him to say "white Alabamians," but this was no states' rights appeal. His invocation of the "equal protection" clause of the Fourteenth Amendment betrayed the real message—if blacks could go to court to ensure that they were not singled out and treated unfairly, then whites could too. This rhetoric, along with pledges to support groups like STAND and Concerned Parents, again reinforced and encouraged defiance at the local level.[59]

When schools opened in September, white parents across Jefferson County chose to send their children to their previously assigned white schools or to just keep them home. This was particularly true where white students had been assigned to previously all-black schools. For example, only 59 white students out of a projected 428 showed up at newly renamed Graysville High—the formerly all-black Alden High. At some schools, no white students showed up. In total about one thousand students defied their assignment. Parents whose children did attend formerly all-black schools began to complain about outdoor toilets, broken windows, lack of lunchrooms, and other inconveniences that black students had dealt with for decades. The school board started granting special exemptions allowing certain students to attend schools outside their assigned zone. More than four hundred of these "out of zone" students joined the one thousand protesting students, who were allowed to remain in the schools of their choice as "visiting" pupils.[60]

As administrators grappled with defiance, the Supreme Court rendered its decision in *Alexander v. Holmes*. On October 29, after an expedited review, the court held that the appellate and trial courts "should have denied all motions for additional time because continued operation of segregated schools under a standard of allowing 'all deliberate speed' for desegregation is no longer constitutionally permissible." The court, in the first major decision with Nixon appointee Warren Burger as chief justice, directed the appellate judges to order the immediate implementation of the originally approved desegregation plans for each of the thirty-three Mississippi school districts covered by the appeal. The Justice Department was obliged to enforce the decision, so the CRD subsequently sought a statewide decree for Mississippi similar to that issued in *Lee v. Macon County* in March 1967.[61]

The Fifth Circuit Court of Appeals found itself in an unfamiliar position—it had been reversed and forced to accelerate desegregation. The effect of this rebuke was soon felt not only in *Alexander* but also in the thirteen consolidated LDF appeals, which included *U.S. v. Jefferson*, *Davis v. Mobile*, and *U.S. v. Bessemer*. On December 1, the court issued a ruling under the familiar styling of *Singleton v. Jackson Municipal Separate School District* (the third major decision under that name). The court acknowledged that the Supreme Court's recent decision in *Alexander* "supervened all existing authority" and "sent the doctrine of deliberate speed to its final resting place." Desegregation had shifted "from a status of litigation to one of unitary operation pending litigation." School systems would have to fully desegregate first, then litigate details later. The appellate court ordered all systems covered by *Singleton* to immediately desegregate faculty, staff, transportation, services, and extracurricular activities. But, using an approach it had recently taken in the case of *U.S. v. Hinds County*, the court gave them until the following fall, autumn 1970, to execute pupil desegregation.[62]

The effect on the three Alabama cases under the *Singleton* umbrella was mixed. Judges Lynne and Allgood had made almost no modifications to the Jefferson County and Bessemer city plans since the appellate court had remanded those cases over the summer. So the appellate court reversed the decisions of the trial courts and ordered the formulation of plans that comported with *Alexander* and *Hinds County*. In *Davis v. Mobile*, however, the appellate court upheld Judge Thomas's approval of his own plan, insisting only that Thomas apply the new standards to a pupil plan for the fall of 1970. The LDF appealed this decision in *Davis* and three similar decisions in Louisiana cases that had been considered alongside *Alexander*.[63]

On January 14, 1970, the Supreme Court held, "Insofar as the [Fifth Circuit] Court of Appeals authorized deferral of student desegregation beyond February 1, 1970, that court misconstrued our holding in *Alexander v. Holmes*." The court reversed and remanded *Singleton v. Jackson III*, heard as *Carter v. West Feliciana Parish School Board*, and instructed the appellate court to issue judgments in the affected cases "forthwith." Almost twenty years of defiance, evasion, and foot-dragging had left no room for any further delay, for any reason. The day of reckoning finally seemed to be upon much of Alabama and the rest of the white South.[64]

"Our Problem Is Not Race"

The reality of the Supreme Court's decision in *Carter v. West Feliciana Parish* hit segregationists in Alabama like a fist to the face. Albert Brewer continued to decry the fleeting life of freedom-of-choice tokenism and accused the court of "singling out" the state, telling the press, "All I can do is express my wholehearted contempt for this action." He promised, "We shall leave no stone unturned in our determination to fight this order with everything in our power." Black leaders would not let the rhetoric go unchallenged. Joe Reed, the former head of ASTA and president of the all-black Alabama Democratic Conference, explained, "The concept of freedom of choice is good, but in practice it has sometimes proved false. If it had been adopted 15 years ago," he proposed, "it might now be the law of the land." But a lack of genuinely good faith at every stage of implementation, and the failure to foster an acceptance of desegregation as anything other than a miserably unfortunate legal obligation, had left freedom of choice moribund. Brewer and many others refused to accept this.[65]

Birmingham attorney U. W. Clemon echoed Reed's sentiments while speaking at the annual meeting of the Birmingham League of Women Voters that winter. "There are those who think the efforts to desegregate schools are efforts to mix, physically, black and white students," he observed, but "the true aim of desegregation, is to provide equal educational opportunity." Clemon argued that it "really [did not] matter whether black kids [went] to school with white kids." As long as all-black schools continued to exist, there would be "an opportunity to discriminate." In an obvious reference to Brewer (and a possible homage to former SNCC leader H. Rap Brown), Clemon added that "quality education" was being tossed about by the state's politicians because it had an "irresistible appeal," like "religion, motherhood, [or] apple pie." Clemon concluded sardonically that it was "strange" that state leaders had "up until now neglected public education to the point that we're last in providing quality education."[66]

One week after the Supreme Court handed down *Carter*, the Fifth Circuit compelled Judge Thomas to enter an order in *Davis v. Mobile* that would desegregate the system, pupils and all, by February 1. He gave the Mobile school board and HEW four days to submit revised plans. The school board again refused to cooperate. HEW submitted two plans. The Civil Rights Division threw its support behind the more limited of the two. Vernon Crawford and the LDF supported the other, which involved significant busing. Thomas rejected both plans and once again chose to craft his own. In a January 1 order, the judge insisted that he could carry out the Supreme Court's mandate without ordering busing, pairing, or the closure or restructuring of black schools. He explained that he was "unwilling to disregard all common sense and all thoughts to sound education, simply to achieve racial balance in all schools," which he did not believe the law required. He would not be swayed, he argued, by the demands of those who would "stir" litigation "for the sake of litigation, without regard to the rights of children and parents involved."[67]

Thomas warned the city that "drastic measures" were still necessary, but he maintained that he would make it "humanely and educationally possible to operate the schools." He was forced to finally do away with freedom of choice. The high schools east of Interstate 65 would operate under geographic zones for the first time. Thomas redrew some of the existing zones to increase desegregation and called for a few grade realignments and school closures but not nearly to the extent laid out in either of the HEW plans. He also contended that the Supreme Court's command to commence "forthwith" did not mean "instantly," and he set a deadline of February 3 for the school board to publish the zoning maps. When that day came, no maps were published. Mobile superintendent Crawford Burns denied that the board was "deliberately dragging its feet or trying to thwart the implementation of the decree," but he said that it was still in the "preliminary planning stages" of implementation.[68]

Thomas's reluctance had encouraged the school board to continue to delay, which emboldened parents to ask for more of the same. Days after the missed deadline, a white father warned officials, "If they can come in here and tell us our children must go to this particular school, the next thing they are going to tell us is, 'Alright, now you've got to go to a particular church.'" Many blacks were similarly frustrated. Vernon Crawford observed, "It's far from being a desegregation plan. It just creates a little more tokenism." The student bodies at four high schools would remain entirely black. The local director for a Quaker social justice organization described it as "a sham" that "did not come close" to what the law required, adding, "The black community is disgusted with the delays." Some black Mobilians were apprehensive about the fate of black schools too, which had served as centers of community pride and civic engagement, particularly those that had been slated to be rebuilt and renovated. A teacher at a local Catholic school confided to a *New York Times* reporter that the plan appeared to be "designed to create chaos so the blacks would be so upset with it they would say to hell with it."[69]

A small but rapidly growing segment of the black community was indeed so fed up with the entire process that they began to argue for a full return to segregation. This campaign was encouraged by Roy Innis, the national president of the Congress of Racial Equality (CORE). Innis had taken CORE in a new direction since its days of organizing the Freedom Rides, and in March 1970 he brought his message of black separatism to Alabama's port city. Innis proposed creating autonomous black school districts. He argued that the NAACP had been ignoring the wishes of the "little people" in cities like Mobile. He proposed an "all-out war" with "HEW activist-bureaucrats, and possibly the old-line, die-hard, failure-prone civil rights aristocracy." The more chaotic implementation became, and the more clear it became that blacks would bear the heaviest burdens of desegregation, the more people listened to Roy Innis.[70]

Black disillusionment was already palpable. When representatives of the Southern Regional Council interviewed black students in formerly all-white schools, one student argued, "In Mobile integration just won't work because when we go to a white school they treat us like some dog. We never get to be the officers of the class, so we'd rather just stay in our own schools." The black activist group Neighborhood Organized Workers threw its support behind Innis's plan, and CORE was able to facilitate the organization of a new local group, Steps Toward Educational Progress (STEPS). STEPS leaders began trying to persuade black voters that independent black school districts were "a very practicable and sensible solution to providing meaningful quality education for all our children in their own neighborhoods where they relate to their neighbors and where their neighbors relate to them." One STEPS representative explained, "What we're trying to get away from is the notion that the only way a black kid can get a quality education is to sit beside a white kid in school." Unfortunately for Innis, implementation of his plan required the approval of the Mobile school board, which publicly dismissed it as "straight communist doctrine."[71]

Meanwhile, *Carter v. West Feliciana* had also resulted in a reversal of the most recent order in *U.S. v. Jefferson County*. The trial court had been compelled to order the county school board to submit by February 1 a new plan for full and immediate desegregation. The plan involved the restructuring, renaming, and closure of a number of all-black schools and the pairing of some black and white schools. As soon as Judge Lynne approved it, however, the school board petitioned the court for "emergency relief" in the form of certain "temporary modifications" to alleviate a "most unbelievable situation." Superintendent Revis Hall explained that this would allow students to "simply continue to go to school where they are going now." Students who had shown up to the school of their choice, in other words, could stay put. This would, in effect, delay pupil desegregation until the fall. Lynne granted the motion, citing the need to "protect accreditation of the schools and enable the School Board to restore some degree of normal administration."[72]

The LDF and the CRD appealed, targeting not just the emergency relief measure but also the plan, as it was, before the modifications, which plaintiffs' counsel U. W. Clemon had called "an insult to the black community." Four county high schools would remain all-black. The Wenonah High zone would include a full third of the entire county's black pupil population, while the Westfield zone had clearly been created to be almost entirely black. The

Midfield High zone was to remain almost entirely white. Clemon argued, as others had in Mobile, that the plan was designed to create an unnecessary atmosphere of crisis, which would itself justify its postponement.[73]

The independent, suburban city school systems in western Jefferson County got similar "emergency" relief. Judge Grooms allowed the Fairfield school board to reopen two of its closed schools when four hundred white students threatened to withdraw rather than attend the city's formerly all-black high school. And he allowed the board to rechristen the black high school as a mostly black "vocational school." He also refused to enjoin the board's practice of transferring "intact" classes from black to white schools—that is, allowing formerly all-white schools to maintain all-black classes, with black teachers, within a student body that appeared integrated on paper. Bessemer had engaged in similar chicanery, for which the LDF sought a contempt citation, which Judge Lynne denied, asserting, "Any further desegregation of the Bessemer system will seriously disrupt the educational system."[74]

Thousands of white students across the county once again reported to the school of their choice, rather than the one to which they had been assigned. For example, none of the 290 whites assigned to all-black Wenonah, A. G. Gaston, and Oliver High Schools reported there. Concerned Parents for Public Education helped coordinate walkouts at three other high schools on the county's north side, two of which were subsequently evacuated upon receiving bomb threats. In six suburban communities, Concerned Parents also organized "parents' sit-ins" and "vigils" at formerly all-white schools that were set to enroll a significant number of black pupils. One parent offered an apology to a local reporter, arguing, "We are not a bunch of racists, we just want to keep our school the way it is."[75]

White parents again marched on the offices of the Jefferson County school board to make unrealistic demands and to spit jeers, insults, and threats at board members. A representative from Concerned Parents suggested that the board "give serious consideration to resigning" immediately, while others insisted that they would pay any subsequent contempt fines and bail bonds for the board members. When Revis Hall explained that the local officials would probably be removed from office as a result of direct defiance, the crowd cheered wildly in approval. Concerned Parents took out another full-page ad in the *Birmingham News* demanding to know why schools had been "taken over for the purpose of achieving social goals," why schools had to have "a certain racial mix," and why students had to be treated "like pawns on a bureaucratic chess board." The activist group then sent thousands of petitions to the White House, urging President Nixon to support a full return to freedom of choice.[76]

Many of Jefferson County's black parents were angry too, particularly about the closure, restructuring, and renaming of formerly all-black schools. Black parents petitioned the school board and the court for more equitable changes, and students showed up at closed schools, trying to force them back open. One parent described the new desegregation plan as "a lousy, rotten deal" and argued, "It's not fair to close our school and make our children go to a white school." In the eastern suburban city of Leeds, all-black Moton High had been set to house all tenth graders in that part of the county, having previously been slated for closure. The *Birmingham News* described Moton as a shell of its former self, wherein "athletic trophies glimmer[ed] from glass cases in the empty halls" and "class pictures smile[d] out to no one." School tradition at Moton was "deceased," according to the *News*, and for its former students, "identity with one's alma mater [was] a thing of the past."[77]

In a statewide televised address in late February, Governor Brewer reminded white parents and students that theirs was a commitment to law and order and a fight for their constitutional rights. The governor lamented the recent orders in *Jefferson* and *Davis* and decried the fact that teachers and students were being "herded around like cattle to bring about a racial balance in the schools." He warned Alabamians that they would "not get solutions ... in the streets" but rather "through legal processes," and he insisted that "the problem [was] not integration or segregation" but rather "quality education." He condemned those, like Wallace, who had given white Alabamians "false hope" of avoiding desegregation altogether, and he pledged, "I will assert our rights as people to the equal protection clause of the laws—no more, no less—as is our right as citizens of the United States." Brewer then filed a claim on behalf of the state, seeking an injunction against the U.S. attorney general and the secretary of HEW and targeting what he described as regionally biased enforcement of school desegregation. The Supreme Court promptly refused to hear the claim, which Brewer called "infuriating." He followed up with a claim in federal district court alleging that the Justice Department and HEW were violating the Civil Rights Act.[78]

After a conference in Mobile, Brewer and his fellow southern governors issued a statement reaffirming their "determination that no child in any state or any school system shall be mandatorily assigned or bused for the sole purpose of achieving racial balance in our public schools." They resented the fact that the South had been "singled out ... for punitive treatment." Brewer then issued a call for local school boards to "say absolutely 'no' to busing," and he reached out to Concerned Parents to explain that he was going to sponsor a "freedom of choice law" in the state legislature. This new legislative foil was to be color masked and based on claims to equal protection. Brewer called the state legislature into special session for the sole purpose of approving the bill—carefully modeled after a law already in place in New York—which declared, "No student shall be assigned or compelled to attend any school on account of race . . . or for the purpose of achieving equality in attendance, . . . at any school, of persons of any one or more particular races."[79]

At the opening of the session, Brewer proclaimed, "Our problem is not race. As I have said before, the question is not one of integration or segregation. We crossed that bridge several years ago." He insisted, "The question is what kind of education are we going to give our children." The legislators responded with the first of sixteen standing ovations. Brewer described the "demoralizing" situation Alabama found itself in. Alabamians had "reluctantly accepted" freedom of choice, but because "people did not choose the way the court thought they should choose, the court said, 'you can't have freedom of choice.'" He stoked segregationists' fears by suggesting that black students were sabotaging white education. Since compulsory assignment, the children of Alabama were "not getting the kind of education [they] ought to be getting," because teachers could barely "do any more than try and keep order in their classes." A new freedom of choice law would "press the advantage," put the state "on the offensive, finally," and "insure that the school children of Alabama [would] indeed have and enjoy equal justice under the law."[80]

The state legislature unanimously approved the freedom of choice law three days later. The *Birmingham News* praised the governor and legislature for their "workmanlike realism," while also condemning the old Wallace way, with its "danger-packed emotionalism." The "self-destructive" Wallace wanted to "exploit the emotional impact of the issue," but Brewer wanted to "create an answer to the issue." The freedom of choice law was, according to the *News*, the "first constructive effort on the school desegregation problem" after "more than a decade of noisy and hopeless defiance." State officials were cautiously optimistic. One state senator captured the mood of most in the statehouse, saying, "I don't know just how the bill will stand up in court, but the least we can do is try." Brewer himself asserted that previous efforts had "failed to get at the real objective," which was complying with the law but limiting its effect. "The Fourteenth Amendment, in all candor, will prevent getting back to a dual school system," he acknowledged. But the new freedom of choice law could restore the most acceptable system possible, and it actually had "a chance to stand up to court tests."[81]

Local boards of education moved quickly to use the new color-masked law as cover for continuing resistance. The Mobile school board issued a resolution indicating that it would not abide by the court's January 31 order calling for immediate integration. Until the freedom of choice law was "tested and declared unconstitutional," the board would follow it. When the March 16 deadline for implementation of the January 31 order passed with no action by the board,

Judge Thomas issued contempt of court citations for the school board members. Each faced a thousand-dollar-per-day fine if not complying within three days. This had the desired effect, as the board members could then face Mobile's white community and say that they had done all they could. The board agreed to implement the plan by the end of the week, pending an application for a stay of the order, which was subsequently denied by Thomas and the Fifth Circuit.[82]

At the same time, Vernon Crawford, John LeFlore, and the LDF filed a motion in *Davis* asking the court to declare the freedom of choice law unconstitutional and to add Governor Brewer and current (and former) attorney general Macdonald Gallion as defendant parties in the case. Thomas refused to do either, arguing that *Davis* was "not the proper vehicle." Gallion then filed a counterclaim against the United States, however, resulting in the designation of a three-judge court to decide the fate of the law in a separate action. On March 20, the new desegregation plan for Mobile went into effect, and around eight thousand of the system's seventy-three thousand students were told that they had to switch schools. While midsemester shake-ups in other districts across the South led to violence and mass protests, the "chaos and confusion" portended by the Mobile school board did not materialize, save for a small demonstration at formerly all-white Davidson High, where around one hundred white students gathered, ironically, to hang an effigy of Judge Thomas, who had delayed implementation at every turn. One reason for the relative calm was the fact that the board had adopted an "irregular student" policy that allowed white students who had refused transfers to stay put "pending further study."[83]

With a judgment on the freedom of choice law postponed until a summer trial, *Jefferson* awaited a hearing on Judge Lynne's "emergency relief" order, allowing the county school board, which had also adopted an "irregular student" policy, to avoid implementation of much of the system's desegregation plan until at least the fall. A spike in violence that spring nonetheless accompanied midterm transfers, undermining what little faith anxious parents had in compulsory assignment moving forward. In addition to an increase in interracial fights in schools, the school board had to confront vandalism at its facilities. One particular incident in mid-April underscored the lengths to which some would go to dismantle integration. Vandals broke into Graysville High and went on a rampage that resulted in multiple broken television sets, telephones, and clocks, nearly one hundred broken windows, intercom panels ripped from the walls, swaths of ceiling torn down, library equipment smashed, water fountains crushed, raw food strewn about the lunchroom, and sheetrock walls destroyed with an axe.[84]

The school board organized biracial citizen patrols to keep an eye on facilities, though this did not prevent the county from being dropped by its property tax insurer. The board had been quick to publicize the violence, because violence, like overcrowding, provided the "proof" that integration did not work. The vandals and apparently some students understood this. At Bessemer's McAdory High, several white students inflicted superficial razor wounds on themselves and reported that they had been cut by gangs of blacks. They later recanted. Rumor-mongering greatly exaggerated the actual threat from violent outbreaks, and whites' floundering confidence in desegregated schools continued to erode. Instead of positive reinforcement from state or local officials, worried parents got more condemnations of the courts and more legislative schemes designed to blunt or delay desegregation's effect. The white exodus began to accelerate.[85]

In Jefferson County, the idea of severing from the county school system and establishing independent municipal school systems had become increasingly popular. Since the county had been threatened with compulsory assignment, and following Mountain Brook's lead, the all-white western suburbs of Pleasant Grove and Hueytown and the over-the-mountain suburbs of Homewood and Vestavia Hills had initiated the secession process. Newly created systems generally offered jobs to teachers and staff in the existing county-run schools, which they sought to purchase from the county. There could be complications. The City of Homewood had to sue the county in state court, because Shades Valley High School was located outside the city limits, and the county balked at accepting tuition from the city for use of the facility. All-black Rosedale High *was* within the Homewood city limits, but it was slated for closure as part of the county's desegregation plan. The city was able to gain support from its small black population by promising to keep Rosedale open. This served as ammunition for city officials, who characterized severance as a color-blind quest for local control.[86]

By the summer of 1970, the plaintiffs in *Jefferson* had filed a motion seeking an injunction against the secession of the municipalities. The motion initially targeted Pleasant Grove, where city officials had argued that the county desegregation plan allowed the wealthier over-the-mountain schools to remain nearly all-white, while the western section of the county "bore the brunt" of compulsory assignment. It grew to include Homewood and Vestavia Hills when those cities moved to secede as well. Attorney U. W. Clemon observed, "Any community which is a white community, which seeks to withdraw from a school system that is under a desegregation plan, is doing so for racial motives." The *Birmingham News* agreed, acknowledging that it was "obvious" that "municipalities with few or no Negroes would stand to preserve their racial characteristics by going independent."[87]

The population of Birmingham dwindled as the suburbs grew apace. The over-the-mountain suburbs grew faster than ever before. Vestavia Hills finished the decade having experienced 200 percent growth in ten years. Whites sought refuge even farther south too, in southern Jefferson County and northern Shelby County. Leading this great trek was the insurance salesman William Hoover. Hoover's efforts to open segregation academies in the city of Birmingham had floundered. He had moved Hoover Academy several times to new facilities in new parts of town. But many parents, especially in the city's West End, could not afford private school tuition, and the ones who could afford it were leaving the city for the suburbs. To make matters worse, when the school's foundation tried to acquire public school property from the small western suburban city of Brighton, local blacks filed a complaint in federal court to block the purchase. Convinced that a private academy in that section of the county was a lost cause, Hoover turned his gaze south.[88]

Hoover years earlier had envisioned the need to escape. In 1953, while the Supreme Court was considering *Brown*, he had purchased a large tract of land in a quiet enclave known as Green Valley, south of Vestavia Hills, along the recently improved and expanded U.S. Highway 31. He then moved his insurance company south, joined the American States' Rights Association, and established himself as one of the state's preeminent segregationists and anti-Semites. Shortly after the Fifth Circuit's landmark ruling in *U.S. v. Jefferson*, he founded the town of Hoover. The town began to annex unincorporated neighboring communities, and it soon stretched from Vestavia Hills and Mountain Brook, to the north, to the cities of Pelham (incorporated 1964) and Alabaster (1953) to the south. Hoover realized that his city was positioned in the middle of a string of affluent white suburbs along what was to be the Interstate 65 corridor, right where I-65 would intersect with the I-459 Birmingham bypass. Plans were laid for a new country club and a shopping mall. And the city of Hoover, more than anywhere else, became the mecca in which white pilgrims placed their faith.[89]

That summer Judge Lynne issued a ruling on the plaintiffs' motion to block Pleasant Grove, Homewood, and Vestavia from establishing independent municipal school districts, or what were then being called "splinter systems." In what amounted to a deal between the court, the municipalities, and the increasingly reluctant Nixon Justice Department, Lynne allowed the cities to break away, provided they agreed to certain conditions moving forward. Each new school system would have to accept students from surrounding black communities who elected to attend city schools, and each would have to hire enough black teachers to reach a 25 percent desegregated faculty ratio by the beginning of the 1971–72 school year. Lynne had rejected a HEW plan that would have paired new municipal schools with predominantly black schools in the county system. The county, meanwhile, would be left with a depleted tax base as well as a larger proportion of black to white students, which portended more white flight. It also had to pay tuition to the new city systems for any black students who elected to attend city schools.[90]

The LDF appealed Lynne's ruling. The Fifth Circuit appellate court had just issued its ruling in the most recent appeal in *Davis*. The court again overturned Judge Thomas, in what the press began to characterize as a case of "legal ping pong." Thomas was directed to order the Mobile school board to implement a more stringent plan. Knowing that neither Thomas nor the school board would devise such a plan, the court provided some parameters, based on the proposed plan of the CRD. The board would have to alter attendance zones and pair and restructure some schools. It would also have to implement a faculty desegregation program that met the test of *Carr v. Montgomery*—each school would have a faculty race ratio roughly equivalent to that of the system as a whole (60 percent white, 40 black). And it would have to adopt a liberal majority-to-minority transfer program, whereby students could easily change schools if the effect was to further desegregation. Finally, Judge Thomas was ordered to oversee the appointment of a biracial committee to resolve future issues before they came before the court.[91]

Later that month, the state-initiated counterclaim involving the new freedom of choice law came before Judge Thomas. In *State of Alabama v. U.S. and Davis*, the court determined that the state had failed to raise a substantial federal question, given the "settled state" of school desegregation law. It also determined that, insofar as the new state law had been enacted to directly contradict the orders of a federal court, it was unconstitutional. The court decided that the effect of the law would be "to make school administrators neutral on the question of desegregation," and "an unwavering line of Supreme Court decisions" had made it clear that more was required of local officials. The state's latest attempt at defiance was thus summarily brushed aside, and segregationist lawmakers had to go back to the drawing board.[92]

The following month, the *Davis* Ping-Pong ball was back on the Fifth Circuit's side of the table. Judge Thomas had entered the appropriate orders, but these were again appealed. This time the Fifth Circuit upheld them, with only a minor modification. Many white parents in Mobile failed to realize that Thomas was bound by the rulings of the circuit court. More than eighty parents marched on the federal courthouse one day that August and demanded an audience with the judge, a highly unusual request that Thomas, incredibly, granted. Parents filed into the courtroom, one by one, to air grievances that were by then familiar. One declared, "You and no court can make us send our children into areas where there is violence, crime, dope, rape, and what-have-you." Another insisted, "We don't want to get out in the streets or do anything unlawful, but we must have something done. This is beyond tolerance."[93]

In keeping with the irregular nature of the audience, Thomas was shockingly candid in his response. "For nine years I have fought this thing and tried to slow it down," he admitted. The best he could do, he told them, was make one last review of the system's plan before the start of school and provide whatever relief seemed plausible. Later that month Thomas approved the alteration of thirty-two school zones "on the basis of efficient administration." The LDF appealed this decision and entered a formal complaint against the trial judge's biased statements at the impromptu hearing. An exasperated Fifth Circuit panel denied the appeal, ordered the plan implemented as modified, and insisted that no further changes could be made before the start of fall semester in September. Despite the fact that Thomas and Lynne had clearly stretched the limits of the authority of their respective courts in delaying desegregation for nearly a decade, Governor Brewer issued a ridiculous call for the state's trial court judges to defy appellate court rulings. Brewer protested, "I would like to see a federal judge stand up on his hind legs and say he wasn't going to do it, if he felt it violated the law and not what some other judge has said." He probably knew better. He also knew that the average white voter in Alabama did not.[94]

All summer the governor had been battling his old mentor, George Wallace, in the Democratic primary for governor. Wallace and his advisors, including Asa Carter, had decided to appeal to the working class by summoning fond memories of Wallace's past defiance. They realized that desegregation disproportionately affected poorer whites. Brewer was wealthy and well educated, and Ace Carter figured the man he took to calling "Alabama's number one white nigger" would be an easy target. So he convinced Wallace to "throw the niggers around Brewer's neck." Wallace's campaign circulated leaflets featuring a picture of a little white girl on a beach, surrounded by a group of smiling black boys, with the caption, "This could be Alabama Four Years from Now!" The campaign also doctored photographs showing Brewer with the black boxer Cassius Clay and Nation of Islam leader Elijah Muhammad. Wallace started calling Brewer a "sissy britches" who was "soft on integration" and cavorted with other "sissy britches from Harvard" in the Justice Department. He accused Brewer of kowtowing to wealthy businessmen in Mountain Brook who could retreat to their mansions in their "lily white" suburb, where they would "sip on those little martinis with their little fingers high in the air." One Wallace pamphlet simply accused Brewer of being gay and his daughter of having sex with black men.[95]

In many ways, George Wallace and Albert Brewer could not have been more different. Wallace had spent a good portion of his and his wife's terms in office campaigning for the presidency, leaving the administration of state government to subordinates, many of whom were incapable, unqualified cronies. Brewer was a businessman with a hands-on approach to governing and a commitment to efficiency and integrity in administration that the governor's office in Alabama had not seen in quite some time. Though he was committed to preserving tokenism, he sought to increase education spending across the board. By most accounts, Brewer was a decent person and an effective governor, but he was not a flashy politician. Wallace, on the other hand, was the quintessential demagogue and was thus beloved by the people, particularly working-class whites, despite his failures as an administrator and his failure to fulfill his promise of "segregation forever."[96]

In other ways, Wallace and Brewer were the same. They understood the supreme value of racial politics, and they sought to protect white privilege and white rights. Brewer understood that Wallace's reckless defiance had done more harm than good, so he had fully committed himself to the more sensible law-and-order strategy of resistance. Wallace was beginning to come over to the more measured approach himself. And he knew that Richard Nixon, soon to be his rival for president again in 1972, had adopted a similar mindset. Wallace at one point publicly accused Brewer of working with Nixon, which was more true than Wallace might have imagined. Nixon was so fearful that Wallace's next third-party run for the White House would siphon off Nixon votes with the Alabamian's "states' rights" pitch and denunciations of an overbearing federal government that he funneled half a million dollars to the Brewer campaign, which then laundered the money. Nixon also sent the IRS after Wallace's hapless brother Gerald, whose corruption was an open secret. It seemed to help initially. Brewer placed first in the May 5 primary, setting the stage for a showdown with Wallace the following month.[97]

Brewer felt that white voters would realize that Wallace's charades had brought more federal scrutiny upon Alabama, had damaged its ability to recruit new industry, and, most importantly, had not prevented integration. Wallace shrewdly played to those voters who did *not* realize this, while at the same time preparing to move toward Brewer's more effective law-and-order style. By the time of the runoff election that summer, the two men's positions on court-ordered compulsory assignment were the same: parents should ignore revamped desegregation plans and take their children to the schools of their choice. Wallace was free, then, to tout his "standing up for Alabama" in the past, while attacking Brewer's socioeconomic status and mischaracterizing his law-and-order stance as being "soft on integration." Wallace also chose to run one of the most nefarious, race-baiting campaigns in the history of U.S. politics. Albert Brewer refused to stoop quite that low. And he lost.[98]

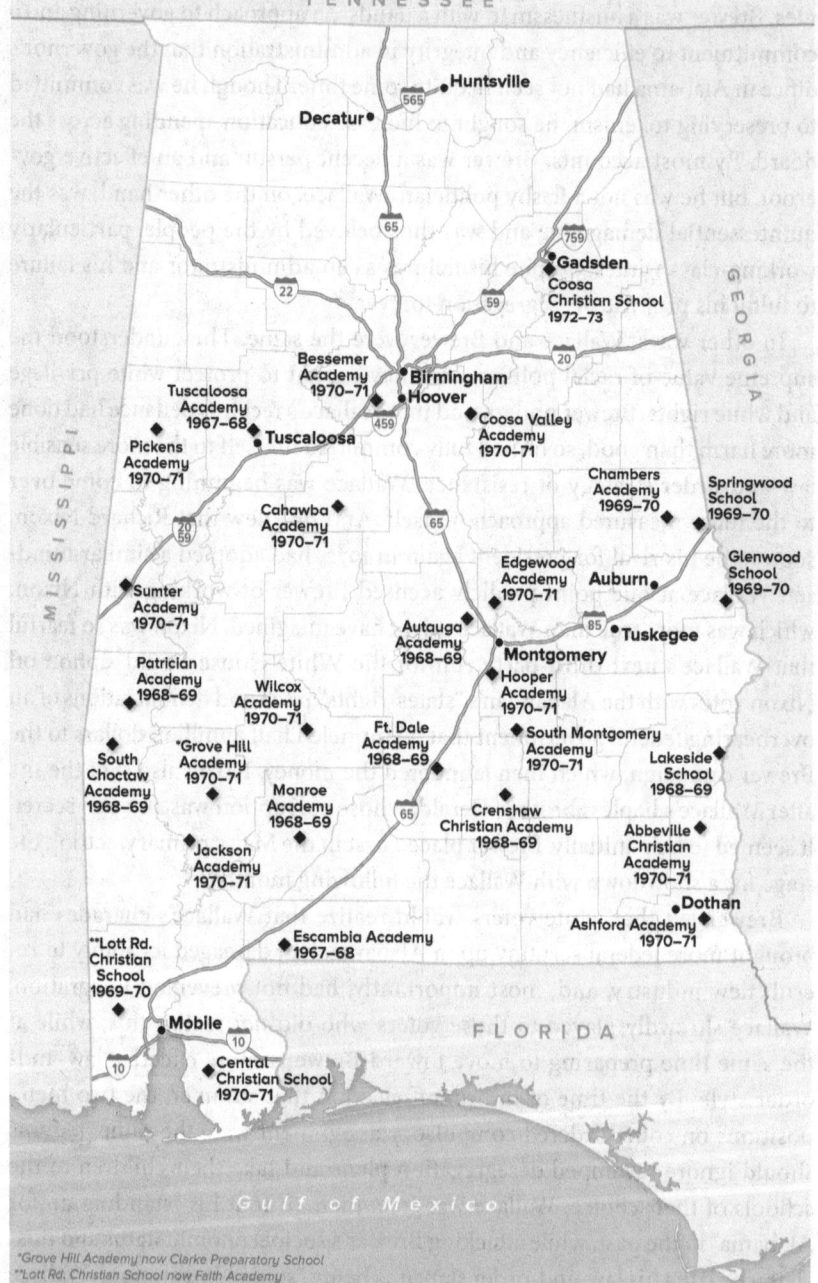

MAP 2. Segregation Academies Opened between 1967 and 1973
Source: *Alabama Independent School Association 2012–13 Directory* (Montgomery: Alabama Independent Schools Association, 2012), http://www.aisaonline.org/.

CHAPTER 6

Swann Song, 1970–1973

On Labor Day, September 7, 1970, over four thousand concerned white citizens of the Mobile area gathered for a rally of resistance in Prichard. Alabama's port city was on the verge of mounting what the *Washington Post* would call "perhaps the strongest challenge of the fall to the federal desegregation drive in the South," and many of those crowded into the city park that evening had come to hear Governor-elect George Wallace preach his new message of law-and-order and white rights. When STAND's Pierre Pelham introduced Wallace, he could not resist taking a jab at the lame duck governor, Albert Brewer—the man who had done more than any other political figure in the state to develop the kind of resistance Wallace was then embracing. Pelham thanked Wallace for taking the state government "out of the hands of the Big Mules," like Brewer, and putting it "in the hands of the people of Prichard, Alabama." Brewer had already denounced the latest court-ordered desegregation plan for Mobile's school system, calling it a "pure case of gerrymandering." But he had been defeated by Wallace, who better understood how to dig into the souls of white folk and tap into their deepest fears.[1]

Pelham's introduction elicited the first of many rebel yells from the crowd, which was rapt when Wallace took the podium. He began, "All you good people take heart and courage. Don't you give up now, you hear. Cause we going to keep on and on and on and on until we get our schools back." He added, "Mr. Nixon, he told us in Charlotte that he was against busing, and now look what's happening." Nixon had campaigned on seeing de jure desegregation through but going no farther, an adoption of Alabama officials' insistence that no one go "beyond the law" in accepting HEW desegregation guidelines. "We going to keep reminding him of what he said," Wallace insisted demonstratively, "And we can get this mess straightened out." They desperately wanted to believe that he was right—that as long as they continued to resist and to put their faith in the law-and-order creed, they could find a way to defeat the courts and the bureaucrats. Wallace advised them, "If I were you, on school day, I would exercise your freedom of choice in the peaceful way you always do things, in the hopes that someday [you] are going to get some relief."[2]

As Wallace continued speaking, members of Mobile's newly organized chapter of Concerned Parents and Citizens went to work among the crowd. They passed out fliers urging parents to heed Wallace's advice and take their children to the school of their choice on registration day. They assured parents that, while the school board was under court order, they personally were not, so they suggested greeting administrators with, "This is the school of my choice. I will not leave until my demands are met!" Parents did not have to sign "conformist papers" and would be "legally within [their] rights" in choosing their child's school. On Wednesday morning, hundreds of parents heeded the call, "Freedom comes first!" Local Concerned Parents chairman Melvin Himes led the way, insisting to reporters that he was simply "exercising [his] constitutional rights," adding, "If we can't enroll [our children] under freedom of choice, we're not going to enroll them."[3]

School systems across the South were preparing for the start of classes that week. Compulsory assignment orders had drastically increased the number of pupils assigned to desegregated schools. In Alabama the number of black students set to attend formerly all-white schools had quadrupled since the fall of 1968. Citizens' advisory committees, set up by the Nixon administration, issued statements calling for peaceful acceptance. The Alabama committee announced, "The federal court orders under which Alabama and other Southern school districts will open this fall are binding and will be enforced, [and] disorder will not cause court-ordered systems to be rescinded or modified." Newspaper editors made similar pleas. The *Birmingham News* urged, "Rules, however unpalatable some may find them, are essential, and [they] will be enforced, and ... order will prevail." Some school boards made efforts to reassure parents that schools would open peacefully. The Birmingham board even set up informational workshops and a hotline for dispelling rumors. But Concerned Parents groups and politicians like Wallace were working even harder to sabotage the opening in the name of white rights.[4]

As both sides fought for the hearts and minds of white parents, the U.S. Supreme Court was preparing to hear the latest appeal in the *Davis v. Mobile* case. Though the Fifth Circuit appellate court had insisted late that summer that Mobile implement the latest court-approved plan without any further delay, the school board had appealed, in the hope of getting relief for the following term. Board members called the plan set to go into effect "stupid," "ridiculous," and "functionally impossible." Vernon Crawford and the LDF had also appealed, insisting that the plan was still inadequate. It left schools in Mobile's urban core largely black, while desegregation of formerly all-white schools west of Interstate 65 remained minimal. The court was set to consider *Davis* alongside appeals involving five other metropolitan areas, including Charlotte, North Carolina. The Charlotte school board contended that its court-ordered desegregation plan was too far-reaching, partly because it involved the significant use of busing. Across the nation that fall, people anxiously awaited—with hope and foreboding—the Supreme Court's omnibus ruling in what was collectively styled *Swann v. Charlotte-Mecklenburg Board of Education*.[5]

"That Doesn't Mean We Are Not Americans"

The fall of 1970 brought new challenges for school systems across the South, but the *Los Angeles Times* observed, "No state in the region has had problems as severe as Alabama." This was particularly true in Mobile and Jefferson County, which were plagued by "non-conformity." On the first day of classes in Mobile, over eleven hundred white students showed up at schools other than those to which they had been assigned. Many of them were accompanied by parents who engaged in sit-in protests, as advised by Concerned Parents volunteers, who set up tables outside schools. One white mother channeled the frustration of generations of black mothers when she explained, "This ridiculous business of having to go miles across town with a school right around the corner has me just about crazy." Concerned Parents organized a protest march to the federal building in downtown Mobile, which drew four thousand whites, some of whom dressed in black judicial robes or carried signs reading, "We Want Our Schools Back" and "The Supreme Court Has Outlawed Our Laws." Mobile mayor Joe Bailey led the group in praying for the federal judiciary.[6]

Nonconformity in Mobile was not limited to those students who showed up at the schools of their choice. Many families hastily moved to whiter school zones, while some used relatives' addresses or otherwise falsified their enrollment applications. As a result, Davidson High, on the mostly white, western outskirts of the city, opened the school year overenrolled by one thousand students. There were also hundreds of students who simply stayed home or enrolled in one of the regions' nearly thirty segregation academies. At formerly all-black Williamson High, 786 white pupils were scheduled to join 323 blacks, but only 219 showed up. At Booker T. Washington Junior High, fewer than 100 white pupils, out of a scheduled 725, attended alongside 800 black students. In Prichard, 150 whites out of 850 actually went to formerly all-black Blount High, with the majority of the remaining 700 opting to attend formerly all-white Vigor High. Nearly 200 of the 1,000 white students assigned to formerly all-white Murphy High refused to attend the school now that it also enrolled 1,200 black students.[7]

Mobile's problems were compounded when Murphy became the epicenter of the state's most serious outbreak of violence that fall. Murphy's scheduled enrollment made it a majority black school in a white neighborhood and therefore a lightning rod for protestors and troublemakers. Nonstudents, white and black, infiltrated the school and roamed its halls. By the third day of class, white students were complaining of being "shaken down" by blacks, and bands of whites had begun inciting fights with blacks, probably none of whom had anything to do with any shakedowns. A series of skirmishes begat an all-out racial brawl by the end of the first full week of class. The Mobile police riot squad restored order and remained on the campus for another week, arresting nine black students for disorderly conduct. By then, fewer than four hundred white students remained, and white teachers threatened a walkout if the local police were not replaced by a permanent group of U.S. marshals.[8]

The chairman of the Mobile school board called the system's desegregation order "an asinine law." In solidarity with the teachers demanding federal protection, he added, "It's theirs, and they can enforce it." The appeals to the Fifth Circuit, meanwhile, resulted in an order insisting that students attending the wrong school could not participate in school activities, take examinations, or receive grades. The school board announced that "nonconforming" students would be granted all other privileges not denied in the order. Judge Thomas surprised the board, however, when he approved the Civil Rights Division's request that the court also prohibit issuing textbooks to nonconforming students and their use of school facilities and equipment. By the third week of classes, school administrators had begun to implore these students to leave, and the number of nonconformers fell to around six hundred pupils, scattered throughout twenty-two schools.[9]

Similar protests unfolded in Birmingham and Jefferson County, where the situation was mitigated by the emergence of the independent white-suburban school systems. Around six thousand white students began the fall in the Pleasant Grove, Homewood, and Vestavia Hills city school systems. No black students were attending Pleasant Grove schools, and fewer than one hundred were attending schools in the other two systems. Nonconformity was rampant elsewhere. Northwest of Birmingham, in the small city of Graysville, one white student out of a scheduled 450 showed up at Graysville High, where 400 black pupils were enrolled. By the end of the first day of classes, the attending student bodies at seven other schools were all black, despite the fact that hundreds of white students had been assigned to each. Just like in Mobile, most of the nonconforming students chose to attend formerly all-white schools nearby or schools with larger white enrollments. Attorney U. W. Clemon estimated that as many as ten thousand students were out of place and argued that the school board was ignoring its responsibility to address the issue.[10]

Birmingham city schools had similar problems. Around four thousand of the system's sixty thousand students refused, in one way or another, to accept their assigned school. Parents at one school occupied classrooms and refused to leave. Teachers staged a walkout at another. Concerned Parents established a Teachers' Defense Fund and encouraged teachers to invoke the state's teacher tenure law, which allowed them to appeal transfers to the state tenure commission. Superintendent Raymond Christian put up a strong rhetorical front, announcing, "I cannot register students who have not been assigned. . . . I cannot accept their fees. I cannot issue them books." Christian also claimed that any teacher who remained "at her old school," instead of reporting to a new assignment, would "in effect be giving up her job." Despite the tough talk, the school board took little action to remove protesting students, parents, or teachers, prompting Clemon and the LDF to petition the court for an order directing the board to do so.[11]

Thirty miles east of Birmingham, in Talladega, a group of white parents commandeered classrooms and began conducted their own all-white classes. One of the parental ringleaders, a local upholsterer named Allen Lockridge, announced that the motivations for the scheme were reports that black boys had been "pulling and pinching" white girls and the fact that marching bands had been asked to stop flying the Confederate battle flag. Someone alerted the CRD, which asked the FBI to investigate the situation. When the FBI furnished the names of Lockridge and others, the CRD asked the district court for a show cause order against the parents. Talladega's desegregation case had recently been severed from *Lee v. Macon County* and assigned to judge Hobart Grooms, who called the parents before the court, where he observed that they were surely "substantially law-abiding" and "decent, upstanding citizens." But he cautioned them, "I try to be tender-hearted and merciful, [but] I just want you to know that the court will not permit defiance." The court, he said, had "no alternative but to obey the laws" and "must have order." He concluded, "I plead with you to obey the law."[12]

Judge Lynne was similarly compelled to act on LDF motions in the Birmingham and Jefferson County cases. He threatened the occupying parents in Birmingham with show cause orders and contempt citations, and he brushed aside protesting teachers' claims, noting that the Fifth Circuit had long since determined, "Local teacher hiring statutes may not be interposed to frustrate a constitutional mandate." The teachers were to report to their assigned posts in five days or be fired. Some teachers mounted a last-ditch effort to obtain an injunction in state court, but this was summarily dismissed, prompting over fifty teachers to resign. Lynne declined to enter contempt citations for Jefferson County superintendent Revis Hall or the county school board. He instead ordered the board to compile a report indicating where students were actually attending. Lynne gave the board so much time to furnish the information to the court that this amounted to a reprieve from any further action for the fall semester.[13]

The nonconformity and turbulence of the fall of 1970 carried over into the following winter and spring. In Jefferson County, U. W. Clemon observed, "In every case where whites have not shown up at a black school, you can go to the nearest white school and find an excess of white students enrolled there." As a result, three out of four black students in the system were attending a school that was 99 percent black, and only twelve of the system's eighty-eight schools had anywhere near the required 30 percent black teacher ratio. Racial violence continued in Mobile. Interracial fistfights remained commonplace. Violence at Vigor High escalated from a brawl, which closed the school for a day in January, to what police called a "general racial melee" involving over one hundred students in early February and then a "major riot" involving nearly three hundred students a week later. Law enforcement officials from Prichard, Mobile, and Chickasaw were called to the latter incident, in which ten students were injured and thirteen arrested. State and local officials offered the unrest as evidence of the wrongheadedness of integration, and the school board petitioned the court for emergency relief due to the "intolerable" situation.[14]

When another major outbreak of violence enveloped Vigor and Murphy late in the semester, dialogue broke down. Many white parents who had initially acquiesced to compulsory assignment removed their children to segregation academies. The school board again insisted that federal marshals ought to be policing the schools. Mobile's state representative, Monty Collins, introduced a new freedom-of-choice bill in the state legislature. Collins called it a "student transfer bill," in a vain attempt to differentiate it from the lately failed choice law of 1970. The law would allow any students who had been "harassed, intimidated, or assaulted" to transfer to the school of their choice. Wallace called it a "must bill."[15]

Black teachers from Mobile went before the U.S. Congress to describe their mounting frustration. One teacher told the Select Committee on Equal Educational Opportunity that black students in Mobile were tired of being disproportionately "suspended, intimidated, harassed, and jailed" while at the same time being blamed for all of desegregation's failures. The city had experienced threats on the lives of black leaders and unsolved bombings, in addition to the violence in schools. Yet the school board had demonstrated "complete unresponsiveness" to the "desires of the black community," such as investigating charges that much of the violence was being instigated by white students. This was, the teacher argued, the reason for the growing popularity of Roy Innis and CORE's plan for black autonomy.[16]

Black students in Mobile were moving forward on their own too. A group of students established the United Student Action Movement of Mobile (USAMM), opened a "center for the advancement of black awareness," and began coordinating direct-action protests. Representatives from USAMM met with the Southern Regional Council in a desegregation workshop after the 1970–71 school year was over and expressed their disappointment, anger, and despair. They insisted that school administrators wanted black students to "become white." They explained that, in majority-white schools, they generally could not get elected to the student council, the cheerleading squad, or other positions because of their race. In rare exceptions to this, the person elected was "invariably the one with the straightest hair." At some schools, they said, blacks were prohibited from forms of racial self-expression, such as wearing their hair in Afros or wearing dashikis, while at those same schools, white boys could wear their hair in ponytails and dress like hippies. "So far," one student said, "integration has only meant humiliation, oppression, and a loss of identity to these black students." And litigation simply meant getting "bogged down." The "only way you can survive," they argued, "is to make white people listen through violence."[17]

While violence in Mobile and suburban white flight in Jefferson County—and "nonconformity" in both—made those situations somewhat different, compulsory assignment proved abhorrent for whites throughout the state. This was particularly clear in the systems still under the *Lee v. Macon* umbrella. They had been working with the court, plaintiffs' counsel, and the USOE to adopt and begin implementing terminal type orders, so that they could have their cases severed for oversight by a single judge. Each of these systems was preparing for major changes in the fall of 1970. Enraged and despairing whites meted out an enormous amount of vitriol to Judge Johnson, who many believed to be the only judge deciding the case. Many segregationists thought compulsory assignment was the result of "edicts" issued by "judicial dictators" who were "unlawfully" assuming control over state education. Vehement denunciations of Johnson and calls for his impeachment were colored by these misunderstandings and encouraged by ongoing condemnations from state leaders like Brewer and Wallace, who continued to insist that whites could "get their schools back" if only judges would "stand up on their hind legs."[18]

Some raised the stakes beyond impeachment. A student at the University of Alabama named Brooks Barganier forwarded Johnson an editorial, insisting that the editor of the *Greenville Advocate* had captured his thinking perfectly. Both Barganier and the editor were disgusted by the implementation of the Butler County desegregation plan, which had resulted in the consolidation of the student bodies of all-white Greenville High and all-black Southside High. Whites had fled the public system for the newly established Fort Dale Academy, and many of those who stayed refused to participate in integrated extracurricular activities. The editor had been moved to publish an open letter to Johnson after witnessing a football game halftime in which the depleted Greenville High marching band was outclassed by its larger rival. White band members had wept "silent, bitter tears" in "humiliation, sorrow and despair," all because Johnson had "gutted the group by edicts and decrees." He lamented the coming of a "spiritless gray world" and concluded, "Damn you, Frank Johnson, damn you." In forwarding the editorial, Barganier informed Johnson that the judge was "despised" throughout the state and added that it was his "sincere hope" that Johnson would "spend an eternity in hell" for "playing God with other people's lives" and sowing "strife and misery."[19]

One woman wrote Johnson in an effort to actually spare the besieged judge from an afterlife of fire and brimstone. She wondered if he had "accepted Jesus as [his] own personal savior." She observed that Johnson did not have to send his son to school with blacks (the younger Johnson attended private school), nor did he "have to eat and sleep with them" like the average white person. She argued that God "did not intend for us to intergrate [sic]," nor for whites to "mix with them." He had put a curse on Cain, after all, and had made his black children "servants of servants." She importuned the judge to consider that he was destined for either hell or heaven and suggested that if he would simply "Get right with the Lord," pray, and ask for God's guidance, then he could "get all of this straightened out" before it was too late for Johnson's own soul and for Alabama. She then offered an example of righteousness as a counterpoint. "You hate George Wallace," she wrote, "But thank God for a man that will stand up and fight for our rights."[20]

The invocation of a racial doomsday did not always involve Johnson's own salvation. A Selma man explained that whites had come to grudgingly accept freedom of choice, but a situation in which they were in the minority in schools was "more than human nature [could] absorb." Parents were "literally afraid for the physical safety of their children." Black students had supposedly warned of violence if schools were fully integrated, and some whites had apparently predicted an "all-out battle." A number of parents had indicated that they would "just as soon die" or go to jail as to send their children to integrated schools. Surely Johnson would understand and help them come to a lawful solution that would prevent a white exodus. Selma's white students had already begun to swell the ranks of John T. Morgan Academy, established in the wake of the first desegregation orders in 1965. By the fall of 1970, the school had added a high school building, science labs, an enlarged cafeteria, a gymnasium, and eight new classrooms. Whites wrote that they feared violence and an "ungodly" scenario in which their children were in the minority, and the rapidly growing segregation academies were buoyed by donations from wealthy locals who chalked up public education as a lost cause.[21]

When the court seemed to turn deaf ears to informal requests for relief, whites surmised that Judge Johnson simply refused to do the sensible thing. One newspaper editor demonstrated not only the distorted understanding of the litigation that plagued the white consciousness but also the enduring power of narratives of miscegenation and racial degradation. Randolph County had been ordered to accept a geographic zoning plan that resulted in black school closure and significant pupil integration for the first time. The editor of the *Randolph Press* observed that all of this was "being done at the pleasure of some federal judge named Frank Johnson, and probably nobody else's." The way he saw it, "One man pointed his finger at the Pleasant Grove School, and it was no more." Johnson had assumed "absolute, near total tyranny in the area" and was forcing the county into a "shotgun marriage," because of his apparent belief that "when blacks and whites are thrown in the common pot and stirred until brown, universal salvation is at hand." Sadly he admitted that there was "no appeal" of Johnson's rulings, unless of course one "dared" to approach HEW. But the editor argued that to "go from one to the other" would only be "crawling further up the anus."[22]

When the Autauga County school board was ordered to pair its all-black and formerly all-white high schools, some white parents began writing letters to the judge, asking if he would want his child taught by a black teacher, surrounded by "discipline problems," or to receive the "standard of education" that a majority black enrollment would produce. "According to the U.S. Constitution," one parent wrote, "everyone has equal rights, just as long as they do not infringe on the rights of others, [but] we feel that if the Negroes are forced upon the students at Hicks . . . they are infringing our rights." A group of parents tried entering a formal motion to intervene in the county's case, but it was denied. By the fall of 1970, the mayor and members of the city council and school board were lobbying all remaining whites in the public system to enroll in Autauga Academy. The ensuing exodus revealed a Black Belt reality—as white community leaders went, so went the white community.[23]

In nearby Wilcox County, the school board had been so obdurate in its refusal to submit a new desegregation plan that Judge Thomas was compelled to surprise the board members at a hearing, ordering them to sit down with HEW officials, right then and there, and hammer one out. The parlay ended with Wilcox superintendent Guy Kelly storming out, telling the bureaucrats, "You will not live to see what you want to do in Wilcox County, not if you live a thousand years." The board subsequently submitted a plan prefaced with the statement, "In order to establish a so-called unitary school system in Wilcox County, the following recommendations are made under duress. These recommendations are educationally unsound and will completely segregate and eventually destroy the Wilcox County School System." The local newspaper praised the board for standing up to the court and endorsed Kelly's argument that race and discrimination were not the real issues, just as the "War between the States" had nothing to do with slavery. This was "about the abridgement of freedom of education," which was "the first and inalienable right and duty of the parent."[24]

The *Lee v. Macon* court began to acknowledge that public schools were bound to become all-black in majority black school districts, because local leaders seemed unwilling to face criticism and work to build acceptance for compulsory assignment plans. In the terminal order for Sumter County, the court declared, "We enter this order in this case with the full realization that . . . the student body in the Sumter County school system will, in all probability, be composed only of Negro students." In the fall of 1970, whites indeed began to flee en masse for Sumter Academy. Jude Wanniski, one-time columnist for the *National Observer* and future advisor to President Ronald Reagan, was covering the efforts to desegregate schools in nearby Marengo County, where the local superintendent had placed his own children in a segregation academy. Wanniski observed, the "lead role in trying to win acceptance for these plans has fallen to the public educators themselves. Where they have given up," he wrote "there may be no integration at all."[25]

In most cases, educators had not only given up on the public schools, they had begun working diligently toward the establishment and growth of private schools. In Lowndes County, private school organizers hired locally legendary football coach Mac Champion to serve as the principal of the recently opened Lowndes Academy, ensuring that the football team members would leave the public high school and then pressure others to do the same. Champion explained the ethos of the white right to freedom of association to reporters. "We don't hate Negroes," he insisted. There was, he argued, a "difference between segregation and discrimination." But, he expounded, "We believe that we have the right to socialize and study the way we please and with whom we please." Champion admitted that it was "not likely" that a black student would be admitted to his school, "because that's the reason for having the school in the first place." Pointing to a portrait of Confederate general Robert E. Lee on his office wall, he claimed, "That doesn't mean we are not Americans. We are good ones down here." And America, he argued, meant the "freedom to choose what school you want to attend."[26]

The number of segregation academies in the South had nearly doubled between the fall of 1969 and the fall of 1970, and Alabama had contributed more than its fair share. In 1965, there were thirty-four private schools in the state that could be identified as such, most of them established in the immediate wake of *Brown* in 1954 or after the first desegregation orders were issued in 1963. By 1970 there were 109. The increase in pupils attending these schools was equally dramatic, if difficult to accurately measure. According to the State Department of Education, the number of students enrolled in private schools in the state increased from 39,524 in 1968–69 to 68,123 in 1970–71. One Alabama educationist utilized data published by the state to determine that 20,500 of those students were enrolled in "private, non-sectarian schools," all of which were segregated. This indicated an increase of nearly 100 percent from the previous fall.[27]

But these figures only represented a portion of the actual number of students in segregation academies. An LDF study concluded that public information on these schools in Alabama was "minimal at best" and that data on enrollment was "incomplete and almost meaningless." In 1970–71, sixty-five schools belonged to the Citizen Council–affiliated Alabama Private School Association. Of these, only thirty-five reported enrollment statistics to the state, which did not enforce laws requiring them to do so. The state did not even recognize the existence of thirteen of the remaining thirty. In other words, the actual number of pupils in the academies was undoubtedly much higher than the figure of 20,500. White students were clearly fleeing public schools, especially when they were in danger of becoming the minority race in a given school system. In districts in which blacks were between 51 and 75 percent of enrollment, 21 percent of whites fled. When blacks were more than 75 percent of the student population, white flight was 54 percent on aggregate—but near total in some cases.[28]

In most Black Belt counties, white flight quickly exceeded 90 percent, as school board members became private school boosters, encouraging parents to forsake the public schools just as they had. The growth of Greene County's Warrior Academy was typical. The school was established in 1965, as HEW initiated desegregation efforts with the county school board. When Greene was added as a defendant party in *Lee v. Macon* in 1969 and forced to implement a compulsory assignment plan, Warrior Academy announced plans to expanded from eight grades to twelve and doubled its enrollment from two hundred to four hundred. Over half of the public school system's white teachers quit, with many taking jobs at the private school. This exacerbated white flight, and Warrior's enrollment jumped to over five hundred the following year. By the fall of 1971, all but twenty white students had left the public system for Warrior Academy or other white schools in surrounding counties.[29]

As enrollment soared at established segregation academies, new ones emerged. Between 1967 and 1973, nearly thirty academies were opened, scattered throughout the state, save for the northern quarter, where whites remained in the solid majority in most areas and where a number of academies had been established when initial desegregation orders came down.[30] The new schools were diverse. Some enrolled upward of five hundred, even approaching one thousand students. Some had fewer than one hundred students. Some were able to occupy former public school facilities, while others were forced to convert old houses or recreation centers, or to hastily build simple sheet metal or cinder block facilities of their own. With financing exclusively from tuition and community fund-raising, some struggled to meet students' basic needs, while others prospered. Some benefited from large donations from wealthy individuals. Others were dependent on barbeques, bake sales, and deer hunts to make ends meet. Where whites fled a city or county entirely, academies were forced to move or close.[31]

Academy founders described the schools as bastions of freedom—freedom of association, freedom from federal government oversight, freedom of religion, or some combination of all three. The editors of the *Citizen* proclaimed, "Nothing is more attractive to the patrons of private schools than the air of freedom." And nothing was more odious to integrationists than "an arrangement which promise[d] potential victims an avenue of liberation." Some of Alabama's segregation academies professed a commitment to "building a school where children could receive a challenging curriculum within a framework of traditional values" or to providing "a comprehensive college preparatory education in a safe and supportive environment." Most were nondenominational, but they nonetheless advertised a "Christian-based" education and championed their ability to compel Bible study and school prayer, which had been prohibited in public schools by recent decisions of the Supreme Court.[32]

In early 1970, it looked for a moment like the federal government's enforcement of tax policy might threaten the segregation academy movement. The schools benefited from federal tax exemption, but black activists in Mississippi filed suit against the IRS in 1969, seeking removal of exemptions for any private schools that discriminated. The trial court in *Green v. Kennedy* enjoined the IRS from granting the exemptions. The Nixon administration announced that the IRS would change its policy, but the appellate court and Supreme Court held that the administration needed to take affirmative steps to determine which schools were discriminating. What looked like a blow for Alabama's academies turned out to be nothing more than a scare, however. The court allowed the IRS to treat the ruling in *Green* as a "law of the case" decision, requiring that it closely scrutinize schools in Mississippi only. And the White House quietly assured southern senators and representatives that the IRS would accept written statements of nondiscrimination at face value.[33]

A similar threat to the new schools came via an appellate court ruling in 1971. In 1969 when William Hoover had attempted to move Hoover Academy to Brighton, where city officials allowed him to lease a former public school facility, black activists had filed suit, arguing that not only was the leasing arrangement unconstitutional but also that the procedure by which the city approved it was dubious (the white mayor had voted twice in order to break a racially divided 3–3 tie in the city council). Judge Grooms ruled in favor of the academy in January 1970, but the Fifth Circuit reversed this the following year. The appellate court rejected the school's assertion that it was nondiscriminatory, calling it a "relic of slavery" and "lily white from its natal day" and arguing that, "in historical context," the court would have to be "naively unsophisticated" to fail to recognize that city officials had made a deal with William Hoover in order to provide a segregated alternative to public schools for white families.[34]

But just as the threat to tax exemption proved to be fleeting, so too did the threat to facilities acquisition. The appellate court ruling was neither statewide nor retroactive. By the spring of 1971, most academies had already acquired public facilities and were not affected. Similarly, tax-exempt status for the academies was most crucial when their foundations were setting up schools through initial land and facilities donations. Existing segregated private schools had little to worry about. Further, most blacks in Alabama were not interested in mounting a prolonged legal challenge to these schools. Many black parents and students were too busy protesting the realities of court-ordered compulsory assignment, almost as vehemently as whites.[35]

More Disillusionment and the "Stand in the School Bus Door"

Despite court oversight, desegregation disproportionately burdened black communities. This came into sharp focus when compulsory assignment plans began to result in the restructuring or closure of formerly black schools. In most cases, courts did not mandate the outright closure of these schools;

they just insisted that they no longer operate as all-black schools. White school boards, however, and in some cases the courts themselves, accepted that whites would not attend formerly all-black schools. Many black schools were therefore closed or turned into vocational centers or alternative, disciplinary schools. When the schools were kept open, they were invariably transformed—black high schools became junior high schools; junior highs became elementary schools. This was usually accompanied by a new name, in the hope that it might help mollify reluctant whites. Alongside widespread attempts to demote or dismiss black teachers and administrators, these changes amounted to what has been called the "dismantling of black education," a process that generated considerable protest from black communities, particularly among the *Lee v. Macon* districts.[36]

The East Alabama city of Opelika provided a compelling example. The city's 1970 desegregation plan called for transforming its black high school, Darden High, into a vocational school called Opelika High–Southside Campus. Only black students chose to attend, but characterizing it as a satellite campus of formerly all-white Opelika High allowed the school board to count those black students toward the Opelika High student body. On paper then, the board had achieved the court-ordered 37 percent black ratio for the supposedly consolidated Opelika High. Neither Fred Gray, the CRD, nor Judge Johnson was fooled by the ruse, and the board was put on notice that the court could not permit the arrangement. Rather than adopt a pairing plan that split an integrated student body evenly between the two schools, the board promised that it would build a new, larger facility within a year. A new Opelika High was thus hastily built. The old Opelika High was rechristened Opelika Middle School, and Darden High was sold to the local Head Start program.[37]

Darden, named for Lee County's first black medical doctor, J. W. Darden, had long been a source of tremendous pride in Opelika's black community. Its loss was widely lamented. One student remembered, "We had a premiere school, even in the fifties, that a lot of students around here didn't have. We kept that building up as if it were our home. You could open up the front door, and the [hardwood] floors would just be sparkling." The school's teachers and administrators were community leaders. School assemblies were community events. Its colors and its mascot and its football team helped provide a shared identity. When it was closed, all of that disappeared. In addition to dealing with that loss, blacks had to confront minority status at the new integrated school, competing with whites for awards and for participation in extracurricular activities. A Darden student who made the transition recalled, "We totally lost everything. For females . . . we lost cheerleading, we lost majorettes. . . . It was not a good time for blacks, because most of us felt like we were forced to change . . . to give up everything. It took a lot of adjusting and a lot of praying to get through."[38]

Black students and their parents often turned to Judge Johnson. Johnson suspected that pressure from white officials sometimes induced blacks to call for the retention of black schools, but this was not always the case. A group of black parents in Enterprise asked the judge to prevail upon the Coffee County school board not to close all-black Coppinville High. One frustrated parent wrote, "We have 60 band members and 10 majorettes. What will become of them when they are transferred to an all-white school?" She added, "It's suppose to be a freedom of choice then why are we going one way." When some rural counties closed black schools, the result was that black children had to travel considerable distances to formerly all-white schools. A father in Chambers County wrote to Johnson to protest, suggesting, "Surely you couldn't have had children in mind, who at the present time is riding a school bus 30 to 40 miles a day."[39]

The principal of the all-black Lockhart No. 2 School in Covington County, in the Wiregrass, expressed similar concern to Johnson. Lockhart was situated in the middle of the black community it served. The white school to which Lockhart's students were to be assigned was over a mile away—too close to compel the school board to provide transportation but too far down a "very long and dangerous highway" to walk. Lockhart was in excellent shape, thanks to the desperate, eleventh-hour efforts of the county board to avoid integration by equalizing facilities. The principal explained, "We have a new lunchroom, new in-door restrooms, water cooler inside, and water fountains outside, televisions and record players in each classroom, movie and film projectors, and the entire school is heated with electric, thermostatic heaters." Each classroom had "bookshelves, books, and maps," and the school had "an automatic time clock." She pleaded, "Judge, your honor, it isn't that we are fighting desegregation, we are just thinking about the safety and welfare of our children. . . . Let us keep this school a little while longer."[40]

The Lockhart No. 2 school was closed despite the principal's plea, as were black schools all over the South. Johnson, along with Judges Grooms and Rives, was sympathetic to the plight of black communities. But he could not act on requests that had not been brought properly before the court. Even then, there was little the *Lee v. Macon* court, or any other court, could do, given the thrust of the litigation and the lingering intransigence of state and local officials. Not all black schools were closed. Many were retained, even in Opelika, where the city's two formerly all-black elementary schools were fully integrated. Most black students ended up in formerly white schools, however. And there they and their parents quickly discovered a host of other problems.[41]

Formerly all-white schools often canceled homecoming dances and proms rather than hold integrated events. Parents' groups subsequently organized their own segregated events. Some schools eradicated entire programs, like marching band, rather than integrate them. But when it came to a school's name, its mascot, its colors, and its traditions, those of the formerly all-white schools were usually retained, while the opposite was true of integrated formerly all-black schools. In some instances, this meant blacks were forced to attend schools that seemed to be haunted by the Confederate past, whether they were nicknamed the Rebels, flew the Confederate flag, or used textbooks that supported a white supremacist interpretation of southern history.[42]

Blacks quickly realized that the recently exposed *Know Alabama* history textbook was not an anomaly. *Alabama History for Schools* argued that, "while the Negro was badly treated as a rule in the foreign slave trade, he was generally very well treated by Alabama farmers," and that, despite some "drawbacks," slavery was "the earliest form of social security in the United States," as slaves "suffered little or no want." Another widely used text, *The Land Called Alabama*, described slavery as "the best means of social and economic control of a subject race ever devised." The text included just two passing references to civil rights protests, alongside a lengthy and triumphal treatment of Wallace's stand in the schoolhouse door. In these and other books, black people were portrayed as passive and content, if not emotional and childlike, while the exploits of the white race were pompously celebrated. Black parents wondered how their children would ever develop a sense of racial pride or how white children could ever learn to see their black counterparts as equals. The NAACP and local parents' groups stepped up pressure on the state to phase out or revise such texts.[43]

Black students assigned to white schools also encountered celebrated symbols of the Confederacy on a daily basis. Confederate flags, particularly the universally recognized battle flag, were commonplace on school flagpoles and in classrooms, in some cases in lieu of the U.S. flag. But few relics of the antebellum past were as powerful and as abhorrent to blacks than the unofficial anthem of the Lost Cause, "Dixie," which was sung at football games, pep rallies, and assemblies. The song was originally part of a parody act in a northern minstrelsy show. A former slave, played by a white man in blackface, lamented his departure from the Old South—"I wish I was in the land of cotton; old times there are not forgotten. Look away, look away, look away, Dixie land." During Redemption, it became the musical expression of the Lost Cause—in this case it was white southerners who yearned for the "land of cotton," unfairly destroyed by "Yankees" and supposedly inept blacks during the war and Reconstruction. By the late 1960s, the song, like the battle flag, enjoyed a resurgence as a defiant retort to the civil rights movement. White students at integrated schools routinely changed the words to the song to include lines like, "Nigger, go back and pick that cotton."[44]

As compulsory assignment spread, protests followed. Black students demanded that school bands cease playing "Dixie." When a group of students in Anniston protested the playing of the song at a November 1969 homecoming ceremony, a melee erupted, and the NAACP's W. C. Patton called on the state to take action. Patton sardonically suggested the novel idea of replacing the battle flag and "Dixie" with the Stars and Stripes and the "Star Spangled Banner." He also helped draft a statement describing the Confederate flag and "Dixie" as "symbolic of a cause, sprit, and hostility which reminds us of division, disunity and an unhappy past." He connected these elements of "heritage" explicitly to the law-and-order creed: "We believe in and seek to participate in law and order as a way of justice and not a rage of bigotry, [and] we reject the concept of 'law and order' in the context of racism, dual justice, and as a cover up for economic and social bigotry."[45]

Tensions over Confederate symbology reached a crescendo in the fall of 1970. In October black students at Butler High in Huntsville walked out of a pep rally in support of that evening's football game the second the band began playing "Dixie." Moments later, about half of them returned, stormed the stage, and attempted to remove and destroy the Confederate flag, prompting violent resistance from white students. Administrators and teachers were driven from the stage in the ensuing brawl, which did not abate until Huntsville police arrived. One week later, white students at West End High in Birmingham staged a walkout in protest of what they characterized as preferential treatment for black students at the seventeen-hundred-student school, which was 60 percent white. The white principal had boldly acceded to the band director's decision to remove two bars from "Dixie." He had also agreed to the naming of a "Mr. and Mrs. Soul," since "Mr. and Mrs. West End" were guaranteed to always be white. The boycotting white students called for the principal's resignation.[46]

In November, Pell City High School in suburban East Birmingham was closed following a series of fights resulting from black students protesting the playing of "Dixie" and white students protesting the appointment of two black cheerleaders to the all-white cheerleading squad. The same day, blacks at Birmingham's Jones Valley High refused to stand for the school's alma mater in protest of the naming of an all-white homecoming court, leading to a brawl and the closure of the school. The ongoing controversy and violence underscored both blacks' increasingly tenuous position in integrated schools and whites' developing sense of white rights. Black students had been forced to abandon black community schools that served as nuclei of their cultural identity, and now they were faced with the adoption of a cultural heritage that was not only alien but downright threatening to them. The *Citizen* ran an editorial that fall lamenting the situation. Censoring "Dixie" and the battle flag, the editors argued, represented a "depressing declination of freedom of speech."[47]

The furor over songs and flags temporarily abated during the winter and spring of 1971, as Frank Johnson and his colleagues on the *Lee v. Macon* court oversaw the long-delayed desegregation and equalization of the state's trade schools and junior colleges. The court issued a ruling requiring substantial desegregation of faculties and strict zoning for some schools, but this generated enough of an uproar that the court reexamined portions of the order and issued a rare modification of its own volition. The *Lee* court essentially allowed the schools to continue on a freedom of choice program, though it was characterized as an "open door" policy. Meanwhile, the U.S. Supreme Court was considering whether or not desegregation orders for K–12 schools should continue to trend in the opposite direction—that is, whether substantial crosstown busing and other means should be used to achieve "racial balance" in schools, particularly in major metropolitan areas. If the answer was yes, then the "northern strategy" might come to fruition, and desegregation might threaten cities across the country outside of the South.[48]

On April 20, 1971, the Supreme Court issued its ruling in *Swann v. Charlotte-Mecklenburg County Board of Education*. The court upheld trial and appellate court rulings and argued that, in cases of plainly de jure segregation, a range of remedies, included busing students beyond the schools nearest to their homes, could be used to effect conversion to a unitary system. Busing had, after all, been a "normal and accepted tool of educational policy" for decades. If in the past it had been used to maintain segregation, then using it now to develop a unitary system was "favorably comparable" and, according to the Fourth Circuit appellate court, "reasonable." The court did note some limits as to "reasonableness," but it insisted that "administratively awkward, inconvenient and even bizarre" arrangements had become the price of eliminating dual school systems. Much of the nation beyond the South would be shielded from the ruling by the de jure distinction, but southern whites had seemingly lost one of their most valuable color-masked crutches—"neighborhood schools."[49]

In the companion opinion in *Davis v. Mobile*, the Supreme Court was compelled to partially reverse the trial and appellate courts. The Mobile school board would no longer be able treat downtown Mobile as a separate area for purposes of pupil assignment. The Fifth Circuit had already forced Judge Thomas to order the implementation of this principle as to the city's junior and senior high schools. But it had not included elementary schools, several of which remained all black or over 90 percent black. Enrollment figures for the previous fall had also revealed that pupil desegregation in the high schools and junior high schools was far below what the school board had projected. A majority of those students still attended all-black schools as well. Accordingly, the Supreme Court held that "neighborhood school zoning," was not "*per se* adequate to meet the remedial responsibility" of the school board. In order to "achieve the greatest possible degree of actual desegregation," Mobile officials would need to consider "all available techniques," including "the possible use of bus transportation and split zoning." Busing was coming to Alabama.[50]

John LeFlore celebrated the ruling, reminding Mobilians that, prior to the filing of the *Davis* case in 1962, "black high school children living in Hillsdale Heights were being transported 52 miles to St. Elmo when Shaw and Davidson were within three and four miles." At a meeting of the school board days later, LeFlore called for unity, for not just whites and blacks but also among blacks themselves. "Those who would keep us divided," he said, "whether they be segregationists or separatists, are rendering our country a serious disservice as they seek to perpetuate the unworkable social experiment of the last 352 years." Segregation could not "provide the answers to the problems in race relations that an accommodating political power structure has helped to create." Representatives of both STAND and CORE in attendance were unmoved. Meanwhile, the leader of the newly consolidated Unified Concerned Parents of Alabama took to the podium to warn the school board of the health hazards inherent in busing, insinuating that "unhealthy" and "unclean" black children would transmit various infectious diseases to white children.[51]

One month later, Richard Nixon came to Alabama, amid escalating tensions between him and George Wallace. The president first flew to Mobile, where he appeared at a ceremony at the state docks to dedicate the Tennessee-Tombigbee Waterway—a canal system that was to link the Tennessee River with Mobile Bay. Nixon began his short speech by thanking "President Wallace"—and here he paused wryly—"of the Tennessee-Tombigbee Development Association." This elicited a hearty laugh from the crowd and from the governor himself. Despite the levity, the White House was then investigating Wallace's brother Gerald for fraud, in the hopes that Wallace might be persuaded to run as a Democrat in the 1972 presidential election. Nixon continued to fear that a third-party Wallace candidacy would significantly damage his chance of reelection. After the brief appearance at the docks, the president flew to Birmingham, where he was poised to deliver a long policy briefing on desegregation before members of the Southern Press Association.[52]

In Birmingham, Nixon gave white Alabamians a fine dose of exactly what they wanted. He said that he had "nothing but utter contempt" for the "double hypocritical standards of those northerners who look at the South and say, 'Why don't those southerners do something about the race problem.'" And he noted that there were more black children in majority white schools in the South than there were anywhere else. Nixon then articulated one of the fundamental tenets of the politics of law and order. Progress had been achieved "because farsighted leaders in the South, black and white, some of whom I am sure did not agree with the opinions handed down by the Supreme Court—which were the law of the land—recognized as law-abiding citizens that they had the responsibility to meet that law of the land, and . . . dealt with the problem." *Swann* presented "some more problems," he admitted, "but I am confident that over a period of time those problems will also be handled in a peaceful and orderly way for the most part." It was the sort of message some white Alabamians had been articulating for years.[53]

Privately Nixon instructed his advisors to tell the leaders of HEW and the CRD to "keep their left-wingers in step with [his] express[ed] policy," which was "to do what the law requires and not one bit more." This application of the law-and-order line allowed the president to lament busing in the South as an unfortunate necessity, while at the same time ensuring that it did not become, on his watch, an even more lamentable necessity outside the South. For his part, Wallace was preparing to counter Nixon's southern strategy with his version of the northern strategy, which included casting busing as a "national matter" and predicting compulsory assignment orders and other federally mandated changes to the status quo for the entire country. Wallace also cast himself as a believer in law and order who was, at the same time, a defiant protector of states' rights and individual rights (to be understood as white rights).[54]

Meanwhile Wallace looked to shore up support at home by developing an anti-busing campaign that the press mordantly dubbed the "stand in the school bus door." The governor had ample help from supporters in the state legislature, as the "freedom of choice" law proposed by Mobile's state representative Monty Collins had come up for debate. The legislation would allow students—specifically white students at Vigor and Murphy High Schools—to transfer out of a given school if they had been "harassed, intimidated, or assaulted." Fred Gray called it an "unconstitutional . . . waste of time and money," doomed to invalidation. Gray and Tuskegee restaurateur Thomas Reed had recently become the first black representatives in the state legislature since Reconstruction. They attempted to mount a last-minute filibuster to block a vote on the bill at the end of the legislative session, but the House speaker refused to recognize Reed and called for a vote over his vehement protests. The bill passed handily with the support of Wallace, who called it one of the "finest ever passed."[55]

The NAACP went after the law immediately. State director K. L. Buford predicted that it would "encourage acts of harassment and intimidation to black students in previously all-white schools in order to force them to transfer back to segregated schools." Buford also wrote to Monty Collins and observed, "It is strange that none of the strong advocates of law and order choose to add the words, 'with justice for all.'" Collins brushed off the criticism and accused Buford of making "his living by trying to make racial turmoil where there [was] none." The feud continued publicly when Buford told a meeting of the Mobile NAACP, to great applause and laughter, "If Monty Collins is naïve enough to sincerely believe that there is no racial turmoil in Alabama," then the electorate had "done all the people of Alabama a great disservice by giving this man of limited knowledge and ability a seat in the Alabama legislature." An LDF challenge soon led to the invalidation of the law. But the politics of white rights had scored points for Collins as well as Wallace, who was not content to stop there.[56]

That summer, the *Swann* and *Davis* rulings resulted in motions for further relief in Alabama's other school cases, providing the governor with an opportunity to broaden his latest defiance. Responding to letters from white parents, Wallace in August 1971 issued executive orders directed at the Jefferson County and Limestone County boards of education. He ordered the Jefferson board to reassign one Pamela Davis, a white girl, to the school of her choice, allowing her to transfer from the formerly all-black school to which she had been assigned, which happened to be twenty miles from her home. The situation in Limestone County allowed Wallace to capitalize on black displeasure over school closures and to reinforce the fiction that his actions were no longer motivated by a desire to preserve white privilege. He ordered the Limestone school board to reopen all-black New Hope Junior High, which had been closed as part of the county's compulsory assignment plan. The governor even offered $30,000 toward the renovation of the school.[57]

Wallace was keen to paint Nixon into a corner. He dryly revealed his strategy to reporters, telling them, "You might say Governor Wallace is working closely with the President to help carry out his desire not to have massive busing." He added a jab about HEW's Leon Panetta and Robert Finch, whom Nixon had been compelled to remove, saying, "People find no credibility in officials pledging no busing and then appointing cabinet officers who openly advocate and push for busing." The governor also knew that his "stand in the school bus door" would invite motions against him and that this would put the Civil Rights Division in an awkward position. Wallace described the potential conundrum by posing a rhetorical question for the press: "Do you think the Justice Department is going to ask for a contempt citation when Nixon is against busing?"[58]

The CRD did not seek a contempt citation, but attorneys for the plaintiff parents in three cases did. Solomon Seay filed a motion in *Lee v. Macon*, but the three-judge court denied it, suggesting that an individual motion against the governor could instead be brought in the severed case against Limestone County. Such a motion was filed and landed before district judge Sam Pointer, a recent Nixon appointee. Rather than grant the motion, Pointer informed the Limestone school board members that if they reopened the closed school, per the governor's order, they could expect contempt citations, which would carry fines of $1,000 per day. The board promptly announced that the school would remain closed. U. W. Clemon brought a similar motion in the *Stout v. Jefferson* case. Pointer heard that plea too, dismissing the governor's executive order as an "expression of free speech" and issuing a similar warning to the Jefferson County school board. The following day the board announced that Pamela Davis's assignment had been a clerical error and that she was being reassigned to a predominantly white school closer to her home.[59]

Pointer thus allowed Nixon to avoid moving on Wallace, who resolved to continue his grandstanding. The nation's second-oldest black-governed municipality must have seemed like an impossibly unlikely location for the him to do so. But he descended upon all-black Hobson City nonetheless for a ceremonial signing of "anti-busing" orders. The residents of Hobson, a tiny satellite of the northeastern Alabama city of Oxford, had been running their own affairs since Reconstruction, with the exception that their all-black schools were administered by the all-white Calhoun County school board. By the time Calhoun was brought under the statewide *Lee v. Macon* order in 1967, Oxford's population of roughly six thousand was 95 percent white. In order to keep its schools all-white, the city and school board had arranged to have its few black students attend Hobson's schools. The application of *Green* in *Lee v. Macon* posed a grave threat to this arrangement. Calhoun County was forced to develop a new plan, prompting Oxford to follow the example set by suburban Birmingham municipalities and break away from the county system. This set up the legal and political battle that would bring Wallace to town in the fall of 1971.[60]

The newly created Oxford board of education had immediately sought control of Oxford High and Oxford Elementary, but Fred Gray and Sol Seay, along with the CRD, had filed motions to block that action. Calhoun County was under a terminal type order, and its case had been transferred from the three-judge *Lee v. Macon* court to the docket of district judge Walter McFadden, a Mississippi native whom Nixon had appointed to replace Hobart Grooms, who had himself taken senior status in 1969. McFadden insisted that Calhoun County and Oxford be treated as one school system for the purposes of desegregation. A panel of the Fifth Circuit appeals court partially affirmed this ruling and held that city systems could not "secede from the county where the effect—to say nothing of the purpose—of the secession [had] a substantial adverse effect on desegregation of the county school district." John Minor Wisdom wrote the opinion, adding, "If this were legally permissible, there could be incorporated towns for every white neighborhood in every city."[61]

Despite their agreement in principle, Wisdom's panel members rejected the desegregation plan that McFadden sanctioned. The Calhoun school board wanted to close Hobson's schools, assuming that whites would not accept assignments there. The plaintiffs had proposed a pairing plan instead. The county then offered a counterproposal that would token integrate Hobson's elementary school and transform its high school into another elementary school, all black. McFadden had approved this plan. The appellate panel cited *Swann* and held, "When historic residential segregation creates housing patterns that militate against desegregation based on zoning, alternative methods must be explored, including pairing of schools." Many Hobson residents wanted their schools to operate as they had in the past and thus rejected both plans. It was for this reason that the Hobson mayor had appealed to Wallace for help. When he arrived in August, the governor was met with a chorus of boos and even pointed heckling: "Get out of town, George, and take the Uncle Tom with you!" The mortified mayor insisted that the rabble had been inspired by outsiders, while Wallace awkwardly signed executive orders directing the county and its municipalities to ignore all orders of the federal courts.[62]

In other appearances that week, Wallace continued to dare Nixon and his attorney general, John Mitchell, to go after him in court. He couched all of his actions as "anti-busing," despite the fact that the situation in Hobson was almost certain to involve no lengthy or otherwise onerous transportation between noncontiguous zones. He criticized Mitchell for "failing to carry out the President's mandate against busing," and suggested, "The only way we're going to bring any solution to this problem is for people in these prestigious offices to come out strong and tell Nixon and the other bureaucrats exactly where they stand." Meanwhile, the bewildered Calhoun County school board appealed to Judge McFadden for instructions, while Judge Pointer again brushed aside the governor's latest executive orders as "legally meaningless." Wallace responded by petulantly telling the media that Pointer did not have "the sense to fry a chicken egg."[63]

Wallace soon turned his focus to legislation. His allies drafted a law that they felt the courts might find more difficult to invalidate than Monty Collins's recently doomed effort, seizing upon the concept of "reasonableness" in the

Swann opinion. The new law would allow parents and students to choose an alternative school in cases where the "time or distance" of their transportation to their assigned school would be "so great" as to "risk the health and safety of the child or significantly impinge upon the educational process," and it would compel local officials to honor those choices. Wallace lauded the bill's passage and vowed to "defer and get out" of the presidential race if Nixon would "stop busing, go back to freedom of choice, and restore neighborhood schools." U. W. Clemon filed a motion in *Jefferson* challenging the new statute. Judge Pointer described it as "a freedom of choice option dressed in slightly different clothing" and declared it invalid without even bothering to ask for the convening of the customary three-judge court. Alabama's lawmakers would have to try something else.[64]

"Preserving the Status Quo of Alabama's Past"

In July 1971, the Mobile board of education announced its "Comprehensive Plan for a Unitary School System," to be implemented that fall per the court's mandate in *Davis*. It caused outrage among whites and blacks. Approximately one thousand white elementary students would be bused east, across I-65, to formerly all-black elementary schools, while a larger number of black elementary students would be bused west into predominantly white schools. White enrollment in formerly all-black schools would be increased annually until it "stabilized." The plan established noncontiguous zones for nineteen elementary schools, five middle schools, and four high schools and called for the busing of roughly nine thousand students on top of the fifty-seven hundred that had been bused into split zones the preceding year. Two black schools would be closed, five would remain all black, five more would be over 90 percent black, and another five would remain over 75 percent black. As experience had shown, these projections were probably just best-case scenarios for the plaintiffs. They had compromised a great deal.[65]

The local attorney representing the LDF, A. J. Cooper, agreed not to challenge the plan or its implementation for three years. Cooper was harshly criticized for this, but he argued that challenging the plan would only mean more years in Daniel Thomas's court of delay, more appeals to the Fifth Circuit, and more time and money wasted. The school board was similarly slammed by whites. William Westbrook of STAND again called for the resignation of the board members. The local Concerned Parents outfit characterized the plan as "reckless" and created for "the sole purpose of attaining a social goal desired only for the benefit of a minority people." There was so much concern for black children, they lamented, but what about white kids who were being "bused, cussed, beaten, shook-down, and utterly deprived of a quality education." It had become "a misfortune to be fortunate," they surmised.⁶⁶

The most passionate condemnation of the new plan came from an organization calling itself the Southerners. The group had originally organized in the aftermath of *Brown* but had fizzled out. It was resurrected in 1970 by then-former Wallace advisor Ace Carter. Within a year, the Southerners could boast nine "divisions" and nearly ten thousand members across Alabama and Mississippi. In their own words, they were a "deliberate group of Anglo Saxon white men," who sought "to promote [their] racial heritage and culture, the knowledge of [their] civilization and the perpetuation of the white race." Mobile's division spent 1971 distributing leaflets calling on the southern white man to face down his "fear and laziness" and meet his "obligation" to "white children and womenfolk." A "war" had been declared, they asserted, "upon an entire generation of little white children, who [were] fighting for their lives, their right to decency, and their heritage of Christian civilization," while the newspapers were "attempting to hide the murder and death of an entire generation of Southern white children."⁶⁷

A telephone number at the bottom of the Southerners' flyers connected callers with a recorded message replete with blatant racism, ludicrous and baseless rumors, fear mongering, and allusions to the Lost Cause. It began, "Today in the so-called public school system of Mobile, Alabama, little white girls are being savagely attacked by gangs of Negroes, [and] white boys are being intimidated, threatened, and severely beaten by roving gangs of blacks." Making matters worse, white children were "having their minds destroyed by the Communistic teachings of a Karl Marx or a Martin Luther King," while "limp-wristed, weak kneed school officials [looked] the other way." The message reminded the caller that, during Reconstruction, the South had been "occupied by nigger troops, governed by northern trash, and prayed for by blue-nosed hypocrites." The voice asked, "Sounds a lot like today doesn't it?" If the white men of Mobile did not do something, the result would be children "with banana-colored skin, wool for hair, and the light blown out in their brains."⁶⁸

The FBI was investigating the Southerners and had uncovered the fact that its "brothers" were preparing for an eventual race war by hoarding weapons and drilling in the Talladega National Forest. The group was also taking more practical and immediate steps. When three thousand members and supporters gathered at the Mobile stockyards for a rally that summer, Ace Carter promised them an escape from the public schools. After railing against federal judges, "that H.E.W. man," and "the Negroid," Carter described his intention to build a church, a "commissary," and a school right there at the stockyards. The profits from the commissary—essentially a segregated grocery store—would provide tuition for white children to attend the Southerners' school, at least "until one single nigger [was] admitted."⁶⁹

Carter's plan to build a segregationist commune in Mobile was doomed in a number of ways. But the most important flaw in his plan, and in his philosophy, was that he and his fellow Southerners had not continued to adapt along with the law-and-order creed. By 1971 the "limp-wristed" politicians that Carter lambasted—including Wallace—had realized that to preserve white privilege and to limit integration, some concessions were necessary beyond simply eschewing violence. Carter and company could not even accept freedom of choice, which for most law-and-order segregationists was the most desirable solution at that point. Strategic segregationists adapted. Implacable, dogmatic ones like Ace Carter gave up or self-destructed.⁷⁰

Carter managed to do both. When the Southerners fell apart in 1973, he disappeared, then resurfaced in Texas under the assumed name Bedford Forrest Carter (a nod to famed Klansman Nathan Bedford Forrest). He grew a mustache, claimed to be part Cherokee, and began a career as a writer. His supposedly autobiographical *Education of Little Tree* would become a *New York Times* best-selling children's book, and his novels *Gone to Texas* and *The Vengeance Trial of Josey Wales* were adapted for the screen as Clint Eastwood's *The Outlaw Josey Wales*. Alabama journalist Wayne Greenhaw wrote a piece in the *New York Times* arguing that Forrest was probably Asa, which others corroborated after seeing Carter on the *Today Show* with Barbara Walters. Carter maintained that Asa was his "no good" brother. Most people believed that lie until long after his death in 1979, when he choked on his own vomit following a drunken feud with one of his sons.⁷¹

Carter's ignominious end mirrored that of his kind of defiance. In the summer of 1971, most segregationists had come to terms with some kind of law-and-order ethos. This included the thousands who continued to escape to the suburbs. At the same time the Southerners were hearing Carter's plan to build a commune, a Fifth Circuit panel was considering the latest appeal in *Stout v. Jefferson County*. Suburban whites were anxious to see what impact the *Swann* decision would have on their newly independent municipal school systems, particularly given the Fifth Circuit's decision in the Calhoun County case just one week prior. Eight cities had seceded from the Jefferson County system by that time. Four of them (Mountain Brook, Tarrant, Bessemer, and Fairfield) had separated prior to the filing of *Jefferson* in 1965, and four (Pleasant Grove, Midfield, Vestavia Hills, and Homewood) had separated since. Judge Lynne had required that each in the latter group accept a token number of black students. But that summer a Fifth Circuit panel reversed that ruling. Writing for the court, Judge Wisdom echoed the Calhoun County opinion. "Where the formulation of splinter school districts . . . have the effect of thwarting the implementation of a unitary school system," he wrote, "the district court may not, consistent with the teachings of *Swann* . . . recognize their creation."⁷²

Jefferson was again remanded to the trial court, where it landed before judge Sam Pointer, whose mandate was to determine which systems were "thwarting implementation." Pointer articulated what would be, in effect, a class-based standard for scrutiny. It was "pretty clear," Pointer observed, that the "demography, the location of people and their colors," was "different" in the southern suburbs than it was in what he called the "midwest"—that is, the western suburbs. The southern region was overwhelmingly white (and affluent). The "midwest" was somewhat more diverse (and working class). "It very well may be," Pointer argued, "that more recognition in that sense of the viability of Homewood and Vestavia can be given than may be given to Midfield and Pleasant Grove, simply because of the reality of the situation of where the people live." According to Pointer, then, Pleasant Grove and Midfield were thwarting Jefferson County's progress toward a unitary system, while Vestavia Hills and Homewood were not. Wealthy whites who had fled over the mountain would be spared anything beyond tokenism.⁷³

Pointer ordered Pleasant Grove to accept approximately four hundred black students from the areas that it had drawn out of its municipal borders and to provide them with transportation. This prompted a judicial back-and-forth that would ultimately result in the city losing control of its schools. The Pleasant Grove school board argued that it could not transport the black students, as it had no buses. Pointer ordered the board to purchase three busses from Jefferson County's fleet, in the same way it had purchased facilities and other equipment, but the board argued that it could not afford to do so and that, in any case, the buses were over the maximum state-sanctioned age of ten years old. Pointer responded to the intransigence by ordering the Jefferson County school board to assume operation of Pleasant Grove's schools in late September. The city's superintendent lamented that the "rights of the citizens of Pleasant Grove [had] been trampled upon and their flourishing school system stripped from them because they would not buy old surplus busses and initiate a student transportation plan."⁷⁴

The Pleasant Grove board appealed the decision, ensuring yet another hearing before the Fifth Circuit. The appellate court was compelled to wait, however, as the Supreme Court was already considering two cases involving splinter systems. The Fourth Circuit appellate court had sanctioned the independence of splinter systems in Virginia and North Carolina in *Wright v. City Council of the City of Emporia* and *U.S. v. Scotland Neck City Board of Education*. The Supreme Court reversed those decisions and approvingly cited the Fifth Circuit's recent rulings in *Calhoun County* and *Jefferson*. With the Supreme Court's vindication, the Fifth Circuit upheld Pointer's order directing the takeover of Pleasant Grove's schools. The appellate panel insisted that "local control" would not be removed "indefinitely" and that the splinter systems would not be "vassals of the county board" forever. They simply had to demonstrate that their "commitment to desegregation [would] not falter." The over-the-mountain systems had no such commitments.[75]

With Jefferson County's most affluent and influential constituents spared the brunt of compulsory assignment, and with Mobile having secured significant concessions from the plaintiffs in *Davis*, George Wallace and his cronies in the legislature turned their attention to rural Alabama. That fall there was a concerted push to develop long-term legislative solutions to the integration problem—ones that would preserve the foundations of white privilege and could withstand a legal test. Some legislators suggested rewriting the state's property tax code. The idea was not new. The seed had been planted when black elected officials attempted to raise taxes prior to the withdrawal of Union troops toward the end of Reconstruction. Both the "Redeemer" constitution that followed the Democrats' takeover in the 1870s and the even more overtly white supremacist constitution of 1901 included provisions that limited property assessment and taxation. White landowners wanted to ensure that their tax dollars would never be used for black advancement, especially education. *Brown* had added a renewed sense of urgency. John Patterson couched his support for school closure in terms of shielding white tax dollars, and Wallace had done the same in supporting tuition grant programs.[76]

Late that fall, the same day that he proposed new anti-busing legislation, Wallace threw his support behind a new property tax bill. It was no accident of timing. Wallace knew that most whites were acutely aware of a potential doomsday scenario portended by four converging federal court mandates. White flight due to compulsory assignment was rapidly resulting in all-black or nearly all-black public school systems in the Black Belt. Federal enforcement of the Voting Rights Act was simultaneously beginning to open the polls to black voting, leading to the election of black officials in those same districts. This was particularly troubling in light of a 1964 ruling of the Supreme Court in the case of *Reynolds v. Sims*. Alabama was ordered to reapportion its state legislative districts, because growing urban districts had been grossly underrepresented for decades. Given white flight from those urban areas, the urban-suburban racial polarization it was creating, and the increasingly robust organizational activity of urban blacks, this looked to contribute to a sharp increase in the number of black elected officials in the state legislature at some point in the near future.[77]

Finally, there was *Weissinger v. Boswell*. A federal trial court had insisted that Alabama develop a statewide ad valorem property tax assessment system that was fair and uniform. State code allowed assessment rates to vary widely. In particular, public utilities land—land owned by companies in the railroad, telephone, oil and gas, water, and power businesses—had been subject to wide disparities between state and local assessment. The three-judge court hearing *Weissinger* invalidated a state statute that allowed for the discrepancies, though it stopped short of striking a statutory system of property classification that allowed certain kinds of property to be assessed differently. The court targeted only wide disparities *within* given classes of property. Utilities property could still constitute a distinct class of property and be assessed at a certain rate, provided that state and local officials adhered to that rate uniformly. The court gave the state eight years to make a fair and full reassessment of property statewide. Alongside legislative reapportionment, black voting, and white flight, that reassessment would constitute a critical threat to white money.[78]

The bill proposed in late 1971 to meet the threat was the brainchild of the chairman of the state senate's Finance and Taxation Committee—Citizens' Council pioneer Walter Givhan, arguably the most fervent and committed segregationist in state history. Givhan and others were especially keen to protect rural farm and timber land. They proposed a constitutional amendment that would enshrine the property classification system, breaking property down into three categories, with each assigned a different assessment rate: utilities property would be assessed at 30 percent of its fair market value; commercial property at 25 percent; and residential, farm, and timber land at 15 percent. There was a "local option" in the bill, which allowed counties and municipalities to increase tax millage rates, but these were subject to local referenda and the approval of the state legislature. The coup de grâce of the bill was a cap, or "lid," on total ad valorem tax revenue that could be collected from a given piece of property. Neither the state nor any local authority could get more than 1.5 percent out of any parcel of land.[79]

The bill passed the legislature easily. That spring, while legislators campaigned for the amendment's approval by way of statewide referendum, Wallace returned to the national campaign trail in support of another bid for the presidency. When he took the podium at a rally outside a shopping mall in suburban Baltimore on June 8, 1972, he assailed "briefcase-carrying bureaucrats" and the "asinine busing decisions" being handed down by federal courts. He called Nixon a hypocrite who would allow the federal government to usurp local control, destroy neighborhood schools, and force-feed the entire country a diet of compulsory assignment. Working-class whites all over the country had begun to see the fiery Alabamian as someone who would fight to keep their hard-earned tax dollars from funding an increasingly burdensome "welfare state." Wallace looked to be the perfect candidate to stand up for white rights. He had already won three Democratic primaries and was poised to win in Maryland as well.[80]

A twenty-one-year-old bus boy from Wisconsin named Arthur Bremer was in the crowd that day. He had been following Wallace's campaign for some time, although he was not so much interested in the politics of white rights, busing, or the threat of federal government overreach. Bremer wanted fame, and he had decided that killing someone important was the way that he would get it. He had at one point strongly considered killing Nixon. Instead it was Wallace he stalked to the rally in Laurel, Maryland, where the governor began lamenting the demise of the rights to freedom of association and freedom of choice. After his short speech, Wallace stepped down to shake hands with well-wishers. Bremer pushed his way toward the front. When he reached point-blank range and Wallace extended his hand, Bremer fired four times. Wallace fell, gravely wounded, along with an Alabama state trooper and a Secret Service agent. That night, as doctors determined that he was paralyzed from the waist down, George Wallace carried Maryland and Michigan. A few weeks later, Alabama voters approved Amendment 325, the first Lid Bill.[81]

As Wallace recovered from the assassination attempt, the twenty-year development of increasingly stringent school desegregation requirements began to grind to a halt. The Supreme Court, newly packed with Nixon appointees, moved to limit the impact of *Swann*. In *San Antonio Independent School District v. Rodriguez*, the plaintiffs argued that poor children in majority-minority suburban school districts constituted a protected class and that strict scrutiny of the Texas school financing system—dependent, as elsewhere, on local taxation—would reveal that it violated the equal protection clause of the Fourteenth Amendment. The trial court agreed and ordered the development of a metropolitan revenue sharing plan. In March 1973, the Supreme Court invalidated that plan, insisting that the Constitution did not "require absolute equality or precisely equal advantages" and that equal educational opportunity was not a "fundamental interest" that would require the strict scrutiny of the courts.[82]

One month later, the Supreme Court heard arguments in *Bradley v. Richmond*. The trial court in the case had ordered the schools of Richmond, Virginia, which were 70 percent black, to merge with the suburban county systems of Chesterfield and Henrico, which were 91 percent white. Blacks were to be bused out of the city to the suburbs and whites bused from the suburbs into the city. But the Fourth Circuit Court of Appeals reversed the decision, maintaining that it could not "compel one of the States of the Union to restructure its internal government for the purpose of achieving racial balance" unless it found evidence of "invidious discrimination in the establishment or maintenance of local government units." The suburban county systems had been established one hundred years earlier, so the appellate court saw no such evidence. The Supreme Court affirmed the appellate panel's decision, a signal of the majority's refusal to sanction compulsory assignment in cases of supposedly de facto segregation.[83]

By that time the NAACP had broadened its implementation efforts beyond the South and had challenged segregation in Detroit. Education in Michigan was not plainly de jure segregated, but the plaintiffs in *Milliken v. Bradley* argued that Detroit and its suburban communities had engaged in or fostered practices, including housing discrimination, that had contributed to the establishment of metropolitan apartheid. The LDF, citing *Lee v. Macon*, convinced the court to order the state to formulate a metropolitan busing plan that would integrate Detroit's black students with suburban whites. The Supreme Court again reversed. Chief Justice Warren Burger wrote for the 5–4 majority, arguing that "the notion that school district lines may be casually ignored or treated as a mere administrative convenience" was "contrary to the history of public education" in the United States. The plaintiffs had failed to demonstrate discrimination on the part of Detroit's suburban school systems, so the busing plan was "wholly impermissible." Dissenting justice Thurgood Marshall channeled the growing frustration of the advocates of desegregation litigation, calling *Milliken* a "solemn mockery" of *Brown* and calling *Rodriguez* a "sham."[84]

Segregationists in Alabama could breathe a sigh of relief. Jefferson County's splinter systems were assured that Judge Pointer's recent order would stand. Along with *Bradley v. Richmond*, *Milliken* and *Rodriguez* ensured that no desegregation order would ever see black students bused out of Birmingham, nor any white tax money bused in. By the fall of 1973, the Birmingham public school system had become 60 percent black, 40 percent white. Forty schools were nearly all black, twenty were nearly all white, and around thirty were substantially integrated. The city itself had also been spared a busing plan, largely because it had never used buses in the past. This had seemed to assuage some whites, and nonconformity and direct action protests by white parents and students had largely disappeared. U. W. Clemon observed that the real reason for relative calm, however, was that the most recalcitrant whites had "either moved out or put their children in private schools." City school superintendent Henry Sparks agreed, saying, "We've done what the courts have said, but I think they realize that a man still has a freedom of choice about where he will live."[85]

Integration in the Jefferson County system was floundering too. If an 80 percent majority of either race represented a segregated school, then fifty-nine of Jefferson's seventy-six schools had not been integrated. Twenty-three of those were between 99.9 and 100 percent one race. The numbers were somewhat better in the combined city-county systems of Montgomery and Mobile, where twenty-four out of fifty schools and twenty-one out of eighty-one, respectively, would fail to meet the standard of 20 percent black. Private schools and suburbs looked to siphon off more whites in short order, however. Whites began moving east, across Mobile Bay, to the growing cities of Daphne, Fairhope, and Spanish Fort in Baldwin County. And they moved from Montgomery north—to Prattville in neighboring Autauga County and Millbrook in Elmore County. Each of those destination counties was operating under a court-ordered desegregation plan, but none was faced with the prospect of whites in majority-black schools. Nor was there a realistic chance that those systems would become majority black, like those in the cities from which whites were fleeing. White flight's motivating factors in those cities became self-fulfilling prophecies, like a stock market crash or a bank run. Whites feared a majority-black system and fled, thereby creating a majority-black system.[86]

Blacks were ostensibly free to flee as well. But federal, state, and local policies, combined with bare racism, especially in the form of housing discrimination, kept most blacks confined to increasingly poverty-ridden cities. Those same policies allowed middle-class whites to escape much more freely and to take crucial tax dollars along with them. Federally funded interstate highways—I-65 in Birmingham and Montgomery, I-85 in Montgomery, and I-10 in Mobile—along with federally guaranteed low-interest mortgages, provided the escape route for whites wealthy enough to own a car. At the same time, housing projects concentrated in segregated, poor communities acted like the ball and chain for blacks in neighborhoods that were often bisected and effectively destroyed by the very same interstate highways that whites were using to get out.[87]

The politics of white rights allowed those who benefited from all of this to see it as the natural consequence of their rise within the middle class. They had begrudgingly and belatedly accepted freedom of choice tokenism and no longer openly lamented the fall of Jim Crow. As they saw it, they were not racists. They had black friends and colleagues. Their children attended school with a few black students. They did not discriminate. So they maintained that their trek to the suburbs was not made possible by white privilege. It was the result of their hard work and the exercise of their right to distance themselves from the problems inherent in the ghettoization of poor blacks, a process for which they bore no individual responsibility.

Wallace and Brewer had nurtured this law-and-order narrative since the turn toward compulsory assignment. And Wallace would soon look to capitalize on the concomitant politics. The assassination attempt, and the realization that he would never walk again, had sapped him of the strength to carry on in the 1972 presidential race, and his inability, or perhaps unwillingness, to carry out the normal duties of a governor had led some to question his fitness for office. As he made almost no preparation for the 1973 regular session of the legislature, he was later blamed for its accomplishing very little. By that time, Wallace had resolved to return to his only real passion—electioneering. He worked to secure an amendment to the state constitution that would allow him to become the first governor of Alabama to serve consecutive terms if elected again in 1974. A significant component of his return to grace would be his recommitment to shoring up white rights and white privilege in the Black Belt.[88]

Despite the ratification of the original Lid Bill amendment, white landowners still had concerns. Wallace aimed to address them, ideally before the eight-year window afforded by *Weissinger* closed and the state had to submit its statewide reassessment of property. Whites feared that black elected officials might one day take advantage of the "local option" in the Lid Bill. If black officials quickly gained control of local governments, they might partner with the state's urban bloc and push through approval of millage rate increases that could offset the ridiculously low assessment rates. Even with the absolute lid on tax revenue in place, the implication was clear—a huge increase in white money for all-black schools. Sam Engelhardt had once asked rhetorically, "If you had a nigger tax assessor, what would he do to you?" That fear, decades later, had finally become very real. The *Mobile Press-Register* more tactfully observed that white legislators were "fearful that the black political leaders, who also enjoy voting majorities, will exercise local options and set property taxes at the highest rates possible in order to raise additional funds for their governmental operations." These taxes would be paid, the *Press-Register* continued, by "white owners of large farms and corporate interests with large timberland holdings."[89]

Black Belt legislators and powerful lobbying groups—namely the Alabama Farm Bureau (later the Alabama Farmers' Federation, or ALFA), the Alabama Forestry Association, and the Associated Industries of Alabama—began to push for a new Lid Bill, one that would go even further in protecting white property from black taxation. When Wallace went before the legislature to oppose tax increases for education at the state level, he railed against Frank Johnson and *Weissinger*, but beyond that he tread carefully. He told legislators, "The people of Alabama are simply turned off on education and some educators because of what the Federal Courts and HEW have done to their children from Huntsville to Mobile. Every one of you know I am telling you the truth when I tell you that." He insisted that a "breakthrough in education" could come "under existing revenues." It was a message with a foundation in Redemption itself. Everyone knew just exactly what the governor meant.[90]

As soon as he was reelected in 1974, Wallace started building support for the new Lid Bill. Like its predecessor, it was the legislative offspring of the politics of white rights and would therefore function as a legally sanctioned form of economic reprisal and a safeguard for continuing white privilege. No mention would be made of race, of course. Lawmakers finally knew better than to open their efforts to legal challenges by revealing their goals too explicitly. If Alabama's white voters did not understand the intent, Wallace sought to underscore the message, telling Black Belt parents, "I think it's a horrible thing that you people have to pay taxes to support *public schools*. Then you have to dig in again to pay for *quality education* for your children in a *private school*." He assured them that the newly proposed Lid Bill would protect their money in several ways.[91]

First, it retained the classification system that allowed farmland and timberland to be assessed at a lower rate than any other form of property, and it lowered that rate from 15 to 10 percent. It also gave landowners the option to have their land assessed based on its "current use" value, as opposed to its fair market value. This meant that farmland and timberland could be assessed based on the revenue it generated, not on what its value might be, given development or optimal use—in other words, what a potential buyer would be willing to pay for the land. There would even be limitations on calculating current use value. The product actually being grown on farmland, for example, could not be considered, nor could the proximity of timberland to transportation facilities, factors that would almost certainly increase the property's fair market value. ALFA and other special interest groups effectively determined the per-acreage current use values they thought were acceptable, then tailored a formula, using rough categories of soil quality and a handful of other factors, to arrive at those figures. Large landholders would end up paying a tiny fraction of what average homeowners would pay on their property.[92]

The new bill also lowered the existing "lid" on total tax revenue, state or local, that could be generated from any piece of property. The cap on farmland and timberland revenue was lowered from 1.5 percent to 1 percent of fair market value or 1 percent of current use value. And property owners would almost always choose to have their property assessed based on its current use value. Tax assessors did have some discretion in granting current use status, but they would face intense pressure and intimidation from the lobbies and their political allies. And if black elected officials wanted to raise millage rates, the tax dollars they could extract from landowners were still limited to 1 percent of the supposed value of the land. The potential effects were staggering. Timberland alone constituted around 70 percent of land in the state. Almost all of it was white owned, and much of it was simply reserved for recreational hunting. Its current use value would be substantially lower than its fair market value, and it would be assessed at 10 percent of that already low current-use value. The new bill would ensure that tax revenues collected from such land would remain miniscule and account for only a tiny fraction of all property tax revenue generated across the state, regardless of the millage rates, for decades to come.[93]

Despite the measure's benefits afforded to wealthy landowners, many of them corporations, and lack of tangible benefit for the average white homeowner, state voters overwhelmingly approved Amendment 373 near the end of Wallace's term on November 7, 1978. Massive resistance had undergone a superficial transformation in twenty years of fighting activist-litigants. Segregationists had been forced to concede token desegregation as the "law of the land." They had been forced to abandon violent resistance and certain forms of economic reprisal. But they never capitulated. Rather than repudiate white privilege, they committed themselves to a defense of white rights. Two decades of combating school desegregation litigation had trained them to craft a legally sound defense of these rights using color-masked language. The Lid Bills were born of this metamorphosis—from traditional massive resistance to a commitment to law and order and the defense of white rights. More than anything else, the second Lid Bill became what one legal scholar called "the instrument preserving the status quo of Alabama's past."[94]

EPILOGUE

"If Ever Is Going to Happen," 1973–2017

In the 2010s—forty years after *Swann*, fifty years after *Lee v. Macon*, and sixty years after *Brown*—the goal of equal educational opportunity remained elusive. School desegregation litigation dragged on in courts in Alabama and across the country. An analysis of data compiled and published by the nonprofit news organization ProPublica in 2014 indicated that 46 school systems in Alabama and 340 nationwide had failed to achieve "unitary status" and remained under court orders. Thousands of systems across the United States had seen their cases closed in the 1990s and 2000s, but, as scholars at Stanford University found in a 2012 study, the effects of court-ordered desegregation "fade[d] over time in the absence of continued court oversight." As school systems were released from court orders, many quickly resegregated.[1]

By 2014, 53 percent of black students in districts relieved of court scrutiny attended schools with minority populations of over 90 percent. Twelve percent attended schools that were 99 percent nonwhite, many of them in the Northeast and Midwest. Suburbs, in general, had become increasingly diverse, but in many metropolitan areas this meant all-black suburban municipalities that had once been exclusively white, suburbs that were majority Asian or Latino, and far-flung exurbs filled with wealthier whites. In a few urban districts, school boards and community leaders had engaged in vigorous efforts to mitigate racial isolation, while in others the opposite was true. Proponents of integration, in any case, had been dealt a blow in 2007, when the Supreme Court, in *Parents Involved in Community Schools v. Seattle School District No. 1*, held that race could not be the sole determining factor in student placement if the goal was to achieve "racial balance" in schools.[2]

Federal enforcement of desegregation had not changed much since the 1970s. The Ford administration condemned busing and refused to send federal troops to Boston and Louisville when whites reacted violently to compulsory assignment orders. The Carter administration also opposed busing, though it ratcheted up enforcement of civil rights law and sent the IRS after the segregation academies. The Supreme Court, in *Runyon v. McCrary* in 1976, held that private schools could not legally deny applications on account of race. The Carter IRS then informed private schools that had been established soon after a desegregation order, and that enrolled an "insignificant number of minority students," that they would have to demonstrate affirmative efforts to recruit minority students in order to maintain tax-exempt status.[3]

The impact of the *Runyon* decision was blunted, however. Many segregation academies proved willing to accept a token number of black students in order to avoid trouble. Some in Alabama were actually forced to consider it in order to boost revenue. A Lowndes Academy teacher explained her school's rationale: "While they don't want a preponderance of blacks at Lowndes Academy, they will accept a black." A widespread push for black admission to the academies never came, though. The *Montgomery Advertiser* presciently observed that "the legal scenario for making the [*Runyon*] ruling effective nationwide would probably be a repeat of public school desegregation efforts of the past 20 years—and might take as long." Regardless, the more robust efforts in civil rights enforcement undertaken by Carter were doomed to immediate reversal by the Reagan administration.[4]

Ronald Reagan castigated compulsory assignment, instead trumpeting "voluntary integration" via magnet school programs. In addition to rolling back civil rights enforcement, his administration diverted federal funds intended for desegregation programs. And when litigation aimed at removing tax-exempt status for segregated sectarian schools reached the Supreme Court, the Reagan Justice Department argued that such action would infringe upon the First Amendment rights of those schools. Reagan himself, in his efforts to court the religious right, argued that his predecessor had a "vendetta" against Christian schools. In *Bob Jones University v. United States*, and in the reopened *Green v. Kennedy* case, the Supreme Court ruled against the administration and held that the IRS had the statutory authority and duty to hold those schools accountable for discrimination. It subsequently sided with the administration, however, when it denied certiorari in the case of *Riddick v. School Board of the City of Norfolk*. This allowed the Norfolk school board to dismantle its desegregation plan upon achieving unitary status, a watershed moment in the era of resegregation.[5]

George H. W. Bush maintained the Reagan approach. His Justice Department supported diminished standards for lifting court orders in *Oklahoma City v. Dowell*, in which the Supreme Court affirmed the principle it had implicitly approved in *Riddick*. And in *Freeman v. Pitts*, the Supreme Court held that trial courts could withdraw supervision in areas where school systems had met the requirements set out in *Green*, even if they had not achieved unitary status. Bill Clinton increased investigations of civil rights complaints and targeted overrepresentation of minority students in special education classes and their underrepresentation in "gifted" classes. The Clinton Justice Department also opposed the removal of court oversight in the case of *Missouri v. Jenkins*, wherein the Supreme Court held that judicially mandated funding increases for magnet programs went beyond the court's remedial authority. Clinton ultimately concluded that desegregation was a matter best left to the states, though, and many school systems obtained unitary status under lowered standards, even where courts acknowledged that resegregation would likely occur.[6]

George W. Bush made a commitment to increased federal funding for education via a bipartisan renewal of the Elementary and Secondary Education Act dubbed No Child Left Behind (NCLB). In crafting the legislation, lawmakers ignored segregation and referred only to "failing schools" and "high-poverty schools." They tethered access to federal funding to "adequate yearly progress" in students' standardized test scores in reading and math. If schools continued to "fail," parents could enroll their students in more "successful" ones, and states could place increasingly stringent sanctions on the "failing" ones, from mandatory tutoring to school takeover. By forcing states to institute some measure of accountability, including tracking test scores by race, the new law increased awareness of achievement gaps, which allowed some states to focus on assisting minority students. The prospect of falling into the "failing" category, however, was not a catalyst to success, nor were the required reforms. Myriad cheating scandals became the public face of the legislation, and more schools began to "fail."[7]

As a 2014 deadline approached for students to achieve proficiency in reading and math, the Obama administration began issuing waivers to the states, staying the deadline and relieving them of some requirements but then imposing new ones, like adopting the set of educational standards known as Common Core. In 2015, after eight years of partisan rancor, Congress replaced No Child Left Behind with Every Child Succeeds. The new law maintained federal requirements for annual testing and the reporting of scores. But it eliminated the federal mandates imposed through the waiver program, and it left to the states the tasks of setting academic standards and determining how to deal with underperforming schools. In Alabama this ensured that segregation would not be among the concerns addressed by the state legislature. Instead lawmakers would use the opportunity to further implement a color-masked state law that they had begun rolling out a couple of years before.[8]

By 2013 Alabama, like most of the South, had become solidly Republican. The Democratic Party had weathered a wave of defections in the 1960s and 1970s, when Kennedy's and Johnson's support for civil rights legislation and welfare state programs cost the party southern white votes in presidential elections. The Democrats held on to state-level offices until the 1990s, when the growth of middle-class suburbs, the politicization of the religious Right, and the increasing association of the state Democratic Party with black voters began to drive remaining whites out. Redistricting schemes, designed to ensure black representation commensurate with—and thus not exceeding—the state's black population, then reduced black support for Democratic candidates in districts that became overwhelmingly white and quickly drifted toward the Republicans.[9]

George Wallace governed the state off and on into the late 1980s as a Democrat. He was succeeded by a series of inept governors, Democratic and Republican, plagued by ethics scandals. Guy Hunt won for the GOP in 1986 and 1990 but resigned under indictment in 1993. Big Jim Folsom's son, Jim Folsom Jr., served out his term. Folsom was succeeded by Republican Fob James, who had previously served a gubernatorial term as a Democrat. That year, as Democrats lost control of the U.S. House of Representatives for the first time in forty years, twenty-three other Alabama elected officials defected to the Republicans, including then-junior U.S. senator Richard Shelby. Thirty more had switched sides by 1998, by which time the GOP was in the process of taking over local courthouses and, most importantly, the state legislature.[10]

It was thus Republican state legislators who, in 2013, engineered the passage of what they called the Alabama Accountability Act (AAA). Like NCLB, it purported to hold "failing schools" "accountable" for their failure. Any school that found itself in the bottom 10 percent of schools in the state, or which had earned consecutive Ds or Fs on state report cards, was added to the list of schools already deemed "failing" by the U.S. Department of Education. The legislation granted $3,500 income tax credits—funded via the tax-based Education Trust Fund—to families moving their children from a failing school to a better-performing public school or a participating private school. Students from poorer families that did not make enough to qualify for the income tax credit could apply for scholarships funded by private donors, who also received hefty tax credits for contributing to a handful of private scholarship funds.[11]

The speaker of the state house of representatives, Mike Hubbard, argued that the bill would "provide some competition for these failing schools." Hubbard, a businessman who would soon be convicted of numerous felony ethics violations and be removed from office in disgrace, explained, "In the business world if you are not doing a good job, and someone comes in and does a better job, you either get better or you go out of business." Republican governor Robert Bentley, who would himself resign amid a sex and ethics scandal, made no mention of race in trumpeting the new law as "historic education reform" that would "benefit students and families across Alabama regardless of their income and regardless of where they live." He added, "I'm so proud we have done this for the children of this state and especially the children who are in failing school systems and had no way out. Now, they have a way out."[12]

The legislation was originally introduced as an eight-page "Local Control School Flexibility" bill designed to allow public schools to seek waivers freeing them from certain state policies. It was sent to a Republican-controlled conference committee, which then reported a substantially altered twenty-seven-page version, prepared in advance by Republicans, that included the "failing schools" designation and the tax credit and scholarship provisions. The state senate approved the bill amid shouting, cursing, and accusations of blatant deception from enraged Democrats. The longtime leader of the Alabama Education Association (AEA), Paul Hubbert, called the move "totally unacceptable," and Democratic legislators variously described it as "sleazy," a "bait and switch," and "the worst thing that has ever hit public education." Birmingham representative Mary Moore announced, "Welcome to the new Confederacy, where a bunch of white men are now going to take over black schools."[13]

Republican legislators subsequently secured passage of an amendment to the act that made the donor-funded scholarship money available to students in *non*-failing school zones. Weeks later, the first list of failing schools was announced. Of the seventy-seven schools listed, thirty-two were in Black Belt systems, and forty-one were in the urban systems of the state's four largest metropolitan areas. Nearly all of them were predominantly black or all black. State education superintendent Tommy Bice, an opponent of the bill, acknowledged, "Almost all of the schools on the list are Title I schools that have high numbers of free and reduced lunch [students] and are typically in school systems that have little local funding." The law would theoretically allow any student to transfer out of those schools and either get a tax credit or a scholarship. For many poor black families, though, these options were useless. Either they could not afford to pay private school tuition up front, or they could not afford to arrange for out-of-district transportation. They could apply for scholarships, but lack of transportation, lack of nearby participating private schools, and admission were still roadblocks.[14]

Since state funding for schools was based on enrollment, critics of the act argued that it would siphon money from the poorest school districts, make failing schools worse, and function as the freedom of choice and tuition grant programs that whites had been trying to establish for half a century. Alabama NAACP president Bernard Simelton mockingly thanked Republican legislators for discovering "the cure for our failing public schools," which was "to cut the funding to public schools, and take away some of their resources and give it to the private schools," thereby "magically turn[ing] those failing public schools into thriving academic powerhouses." State senate president pro tem Del Marsh demurred, claiming, "It's important to make sure parents in those [failing] schools know that they have a choice; they've never had a choice before."[15]

When the results of the law's first year of implementation were released in the fall of 2014, opponents noted that the state had approved just seventy-one applications for tax credits, totaling $142,365, to students who transferred from failing schools. But donors gave nearly $25 million—the legally established maximum—to various scholarship funds like Alabama Opportunity, which alone approved over twenty-five applications for scholarships. Less than half of the scholarships went to students from failing schools. One official with AEA wondered, "If over half of the students are not from failing schools, exactly what was the intent?"[16]

The AEA, along with the Lowndes County school board and state senator Quentin Ross, challenged the AAA in state circuit court. The plaintiffs alleged that the "flexibility" bill had been fundamentally altered without due legislative process and that it unconstitutionally appropriated public funds for use by private organizations. In May 2014, circuit judge Gene Reese found for the plaintiffs in *Boyd v. Magee*. In the 1990s, Reese had sided with the plaintiffs in *Alabama Coalition for Equity v. James*, a suit aimed at addressing miserable conditions in public schools through more equitable funding. The ruling had been rendered meaningless by partial reversal by the Supreme Court of Alabama and legislative inaction, however. In *Boyd*, Reese argued that what amounted to a "redirection" of public funds was a clear case of the legislature "doing indirectly what it [was] forbidden to do directly," quoting an opinion from the 1950s involving John Patterson. Reese also agreed that the net effect would be to further devastate failing schools by reducing already desperately needed funding. The court enjoined the enforcement of the AAA, and the state appealed.[17]

The Southern Poverty Law Center (SPLC) organized a separate suit in which eight Black Belt students and their parents challenged the AAA on equal protection grounds. The plaintiffs argued that the act created "two classes of students assigned to failing schools—those who can escape them because of their parents' income or where they live, and those, like the plaintiffs here, who cannot."

SPLC president Richard Cohen accused Republican legislators of making "empty promise[s]" when touting it as a color-blind piece of legislation that would benefit all students. "The reality is just the opposite," Cohen insisted. "Children in Alabama's Black Belt, most of them African-Americans, are still trapped in failing schools, still being given the short end of the stick." None of the plaintiff families could afford to send their children to private schools, even with the accountability act incentives, and even if they could, Cohen maintained, there were no participating private schools within thirty miles of some of them.[18]

District judge Keith Watkins dismissed the SPLC suit, *Marshall v. Bentley*. Watkins called the request for an injunction against the accountability act "arguably mean," in that it simply denied some students a way out, while leaving the others no better off. An injunction, he wrote, would "leave the plaintiffs in exactly the same situation to which they [were] currently subject, but with the company of their better-situated classmates." This was, he determined, "equally bad treatment." Mike Hubbard applauded the dismissal of what he described as a "misguided, left-wing lawsuit," as did Del Marsh, who had himself characterized it as an effort "to maintain the status quo." All eyes turned to the state's appeal in the *Boyd* case.[19]

In March 2015, the all-Republican state supreme court reversed the circuit court on the major issues in *Boyd*. The court determined that the procedural challenge was invalid because the bill as passed and the bill as originally proposed shared the "general purpose" of "education reform and accountability." The claims of unconstitutional appropriation of state funds for private education were similarly invalid, according to the court, because "appropriations" involved funds that actually passed through the state treasury, ruling out tax credits and private donations to charitable organizations. Marsh called it "a loss for activist judges and status quo union bosses," referring to Judge Reese and the recently deceased Paul Hubbert.[20]

As of 2017, seventy-five schools were deemed to be "failing" in Alabama, all but three of which were in the Black Belt or in the cities of Birmingham, Mobile, Montgomery, Huntsville, and Tuscaloosa. The student bodies at those schools were overwhelmingly black. Nearly four thousand students were receiving scholarships for 144 participating private schools that school year, but only a third of those pupils had transferred from a "failing" school, and a quarter of them were already enrolled in a private school when they were awarded the scholarship. Lawmakers had used the lessons of half a century to craft legislation that could withstand litigious challenges and deliver to white parents those most elusive of goals—the right to send their children to a school unburdened by the albatross of the African American poor, and the guarantee that their money could be funneled toward the former, without being wasted on the latter.[21]

Alabama's property tax system delivered in this regard too. The Lid Bill amendments continued to shield the money of white landowners from funding all-black public schools. The first attempt to enjoin the state from enforcing the Lid Bills had been initiated within the *Knight v. Alabama* litigation in the 1990s. In 2004 a federal court had agreed that the Lid Bills had a sordid racial history, but it had refused to enjoin their enforcement, insisting that *Knight*, a higher education case, was not the vehicle in which to do it. The Eleventh Circuit Court of Appeals agreed in 2007, and the Supreme Court declined to hear the case. The plaintiffs' attorneys then engineered a new case, *Lynch v. Alabama*, which took direct aim at the Lid Bills.[22]

The initial claim in *Lynch* was filed in 2008 by Jim Blacksher, a veteran civil rights lawyer from Mobile who had taken over the *Davis v. Mobile* case from Vernon Crawford in the 1970s. Blacksher argued that the 1978 Lid Bill amendment kept property tax revenues so low that K–12 schools were chronically underfunded, particularly in rural, black school districts, and that black public school children faced a crippling disadvantage as a result. Average assessment of residential, forest, and agricultural lands hovered around 8 percent, and there was an abysmally low cap on tax revenue that could be generated from it, regardless of millage rate increases. As a result, Alabama's property tax revenues were not only the lowest in the United States, they were three times lower than the national average and twice as low as the next lowest state. Timber acreage accounted for more than 70 percent of all land in the state, and in the fiscal year 1999–2000 owners of such property paid between fifteen and thirty-five cents per acre in property taxes. Property tax revenues accounted for a mere 5 percent of the state's total tax haul. Most of the rest came from regressive sales and income taxes—another blow for poor black districts.[23]

When *Lynch* finally made it to trial in 2011, the defendant state officials maintained that lawmakers had no "discriminatory intent" in drafting the Lid Bill amendments. This was a defense strategy that Blacksher had seen before. The City of Mobile had been able to hide behind this rationale in a case involving its use of at-large voting districts in the 1980s. Congress, however, had subsequently amended the language of the Voting Rights Act, replacing "discriminatory intent" with "discriminatory results." Blacksher had then asked the court to use the statewide, structural injunctive relief strategy developed in *Lee v. Macon* to have this new standard applied to voting districts across the state, in *Dillard v. Crenshaw County*. The state's attorneys in *Lynch* knew, then, that this defense had failed when it came to voting rights. But there was no federal statute that established the "discriminatory results" standard for education.[24]

During a four-week trial in Huntsville in the spring of 2011, the defense in *Lynch* contended that Alabamians had a historical antipathy toward taxation that was wholly independent of race. Blacksher countered by reinforcing the expert testimony in *Knight* with that of additional scholars, all of whom agreed that the legislation was the product of one hundred years of racially motivated lawmaking. District judge Lynwood Smith, a Clinton appointee from Talladega, issued an 875-page opinion that fall, in which he lambasted Alabama's property tax scheme and the current condition of education in the state. Smith argued that lawmakers had seen "little benefit from investing in a quality statewide public school system, because the children of their most influential constituents [were] generally enrolled in exclusive suburban school systems, with large local tax bases, or in private schools," almost all of which were the product of white flight.[25]

Smith, however, refused to conclude that any of this disproportionately affected blacks. The issue was class, he claimed, not race. The Lid Bills "also punish[ed] many white students who remain[ed] in the public school systems," Smith wrote. The "children of the rural poor, whether white or black," were "left to struggle" in "underfunded, dilapidated schools." Blacksher and the plaintiffs understood that class and race were inextricably linked in Alabama history—blacks were disproportionately represented among the rural poor and constituted almost the entirety of the urban poor. Smith remained unmoved, though, despite testimony that suggested that rural blacks in Alabama had always struggled in underfunded, dilapidated schools, and despite the fact that many poor, rural whites had chosen to attend shoddy private schools rather than attend any schools with blacks.[26]

According to Smith, the court was restrained by *San Antonio Independent School District v. Rodriguez*. During *Brown* enforcement, state governments had given "the appearance of complying with federal decrees," Smith explained, while at the same time ensuring that "only the wealthy [could] access a quality education for their children, either by moving into exclusive suburbs with public schools well-funded by local tax revenues, or by paying for their children to attend private schools." White lawmakers then chose not to "incur voter disapproval of increased tax levies for the support of an integrated public school system." The Supreme Court in *Rodriguez* determined that equal educational opportunity was not a fundamental right, and in so doing, according to Smith, it "blessed this terrible choice and eviscerated the vision of *Brown*."[27]

Jim Blacksher could only call the decision "regrettable" for "schoolchildren in the Black Belt and other rural counties," who would "continue to receive an inferior education relying on an inadequate tax base." He appealed to the Eleventh Circuit, which heard the appeal in December 2012 and issued its opinion in 2014. Circuit judge Adalberto Jordan began with a reference to Voltaire. "In the 'best of all possible worlds,'" Jordan wrote, "state and local governments would ensure adequate funding for all facets of their public school systems. In the world in which we live, however, the reality is that some public school systems do not have sufficient resources to educate the children entrusted to their care." The court was "cognizant of Alabama's deep and troubled history of racial discrimination," which had been "illustrated vividly by the plaintiffs at trial." But Jordan concluded, "Courts . . . are not always able to provide relief, no matter how noble the cause." The three-judge panel upheld Smith's determination that the 1978 Lid Bill was "financially, and not discriminatorily motivated."[28]

Smith had relied on evidence that the real motivators behind the Lid Bills were "massive resistance to substantial property tax increases . . . heavy support from the Alabama Farm Bureau Association . . . and a clash between rural and urban interests." The appellate court argued that it could find no fault in that determination. It also made a distinction between the property tax classification system, protected by that finding, and the millage rate caps, which were more susceptible to the charge of discriminatory intent. The circuit judges determined that the plaintiffs lacked standing to challenge the caps, because there was no indication that eliminating them would actually lead to properly funded public schools and "upward mobility" for poor black schoolchildren. Voters in Lawrence and Sumter Counties had recently rejected millage rate increases to support public schools. So the court reasoned that, if black voters were unwilling to support higher rates, there was no guarantee that lifting the millage rate cap would do any good.[29]

State attorney general Luther Strange proclaimed, "Today's ruling in *Lynch v. Alabama* again confirms . . . that the citizens of Alabama have a right to structure their own tax system" and insisted that his office was "committed to defending and vindicating this important right whenever necessary." Later that fall, the U.S. Supreme Court declined to hear the case. Jim Blacksher acknowledged defeat but took bitter solace in the fact that the Eleventh Circuit was "the fourth court to agree" that the Lid Bills were "steeped in historical racial discrimination." He lamented, "The courts are just saying there's nothing we can do about it for various technical and legal reasons." This was the intention from the moment lawmakers had seen a "perfect storm" developing in the early 1970s that threatened to send their money to black schools. Blacksher suggested that it was finally "time to turn to the political process" if any kind of meaningful tax reform was ever to happen. "The people of Alabama are going to have to demand a fix," he said, "but that will be difficult."³⁰

By the time *Lynch* hit a dead end, the majority of Alabama's public school systems had seen their desegregation cases closed and court scrutiny removed. White communities and elected officials surmised that the issue of integration was history and that the idea of equal educational opportunity for minorities was obsolete. This led, as one scholar put it, to a "quiet reversal" of the gains made through decades of litigation—or to "sleepwalking back to *Plessy*." Certainly this was not the case everywhere. Schools in many systems were substantially integrated. And some scholars have suggested that sustained interracial contact in schools ought to be a principle goal of integration litigation and policy. Sol Seay called it the "mixing bowl theory"—if white and black students could grow up together, understand one another, possibly even befriend each other, then the next generation of policy makers would be more racially enlightened than the last. If this were the case, Alabama could at least offer some limited success stories, despite the failures of *Lynch*, *Boyd*, and *Marshall v. Bentley*.³¹

In the East Alabama city of Opelika, a vibrant segregation academy did not completely drain white students from the public schools. This was partly because the city did not have a majority-black population, so whites were not faced with the prospect of minority status in government. Opelika did have a moderate white leadership that fought alongside black community leaders to maintain an integrated public system. Compulsory assignment orders did compel some white families to choose Opelika's Scott Academy or neighboring Auburn's Lee Academy, which later merged to become Lee-Scott. But most elected to stay in the public system. Between the 1970s and early 2000s, enrollment in Opelika city schools remained roughly 35 percent white and 65 percent black. The school board was able to obtain unitary status and see its *Lee v. Macon* case closed in 2002, after which leaders continued to push to avoid resegregation.³²

Opelika's story was more exception than the rule, however. Fifteen miles to its southwest, the portion of I-85 dubbed the "Ray Bass Highway" subtly bypassed the city of Tuskegee. As highway director under George Wallace, the Lowndes County segregation academy pioneer Bass had helped ensure that Tuskegee was a forlorn city as far as whites were concerned. When blacks took control of the city government in the 1970s, whites simply fled the city itself—completely. By 2010 the city's white population was less than 2 percent. This had forced Macon Academy to move west, toward Montgomery's eastern suburbs, in order to survive. Its enrollment dipped to 115 students in the 1990s, but with the benefit of increasing white flight from the state capitol, newly christened Macon-East Montgomery Academy enrolled 409 students in 2013–14, 279 white and 9 black.[33]

Montgomery's public schools by the 2010s were among the most segregated in the state. Whites had fled the city for the eastern and northern suburbs when compulsory assignment hit in the 1970s, but the racial breakdown of the city initially hovered around 55 percent white and 45 percent black. As class-based city politics gave way to a fully racial divide, though, propelled by two high-profile incidents of abuse of white police power in the late 1970s and early 1980s, more whites chose to leave. In 2010, with efforts to annex white suburban neighborhoods floundering, the city's population was 37 percent white. The public school system was over 90 percent black. Most whites who remained in the city's increasingly tiny, affluent white enclaves enrolled their children in one of its large segregation academies, each of which accepted a token number of black students—Montgomery Academy, 27 black students among 819; St. James School, 49 out of 996; and Trinity Presbyterian, just 1 of 906. A few miles to the southwest of Trinity sat Harrison Elementary, the first school blacks had attempted to desegregate, forty-six years before. Its enrollment: 229 black students, 1 white.[34]

Farther west on U.S. Highway 80—a corridor designated by the National Park Service as the "Selma to Montgomery National Voting Rights Trail" but designated by the Alabama legislature as the Walter C. Givhan Highway—lay Lowndes County. Here Ray Bass, with Givhan's help, had established Lowndes Academy in 1966. More than anywhere else, compulsory assignment in the Black Belt had led to massive white flight from public systems. By 2013–14 Lowndes Academy enrolled 201 students, 5 of whom were black, while Lowndes County Central High School enrolled 247 students, 1 of whom was white. In nearby Wilcox County, the public schools enrolled 1,801 students, every single one of whom was black, while Wilcox Academy enrolled 268 students, all white. It was similar across the region, as desegregation cases were closed on account of there not being any white students left in the public schools with whom to integrate.[35]

As of 2018, Sumter County appeared set to offer something of an alternative. A biracial group of administrators and faculty at the University of West Alabama were among the first to take advantage of a 2015 state decision to allow for the creation of public charter schools, subject to the approval of either local school boards or a state commission. They established University Charter School, to open in the fall of 2018, and insisted that it would be an integrated institution. Enough white students planned to enroll that Sumter Academy was forced to close. While the closure of a segregation academy and the prospect of anything other than apartheid offered real hope for proponents of integration, the new school could not hope to accommodate more than a fraction of the almost sixteen hundred students attending existing public schools in the county, which were sure to remain 99 percent black. Elsewhere charter school applications looked like they would create acrimony between local school boards and the state commission, as in Birmingham, or complicate ongoing litigation, as in Huntsville.[36]

In Mobile litigation had finally been terminated. The school board had initially sought dismissal of the *Davis* case in 1979, but district judge Brevard Hand instead called for the appointment of biracial community committees to formulate a new desegregation plan for the county. The committees' efforts were contentious, as the plaintiffs' urged continued use of busing, which was vehemently opposed by community representatives, white and black, and the Reagan Justice Department. The committees reported to Hand in 1983 that they could not devise a plan. The case returned to court, and three years later Hand ruled that, despite continued use of busing, Mobile had not successfully integrated its pupils. The then-integrated school board developed a plan that reduced busing in favor of a robust magnet school program, hoping that fine arts or math and science programs might entice white students to attend majority-black schools. Jim Blacksher and the plaintiffs supported the plan, and Hand approved it in 1988. The board struggled with implementation in the 1990s, but by 1997 all parties had agreed to end the litigation. Hand dismissed the case upon the signing of an agreement holding the board to maintaining the magnet program.[37]

Mobile managed to avoid total white flight. As of 2014–15, formerly all-white Murphy High, once the scene of repeated episodes of racial violence, enrolled 450 white students and 1,662 black students. However, most of the city's affluent white families enrolled their children in private schools. This included two schools established prior to *Brown* that, like Trinity in Montgomery, had nonetheless reaped the benefits of white flight. UMS-Wright Preparatory had a 2013–14 enrollment of 1,150, with 28 black students, and St. Paul's Episcopal had an enrollment of 1,405, with 39 black students. The suburb of Prichard had become virtually all black. Its primary public high school, formerly all-white Vigor, enrolled 758 black students and just 19 white students in 2014. Whites there, and quite a few in Mobile proper, had begun looking east years before. Construction had been completed on I-10's George Wallace Tunnel in 1973. The Wallace tunnel had been carrying drivers across Mobile Bay, out of the city, and into suburban Baldwin County ever since.[38]

Four hours up I-65, Birmingham saw comparatively little white flight to private schools but almost total white flight from the city itself. The reasons were myriad, including corruption in the regime of the city's first black mayor, Richard Arrington; the Rust Belt–style effects of industrial decay, especially due to the departure of U.S. Steel; and, most significantly, the opportunity afforded by the suburbs. Whites escaped what they saw as widespread decline because they could. Along with those families and pupils went precious sales tax and property tax dollars. Not only did Birmingham's schools become the most racially exclusive of any in the state outside the Black Belt, the system was beset with massive fiscal shortfalls, dreadfully "underachieving" schools, and violence and drug problems. In 2012–13, per the punitive options established as part of NCLB, there was even talk of a state takeover of the system, amid widespread layoffs and school closures.[39]

By that time the over-the-mountain suburbs had lured tens of thousands of white families. None of the municipalities was less than 75 percent white, and each either had its own school system or was part of the predominantly white Shelby County system. White suburbs had grown up to the east of the city as well, including Trussville, which was 90 percent white and successfully severed itself from the Jefferson County school system in 2005. Jefferson County's desegregation case remained active, and each municipality that sought to secede had been forced to satisfy the court before doing so, though this had not been difficult. Despite much splintering, the county's schools remained among the most integrated in the state. Working-class whites in places like Pleasant Grove and Hueytown on the west side, and Fultondale and Gardendale to the north, had chosen to stick with county schools. At least initially.[40]

In 2012 organizers in Gardendale initiated plans to separate from the county system. City voters approved the plan in late 2013, and a board of education was in place by 2014. Plaintiffs' counsel in the *Stout and U.S. v. Jefferson County* case, including then-former federal judge U. W. Clemon, moved to block the secession, adding local student Kymiyah Reeves and her parents Rickey and Alene to the fifty-three-year-old class-action suit and petitioning the trial court in Birmingham for an injunction. In April 2017, district judge Madeline Haikala, an Obama appointee, found that, despite city leaders' claims to the contrary, "race was a motivating factor" in their efforts. She noted especially their desire to be free of black students from neighboring communities, in the words of white organizers, who were transferring into Gardendale schools under the terms of NCLB and "consum[ing] the resources" of their "schools and teachers, and resident students." There were also, Haikala explained, "blatant public statements from separation organizers, like 'we don't want to become' what [then-predominantly black] Center Point has become,' and we need separation to provide 'better control of the geographic composition of the student body.'" Nonetheless, Haikala conditionally approved Gardendale's bid to sever.[41]

The judge admitted, "Some of the circumstances surrounding Gardendale's attempt to separate are deplorable." But she insisted, "A number of practical considerations counsel against" denying the city's request, including black students in the city's schools who would face a backlash over the denial, the fact that the racism exposed at trial might actually make it more difficult for Jefferson County to obtain unitary status if Gardendale remained, and finally the fact that some parents and organizers had valid, nonracial motivations. Haikala's order allowed for the city to operate only its two elementary schools for three years, after which it could take over the remaining schools, provided the school board had by then presented an acceptable desegregation plan, added a black member, and paid the county $33 million for the city's brand-new high school.[42]

The city and the plaintiffs appealed the decision and applied for a stay of the order, which Haikala granted. An Eleventh Circuit appellate panel subsequently found that Haikala had "abused [the trial court's] discretion" by allowing the city to secede under her own plan and reversed the decision. Gardendale school board president Michael Hogue quickly announced the city's intention to appeal in order to "vindicate the rights of our residents." After fifty years in court, Clemon observed with reflective frustration, "The battle is just not over."[43]

Clemon probably knew as well as anyone. He was still litigating the *Hereford v. Huntsville* desegregation suit too. The CRD, the LDF, and the Huntsville school board had for decades been operating under consent decrees and negotiating new school construction, magnet program development, and other matters via mediation. Then, fifty-one years after Sonnie Hereford and Orzell Billingsley filed the initial complaint, and twenty-seven years since any adversarial proceedings, the parties found themselves again in the courtroom. In 2013, in preparation for the opening of several newly built schools, the Huntsville school board drafted a rezoning plan, which it filed with Haikala's Northern District court in early 2014. The Obama Justice Department opposed the plan.[44]

The CRD argued that the plan would "cement the boundaries" between the district's identifiably black and white schools and place hundreds of students in more segregated environments. The school board argued that it could not be responsible for the "private choices" of people who elected to live in segregated neighborhoods—a position sanctioned by the Supreme Court in *Freeman v. Pitts*. The longtime attorney for the LDF, Norman Chachkin, who also represented the LDF in *Stout v. Jefferson*, sided with the school board, arguing that the new plan would actually benefit the plaintiff class by increasing minority enrollment at magnet schools and in Advanced Placement courses, and by increasing transportation opportunities. The local NAACP opposed the plan, however. The school board was in the process of closing virtually all-black Butler High and Terry Heights Elementary, and it was building a new school, Hereford Elementary. With Butler gone, the board wanted to feed the Hereford students into largely black Johnson High instead of nearby Huntsville High, a predominantly white school that some felt was the logical choice.[45]

Sonnie Hereford sided with the local NAACP and retained Clemon as his counsel. Hereford argued that the case had technically never been certified as a class action and that he no longer had a vested interest in the litigation. Judge Haikala allowed him to withdraw as a plaintiff, asserting that the litigation had long been a public action involving Huntsville and the Justice Department. This left no role for the LDF, forcing Chachkin out of the litigation and removing any support for the school board's plan. The court then sided with the CRD and ordered Huntsville to adopt and implement the division's zoning plan. The ordeal left many embittered. Locals, black and white, bristled at having to swallow yet another federal plan. Some worried that whites would flee the Huntsville High zone; others worried that gentrification would drive blacks from the Terry Heights neighborhood. All could be certain that race would remain at the center of public debates over education in Huntsville.[46]

The same could be said of Tuscaloosa. In the 1980s and 1990s, Tuscaloosa had boasted one of the most successfully integrated school systems in the country. In 1979, the school board had met the demands of the court by pairing all-black Druid High with formerly all-white Tuscaloosa High, to form one Central High, with a split campus—ninth and tenth grade at the old Druid, eleventh and twelfth at the old Tuscaloosa High. With twenty-three hundred students, Central was a megaschool, and it became a model for integrated education. Though racially disproportionate "tracking" of students into vocational and "honors" programs remained an issue, black and white students racked up accolades from math and debate team successes to cheerleading and football championships. The school produced a staggering number of National Merit Scholars, and its dropout rate was under half the national average. But it all fell apart.[47]

In the late 1990s, the school board cut a deal with leading figures among Tuscaloosa's black elite. The city had recently missed out on landing a Saturn automobile plant, but it was being considered as a site for a Mercedes-Benz plant. White flight had left the Tuscaloosa public schools with a black majority, and many felt that a lack of majority white schools had turned Saturn away. To prevent further white exodus and boost the city's recruitment capabilities, the board decided to open an elementary school in an affluent white-flight enclave on the north bank of the Black Warrior River. The school board arranged a quid pro quo: it promised new schools in the working-class, all-black West End in exchange for black support for the new white elementary school. The court approved the deal and agreed to close Tuscaloosa's desegregation case in 2000. Black leaders who supported the arrangement had surmised, "The answer cannot be 'The only way to get good schools is to have white people in them.'" They also felt that a release from court oversight was inevitable and wanted to get tangible concessions before their ability to bargain was gone. Race and class would soon converge, however, to destroy educational opportunity for black students in the West End.[48]

Central High was quickly dismantled. Two significantly integrated high school attendance zones were drawn up, one in the affluent, white northern part of town near the University of Alabama, and another on the east side. A third zone was carved around West End, where students would attend the old Central, which became not only 99 percent black but also almost exclusively poor. The majority of the city's middle-class and upper-class black students were zoned into Northridge High or Paul W. Bryant High. By 2014, 80 percent of Central's students qualified for Title I free or reduced-cost lunches. White former school officials admitted that the school had become a "dumping ground" for bad teachers. For years it offered no AP courses or even a school newspaper or yearbook program. After the passage of the Accountability Act, Central was declared a failing school. As of 2016, Tuscaloosa had five private schools participating in the AAA, all of which were majority white, with two being over 96 percent white. Ninety-six students received scholarships to attend them, but only eleven of these were from failing schools.[49]

It could hardly be said that *Brown* had led to the integration of Alabama's schools. If the primary goal of black activist-litigants was as modest as the elimination of plainly de jure segregation, they had been successful. Prior to *Brown*, there was widespread disregard for the law. After the decades-long fight to enforce the decision, there was technically widespread compliance. At the same time, the tortured compliance years revealed that litigation could only do so much. Scholars on both sides of the *Brown* debate have agreed that litigation cannot by itself effect social justice. Litigation in the 2010s demonstrated that the goals of many advocates for racial justice in Alabama went beyond simply dismantling the old de jure dual school system. Equal educational opportunity had been the aim of some all along. But the maturation of defiance and the ability of segregationists to craft a seemingly compliant strategy of enduring massive resistance limited the effect of school desegregation litigation to prima facie enforcement of the law. And the narrative and legal strategy of defending white constitutional rights rendered that fortress of resistance ultimately unassailable.⁵⁰

A long series of disingenuous claims in the unspoken name of segregation and white privilege gave way in Alabama to a genuine belief that whites who had avoided integration had simply exercised their constitutionally mandated and God-given individual rights. Those in elite white academies felt no pang of responsibility for poor blacks in failing schools. Rural whites in struggling segregation academies refused to accept responsibility for the sorry state of both public and private education in the Black Belt. Suburban whites did not acknowledge that they enjoyed the benefit of white privilege, buttressed by state and federal government policies. They were exonerated, choosing to maintain law and order by eschewing violent resistance, by acting through political channels to further their interests, and by asserting their rights to freedom of choice, freedom of association, and freedom from black taxation. The ultimate victory for their resistance, though, came in convincing others that there was nothing against which to speak out. Violence and even early massive resistance were easily condemnable. The solutions produced by the law-and-order movement to protect white rights were not. Decades of fighting school desegregation litigation had ensured that.

◉ ◉ ◉

Solomon Seay recounted much of the preceding story to me at his dining room table in 2012. He talked about where historians had gotten it right and wrong. About the legacy of Judge Johnson. About the various shades of segregationists against whom he had squared off. About the many local officials with whom he had worked. He was passionate about the efficacy of litigation and deeply frustrated by the lack of attention given to its role in the civil rights movement. Toward the end of the interview, though, he began to share a different kind of personal story, one that pointed toward the limits of litigation when it was up against the weight of history, the power of narrative, and the stubbornness of human nature. He began to describe an encounter in one of the *Lee v. Macon* cases—the case against Marengo County, which he had once called the "most recalcitrant" school system in Alabama, whose superintendent had called him a Mickey Mouse lawyer.

Near the conclusion of a particularly contentious hearing in the case, Seay found himself, as he sometimes did, on the witness stand, this time before judge Brevard Hand. Hand asked him, "Seay, do you think we will ever get to the point in this country where race makes no difference?" Seay knew his answer but feigned introspection for just a moment. "Sure," he finally replied confidently, "Because 'ever' is a long, long time, and it's bound to happen ever."

He paused again, then added, "But it will not happen in your lifetime or mine." Judge Hand was taken aback. He wanted to know why Seay felt that way. "Judge, I'm really not sure," he admitted, matter-of-factly, "but maybe it's because I've been black too long, and you've been white too long." Recounting the story to me years later, Seay mused, "If ever is going to happen, it's going to be because these youngsters begin to communicate with each other. You and I can't do it."[51]

NOTES

Abbreviations

ACHR	Alabama Council on Human Relations
ADAH	Alabama Department of Archives and History, Montgomery, Alabama
BN	*Birmingham News*
BOE	Board of Education
CRD	Civil Rights Division
DOJ	Department of Justice
FMJP	Frank M. Johnson Papers, Library of Congress, Manuscript Division
FOIA	Freedom of Information Act
GAAF	Governors Administrative Assistant Files, ADAH
GPO	Government Printing Office
HEW	U.S. Department of Health, Education, and Welfare
LAT	*Los Angeles Times*
LVMCF	*Lee v. Macon County* BOE Case File, FMJP
LVMTR	*Lee v. Macon County* BOE Trial Record, Federal District Court House, Montgomery, Alabama
MA	*Montgomery Advertiser*
NYT	*New York Times*
PNAACP	*Papers of the NAACP*, ed. John H. Bracy et al., Bethesda, Md.: University Publications of America, 1981–present
RRLR	*Race Relations Law Reporter*
RRLS	*Race Relations Law Survey*
SDSBS	*School Desegregation in the Southern and Border States*
SSN	*Southern School News*
TN	*Tuskegee News*
TRO	Temporary Restraining Order
USCCR	United States Commission on Civil Rights
USOE	United States Office of Education, HEW
WP	*Washington Post*

Introduction

1. Solomon Seay, interview with author, Feb. 1, 2012, digital recording and transcript in possession of the author.

2. Ibid.

3. Ibid.

4. *LAT*, Aug. 12, 1994; Docket Report, *LVMTR*; Lee v. Randolph County BOE, 160 F.R.D. 642, 885 F.Supp. 1526 (M. D., Ala., 1995). On miscegenation, see Sheryll Cashin,

Loving: Intimacy in America and the Threat to White Supremacy (New York: Beacon Press, 2017).

5. *LAT*, Aug. 12, 1994; *NYT*, Jan. 11, 1995; Vickie Cox Edmondson, ed., *No Mistakes, No More Tears: The ReVonda Bowen Story* (Bloomington, Ind.: Author House, 2005).

6. *LAT*, Aug. 12, 1994; *NYT*, Jan. 11, 1995; *Tuscaloosa News*, Aug. 2, 1994; Lee v. Randolph County BOE, 885 F.Supp. 1526 (M. D., Ala., 1995).

7. Ibid.

8. Lee v. Randolph County BOE, 2011 U.S. Dist. LEXIS 34645 (M. D., Ala., 2011), 2012 U.S. Dist. LEXIS 110774 (M. D., Ala., 2012), Lexis-Nexis Academic, http://www.lexisnexis.com; Seay interview.

9. On southern exceptionalism, see Joseph Crespino and Matthew Lassiter, eds., *The Myth of Southern Exceptionalism* (New York: Oxford University Press, 2009); Thomas Sugrue, *Sweet Land of Liberty: The Forgotten Struggle for Civil Rights in the North* (New York: Random House, 2008); Thomas Sugrue, *The Origins of the Urban Crisis: Race and Inequality in Postwar Detroit* (Princeton: Princeton University Press, 2010); Michelle Nickerson and Darren Dochuk, eds., *Sunbelt Rising: The Politics of Space, Place, and Region* (Philadelphia: University of Pennsylvania Press, 2011); and John Egerton, *The Americanization of Dixie: the Southernization of America* (New York: Harper's Magazine Press, 1974).

10. Knight v. Alabama, 787 F.Supp. 1030 (N. D., Ala., 1991); Susan Pace Hamill, "*Knight v. State of Alabama*," *Encyclopedia of Alabama*, Feb. 12, 2015, http://www.encyclopediaofalabama.org/article/h-1480; Alabama State Teachers Association v. Alabama Public School and College Authority, 289 F.Supp. 784 (M. D., Ala., 1969), affirmed 393 U.S. 400 (1969).

11. Knight v. Alabama, affirmed in part, 14 F.3d 1534 (11th CCA, 1994), 900 F.Supp 272 (N. D., Ala., 1995) (Knight II); Knight v. Alabama Plaintiffs' Post-Trial Proposed Findings of Fact and Conclusions of Law, June 7, 2004, at Plaintiffs' Knight & Sims vs. Alabama Website, https://web.archive.org/web/20071117023103/http://www.knightsims.com/pdf/04_06_09/Plaintiffs%20proposed%20FOF%20and%20COL%205.doc; Hamill, "*Knight v. State of Alabama*."

12. Hamill, "*Knight v. State of Alabama*." Expert witness historians were Robert J. Norrell and J. Mills Thornton.

13. Ibid.

14. Knight v. Alabama Plaintiffs' Post-Trial Findings; Hamill, "*Knight v. State of Alabama*." On color blindness, see Matthew Lassiter, *The Silent Majority: Suburban Politics in the Sunbelt South* (Princeton University Press, 2006), 1–20, 30, 148; and William Hustwit, *James J. Kilpatrick: Salesman for Segregation* (Chapel Hill: University of North Carolina Press, 2013), 4, 226.

15. Knight v. Alabama, 458 F.Supp.2d 1273 (N. D., Ala., 2004) (Knight III), 1286–99, 1311; Hamill, "*Knight v. State of Alabama*." See also Susan Pace Hamill, "Constitutional Reform in Alabama: A Necessary Step toward Achieving a Fair and Efficient Tax Structure," *Cumberland Law Review* 33 (2003): 437.

16. Knight v. Alabama, 458 F.Supp.2d 1273 (N. D., Ala., 2004), 1311–14, affirmed 476 F.3d 1219 (11th CCA, 2007), cert. denied, 127 S.Ct. 3014 (2007); Hamill, "*Knight v. State of Alabama*."

17. Jacqueline Dowd Hall, "The Long Civil Rights Movement," *Journal of American History* 91 (2005): 1231.

18. On the NAACP, see Brian Dougherty and Charles Bolton, *With All Deliberate Speed: The Implementation of Brown v. Board of Education* (Fayetteville: University of Arkansas

Press, 2008); and J. Mills Thornton, *Dividing Lines: Municipal Politics and the Struggle for Civil Rights in Montgomery, Birmingham, and Selma* (Tuscaloosa: University of Alabama Press, 2002). On massive resistance to desegregation, see Jason Morgan Ward, *Defending White Democracy: The Making of a Segregationist Movement and the Remaking of Racial Politics, 1936–1965* (Chapel Hill: University of North Carolina Press, 2011); James Patterson, *Brown v. Board of Education: A Civil Rights Milestone and Its Troubled Legacy* (New York: Oxford University Press, 2001); Clive Webb, ed., *Massive Resistance: White Opposition to the Second Reconstruction* (New York: Oxford University Press, 2001); Numan Bartley, *The Rise of Massive Resistance: Race and Politics in the South during the 1960s* (Baton Rouge: Louisiana State University Press, 1969, 1997); George Lewis, *Massive Resistance: The White Response to the Civil Rights Movement* (New York: Oxford University Press, 2010); Harvie Wilkinson, *From Brown to Bakke: The Supreme Court and School Integration, 1954–1978* (New York: Oxford University Press, 1981).

19. On rationalized acceptance of tokenism, see Glen Eskew, *But for Birmingham: The Local and National Movements in the Civil Rights Struggle* (Chapel Hill: University of North Carolina Press, 1997); Thornton, *Dividing Lines*; Jeff Roche, *Restructured Resistance: The Sibley Commission and the Politics of Desegregation in Georgia* (Athens: University of Georgia Press, 1998).

20. On strategic accommodations, see Joseph Crespino, *In Search of Another Country: Mississippi and the Conservative Counterrevolution* (Princeton: Princeton University Press, 2009), 1–3. On freedom of association, see Kevin M. Kruse, "The Fight for 'Freedom of Association': Segregationist Rights and Resistance in Atlanta," in Webb, *Massive Resistance*, 99–116; and Kevin M. Kruse, *White Flight: Atlanta and the Making of Modern Conservatism* (Princeton University Press, 2005), 1–15, 161–79, 234–58. On the failure of moral awakening, see Tony Freyer, *The Little Rock Crisis: A Constitutional Interpretation* (New York: Greenwood Press, 1984); and Tony Freyer, *Little Rock on Trial: Cooper v. Aaron and School Desegregation* (Lawrence: University Press of Kansas, 2007).

21. On the southern strategy, see Dan Carter, *The Politics of Rage: George Wallace, the Origins of the New Conservatism, and the Transformation of American Politics*, 2nd ed. (Baton Rouge: Louisiana State University Press, 2000); Dan Carter, *From George Wallace to Newt Gingrich: Race in the Conservative Counterrevolution, 1963–1994* (Baton Rouge: Louisiana State University Press, 1999); and Egerton, *The Americanization of Dixie*. For the new school, see Kruse, *White Flight*; Lassiter, *Silent Majority*; Crespino, *In Search of Another Country* and *Strom Thurmond's America* (New York: Hill and Wang, 2012); Sugrue, *Sweet Land of Liberty* and *Origins of the Urban Crisis*; Nickerson and Dochuk, *Sunbelt Rising*; and Lisa McGirr, *Suburban Warriors: The Origins of the New American Right* (Princeton: Princeton University Press, 2001).

22. Brian K. Landsberg, "*Lee v. Macon County Board of Education*: The Possibilities of Federal Enforcement of Equal Educational Opportunity," *Duke Journal of Constitutional Law and Public Policy* 12, no. 1 (2016): 1–52; Paul Finkelman, "The Centrality of Brown," in *Choosing Equality: Essays and Narratives on the Desegregation Experience*, ed. Robert L. Hayman Jr. and Leland Ware (State College: Penn State University Press, 2009); Paul Finkelman, "Civil Rights in Historical Context: In Defense of Brown," *Harvard Law Review* 118 (2004–5): 917; and Martha Minow, *In Brown's Wake: Legacies of America's Educational Landmark* (New York: Oxford University Press, 2010).

23. For the backlash thesis, see Michael Klarman, *From Jim Crow to Civil Rights: The Supreme Court and the Struggle for Racial Equality* (New York: Oxford University Press,

2004), especially 342–43, 360, 363. See also Michael Klarman, "Why Massive Resistance?," in Webb, *Massive Resistance*, 21–38. Other detractors are Charles Ogletree, *All Deliberate Speed: Reflections on the First Half-Century of Brown v. Board of Education* (New York: Norton, 2004); and Derrick Bell, *Silent Covenants: Brown v. Board of Education and the Unfulfilled Hopes of Racial Reform* (New York: Oxford University Press, 2004). Competing interpretations include Finkelman, "The Centrality of Brown" and "Civil Rights in Historical Context: In Defense of Brown"; Minow, *In Brown's Wake*; Kenneth Mack, "The Myth of Brown?" *Yale Law Journal Pocket Part*, Nov. 1, 2005, https://perma.cc/858Z-GLTW; and Hayman and Ware, *Choosing Equality*. On the Supreme Court and social change, see Gerald Rosenberg, *The Hollow Hope: Can Courts Bring about Social Change?* (Chicago: University of Chicago Press, 1991, 2008); and David A Schultz, ed., *Leveraging the Law: Using Courts to Achieve Social Change* (New York: Peter Lang, 1998).

24. Klarman, *From Jim Crow to Civil Rights*, 342, 360–63.

25. Tony Freyer and Timothy Dixon, *Democracy and Judicial Independence: A History of Federal Courts in Alabama, 1820–1994* (New York: Carlson, 1995), 252–55; Jack Bass, *Unlikely Heroes: The Dramatic Story of the Southern Judges of the Fifth Judicial Circuit Who Translated the Supreme Court's Brown Decision into a Revolution for Equality* (New York: Simon and Schuster, 1981).

Chapter 1. "The NAACP Organized—Why Not You"

1. *MA*, Sept. 2, 3, 1954.

2. Ibid.

3. *SSN*, Oct. 1, 1954; *MA*, Sept. 2, 3, 1954; Robert Heinrich, "Montgomery: The Civil Rights Movement and Its Legacy" (PhD diss., Brandeis University, 2008), 16–20.

4. *SSN*, Oct. 1, 1954; *MA*, Sept. 2, 3, 1954; *NYT*, Sept. 3, 1954.

5. *SSN*, Oct. 1, 1954; *MA*, Sept. 3, 4, 1954; Fred Gray, *Bus Ride to Justice: Changing the System by the System* (Selma: Black Belt Press, 1995), 204–5.

6. *MA*, Sept. 4, 1954.

7. *SSN*, Oct. 1, 1954; *MA*, Sept. 3, 4, 1954; *Washington Afro-American*, May 25, 1954; *MA*, Sept. 4, 1954; *NYT*, Sept. 3, 1954; *BN*, Oct. 31, 1954; Fred Gray, *Bus Ride to Justice*, 204–5.

8. Roy Wilkins, "The Role of the NAACP in the Desegregation Process," *Social Problems* 2, no. 4 (April 1955): 201–3; Ruby Hurley to Southeast Regional Branches, June 7, 1954, and Elizabeth Gayer to Harriet Crowley, Jan. 21, 1955, *PNAACP*, part 25, series A.

9. Ruby Hurley to Southeast Regional Branches, June 7, 1954; *News and Action*, NAACP Southeast Regional Office Newsletter, July 1954; Ruby Hurley, Statement for Broadcast-WJRD, July 22, 1954—all in *PNAACP*, part 25, series A.

10. Ruby Hurley to Branch Officers, Sept. 24, 1954, *PNAACP*, part 25, series A; *Huntsville Times*, Sept. 24, 1954, Oct. 15, 1954; John Dittmer, *Local People: The Struggle for Civil Rights in Mississippi* (Urbana: University of Illinois Press, 1994).

11. NAACP press release, Dec. 12, 1954, and Memorandum from Moon to Current, Dec. 9, 1954; Ruby Hurley to Field Secretaries, July 26, 1955—both in *PNAACP*, part 25, series A. NAACP press release, Southeast Regional Office, Feb. 3, 1955; *News and Action*, Newsletter of the NAACP Southeast Regional Office, March 1955—both in *PNAACP*, part 2, series A.

12. *SSN*, Jan. 6, 1955; *MA*, Nov. 29, 1954; Jason Morgan Ward, *Defending White Democracy: The Making of a Segregationist Movement and the Remaking of Racial Politics,*

1936–1965 (Chapel Hill: University of North Carolina Press, 2011); Neil R. McMillen, *The Citizens' Council: Organized Resistance to the Second Reconstruction* (Urbana: University of Illinois Press, 1971), 43.

13. *SSN*, Jan. 6, 1955; McMillen, *Citizens' Council*, 43.

14. *SSN*, Jan. 6, 1955; *BN*, Dec. 3, 1954; *Pittsburgh Courier*, Dec. 15, 1955; *Nashville Tennessean*, Nov. 28, 1954.

15. *MA*, Feb. 1, 1955; McMillen, *Citizens' Council*, 16–25.

16. *SSN*, Sept. 1955; *BN*, Aug. 4, 11, 16, 20, Sept. 2, 1955; *MA*, Aug. 13, 21, 1955.

17. *SSN*, Oct. 1955; *BN*, Aug. 4, 24, 1955; *MA*, Sept. 9, 1955. *News and Action*, March 1955; and Memorandum from Lucille Black to Gloster Current, June 3, 1955—both in *PNAACP*, part 2, series A.

18. *SSN*, Oct. 1955; *MA*, Sept. 9, 1955; Affidavits of Ernest Doyle, Richard Winston, Daniel Stevens, S. W. Boynton, and H. W. Shannon, *PNAACP*, part 20, reel 4.

19. *SSN*, Oct. 1955; *MA*, Sept. 9, 1955; *BN*, March 8, 1955; *Louisville Courier-Journal*, Sept. 8, 1955; McMillen, *Citizens' Council*, 44–45.

20. *News and Action*, NAACP Southeast Regional Office Newsletter, Sept. 1955; and NAACP press release, "Schools No. 1 Object of Southern NAACP," Dec. 15, 1955—both in *PNAACP*, part 25, series A.

21. *NYT*, Feb. 7, 1956; *BN*, June 23, Oct. 4, Nov. 9, 1955, Jan. 17, 1956; *SSN*, Oct. 1956; *Memphis Commercial Appeal*, Feb. 18, 1956.

22. *SSN*, Oct. 1956; *BN*, Nov. 21, 1955; McMillen, *Citizens' Council*, 44–45; Citizens' Council ad, "Time for all White People to Be Counted," in *PNAACP*, part 23, reel 4.

23. Halberstam changed not only the names of those involved but also the name of the town itself, which he called Clifford.

24. David Halberstam, "The White Citizens Councils: Respectable Means for Unrespectable Ends," *Commentary*, Oct. 1956, https://www.commentarymagazine.com/articles/the-white-citizens-councilsrespectable-means-for-unrespectable-ends.

25. William Thomas, president, Bessemer NAACP Branch, to Roy Wilkins, Feb. 7, 1956, Citizens' Council Leaflet attached, *PNAACP*, part 20, reel 13; *Columbus (Ga.) Ledger-Enquirer*, Sept. 2, 1956; *Atlanta Constitution*, Sept. 9, 1956; *NYT*, Feb. 18, 1956.

26. *BN*, Nov. 1, Dec. 4, 1955, March 5, 1956; *Louisville Courier-Journal*, March 11, 1956; McMillen, *Citizens' Council*, 49–56; Dan Carter, *Politics of Rage*, 2nd ed., 105–9; Joseph E. Lowndes, *From the New Deal to the New Right: Race and the Southern Origins of Modern Conservatism* (New Haven: Yale University Press, 2009), 140–54; Newman Douglas, Laura Browder, and Marco Ricci, *The Reconstruction of Asa Carter*, television documentary (Corporation for Public Broadcasting, 2010).

27. *BN*, Nov. 1, Dec. 4, 1955; McMillen, *Citizens' Council*, 52–55.

28. *MA*, Feb. 11, 1956; *St. Louis Post-Dispatch*, Feb. 28, 1956; *SSN*, March 1956; Jan Gregory Thompson, "A History of the Alabama Council on Human Relations, from Roots to Redirection, 1920–1968" (PhD. diss., Auburn University, 1983), 39–41.

29. Thompson, *History of the Alabama Council on Human Relations*, 1–29, 39–44.

30. Ibid.

31. Charles J. Bloch, *The Need for States Rights Councils and Citizens Councils* (Atlanta: States Rights Council of Georgia, 1957); Central Alabama Citizens' Council Membership Card, on display at the Tuskegee Human and Civil Rights Multicultural Center; Clive Webb, "Charles Bloch: Jewish White Supremacist," *Georgia Historical Quarterly* 83,

Summer 1999: 267–92; David Chappell, *Stone of Hope: Prophetic Religion and the Death of Jim Crow* (Chapel Hill: University of North Carolina Press, 2004), 166, 259–42.

32. Senate Joint Resolution No. 894, Sept. 19, 1953, p. 51, quoted in Trial Brief of the U.S., Jan. 5, 1967, LVMCF, FMJP, C19, F5; *SSN*, Oct. 1, 1954; Thomas Gilliam, *The Second Folsom Administration: The Destruction of Alabama Liberalism, 1954–1958* (PhD diss., Auburn University, 1975), 107.

33. *SSN*, Sept. 1, 1954; *Birmingham Post-Herald*, July 10, 1954, emphasis added.

34. Gilliam, *Second Folsom Administration*, 103–4; Carl Grafton and Anne Permaloff, *Big Mules and Branchheads: James E. Folsom and Political Power in Alabama* (Athens: University of Georgia Press, 1985), 161–80; *BN*, June 22, 23, 1955. On "law and order" and preserving the city's image, see Glen Eskew, *But for Birmingham: The Local and National Movements in the Civil Rights Struggle* (Chapel Hill: University of North Carolina Press, 1997), 53–84; and Robin D. G. Kelley, *Hammer and Hoe: Alabama Communists during the Great Depression* (Chapel Hill: University of North Carolina Press, 1990), 119–37.

35. Wayne Flynt, *Alabama in the Twentieth Century* (Tuscaloosa: University of Alabama Press, 2004), 29–66. See also Gilliam, *Second Folsom Administration*; and Grafton and Permaloff, *Big Mules and Branchheads*.

36. *SSN*, Nov. 4, 1954; Gilliam, *Second Folsom Administration*, 187.

37. *SSN*, Oct. 1, 1954, Nov. 4, 1954.

38. *SSN*, Nov. 4, 1954; Gilliam, *Second Folsom Administration*; Grafton and Permaloff, *Big Mules and Branchheads*; George E. Sims, *The Little Man's Big Friend: James E. Folsom in Alabama Politics, 1946–1958* (Tuscaloosa: University of Alabama Press, 1985).

39. *SSN*, March 3, 1955; Harvie Wilkinson, *From Brown to Bakke: The Supreme Court and School Integration, 1954–1978* (New York: Oxford University Press, 1981), 17–18; Patterson, *Brown v. Board of Education*, 82–85; *SSN*, Oct. 1, 1954.

40. *SSN*, June 8, 1955.

41. See full text of the placement law at *RRLR* 1, no. 1 (Feb. 1956): 235–37. See summaries at *SSN*, Feb. 3, 1955; and Gilliam, *Second Folsom Administration*, 175–76.

42. *RRLR* 1, no. 1 (Feb. 1956): 235–37.

43. Ibid.; *SSN*, Feb. 3, 1955; Gilliam, *Second Folsom Administration*, 175–76.

44. *Birmingham World*, June 14, 1955; Wilkinson, *From Brown to Bakke*, 83–84; J. W. Peltason, *Fifty-Eight Lonely Men: Southern Federal Judges and School Desegregation* (New York: Harcourt, Brace and World, 1961), 78; Gilliam, *Second Folsom Administration*, 181.

45. *SSN*, May 4, June 8, Sept. 1955.

46. Wilkinson, *From Brown to Bakke*, 82, quoting Briggs v. Elliott, 132 F.Supp. 776 (E. D., S.C., 1955), 777.

47. Ibid., 84, quoting Carson v. Warlick, 238 F.2d 724, 728 (4th CCA, 1956); Patterson, *Brown v. Board of Education*, 54–55; *RRLR* 1, no. 1 (Feb. 1956): 4.

48. *SSN*, Feb. 1956; *Atlanta Journal*, Jan. 20, 1956; William Hustwit, "From Caste to Colorblindness: James J. Kilpatrick's Segregationist Semantics," *Journal of Southern History* 77, no. 3: 639–72, including "encroachments"; William Hustwit, *James J. Kilpatrick: Salesman for Segregation* (Chapel Hill: University of North Carolina Press, 2013), 41–66; Chappell, *Stone of Hope*, 168–70; Grafton and Permaloff, *Big Mules and Branchheads*, 189–90; Gilliam, *The Second Folsom Administration*, 316; Wilkinson, *From Brown to Bakke*, 82–83, 98–99; Bartley, *Rise of Massive Resistance*, 126–31.

49. *SSN*, Feb. 1956; *BN*, Feb. 2, 1956; Gilliam, *Second Folsom Administration*, 324–27. See *RRLR* 1, no. 2 (April 1956): 437–38 (full text of Alabama resolution) and 465–98 (on interposition and nullification generally).

50. *SSN*, April 1956; *Atlanta Journal*, Jan. 26, 1956; Grafton and Permaloff, *Big Mules and Branchheads*, 194–98; E. Culpepper Clark, *The Schoolhouse Door: Segregation's Last Stand at the University of Alabama* (Tuscaloosa: University of Alabama Press, 2007), 17–22.

51. *BN*, Feb. 8, Aug. 8, 16, 24, 1956; *MA*, Feb. 8, 1956; *Atlanta Journal*, Feb. 12, 1956; *SSN*, March 1956; Gilliam, *Second Folsom Administration*, 319–20, including "down to earth."

52. *SSN*, March, April 1956; *BN*, Feb. 28, 1956; Gilliam, *Second Folsom Administration*, 328–32; Sims, *Little Man's Big Friend*, 184; Bartley, *Rise of Massive Resistance*, 116; John Kyle Day, *The Southern Manifesto: Massive Resistance and the Fight to Preserve Segregation* (Jackson: University Press of Mississippi, 2014); Keith Finley, *Delaying the Dream: Southern Senators and the Fight Against Civil Rights, 1938–1965* (Baton Rouge: Louisiana State University Press, 2010).

53. *MA*, March 10, 1956; *SSN*, April, June 1956; Glenn Feldman, *The Great Melding: War, the Dixiecrat Rebellion, and the Southern Model for America's New Conservatism* (Tuscaloosa: University of Alabama Press, 2014); Kari Frederickson, *The Dixiecrat Revolt and the End of the Solid South, 1932–1968* (Chapel Hill: University of North Carolina Press, 2001).

54. Samuel L. Webb and Margaret E. Armbrester, eds., *Alabama Governors: A Political History of the State* (Tuscaloosa: University of Alabama Press, 2001), 210–15; Gene Howard, *Patterson for Alabama: The Life and Career of John Patterson* (Tuscaloosa: University of Alabama Press, 2008).

55. Webb, *Alabama Governors*, 210–15; Howard, *Patterson for Alabama*, 97.

56. Howard, *Patterson for Alabama*, 99–101.

57. *BN*, June 1, 1956; *Charlotte News*, June 1, 1956; Alabama ex rel. Patterson v. NAACP, *RRLR* 1, no. 4 (Aug. 1956): 706.

58. *MA*, Nov. 26, 1956, Feb. 26, 1958; *Jackson (Miss.) Daily News*, May 20, 1957; James McWhorter Pruitt Jr., "Thomas Goode Jones," *Encyclopedia of Alabama*, February 13, 2008, http://www.encyclopediaofalabama.org/article/h-1463; Walter B. Jones, *Citizenship and Voting in Alabama* (Montgomery: American Citizen's Press, 1947). On the Lost Cause, see David Goldfield, *Still Fighting the Civil War: The American South and Southern History* (Baton Rouge: Louisiana State University Press, 2002).

59. *MA*, Nov. 26, 1956, Feb. 26, 1958; *Jackson (Miss.) Daily News*, May 20, 1957.

60. *SSN*, Jan. 6, 1955, Aug. 1958.

61. Alabama ex rel. Patterson v. NAACP, *RRLR* 1, no. 4 (Aug. 1956): 706; *SSN*, July 1956.

62. Browder v. Gayle, 142, F.Supp 707 (1956), affirmed, 352 U.S. 903 (1956).

63. *MA*, June 7, 1956; *BN*, June 10, 1956; Gray, *Bus Ride to Justice*, 1–90.

64. Tony Freyer and Timothy Dixon, *Democracy and Judicial Independence: A History of Federal Courts in Alabama, 1820–1994* (New York: Carlson, 1995), 215–55; Jack Bass, *Taming the Storm: The Life and Times of Judge Frank M. Johnson, Jr. and the South's Fight over Civil Rights* (New York: Doubleday, 1993); Tinsley Yarborough, *Judge Frank Johnson and Human Rights in Alabama* (Tuscaloosa: University of Alabama Press, 1981); Frank Johnson, *Defending Constitutional Rights*, edited by Tony Freyer (Athens: University of Georgia Press, 2001); Peltason, *Fifty-Eight Lonely Men*.

65. *MA*, June 7, 1956; *BN*, June 10, 27, 1956; *Birmingham World*, June 30, 1956; Gray, *Bus Ride to Justice*. On Rives, see Jack Bass, *Unlikely Heroes: The Dramatic Story of the Southern Judges of the Fifth Judicial Circuit Who Translated the Supreme Court's Brown Decision into a Revolution for Equality* (New York: Simon and Schuster, 1981), 70–77; Freyer and Dixon, *Democracy and Judicial Independence*, 205–13; Peltason, *Fifty-Eight Lonely Men*, 84.

66. *SSN*, Aug. 1956; *BN*, July 6, 1956; *MA*, July 6, 9, 1956; Howard, *Patterson for Alabama*, 100–102, 106; *Black Dispatch* (Oklahoma City), Aug. 3, 1956.

67. *RRLR* 1, no. 5 (Oct. 1956): 917; *SSN*, Aug. 1956; *MA*, July 31, 1956; *Memphis Commercial Appeal*, Aug. 5, 1956.

68. Andrew Manis, *A Fire You Can't Put Out: The Civil Rights Life of Birmingham's Reverend Fred Shuttlesworth* (Tuscaloosa: University of Alabama Press, 1999), 93; Nancy C. Curtis, *Black Heritage Sites: The South* (New York: New Press, 1990), 35; "Fourth Avenue History Hunt: The Black Business District," Birmingham Historical Society, http://www.bhistorical.org/education/Hh_4a.pdf.

69. Manis, *Fire You Can't Put Out*, 94–96; J. Mills Thornton, *Dividing Lines: Municipal Politics and the Struggle for Civil Rights in Montgomery, Birmingham, and Selma* (Tuscaloosa: University of Alabama Press, 2002), 197; *SSN*, July 1956 (emphasis added).

70. *SSN*, Sept. 1957; *BN*, Aug. 29, 1957; Thornton, *Dividing Lines*, 204, 216.

71. Thornton, *Dividing Lines*, 216; Manis, *Fire You Can't Put Out*, 145–47; *SSN*, Sept., Oct., Dec. 1957.

72. *BN*, Sept. 9, 1957.

73. *SSN*, Oct. 1957; *BN*, Sept. 9, 10, 1957; *Christian Science Monitor*, Sept. 10, 1957. See accounts of Pat and Ricky Shuttlesworth in Ellen Levine, ed., *Freedom's Children: Young Civil Rights Activists Tell Their Own Stories* (New York: Puffin Books), 37–40; Manis, *Fire You Can't Put Out*, 145–61; and Thornton, *Dividing Lines*, 216–17.

74. *SSN*, Nov., Dec. 1957, Jan. 1958; *WP*, Nov. 22, 1957.

75. *SSN*, Jan. 1958; Peltason, *Fifty-Eight Lonely Men*, 84–85; Jack Bass, *Unlikely Heroes*, 61, 181, 91; Freyer and Dixon, *Democracy and Judicial Independence*, 140–44, 202–13; Thornton, *Dividing Lines*, 203–6; Brian Landsberg, *Free at Last to Vote: The Alabama Origins of the Voting Rights Act* (University of Kansas Press, 2007), 53–55.

76. Wilkinson, *From Brown to Bakke*, 83–84; Shuttlesworth v. Birmingham BOE, *RRLR* 3, no. 3 (June 1958): 425–34 (see also at 162 F.Supp. 172).

77. *SSN*, Aug., Sept. 1958; *BN*, Aug. 31, 1958.

78. Shuttlesworth v. Birmingham BOE, 358 U.S. 101 (1958); Peltason, *Fifty-Eight Lonely Men*, 85–86, including "court observer" quotations; Bartley, *Rise of Massive Resistance*, 291–92; Bass, *Unlikely Heroes*, 125–26; *NYT*, Dec. 30, 1958; *RRLR* 3: 917; *RRLR* 4: 281; *RRLR* 5: 343–49.

79. *SSN*, Dec. 1958; *BN*, Nov. 25, 26, 1958; *Atlanta Journal*, Nov. 25, 30, 1958; *MA*, Nov. 25, 1958.

80. *MA*, Dec. 12, 1958; Cooper v. Aaron, 358 U.S. 1 (1958); James v. Almond, 170 F.Supp. 331 (E. D., Va., 1959); Bartley, *Rise of Massive Resistance*, 244.

81. *MA*, Aug. 30, 1959; Thornton, *Dividing Lines*, 103–4.

82. *MA*, Nov. 9, 1958, Dec. 31, 1959, May 16, 1960.

83. *WP*, April 3, 1960; Thornton, *Dividing Lines*, 104–7, 392–98; *NYT*, Sept. 27, 1959; *BN*, July 27, Sept. 1, 1959; *MA*, Feb. 1, 8, 20, 22, March 20, April 10, May 22, July 27, 28, Dec. 31, 1959.

84. *BN*, Feb. 24, 1959; Glen Eskew, "The Classes and the Masses: Fred Shuttlesworth and Birmingham's Black Middle Class," in *Birmingham Revolutionaries: The Reverend Fred Shuttlesworth and the Alabama Christian Movement for Human Rights*, ed. Marjorie White and Andrew Manis (Macon, Ga.: Mercer University Press, 2000), 32–47; Eskew, *But for Birmingham*, 147–48; Thornton, *Dividing Lines*, 217–27.

85. *MA*, Oct. 31, Nov. 4, 1959; *BN*, Nov. 24, 1959; *SSN*, July 1960.

86. Horace Huntley and John W. McKerley, eds., *Foot Soldiers for Democracy: The Men, Women, and Children of the Birmingham Civil Rights Movement* (Urbana: University of Illinois Press, 2009), 35–44.

87. *A Statistical Summary of School Segregation-Desegregation in the Southern and Border States* (Nashville: Southern Education Reporting Service, 1961), 3–4; Peltason, *Fifty-Eight Lonely Men*, 132; United States v. United States Klans, 194 F.Supp. 897; *BN*, March 31, 1963.

Chapter 2. "Our Most Historical Moment"

1. Alabama Governors, Inaugural Addresses and Programs, SP194, ADAH (see full text also at *MA*, Jan. 15, 1963); Dan Carter, *The Politics of Rage: George Wallace, the Origins of the New Conservatism, and the Transformation of American Politics*, 2nd ed. (Baton Rouge: Louisiana State University Press, 2000), 14.

2. Ibid.

3. Ibid.

4. Ibid.

5. *NYT*, Sept. 8, 1963.

6. *BN*, July 9, 11, 1962, Dec. 19, 2001; Nelson v. Birmingham BOE, *RRLR* 7, no. 3 (Fall 1962): 659–62; *SSN*, Aug. 1962; J. Mills Thornton, *Dividing Lines: Municipal Politics and the Struggle for Civil Rights in Montgomery, Birmingham, and Selma* (Tuscaloosa: University of Alabama Press, 2002), 176–77, 206, 212, 218.

7. Nelson v. Birmingham BOE, and Nelson v. The Honorable H. H. Grooms, *RRLR* 7, no. 3 (Fall 1962): 659–62; Decision on Petition for Writ of Mandamus, Aug. 17, 1962, ibid., 660–62; *BN*, Aug. 10, 18, 1962; *SSN*, Sept. 1962; Thornton, *Dividing Lines*, 218–19.

8. Jack Bass, *Unlikely Heroes: The Dramatic Story of the Southern Judges of the Fifth Judicial Circuit Who Translated the Supreme Court's Brown Decision into a Revolution for Equality* (New York: Simon and Schuster, 1981), 15–25; Constance Baker Motley, *Equal Justice under Law: An Autobiography* (New York: Farrar, Strauss, and Giroux, 1998), 133–35; "That Fascinating and Frenetic Fifth," *Time*, Dec. 4, 1964; "Interpreter in the Front Line," *Time*, May 12, 1967, 72; J. W. Peltason, *Fifty-Eight Lonely Men: Southern Federal Judges and School Desegregation* (New York: Harcourt, Brace and World, 1961), 26–28, 118; Harvie Wilkinson, *From Brown to Bakke: The Supreme Court and School Integration, 1954–1978* (New York: Oxford University Press, 1981), 81; Jack Greenberg, *Crusaders in the Courts: How a Dedicated Band of Lawyers Fought for the Civil Rights Revolution* (New York: Basic Books, 1994), 352.

9. Emphasis in original. *BN*, Aug. 13, 20, 29, 1962; Bush v. Orleans Parish School Board, 308 F.2d 491 (5th CCA, Aug. 1962), 491–99; Augustus v. Board of Public Instruction of Escambia County, 306 F.2d 862 (5th Cir., July 1962), 499, 869.

10. *BN*, Sept. 5, 1962; *SSN*, Sept., Nov. 1962.

11. *BN*, Sept. 5, 1962; *Atlanta Journal*, Sept. 5, 1962; "Segregation in Public Schools Built with Federal Funds," files of W. Wilson White, 1958–1959, Memorandum from White to

Deputy Attorney General, May 19, 1959, Files of Joseph M. F. Ryan, 1958–1960, *Records of the United States Department of Justice's Civil Rights Division, 1958–1973*, in *The Civil Rights Movement and the Federal Government* [microfilm] (Bethesda, Md.: LexisNexis, 2008) [hereafter DOJ CRD Records].

12. Memorandum from Marshall to Barrett, July 10, 1962, Files of Joseph M. F. Ryan, 1958–1960, DOJ CRD Records; Michael R. Belknap, ed., *Civil Rights, the White House, and the Justice Department, 1945–1968*, vol. 17, *Administrative History of the Civil Rights Division of the Department of Justice During the Johnson Administration* (New York: Garland, 1991), 5–8; Brian Landsberg, *Enforcing Civil Rights: Race Discrimination and the Department of Justice* (Lawrence: University of Kansas Press, 1997), 1–5, 135–38; Carl Brauer, *John F. Kennedy and the Second Reconstruction* (New York: Cambridge University Press, 1977), 124–46; St. John Barrett, *The Drive for Equality: A History of Civil Rights Enforcement* (Baltimore: Publish America, 2009); *WP*, June 17, 2012 (Barrett obituary).

13. Memorandum from Marshall to Robert Kennedy, "re Huntsville Alabama School Situation," July 31, 1962, and Barrett, Memorandum, "Legal Action on Impacted Area Schooling," Aug. 24, 1962, in *Civil Rights, The White House, and the Justice Department, 1945–1968*, vol. 7, *Desegregation of Public Education*, ed. Michael Belknap (New York: Garland, 1991), documents 64–65.

14. *SSN*, Nov. 1962; Thornton, *Dividing Lines*, 218–19; *NYT*, Oct. 23–27, 1962.

15. *SSN*, Nov. 1962; *BN*, Oct. 26, 1962; Thornton, *Dividing Lines*, 218–19. On Critz, see John Jackson, *Science for Segregation: Race, Law, and the Case against "Brown v. Board of Education"* (New York: New York University Press, 2005).

16. Petition to the BOE of Mobile in DOJ-CRD's Historical Documents Online, FOIA Electronic Reading Room, Desegregation of Schools, Alabama (reel 037, parts 1–6), http://www.justice.gov/crt/foia/readingroom [hereafter DOJ-CRD FOIA Records Online]; *MA*, Nov. 15, 1962; *SSN*, Dec. 1962; Scotty E. Kirkland, "Pink Sheets and Black Ballots: Politics and Civil Rights in Mobile, Alabama, 1945–1985" (master's thesis, University of South Alabama, 2009), 30–37, 102.

17. Carter, *Politics of Rage*, 98–109; In re: Wallace, Stokes, Rogers, Livingston, Evans, and Spencer, Dec. 11, 1958–Jan. 26, 1959, *RRLR* 4, no. 1 (Spring 1959): 97–122; *SSN*, Oct. 1963; *BN*, Oct. 3, 1962.

18. *SSN*, Nov., Dec. 1962, Jan. 1963; "Let's Work Together," pamphlet of the ACMHR, Southern Education Reporting Service, *Facts on Film*, 1962–1963 supplement, under "Misc. Materials." On business moderates, see Glen Eskew, *But for Birmingham: The Local and National Movements in the Civil Rights Struggle* (Chapel Hill: University of North Carolina Press, 1997); and Thornton, *Dividing Lines*. On clergy, see Wayne Flynt, *Alabama Baptists: Southern Baptists in the Heart of Dixie* (Tuscaloosa: University of Alabama Press, 1998), 517–20; David Chappell, *Stone of Hope: Prophetic Religion and the Death of Jim Crow* (Chapel Hill: University of North Carolina Press, 2004), 107, 131.

19. Mobile Board to Petitioners, Jan. 15, 1063, DOJ-CRD FOIA Records Online, Desegregation of Schools, Alabama, part 6; *MA*, Jan. 16, 1963; *Jackson Daily News*, Jan. 16, 1963.

20. U.S. v. Madison County BOE, *RRLR* 8, no. 2 (Summer 1963): 490; *SSN*, Feb., April 1963; *MA*, Feb. 1, 2, 8, 1963; *BN*, Feb. 7, 1963.

21. Bride Mae Davis et al. v. Board of School Commissioners of Mobile County, C.A. 3003, Original Complaint, in DOJ-CRD FOIA Records Online; *SSN*, Feb., April 1963; *MA*, Feb. 1, 2, 8, 1963; *BN*, Feb. 7, 1963.

22. *SSN*, April 1963; *NYT*, March 26, 2011; *WP*, March 27, 2011; Frye Gaillard, *Cradle of Freedom: Alabama and the Movement That Changed America* (Tuscaloosa: University of Alabama Press, 2004), 185–86; Sheryll Cashin, *The Agitator's Daughter: A Memoir of Four Generations of One Extraordinary African-American Family* (New York: Public Affairs, 2012).

23. Anthony Lee, interview with the author, Nov. 14, 2011, digital recording in possession of the author; Anthony Lee, interview with Brian Landsberg, Sept. 6, 2012, transcript in possession of the author; *SSN*, Feb. 1963; Fred Gray, *Bus Ride to Justice: Changing the System by the System* (Selma: Black Belt Press, 1995), 208–9; Robert J. Norrell, *Reaping the Whirlwind: The Civil Rights Movement in Tuskegee* (New York: Knopf, 1985), 57, 137–38, 166–69; Solomon Seay Jr., *Jim Crow and Me: Stories from My Life as a Civil Rights Lawyer* (Montgomery: New South, 2008), 89, 91, 97; Lee v. Macon County BOE (Civil Action 604-E), Original Complaint, filed Jan. 28, 1963, LVMTR; *Baltimore Afro-American*, March 2, 1963; *SSN*, April, 1963.

24. The Birmingham Truce Agreement, DOJ-CRD FOIA Records Online; Eskew, *But for Birmingham*, 217–97; *BN*, June 22, 23, 1955; Thornton, *Dividing Lines*, 218–19, 231–333; Brauer, *John F. Kennedy and the Second Reconstruction*, 278; Diane McWhorter, *Carry Me Home: Birmingham, Alabama: The Climactic Battle of the Civil Rights Revolution* (New York: Simon and Schuster, 2001), 303–570.

25. *SSN*, June 1963; Lucy v. Adams, Malone v. Mate, and U.S. v. Wallace, June 5, 1963, all in *RRLR* 8, no. 2 (Summer 1963): 448–52, 453–55.

26. *SSN*, June 1963; *NYT*, Sept. 12, 2000 (Lynne obituary).

27. *SSN*, April, June, July, 1963; U.S. v. Wallace, *RRLR* 8, no. 2 (Summer 1963): 54; Carter, *Politics of Rage*, 133–55, 150–51; E. Culpepper Clark, *The Schoolhouse Door: Segregation's Last Stand at the University of Alabama* (Tuscaloosa: University of Alabama Press, 2007).

28. John F. Kennedy, "Radio and Television Report to the American People on Civil Rights, 11 June 1963," Kennedy Presidential Library and Museum, http://www.jfklibrary.org/; Brauer, *John F. Kennedy and the Second Reconstruction*, 247–64.

29. *NYT*, May 29, 2963; *MA*, July 21, 1963; *SSN*, July 1963; *BN*, May 28, Sept. 1, 1963; Armstrong v. the BOE of the City of Birmingham, *RRLR* 8, no. 2 (Summer 1963): 460–65. See also 220 F. Supp. 217 (N. D., Ala., 1963).

30. *NYT*, May 29, 1963; *MA*, May 29, 1963; *BN*, May 29, June 26, 1963; Bass, *Unlikely Heroes*, 159–60, 227; Stell v. Savannah-Chatham County BOE, 318 F.2d 425 (5th CCA, 1963); Watson v. Memphis, 373 U.S. 526 (1963); Goss v. BOE of the City Knoxville, 373 U.S. 683 (1963).

31. *BN*, May 29, 1963; *MA*, June 28, 1963.

32. Tony Freyer and Timothy Dixon, *Democracy and Judicial Independence: A History of Federal Courts in Alabama, 1820–1994* (New York: Carlson, 1995), 137–45, 278; Brian Landsberg, *Free at Last to Vote: The Alabama Origins of the Voting Rights Act* (Lawrence: University of Kansas Press, 2007), 117–20; Motley, *Equal Justice under Law*, 147; Brian Landsberg, interview with the author, March 29, 2012, digital recording in possession of the author.

33. Davis v. Board of School Commissioners of Mobile County, *RRLR* 8, no. 2 (Summer 1963): 480–85; *SSN*, May, July, July 1963; *BN*, June 10, 25, 1963; *MA*, June 11, 25, 1963. For Davis case, see also 318 F.2d 63 (5th CCA, 1963); and 219 F.Supp. 542 (S. D., Ala., 1963).

34. Davis v. Board, *RRLR* 8, no. 2 (Summer 1963): 485–88, see also at 322 F.2d 356 (5th CCA, 1963); Armstrong v. BOE, *RRLR* 8, no. 2 (Summer 1963): 466–80, see also at 323 F.2d 333 (5th CCA, 1963); *SSN*, Aug. 1963; *BN*, June 27, 29, 1963; Bass, *Unlikely Heroes*, 227–30; Thornton, *Dividing Lines*, 219–20; Freyer and Dixon, *Democracy and Judicial Independence*, 203–5; *NYT*, Sept. 11, 1963.

35. Armstrong v. BOE, *RRLR* 8. no. 2 (Summer 1963): 470–80, see also at 323 F.2d 333 (5th CCA, 1963); *SSN*, Aug. 1963.

36. Armstrong v. BOE, *RRLR* 8, no. 3 (Fall 1963): 890–96, see also at 323 F.2d 333, 352; Bass, *Unlikely Heroes*, 231–47; Frank Read and Lisa McGough, *Let Them Be Judged: The Judicial Integration of the Deep South* (Metuchen, N.J.: Scarecrow Press, 1978), 261–80.

37. Bass, *Unlikely Heroes*, 229–31; Read and McGough, *Let Them Be Judged*, 407; Armstrong v. BOE of the City of Birmingham, *RRLR* 8, no. 3 (Fall 1963): 888–89; Davis v. Board of School Commissioners, *RRLR* 8, no. 3 (Fall 1963): 901–4, stay denied, 84 S.Ct. 10; Hereford v. Huntsville BOE, *RRLR* 8, no. 3 (Fall 1963): 908–9; Docket Report, Hereford v. Huntsville Case File, U.S. District Court, N. D., Alabama.

38. "Interpreter in the Front Line," *Time*, May 12, 1967, 84–93; Freyer and Dixon, *Democracy and Judicial Independence*, 215–55; Landsberg, *Free at Last to Vote*, 92–93; Landsberg interview; Solomon Seay, interview with author, Feb. 1, 2012, digital recording and transcript in possession of the author.

39. Lee v. Macon County BOE, Order of July 16, 1963, LVMTR; Landsberg interview.

40. David Norman to St. John Barrett, August 15, 1963, DOJ CRD Case Files, Lee v. Macon County (Case # 144-100-2-1), section 2, National Archives and Records Administration, College Park, Md.; Johnson, Handwritten Notes from Aug. 13, 1963 Hearing, Brief in Support of Defendants' Motion, May 24, 1963, Johnson, Handwritten Notes on Armstrong v. BOE Opinion, LVMCF, FMJP, C20, Fs 9, 10; Lee v. Macon, Order of August 22, 1963, *RRLR* 8, no. 3 (Fall 1963): 909–12, also at 221 F.Supp. 297.

41. Norrell, *Reaping the Whirlwind*, 138–39; "Applications for Transfer to Tuskegee Public School, Term Beginning September 2, 1963, Approved and Denied," LVMCF, FMJP, C20, F9.

42. Willie Wyatt, interview with the author, Jan. 4, 2012, digital recording and transcript in possession of the author; Landsberg, *Free at Last to Vote*, 27–28.

43. Memorandum from Captain R. W. Godwin and Lieutenant E. J. Dixon to Major W. R. Jones, Commander, Investigative and Identification Division, Aug. 29, 1963, GAAF, SG 19974, ADAH; Norrell, *Reaping the Whirlwind*, 140–43; *NYT*, Sept. 1, 1963; *TN*, Feb. 9, 2012.

44. Memorandum from Godwin/Dixon to Jones, Aug. 29, 1963, GAAF, SG 19974, ADAH; Norrell, *Reaping the Whirlwind*, 140–43; *NYT*, Sept. 1, 1963; Thornton, *Dividing Lines*, 339; Carter, *Politics of Rage*, 167.

45. Burke Marshall to St. John Barrett, August 13, 1963, and Burke Marshall to J. Edgar Hoover, Aug. 16, 1963, DOJ-CRD FOIA Records Online, part 1; *BN*, July 15, 16, 18, Aug. 21, 28, Sept. 1, 1963; *SSN*, Aug. 1963.

46. *BN*, July 10, 15, 23, 24, Aug. 10, 17, 21, 25, 28, Sept. 1, 1963; *MA*, July 5, 23, 1963.

47. *MA*, July 3, Sept. 1, 1963; Thornton, *Dividing Lines*, 336–40. On Stoner, see Clive Webb, *Rabble Rousers: The American Far Right in the Civil Rights Era* (Athens: University of Georgia Press), 153–83; Carter, *Politics of Rage*, 164–68.

48. Armstrong v. BOE of the City of Birmingham, *RRLR* 8, no. 3 (Fall 1963): 899–901; Petition for Intervention and Stay, 323 F.2d 333 (5th CCA, 1963); Cooper v. Aaron, 358 U.S. 1 (1958); *SSN*, Aug., Sept. 1963; Carter, *Politics of Rage*, 167–69.

49. Davis v. Board of School Commissioners, Approval of Plan, August 23, 1963, *RRLR* 8, no. 3 (Fall 1963): 907–8; *BN*, July 15, 16, 18, 1963; *SSN*, Aug., Sept. 1963; Richard Pride, *The Political Use of Racial Narratives: School Desegregation in Mobile, Alabama, 1954–1997* (Urbana: University of Illinois Press, 2002), 38–45; Kirkland, *Pink Sheets and Black Ballots*, 49–51, 88, 114.

50. *MA*, Aug. 23, 1963; *BN*, Aug. 30, 1963; Pride, *Political Use of Racial Narratives*, 39–40; *NYT*, Sept. 1, 1963.

51. Ennis Sellers, "My Four Years Serving the Tuskegee United Methodist Church," unpublished manuscript in possession of author and ADAH, 4–5.

52. Marshall to Director, FBI, Aug. 19, 1963, Doar to Barrett, Aug. 21, 1963, DOJ-CRD FOIA Records Online, part 2.

53. Executive Order Nine and Ten, in GAAF, SG 19974, ADAH; Testimony of C. A. Pruitt, Trial Transcript, U.S. v. George Wallace et al., Sept. 24, 1963, in DOJ-CRD FOIA Records Online, part 3; Sellers, "My Four Years Serving the Tuskegee United Methodist Church," 5; *NYT*, Sept. 8, 1963; Norrell, *Reaping the Whirlwind*, 145–7; Carter, *Politics of Rage*, 162–63; Brauer, *John F. Kennedy and the Second Reconstruction*, 292–3.

54. Sellers, "My Four Years Serving the Tuskegee United Methodist Church," 5–6; *TN*, Feb. 9, 2012; *SSN*, Sept., 1963; Norrell, *Reaping the Whirlwind*, 144–45.

55. *SSN*, Sept., 1963; Norrell, *Reaping the Whirlwind*, 144–5; Wallace, Statement on Executive Order Number Nine, GAAF, SG 19974, ADAH.

56. Thornton, *Dividing Lines*, 336–40; Carter, *Politics of Rage*, 164–69.

57. Telegram, Shuttlesworth et al. to Attorney General Robert Kennedy, Sept. 4, 1963, Richard Wasserstrom to Burke Marshall (2), Aug. 30, 1963, St. John Barrett, Memorandum to Personal File, Aug. 31, 1963, all in DOJ-CRD FOIA Records Online, part 6; Thornton, *Dividing Lines*, 340–1; *SSN*, Sept., 1963; *LAT*, Sept. 8, 1963.

58. Thornton, *Dividing Lines*, 341–3; *NYT*, Sept. 8, 1963; *SSN*, Sept., 1963; Carter, *Politics of Rage*, 169–71.

59. Thornton, *Dividing Lines*, 341–43; *NYT*, Sept. 8, 1963; *SSN*, Sept., 1963; Carter, *Politics of Rage*, 169–71.

60. Motion for Issuance of an Order to Show Cause, Sept. 6, 1963, Hereford v. Huntsville BOE, DOJ-CRD FOIA Records Online; Hereford v. Huntsville BOE Docket Report; *NYT*, Sept. 7, 8, 1963; *LAT*, Sept. 8, 1963; *SSN*, Sept., 1963.

61. *NYT*, Sept. 8, 1963; *MA*, Sept. 7, 8, 1963; *BN*, Sept. 9, 1963; Hereford v. Huntsville Docket Report; Brauer, *John F. Kennedy and the Second Reconstruction*, 293.

62. *NYT*, Sept. 8, 1963; *MA*, Sept. 7, 8, 1963; *BN*, Sept. 9, 1963; *St. Louis Post-Dispatch*, Sept. 9, 1963, *Baltimore Afro-American*, Sept. 14, 1963; Thornton, *Dividing Lines*, 344.

63. Executive Orders Eleven and Twelve, in GAAF, SG 19974, ADAH; *St. Louis Post-Dispatch*, Sept. 9, 1963; *NYT*, Sept. 10, 1963.

64. *BN*, Sept. 9, 1963; Pride, *Political Use of Racial Narratives*, 40–41; *St. Louis Post-Dispatch*, Sept. 9, 1963; *NYT*, Sept. 10, 1963, *SSN*, Oct. 1963.

65. *BN*, Sept. 9, 1963; *St. Louis Post-Dispatch*, Sept. 9, 1963; *NYT*, Sept. 10, 1963.

66. Testimony of C. A. Pruitt, trial transcript, United States v. George Wallace et al., Sept. 24, 1963, in DOJ-CRD FOIA Records Online, part 3; Memorandum from Captain C.S. Prier to Colonel Albert J. Lingo, Sept. 11, 1963, in GAAF, SG 19974, ADAH; Wyatt interview.

67. *St. Louis Post-Dispatch*, Sept. 9, 1963; *WP*, Sept. 10, 1963; Thornton, *Dividing Lines*, 344.

68. Draft Memorandum to Burke Marshall, Prepared by Ben Hardeman and St. John Barrett, in DOJ-CRD FOIA Records Online, part 1; Brauer, *John F. Kennedy and the Second Reconstruction*, 294; *BN*, Sept. 10, 1963; *MA*, Sept. 10, 1963; U.S. v. Wallace, Civ. A. No. 1976-N (M. D., Ala., 1963).

69. Brauer, *John F. Kennedy and the Second Reconstruction*, 294; *BN*, Sept. 10, 1963; *MA*, Sept. 10, 1963; U.S. v. Wallace, Civ. A. No. 1976-N (M. D., Ala., 1963), TRO of Sept. 9, 1963, *RRLR* 8, no. 3 (Fall 1963): 816–18, see also in GAAF, SG 19974, ADAH; Thornton, *Dividing Lines*, 344.

70. Testimony of Donald D. Forsht, U.S. marshal, in Trial Transcript, U.S. v. Wallace, DOJ-CRD FOIA Records Online, part 3; *BN*, Sept. 10, 1963; *MA*, Sept. 10, 11, 1963; Thornton, *Dividing Lines*, 344.

71. Forsht Testimony and Testimony of Alfred C. Harrison, Adjutant General, in U.S. v. Wallace Trial Transcript, DOJ-CRD FOIA Records Online, part 3; Executive Order Number Thirteen, GAAF, SG 19974, ADAH; *BN*, Sept. 10, 1963; *MA*, Sept. 10, 11, 1963; Thornton, *Dividing Lines*, 344.

72. Presidential Proclamation 3554 and Executive Order 11118, *RRLR* 8, no. 3 (Fall 1963): 919–20; Harrison Testimony, U.S. v. Wallace Trial Transcript; *BN*, Sept. 10, 1963.

73. *BN*, Sept. 10, 12, 17, 1963; *MA*, Sept. 13, 14, 1963; Pride, *Political Use of Racial Narratives*, 43; *NYT*, Sept. 11, 14, 1963.

74. *NYT*, Sept. 11, 1963; *WP*, Sept. 11, 1963; *MA*, Sept. 11, 1963; *SSN*, Oct. 1963; Thornton, *Dividing Lines*, 345.

75. *NYT*, Sept. 11, 1963; *WP*, Sept. 11, 1963; *MA*, Sept. 11, 1963; *SSN*, Oct. 1963; Thornton, *Dividing Lines*, 345.

76. *TN*, Sept. 5, 12, 19, 1963; *SSN*, Oct. 1963; Norrell, *Reaping the Whirlwind*, 148–50; Andy Sharpe and Andy Hornsby, correspondence with author, June 18, 2014; Sharpe's unpublished manuscript in possession of the author.

77. Sharpe manuscript.

78. *TN*, Sept. 5, 12, 19, 1963; *SSN*, Oct. 1963; Norrell, *Reaping the Whirlwind*, 148–50.

79. Sellers, "My Four Years Serving the Tuskegee United Methodist Church," 6–8; *TN*, Sept. 5, 19, 1963; *SSN*, Oct. 1963; Norrell, *Reaping the Whirlwind*, 103–5, 148–50; Hall v. St. Helena Parish School Board, 197 F. Supp. 649 (E. D., La., 1961), affirmed, 368 U.S. 515 (1962).

80. *TN*, Sept. 19, 1963; Gallion to Wallace, GAAF, Macon Academy, SG 19969, ADAH.

81. *NYT*, Sept. 14, 1963; *SSN*, Oct. 1963; Thornton, *Dividing Lines*, 345.

82. *NYT*, Sept. 14, 1963; *Knoxville News-Sentinel*, Sept. 23, 1963; *BN*, Sept. 20, 24, 1963; *SSN*, Oct. 1963; Thornton, *Dividing Lines*, 345.

83. *MA*, Sept. 16, 1963; Carter, *Politics of Rage*, 181–82; Thornton, *Dividing Lines*, 146–47; Eskew, *But for Birmingham*, 318–21.

84. *MA*, Sept. 16, 1963; Carter, *Politics of Rage*, 181–82; Thornton, *Dividing Lines*, 146–47; Eskew, *But for Birmingham*, 318–21.

85. Allen G. Breed and Holbrook Mohr, AP, "FBI Says the End Is Near for Investigations into Civil Rights Era Cold Cases," *Huffington Post*, Nov. 5, 2011, http://www.huffingtonpost.com/; Tim Padgett and Frank Sikora, "The Legacy of Virgil Ware," *Time*, Sept. 22, 2003, 53–59.

86. *MA*, Sept. 16, 1963; *SSN*, Oct. 1963; *BN*, Sept. 21, 1963; Eskew, *But for Birmingham*, 318–21; Carter, *Politics of Rage*, 181–82; Thornton, *Dividing Lines*, 146–47, 347.

87. Carter, *Politics of Rage*, 181–82; *SSN*, Oct. 1963; *BN*, Sept. 21, 1963, reprinting editorials from the Talladega and Cullman newspapers; *Alabama Baptist*, Sept. 19, 1963; Thornton, *Dividing Lines*, 347.

88. *SSN*, Oct. 1963; *BN*, Sept. 21, 1963, reprinting editorials from cited newspapers; *Alabama Baptist*, Sept. 19, 1963; Thornton, *Dividing Lines*, 347.

89. *BN*, Sep. 16, 21, 29, 1963; *SSN*, Oct., 1963; *MA*, Sept. 17, 1963; Carter, *Politics of Rage*, 181–82.

90. *BN*, Sept. 21, 28, 1963, reprinting editorials from the Talladega, Huntsville, and Tuscaloosa newspapers; *SSN*, Oct. 1963; *Alabama Baptist*, Sept. 19, 1963.

91. *BN*, Sept. 19, 1963.

92. Andrew Cohen, "The Speech That Shocked Birmingham the Day after the Church Bombing," *Atlantic*, Sept. 13, 2013; *SSN*, Oct. 1963; Carter, *Politics of Rage*, 181–82; Eskew, *But for Birmingham*, 318–21. Morgan obituaries: *WP*, Jan. 9, 2009; *NYT*, Jan. 9, 2009; *LAT*, Jan. 12, 2009.

93. *BN*, Sept. 30, 1963, reprinted as Southern Regional Council Report L-46, Nov. 15, 1963, *Facts on Film*, *1963–64 Supplement*, Misc. Materials.

94. Carter, *Politics of Rage*, 189–95; Thornton, *Dividing Lines*, 145; *SSN*, Oct. 1963; U.S. v. Wallace, Preliminary Injunction of Sept. 24, 1963, *RRLR* 8, no. 3 (Fall 1963): 920–24; Padgett and Sikora, "Legacy of Virgil Ware"; Cohen, "The Speech That Shocked Birmingham the Day after the Church Bombing."

95. *BN*, Sept. 23, 1963.

Chapter 3. "Now a Single Shot Can Do It"

1. *BN*, Jan. 14, 1964; *MA*, Sept. 17, 1963; Robert J. Norrell, *Reaping the Whirlwind: The Civil Rights Movement in Tuskegee* (New York: Knopf, 1985), 153–60.

2. Amended and Supplemental Complaint, Feb. 3, 1964, and Writ of Injunction, Temporary Restraining Order, Feb. 3, 1964, LVMCF, FMJP, C28, F5; *BN*, Jan. 12, 14., 1964; *MA*, Sept. 17, 1963; Norrell, *Reaping the Whirlwind*, 153–60.

3. *TN*, Jan. 30, 1964; *SSN*, Feb. 1964.

4. Merle Black and Earl Black, *Politics and Society in the South* (Cambridge: Harvard University Press, 1989), 8–15; Wayne Flynt, *Alabama in the Twentieth Century* (Tuscaloosa: University of Alabama Press, 2004), 318–25.

5. *A Statistical Summary of School Segregation-Desegregation in the Southern and Border States* (Nashville: Southern Education Reporting Service, 1961), 4–6; *SSN*, Feb., May, June 1964; *BN*, Nov. 9, 1963; *MA*, Nov. 13, 16, 1963; Richard Pride, *The Political Use of Racial Narratives: School Desegregation in Mobile, Alabama, 1954–1997* (Urbana: University of Illinois Press, 2002), 48–53.

6. Amended and Supplemental Complaint, Writ of Injunction, and Temporary Restraining Order, Feb. 3, 1964, LVMCF, FMJP, C28, F5; Norrell, *Reaping the Whirlwind*, 160.

7. Amended Complaint, Injunction, TRO, Feb. 3, 1964, LVMCF, FMJP, C28, F5; *MA*, Feb. 4, 6, 1964; Fred Gray, *Bus Ride to Justice: Changing the System by the System* (Selma: Black Belt Press, 1995), 213–14; Norrell, *Reaping the Whirlwind*, 160.

8. Amended LVM Complaint; *BN*, Feb. 3, 1964; *MA*, Feb. 4, 1964.

9. Writ of Injunction and TRO, Feb. 3, 1964, LVMCF, FMJP, C28, F5.

10. Amendment to Amended Complaint, Feb. 10, 1964, LVMCF, FMJP, C28, F5; Brief of the U.S. in Support of Plaintiffs' Motion, March 13, 1964, and Memorandum Brief of

Plaintiffs in Support of Their Motion, March 23, 1964, LVMCF, FMJP, C19, F9; Petition Seeking Instructions, Feb. 6, 1964, LVMCF, FMJP, C28, F5; *MA*, Feb. 6, 1964.

11. *BN*, Feb. 5, 6, 1964; *NYT*, Feb. 6, 1964.

12. U.S. v. Rea, 231 F.Supp. 772 (M. D., Ala., 1964), 773–74, see also at *RRLR* 9, no. 1 (Spring 1964): 156–58; Notasulga, Alabama, Ordinances of Feb. 3, 1964, *RRLR* 9, no. 1 (Spring 1964: 154–55; *SSN*, Feb. 1964; *BN*, Feb. 5, 6, 1964; *NYT*, Feb. 6, 1964.

13. *SSN*, Feb. 1964; *BN*, Feb. 5, 6, 1964; *NYT*, Feb. 6, 1964.

14. *BN*, Feb. 5, 6, 1964; *NYT*, Feb. 6, 1964; *Jackson Daily News*, Feb. 6, 1964; *WP*, Feb. 6, 1964.

15. *BN*, Feb. 5, 6, 1964; *NYT*, Feb. 6, 1964; *Jackson Daily News*, Feb. 6, 1964; *WP*, Feb. 6, 1964.

16. *NYT*, Feb. 6, 1964; *BN*, Feb. 6, 1964; *MA*, Feb. 6, 1964; *Jackson Daily News*, Feb. 6, 1964; *WP*, Feb. 6, 1964; *St. Petersburg Times*, Feb. 6, 1964; Willie Wyatt, interview with the author, Jan. 4, 2012, digital recording and transcript in possession of the author; Anthony Lee, interview with the author, Nov. 14, 2011, digital recording in possession of the author; *SSN*, Feb. 1964; Norrell, *Reaping the Whirlwind*, 161.

17. *NYT*, Feb. 6, 1964; *BN*, Feb. 6, 1964; *MA*, Feb. 6, 1964; *Jackson Daily News*, Feb. 6, 1964; *WP*, Feb. 6, 1964; *St. Petersburg Times*, Feb. 6, 1964; *SSN*, Feb. 1964; Norrell, *Reaping the Whirlwind*, 161.

18. U.S. v. Rea, 231 F.Supp. 772 (M. D., Ala., 1964), 773–74, see also at *RRLR* 9, no. 1 (Spring 1964): 156–58; Amendment to Amended Complaint, LVMCF, FMJP, C28, F5; *NYT*, Feb. 6, 1964; *BN*, Feb. 6, 1964; *MA*, Feb. 6, 1964; *Jackson Daily News*, Feb. 6, 1964; *St. Petersburg Times*, Feb. 6, 1964; Wyatt interview; Lee interview; *SSN*, Feb. 1964; Norrell, *Reaping the Whirlwind*, 161.

19. *RRLR* 9, no. 1 (Spring 1964): 156–58; Amendment to Amended Complaint, LVMCF, FMJP, C28, F5; *MA*, Feb. 6, 15, 1964; *BN*, Feb. 6, 7, 14, 16, 1964; *TN*, Feb. 20, 1964; *Jackson Daily News*, Feb. 10, 1964; *NYT*, Feb. 13, 1964; Norrell, *Reaping the Whirlwind*, 161.

20. Alabama Supreme Court Advisory Opinion, Feb. 18, 1964, *RRLR* 9, no. 1 (Winter 1964): 159–61; Resolution of the Alabama State BOE, Feb. 18, 1964, LVMCF, FMJP, C21, F6; *BN*, Feb. 8, 1964; *MA*, Feb. 19, 1964; John Hayman, *Bitter Harvest: Richmond Flowers and the Civil Rights Revolution* (Montgomery, AL: River City Publishing, 1996), 182–85.

21. U.S. v. Rea, 231 F.Supp. 772 (M. D., Ala., 1964), see also *RRLR* 9, no. 1 (Winter 1964): 156–58; *SSN*, March 1964; *Auburn Plainsman*, Feb. 12, 1964; *BN*, Feb. 11, 16, 1964; *MA*, Feb. 15, 1964; Richard Rives to Elbert Tuttle, Jan. 30, 1963, and Elbert Tuttle to Rives and Johnson, Feb. 3, 1964, LVMCF, FMJP, C21, F1; Feb. 7, 1964, Order of the Fifth Circuit Court of Appeals Designating a Three-Judge Court, LVMTR.

22. Frank Johnson, Handwritten Notes from Feb. 21–22 Hearing, LVMCF, FMJP, C28, F5; *BN*, Feb. 22, 1964; *MA*, Feb. 22, 1964.

23. Frank Johnson, Handwritten Notes from Feb. 21–22 Hearing, LVMCF, FMJP, C28, F5; *BN*, Feb. 22, 1964; *MA*, Feb. 22, 1964.

24. *BN*, Feb. 21, 1964; *MA*, Feb. 21, 23, 1964; Motion of Attorney General of the State, Answer of Defendant State BOE, Feb. 20, 1964, Motion to Dissolve or Modify TRO, Feb. 5, 1964, LVMCF, FMJP, C28, F5.

25. Issues on Which Briefs Are Requested, LVMCF, FMJP, C28, F4.

26. Memorandum Brief of the U.S., March 13, 1964, Memorandum Brief of Plaintiffs, March 23, 1964, LVMCF, FMJP, C19, F9.

27. Memorandum Brief of the U.S., March 13, 1964, LVMCF, FMJP, C19, F9.
28. Memorandum Brief of the U.S., March 13, 1964, 36–45; Memorandum Brief of the State BOE, April 10, 1964, 7–41; Reply Brief of the U.S. in Support of Plaintiffs' Motion, April 22, 1964, 8, 11, 21—all in Johnson Papers: LVCM, C19, F9; *MA*, March 14, 17, 1964; *BN*, March 17, 1964.
29. Plaintiffs' Motion for Additional Relief, April 24, 1964, LVMCF, FMJP, C28, F4; Memorandum Opinion and Injunction, April 28, 1964, LVMTR; *TN*, April 9, 1964; Norrell, *Reaping the Whirlwind*, 161; *MA*, May 1, 1964.
30. *MA*, March 13, April 18, 19, 24, 1964; *NYT*, March 14, June 14, 1964; *BN*, April 18, 19, 21, 1964; Lee interview, Wyatt interview.
31. *TN*, May 7, June 11, 1964; *MA*, June 13, 1964. On Kilpatrick, see William Hustwit, *James J. Kilpatrick: Salesman for Segregation* (Chapel Hill: University of North Carolina Press, 2013).
32. Griffin v. County School Board of Prince Edward, 377 U.S. 218 (1964); Calhoun v. Lattimer 377 U.S. 263 (1964); Harvie Wilkinson, *From Brown to Bakke: The Supreme Court and School Integration, 1954–1978* (New York: Oxford University Press, 1981), 98–101; Jack Greenberg, *Crusaders in the Courts: How a Dedicated Band of Lawyers Fought for the Civil Rights Revolution* (New York: Basic Books, 1994), 581n382.
33. *SSN*, June, July, 1964; Armstrong v. Birmingham BOE, 333 F.2d 47; Davis v. BSC of Mobile County, 333 F.2d 53; *RRLR* 9, no. 2 (Summer 1964): 620–26; *MA*, Aug. 4, 8, 1964; Bennett v. Madison County BOE (N. D.); Carr v. Montgomery County BOE, 232 F.Supp. 705 (M. D.); Harris v. Bullock County BOE, 232 F.Supp 959 (M. D.); Miller v. BOE of Gadsden; *RRLR* 9, no. 3 (Fall 1964): 1163–98.
34. Lee v. Macon Opinion and Decree of July 13, 1964, 231 F.Supp. 743; *RRLR* 9, no. 2 (Summer 1964): 626–38; *NYT*, July 14, 1964; *BN*, July 14, 1964; *MA*, July 14, 1964.
35. Lee v. Macon Opinion and Decree of July 13, 1964, 231 F.Supp. 743.
36. Ibid., emphasis in original.
37. Ibid.
38. *SSN*, Aug. 1964; *NYT*, July 14, 1964; *MA*, July 14, 15, 1964; *BN*, July 14, 15, 17, 1964.
39. *BN*, July 18, 1964.
40. *BN*, July 5, 1964; *The Citizen*, July–Aug. 1964, 7; Katzenbach v. McClung, 379 U.S. 294 (1964), Heart of Atlanta Motel v. United States, 379 U.S. 241 (1964); Richard C. Cortner, *Civil Rights and Public Accommodations: The Heart of Atlanta Motel and McClung Cases* (Lawrence: University of Kansas Press, 2001).
41. Roy Wilkins, "The Role of the NAACP in the Desegregation Process," *Social Problems* 2, no. 4 (April 1955); Wilkinson, *From Brown to Bakke*, 101–7; Carl Brauer, *John F. Kennedy and the Civil Rights Revolution* (New York: Cambridge University Press, 1977), 250; Brian K. Landsberg, "The Kennedy Justice Department's Enforcement of Civil Rights: A View from the Trenches," in *John F. Kennedy, History, Memory, Legacy: An Interdisciplinary Inquiry*, ed. John D. Williams et al. (University of North Dakota Press Online), http://www.und.nodak.edu/instruct/jfkconference, 2012, pp. 4–10; Beryl A. Radin, *Implementation, Change, and the Federal Bureaucracy: School Desegregation Policy in HEW, 1964–1968*, Policy Analysis and Education Series (New York: Teachers' College Press, 1977), 4–7; *The Citizen*, Sept. 1964, 2.
42. *SSN*, Sept., Oct., Nov., Dec., 1964; *NYT*, Sept. 9, 1964; *BN*, Sept. 1, 3, 6, 8, 1964; *MA*, Aug. 27, Sept. 3, 6, 9, 1964; Norrell, *Reaping the Whirlwind*, 168. Harold Franklin, a graduate

student, was the first to desegregate Auburn. See Franklin v. Parker, 223 F.Supp 724 (M. D., Ala., 1963), mod. 331 F.2d 84 (5th CCA, 1963); and Gray, *Bus Ride to Justice*, 195-96.

43. *SSN*, Sept., Oct., Nov., Dec. 1964; *NYT*, Sept. 9, 1964; *BN*, Sept. 1, 3, 6, 8, 1964; *MA*, Aug. 27, Sept. 3, 6, 9, 1964; Ellen Levine, ed., *Freedom's Children: Young Civil Rights Activists Tell Their Own Stories* (New York: Puffin Books), 50-51.

44. *SSN*, Sept., Oct. 1964, Jan. 1965; *NYT*, Sept. 9, 1964; *BN*, Sept. 8, 1964; *Dallas Times-Herald*, Sep. 3, 1964; *MA*, Sept. 9, 1964.

45. *SSN*, Oct. 1964. On the New Right, see, among others, Joseph E. Lowndes, *From the New Deal to the New Right: Race and the Southern Origins of Modern Conservatism* (New Haven: Yale University Press, 2009); Joseph Crespino, *Strom Thurmond's America* (New York: Hill and Wang, 2012); Joseph Crespino, *In Search of Another Country: Mississippi and the Conservative Counterrevolution* (Princeton: Princeton University Press, 2009); Kevin M. Kruse, *White Flight: Atlanta and the Making of Modern Conservatism* (Princeton University Press, 2005); Glenn Feldman, *The Great Melding: War, the Dixiecrat Rebellion, and the Southern Model for America's New Conservatism* (Tuscaloosa: University of Alabama Press, 2014); Kari Frederickson, *The Dixiecrat Revolt and the End of the Solid South, 1932-1968* (Chapel Hill: University of North Carolina Press, 2001).

46. *SSN*, Dec. 1964, Feb. 1965.

47. Brian Landsberg, *Enforcing Civil Rights: Race Discrimination and the Department of Justice* (Lawrence: University of Kansas Press, 1997), 108-9; Wilkinson, *From Brown to Bakke*, 104-7; *SSN*, Jan. 1965; *BN*, Aug. 18, 1966.

48. *SSN*, Feb., March 1965; Trial Brief of the U.S., Jan. 5, 1967, LVMCF, FMJP, C19, F5, p. 14.

49. *SSN*, Feb., March 1965.

50. *SSN*, March, April 1965; David Garrow, *Protest at Selma: Martin Luther King, Jr., and the Voting Rights Act of 1965* (New Haven: Yale University Press, 1978); Brian Landsberg, *Free at Last to Vote: The Alabama Origins of the Voting Rights Act* (Lawrence: University of Kansas Press, 2007); Williams v. Wallace, 240 F.Supp. 100 (M. D., Ala., 1965).

51. *SSN*, March, April 1965; City of Bessemer BOE v. Gardner, C.A. 65-180 (N. D., Ala.).

52. *Profile of ESEA*, PL 89-10, HEW, USOE (Washington D.C.: GPO, 1966), 5-7, 26.

53. *General Statement of Policies under Title VI of the Civil Rights Act of 1964 Respecting Desegregation of Elementary and Secondary Schools*, HEW, USOE (Washington D.C.: GPO, 1965); *The First Year of School Desegregation under Title VI in Alabama: A Review with Observations and Conclusions*, Special Report of the ACHR (Huntsville, Ala.: ACHR, 1965).

54. *SSN*, April, May, June 1965.

55. *SSN*, June 1965; *Alabama Council Bulletin*, ACHR, May 18, 1965; *WP*, June 30, 1965; *BN*, June 26, 27, 1965; Trial Brief of the United States, Jan. 5, 1967, LVMCF, FMJP, C19, F5, pp. 16-17.

56. U.S. Brief in Support, Oct. 19, 1966, LVMCF, FMJP, C21, F6; *The First Year of School Desegregation under Title VI in Alabama*, ACHR; *School Desegregation in the Southern and Border States* [hereafter *SDSBS*], Sept. 1965; SERS; *The Citizen*, June, 1965; *MA*, June 11, 1965; *BN*, June 11, 1965.

57. U.S. Brief in Support, Oct. 19, 1966, LVMCF, FMJP, C21, F6; *BN*, May 25, June 5, 1965; *SSN*, June 1965.

58. *BN*, May 25, June 5, 1865; *SSN*, June 1965; Brown and U.S. v. BOE of the City of Bessemer, Stout and U.S. v. Jefferson County BOE, and Boykins and U.S. v. Fairfield; "Status

Report of School Cases," March 9, 1967, DOJ CRD Records, entry 306 F, Records of John Doar (boxes 1–2); Singleton v. Jackson, 348 F.2d 729, 731; Wilkinson, *From Brown to Bakke*, 111–12.

59. Affidavit of Jordan Gully, taken by Student Nonviolent Coordinating Committee (SNCC) and filed with the Alabama State Advisory Committee, U.S. Commission on Civil Rights (USCCR), in *The Civil Rights Movement and the Federal Government: Records of the U.S. Commission on Civil Rights, School Desegregation in the South, 1965–66* (microfilm) (Bethesda, Md.: LexisNexis, 2009) [hereafter, USCCR Alabama State Advisory Committee Files]: Alabama, Complaints, 1965 (1), reel 2, frame 113.

60. Ibid.

61. Robert Harris, Eli Logan, Willie Joe White, Cato Lee, and [illegible], Sworn Affidavits to SNCC; Bernice Johnson to Nicholas Katzenbach, Aug. 2, 1965—both in USCCR Alabama State Advisory Committee Files: Alabama, Complaints (1), 1965; Hasan K. Jeffries, *Bloody Lowndes: Civil Rights and Black Power in Alabama's Black Belt* (New York: New York University Press, 2009).

62. T. Y. Rogers to USCCR, Sept. 17, 1965; Alabama State Advisory Committee, Complaint Submitted to Mid-South Regional Office, Aug. 20, 1965; T. Y. Rogers to USCCR., Aug. 20, 1965; Henry McCaskill to State Advisory Committee, Aug. 18, 1965; Affidavit of Elizabeth Hutton, Aug. 28, 1965; "School Integration Attempt (Unsuccessful)," Sept. 11, 1965; Affidavit of Ginger Dunnican, Aug. 27, 1965; Affidavits of Annie Bryant and Dorothy Mae Bryant, Aug. 27, 1965; Affidavit of Dolores Ann Williams, Aug. 27, 1965—all in USCCR Alabama State Advisory Committee Files: Special Subjects, Alabama, Complaints (1), 1965; *SDSBS*, Feb. 1966.

63. "School Desegregation in Anniston Alabama," Robert Amidon and Jacques E. Wilmore, Oct. 1965, USCCR Alabama State Advisory Committee Files: Anniston, Alabama Report, reel 1, frame 208.

64. *The First Year of School Desegregation under Title VI in Alabama*, ACHR; *SDSBS*, Sept. 1965; Joseph Bagley, "A Meaningful Reality: The Desegregation of the Opelika, Alabama City School System, 1965–72" (master's thesis, Auburn University, 2007), 26.

65. Telegram from Governor Wallace et al. to R. A. Thornton, Superintendent, Lauderdale County, Sept. 3, 1965, *PNAACP*, supplement to part 23, LDCF, 1965–1972, Series A: The South, Section I: Alabama, reel 8, frame 0247; *The First Year of School Desegregation under Title VI in Alabama*, ACHR; Trial Brief of the U.S., Jan. 5, 1967, LVMCF, FMJP, C19, F5, pp. 17–18.

66. *The First Year of School Desegregation under Title VI in Alabama*, ACHR; *SDSBS*, Sept. 1965.

67. *SDSBS*, Oct., Nov., Dec. 1965.

68. *SDSBS*, Dec. 1965.

69. "Status Report of School Cases," March 9, 1967, in DOJ CRD Records, reel 8, frame 615, entry 306 F, Records of John Doar; *SDSBS*, Jan., Feb, March 1966; *RRLR* 11, no. 2 (Summer 1966): 682–93.

70. "Revised Statement of Policies for School Desegregation Plans under Title VI of the Civil Rights Act of 1964," 0-206-939, HEW (Washington, D.C.: GPO, 1966); John Gardner to Members of Congress, April 1966, in DOJ CRD Records: Records of John Doar, Policy Correspondence, 1965–66, reel 8, frame 615; *SDSBS*, March 1966.

71. Singleton v. Jackson MSSD, 355 F.2d 865 (5th CCA, 1966), 882; "Revised Statement of Policies," HEW; Gardner to Congress, April 1966, and Doar to U.S. Attorneys, April 21, 1966, DOJ CRD Records: Records of John Doar, Policy Correspondence, 1965–66.

72. "Revised Statement of Policies," HEW.

73. *SDSBS*, April 1966; Gardner to Congress, April 1966, Harold Howe, USOE, to School Superintendents and Chief State School Officers, April 9, 1966, in DOJ CRD Records: Records of John Doar, Policy Correspondence, 1965–66.

74. *SDSBS*, March 1966; *BN*, March 11, 12, 17, 1966.

75. *BN*, March 22, April 14, 1966; *SDSBS*, March, April 1966.

76. Civil Rights Commission Memorandum, Minutes of Closed Meeting of Alabama State Advisory Committee (ASAC), Birmingham, March 17, 1966, in USCCR, ASAC Files: Special Subjects; Summary Report, ASAC to the USCCR, Report of Open Meeting at Montgomery, Feb. 26, 1965, in USCCR, ASAC Files: Special Subjects; *BN*, March 22, April 14, 1966; *SDSBS*, March, April 1966.

77. *SDSBS*, April 1966; *BN*, April 11, 1966.

78. *SDSBS*, May 1966.

79. *SDSBS*, May 1966; Trial Brief of the U.S., Jan. 5, 1967, LVMCF, FMJP, C9, F5, pp. 23–4.

80. Resolution of May 19, 1966, Meeting Agenda and Minutes of the State BOE, Department of Education Files, SG20904–5, ADAH; Resolution of the Alabama State Legislature, July 26, 1966, in Special Session, *Journal of the House of Representatives of the State of Alabama* (Montgomery: Brown Printing, 1966); John R. Durr, "Title VI, the Guidelines and Desegregation in the South," *Virginia Law Review* 53, no. 1 (Jan. 1967); *SDSBS*, May 1966.

81. HEW Memorandums, Richard Fairley to David Seeley, May 13, 1966, and Fairley to Harold Williams, May 24, 1966; USOE Telephone/Conference Records, Alan Ellis to Calhoun County BOE, July 1, 1966, Richard Sable to Harry Weaver, July 1, 1966, and Lawrence Crowder to Nelson Swinea, July 8, 1966—all in *PNAACP*, supplement to part 23, Legal Department Case Files, 1960–1972, series A, section I, reels 3–9 [NAACP Lee v. Macon Files]; Trial Brief of the U.S., Jan. 5, 1967, LVMCF, FMJP, C19, F5, pp. 26.

82. USOE Telephone/Conference Records, Alan Ellis to Supt. Garner, Brewton, July 7, 1966; Martin Cooper to David Brown, Colbert County, July 19, 1966; John Deason to Richard Fairley, Aug. 26, 1966; Harold Howe to Austin Meadows, June 3, 1966—all in NAACP Lee v. Macon Files, Background Information; Trial Brief of the U.S, Jan. 5, 1967, LVMCF, FMJP, C19, F5, pp. 27–30, 32; Jeffrey Frederick, "Command and Control: George Wallace, Governor of Alabama, 1963–72" (PhD diss., Auburn University, 2003), 310.

83. Complaint Submitted to Mid-South Regional Office, USCCR, March 30, 1966, "Questionnaire" attached; Walter Lewis to Rev. Henry McCaskill and Mrs. Sarah Daniel, Oct. 1, 1965; Frank Smith to Jacques Wilmore, Dec. 3, 1966; Walter Lewis to Samson Crum, Nov. 14, 1966; Donald Jelinek to Charles Grant, Sept. 28, 1966; Complaint submitted to Secretary of Agriculture regarding Mr. and Mrs. Roosevelt Bracey, May 2, 1966; Collins Harris to John Doar, May 30, 1966—all in USCCR, ASAC Files: Special Subjects, Alabama, Complaints, 1965–1966; NAACP LDF Fundraising Literature, "Wetumpka Has Everything," in *Facts on Film, 1966–1967 Supplement*, Misc. Materials.

84. House Bill 446, Approved Sept. 2, 1966, *PNAACP*, supplement to part 23, series A, section 1, reel 3; LVMCF, FMJP, C28, F8; *BN*, Aug. 18, 19, 21, 1966; *MA*, Sept. 3, 1966.

85. House Bill 446, Sept. 2, 1966.

86. *SDSBS*, Sept. 1966; *BN*, Aug. 19, Sept. 11, 15, 1966; *MA*, Sept. 18, 1966.

87. Trial Brief of the U.S., Jan. 5, 1967, LVMCF, FMJP, C19, F5, pp. 44–45, 47.

88. Act 687, Amended Sept. 1, 1966 as Act 170, 1966 Regular Session, see U.S. Brief in Support, Oct. 19, 1966, LVMCF, FMJP, C21, F6; Stipulation and Supplemental Stipulation of Facts, Sept. 30, 1966, LVMCF, FMJP, C28, F8; *SDSBS*, March, April 1966; *BN*, July 27, Aug. 3, 10, 11, 18, 1966.

89. Stipulation of Facts, Sept. 30, 1966, U.S. Brief in Support, Oct. 19, 1966, Johnson Papers; *SDSBS*, May 1966; *WP*, June 2, 1966; *BN*, May 18, 27, 28, Aug. 14, 1966; *MA*, May 27, 29, 1966; *Chattanooga Times*, Aug. 19, 1966.

90. *Statistical Summary of School Desegregation in the Southern and Border States, 1966–1967* (Nashville: SERS, 1966); *SDSBS*, Sept. 1966; *BN*, Aug. 28, 1966.

91. Alton A. Turner to James A. Devlin, Oct. 4, 1966; J. R. Pittard to David Seeley, Oct. 11, 1966; H. L. Terrell to David Seeley, Sept. 29, 1966; HEW-USOE EEOP Official Files, Telephone/Conference Records; "Alabama School Districts Which Have Experienced Political Pressure and Influence"—all in NAACP Lee v. Macon Files, Background Information, reel 3; *BN*, Sept. 24, 1966.

92. Motion for Leave to Intervene, Aug. 30, 1966, and Supplemental Complaint, Aug. 31, 1966, LVMCF, FMJP, C28, F3; *BN*, Sept. 12, 15, 29, 1966; *MA*, Sept. 13, 18, 1966; Amendment to Complaint, NAACP v. Wallace, C.A. 2457-N (N. D., Ala.), in NAACP Lee v. Macon Files, General Case Material, Sept. 1966, reel 6; Motion for an Order to Show Cause, Sept. 22, 1966, LVMCF, FMJP, C28, F8; *BN*, Sept. 12, 15, 23, 1966.

93. *MA*, Sept. 13, 1966; *BN*, Sept. 28, 1966.

Chapter 4. "More Than a Mere Word of Promise"

1. Transcript of Proceedings, Lee v. Macon County BOE and NAACP v. Wallace, Nov. 30, 1966, NAACP Lee v. Macon Files, Transcripts, Nov. 1966, reel 9, pp. 78–82; State Department of Education Release (Meadows memo), July 1, 1966, NAACP Lee v. Macon Files, Depositions, reel 4; *LAT*, Dec. 1, 1966; National Register of Historic Places Registration Form, Continuation Sheet and Accompanying Photos for U.S. Post Office and Courthouse (Frank M. Johnson Federal Building), http://nrhp.focus.nps.gov; *Farmer's Almanac* Historical Weather online, http://www.farmersalmanac.com/weather-history; "Interpreter in the Front Line," *Time*, May 12, 1967, 72.

2. Transcript of Proceedings, Lee v. Macon County BOE and NAACP v. Wallace, Nov. 30, 1966, NAACP Lee v. Macon Files, Transcripts, Nov. 1966, reel 9, pp. 78–82.

3. Ibid.
4. Ibid.
5. Ibid.
6. Ibid.

7. *BN*, Oct. 1, 1966; Order of Oct. 13, 1966, NAACP Lee v. Macon Files, General Case Material, 1966, reel 7; *SDSBS*, Oct., Nov. 1966.

8. Mark A. Chesler, *In Their Own Words: A Student Appraisal of What Happened after School Desegregation* (Atlanta: Southern Regional Council, 1967), see copy in Facts on Film, 1966–1967 Supplement, Misc. Materials; *WP*, April 23, 1967; *LAT*, April 30, 1967; *BN*, Dec. 18, 1966.

9. Chesler, *In Their Own Words*, 2–5; *LAT*, Dec. 16, 1966.

10. Chesler, *In Their Own Words*, 5–9, 12; reflections of Arlam Carr and Delores Boyd in Ellen Levine, ed., *Freedom's Children: Young Civil Rights Activists Tell Their Own Stories* (New York: Puffin Books), 50–55; *LAT*, Dec. 16, 1966; *Southern School Desegregation*,

1966–67, Report of the USCCR (Washington, D.C.: GPO, 1967), 57; *Atlanta Daily World*, Nov. 18, 1967.

11. Chesler, *In Their Own Words*, 9–14; Joseph Bagley, "A Meaningful Reality: The Desegregation of the Opelika, Alabama City School System, 1965–72" (master's thesis, Auburn University, 2007), 58–59.

12. Chesler, *In Their Own Words*, 12–15.

13. J. Frank Owsley et al., *Know Alabama: An Elementary History* (Birmingham: Colonial Press, 1957), copy in Special Collections and Archives, Draughon Library, Auburn University; Solomon Seay, interview with the author, Feb. 1, 2012, digital recording and transcript in possession of the author; *NYT*, Feb. 9, 1970; Bagley, *Meaningful Reality*, 56–59; Owsley, "The Irrepressible Conflict," in *I'll Take My Stand: The South and the Agrarian Tradition* (1930; repr., Baton Rouge: Louisiana State University Press, 2006), 61–91; Orville Vernon Burton, "Frank Lawrence Owsley," *American National Biography Online*, Oxford University Press, http://www.anb.org/. On textbook and curricula controversies in the long civil rights movement, see Kevin Boland Johnson, "Guardians of Historical Knowledge: Textbook Politics, Conservative Activism, and School Reform in Mississippi, 1928–1982" (PhD diss., Mississippi State University, 2014); and Charles Eagles, *Civil Rights Culture Wars: The Fight over a Mississippi Textbook* (Chapel Hill: University of North Carolina Press, 2017).

14. Owsley et al., *Know Alabama*, 93–98.

15. Ibid., 111–15, 142–47.

16. *NYT*, Feb. 9, 1970; *LAT*, March 25, 1970; *Atlanta Constitution*, March 10, 1970; Seay interview; *Alabama Council Bulletin* (Auburn: ACHR), Jan. 16, 1967, 3; *The Citizen*, Oct. 5–6, Nov. 7–8, 1966, in *Facts on Film, 1966–67 Supp.*, Misc. Materials.; Jeffrey Frederick, "Command and Control: George Wallace, Governor of Alabama, 1963–72" (PhD diss., Auburn University, 2003), 297–98.

17. Dan Carter, *The Politics of Rage: George Wallace, the Origins of the New Conservatism, and the Transformation of American Politics* (Baton Rouge: Louisiana State University Press, 2000), 288–92; Frederick, *Command and Control*, 348–49.

18. Order of Nov. 23, 1966, NAACP v. Wallace, Answer and Cross-Claim of George C. Wallace, et al., Nov. 22, 1966, NAACP v. Wallace, PNAACP, supplement to part 23, reel 7; Motion for Preliminary Injunction and Supplemental Complaint, Nov. 21, 1966, Answer of George C. Wallace, Governor, Nov. 29, 1966, LVMCF, FMJP, C8, F7; Lee v. Macon Trial Transcript, Nov. 30–Dec. 2, 1966, NAACP Lee v. Macon Files.

19. Transcripts and Summaries of Depositions, State Dept. of Ed. School Surveys, NAACP Lee v. Macon Files, Depositions, reels 4–6. On the CRD team, see Brian K. Landsberg, "*Lee v. Macon County* BOE: The Possibilities of Federal Enforcement," *Duke Journal of Constitutional Law and Public Policy* 12, no. 1: 1–52, 27–28.

20. Deposition of J. R. Snellgrove, Oct. 21, 1966, 10–11, in NAACP Lee v. Macon Files: Depositions.

21. Lee v. Macon Trial Transcript, Nov. 30, 1966, 21–22.

22. Lee v. Macon Trial Transcript, Nov. 30, 1966, 73; *LAT*, Dec. 1, 1966; *NYT*, Dec. 1, 1966.

23. Lee v. Macon Trial Transcript, Nov. 30, Dec. 1, 1966, NAACP Lee v. Macon Files: Transcripts, Nov.–Dec., 1966, reel 9.

24. Lee v. Macon Trial Transcript; *BN*, Dec. 2, 1966; *LAT*, Dec. 2, 1966; *NYT*, Dec. 2, 1966; "Apologist," *Time*, Oct. 31, 1969, 70.

25. U.S. v. Jefferson County BOE, 372 F.2d 836, 845–62 (1966), emphasis in original; Michael Belknap, ed., *Civil Rights, the White House, and the Justice Department, 1945–1968*, vol. 17, *Administrative History of the Civil Rights Division of Justice during the Johnson Administration* (New York: Garland, 1991), 68–70; "The Courts, HEW, and School Desegregation," comment, *Yale Law Journal* 77 (Dec. 1967): 350–52; *BN*, Jan. 12, 13, 14, 1967; *NYT*, Dec. 29, 1966; Harvie Wilkinson, *From Brown to Bakke: The Supreme Court and School Integration, 1954–1978* (New York: Oxford University Press, 1981), 111–14; Owen Fiss, *Injunctions* (St. Paul, Minn.: Foundation Press, 1972), 649–50; Jack Bass, *Unlikely Heroes: The Dramatic Story of the Southern Judges of the Fifth Judicial Circuit Who Translated the Supreme Court's Brown Decision into a Revolution for Equality* (New York: Simon and Schuster, 1981), 297–310.

26. U.S. v. Jefferson County BOE, 372 F.2d 836, 862–65, emphasis in original.

27. U.S. v. Jefferson County BOE, 372 F.2d 836, 865–98, 905–10; *BN*, Jan. 28, 1967; *SDSBS*, Jan. 1967; Wilkinson, *From Brown to Bakke*, 112–14.

28. *SDSBS*, Jan. 1967; U.S.' Supplemental Complaint, Feb. 26, 1967, in LVMCF, FMJP, C19, F7, p. 8n4. Emphasis in original.

29. *SDSBS*, Feb. 1967; *BN*, Jan. 28, 1967.

30. Johnson to Rives, Grooms, and Pittman, Feb. 15, 1967; Johnson to Rives and Grooms, March 15, 1967—both in LVMCF, FMJP, C28, F6; Supp. Brief of the U.S., Feb. 22, 1967, NAACP v. Wallace, 2–10, in *PNAACP*, supplement to part 23, series A, section I, reel 7.

31. Lee v. Macon County BOE, Opinion, Order, and Decree of March 22, 1967, 267 F.Supp 458, 460–75.

32. Lee v. Macon, 267 F.Supp. 458, 475–78.

33. Lee v. Macon, 267 F.Supp. 458, 478–83.

34. Lee v. Macon, 267 F.Supp. 458, 483–91; "Status Report of School Cases," March 9, 1967, in DOJ CRD Records, Records of John Doar: Desegregation (reel 8).

35. Johnson to Rives and Grooms, March 15, 1967, in LVMCF, FMJP, C28, F6; Brian Landsberg, interview with the author, March 29, 2012, digital recording in possession of the author; excerpts from Fiss interview in Jack Bass, *Taming the Storm: The Life and Times of Judge Frank M. Johnson, Jr., and the South's Fight over Civil Rights* (New York: Doubleday, 1993), 230–35, 480–32.

36. Brian Landsberg, *Enforcing Civil Rights: Race Discrimination and the Department of Justice* (Lawrence: University of Kansas Press, 1997), 140; Landsberg interview; Landsberg, "Lee v. Macon County BOE," 39–40; Bass, *Taming the Storm*, 230–35, 480–32; James Dunn, "Title VI, the Guidelines, and School Desegregation in the South," *Virginia Law Review* 53, no. 1 (Jan. 1967), 88; Fiss, *The Civil Rights Injunction* (Bloomington: Indiana University Press, 1978), 4, 17, 49, 98–18, 101–35, 104–16; Fiss, *Injunctions*, 415–17, 449–50, 645–90; Belknap, ed., *Civil Rights, the White House, and the Justice Department, 1945–1968*, vol. 17, 70–72; *Southern School Desegregation*, USCCR (Washington, D.C.: GPO, 1967), 44, 124–26; Frank Read and Lisa McGough, *Let Them Be Judged: The Judicial Integration of the Deep South* (Metuchen, N.J.: Scarecrow Press, 1978), 398–405.

37. Susan Ashmore, "Wyatt v. Stickney: A Landmark Case for Disability Justice," Alabama in the Age of Aquarius symposium, ADAH, Aug. 19, 2016; Larry Yackle, *Reform and Regret: The Story of Federal Judicial Involvement in the Alabama Prison System* (New York: Oxford University Press, 1989); Phillip J. Cooper, *Hard Judicial Choices: Federal*

District Court Judges and State and Local Officials (New York: Oxford University Press, 1988), 163–204; James v. Wallace (prisons), 382 F.Supp. 1177 (M. D., Ala., 1974); Pugh v. Locke (prisons), 406 F.Supp. 318 (M. D., Ala., 1976); Wyatt v. Stickney (mental health), 344 F.Supp. 373 (M. D., Ala., 1972); "The Wyatt Case: Implementation of a Judicial Decree Ordering Institutional Change," *Yale Law Journal* 84 (May 1975): 1338–79; Dillard v. Crenshaw County, 640 F.Supp. 1347 (M. D., Ala., 1986), 686 F.Supp. 1459 (M. D., Ala., 1988); Payton McCrary et al., "Alabama," in *Quiet Revolution in the South: The Impact of the Voting Rights Act, 1965–1990*, ed. Chandler Davidson and Bernard Grofman (Princeton: Princeton University Press, 1994), 38–66.

38. "The Courts, HEW, and School Desegregation," 362–64.

39. *BN*, March 30, 31, 1967; Landsberg, "*Lee v. Macon County* BOE," 37–38; David Norman, "The Strange Career of the Civil Rights Division's Commitment to Brown," *Yale Law Journal* 93 (May 1984): 987; Bass, *Taming the Storm*, 235 (Fiss quotation); Fred Gray, *Bus Ride to Justice: Changing the System by the System* (Selma: Black Belt Press, 1995), 215–18; Greenberg quoted in NAACP press release, "Alabama Schools Must End Bias," March 24, 1967, in *Facts on Film, 1966–1967 Supplement*, Misc. Materials; Charles Bolton, *The Hardest Deal of All: The Battle over School Integration in Mississippi* (Oxford: University of Mississippi Press, 2005), 128–31; U.S. v. Georgia, 428 F.2d 377 (5th CCA, 1970); U.S. v. Texas, 321 F.Supp. 1043 (E. D., Tex., 1970); U.S. v. Hinds County, Mississippi, 417 F.2d 852 (5th CCA, 1969).

40. U.S. v. Jefferson County BOE, 380 F.2d 385, 389–96; *BN*, March 29, 30, 1967; NAACP LDF press release, April 1, 1967, in *Facts on Film, 1966–1967 Supplement*, Misc. Materials; Fiss, *Injunctions*, 449–50; Bass, *Unlikely Heroes*, 297–310; *Lawlessness and Disorder: Fourteen Years of Failure in Southern School Desegregation*, Special Report of the Southern Regional Council (Atlanta: SRC, 1968), 26, in *Facts on Film, 1968–69 Supplement*, Misc. Materials.

41. U.S. v. Jefferson County BOE, 380 F.2d 385, 397–427; Bass, *Unlikely Heroes*, 303–4. On freedom of association, see Kevin M. Kruse, *White Flight: Atlanta and the Making of Modern Conservatism* (Princeton University Press, 2005), 161; and Kevin M. Kruse, "The Fight for Freedom of Association: Segregationist Rights and Resistance in Atlanta," in *Massive Resistance: White Opposition to the Second Reconstruction*, ed. Clive Webb (New York: Oxford University Press, 2001), 99–116.

42. "Interpreter in the Front Line," *Time*, May 12, 1967, 84–93.

43. Johnson to Doar, March 23, 1967, Johnson Papers, LVMCF, FMJP, C28, F6; *NYT*, March 29, 1967; *WP*, March 29, 1967; *BN*, March 29, 30, 31, 1967; *SDSBS*, March 1967.

44. Address by Governor Lurleen Wallace, March 30, 1967 (with handwritten notes by Johnson) in LVMCF, FMJP, C21, F5; *NYT*, March 29, 1967; *WP*, March 29, 1967; *BN*, March 29, 30, 31, 1967; *SDSBS*, March 1967.

45. Lurleen Wallace address, March 30, 1967, LVMCF, FMJP, C21, F5.

46. "Statements . . . that do not appear to have any basis in fact," LVMCF, FMJP, C21, F6; Plaintiffs' Opposition to Defendants' Application for a Stay, April 13, 1967, and Order Denying, April 15, 1967, LVMCF, FMJP, C29, F2; *WP*, April 16, 1967; *BN*, April 16, 1967.

47. *LAT*, April 23, 1967; Read and McGough, *Let Them Be Judged*, 405; *SDSBS*, April 1967; *BN*, March 24, 30, 31, 1967.

48. Read and McGough, *Let Them Be Judged*, 395–96; *BN*, April 29, 1967.

49. Read and McGough, *Let Them Be Judged*, 395–96; *BN*, April 29, 1967.

50. *SDSBS*, April 1967, SERS; *BN*, March 24, 30, 31, 1967.

51. NAACP v. Wallace, 269 F.Supp 346, 348–52; *SDSBS*, May 1967.

52. Rives to John Brown, April 19, 1967; Johnson to Rives and Grooms, April 4, 1967—both in LVMCF, FMJP, C28, F10; Johnson to Doar, Aug. 16, 1967, LVMCF, FMJP, C29, F3; Rives to Johnson, Aug. 27, 1969, LVMCF, FMJP, C30, F7.

53. State Superintendent's Report, April 17, 1967, Report of the U.S., April 22, 1967, Order Adding Parties Defendant, April 24, 1967, LVMCF, FMJP, C29, F2; Johnson to Rives and Grooms, April 20, 1967, LVMCF, FMJP, C28, 10; Transcript of Proceedings, May 13, 1967, LVMCF, FMJP, C21, F5; Order of May 18, 1967, LVMCF, FMJP, C29, F1; *SDSBS*, April 1967; *BN*, April 13, 1967.

54. Order Adding Parties Defendant, April 24, 1967, LVMCF, FMJP, C29, F2; Transcript of Proceedings, May 13, 1967, LVMCF, FMJP, C21, F5; Order of May 18, 1967, and Report of the U.S., May 25, 1967—both inLVMCF, FMJP, C29, F1; Orders Enjoining Marion BOE and Thomasville BOE, June 14, 1967, LVMCF, FMJP, C29, F5; Docket Report, LVMTR.

55. Motion for More Specific Relief, Aug. 2, 1967, and Motion for an Order Requiring Ernest Stone to Further Implement Section IV, Aug. 2, 1967, LVMCF, FMJP, C29, F4; Order Granting U.S.'s Motions, Aug. 2, 1967, and Johnson to Rives and Grooms, July 19, 1967, LVMCF, FMJP, C20, F6.

56. Johnson to John Doar, Nov. 30, 1967, Stone to Harry L. Weaver, Escambia County, Dec. 1, 1967, Stone to Davis Brown, Colbert County, Nov. 29, 1967, LVMCF, FMJP, C20, F6; Stone to Johnson, Nov. 22, 1967, LVMCF, FMJP, C20, F2.

57. Johnson to Rives and Grooms, April 13, 1967, Johnson to Rives and Grooms, April 24, 1967, LVMCF, FMJP, C23, F3.

58. Johnson to Rives and Grooms, May 4, 1967, Rives to Johnson, April 24, 1967, Grooms to Johnson, April 1, 1967, LVMCF, FMJP, C20, F6; Order Adding Parties Defendant and TRO, July 14, 1967, LVMCF, FMJP, C29, F5; "The Courts, HEW, and School Desegregation," 323–24; *NYT*, May 14, 1967.

59. Order Adding Parties Defendant and TRO, July 14, 1967, LVMCF, FMJP, C29, F5; Prehearing Memorandum with Handwritten Notes, LVMCF, FMJP, C21, F8; Johnson to Rives and Grooms, July 27, 1967, and Johnson to Doar, Aug. (date missing), 1967, LVMCF, FMJP, C29, F3; *NYT*, July 15, 1967.

60. Transcript of Proceedings, July 22, 1967, LVMCF, FMJP, C21, F8 (see Johnson's Handwritten Notes from Hearing at C21, F5); *SDSBS*, July 1967.

61. Transcript of Proceedings, July 22, 1967, LVMCF, FMJP, C21, F8; Opinion and Order, July 28, 1967, Lee v. Macon County BOE, 270 F.Supp. 859, copy with handwritten notes at LVMCF, FMJP, C29, F5; *RRLR* 12, no. 3 (Fall 1967): 1208–14; *SDSBS*, July 1967; *BN*, July 29, 1967; *Atlanta Constitution*, Aug. 2, 1967.

62. *Southern School Desegregation, 1966–67*, Civil Rights Commission, 90–94; *SDSBS*, Sept. 1967; *BN*, Sept. 5, 1967, Jan. 30, 1968.

63. Rives to Grooms and Johnson, Aug. 25, 1967, Addenda to Prehearing Memorandum, Sept. 16, 1967, LVMCF, FMJP, C22, F1; Rives to Grooms and Johnson, April 4, 1967, LVMCF, FMJP, C28, F6; Memo of Phone Call, H. L. Terrell to the Court, Sept. 8, 1967, and Rives to Grooms and Johnson, Sept. 11, 1967, Johnson Papers, LVMCF, FMJP, C29, F7; *SDSBS*, Sept. 1967.

64. Plaintiffs' Motion for Further Relief, Sept. 2, 1967, copy of Alabama Act 285 attached (with handwritten notes), Johnson Papers, LVMCF, FMJP, C22, F1; Lurleen

Wallace to Superintendents of Education, Sept 6, 1967, LVMCF, FMJP, C29, F7; *SDSBS*, Sept. 1967.

65. Plaintiffs' Motion for Further Relief, Sept. 2, 1967, TRO, Sept. 5, 1967, U.S.'s Supplemental Complaint/Motion for PI, Sept. 4, 1967, LVMCF, FMJP, C30, F2; copy of Alabama Act 266 (with handwritten notes), LVMCF, FMJP, C22, F1; *RRLR* 12, no. 3 (Fall 1967): 1215; *SDSBS*, Sept. 1967; *NYT*, Aug. 27, 1967.

66. Plaintiffs' Supplemental Complaint, Sept. 16, 1967, LVMCF, FMJP, C22, F2; Addenda to Prehearing Memorandum, Sept. 16, 1967, LVMCF, FMJP, C22, F1; *SDSBS*, Sept. 1967; *BN*, Sept. 17, 1967; *Atlanta Constitution*, Sept. 17, 1967.

67. Plaintiff-Intervenor's Brief in Support, Sept. 26, 1967, LVMCF, FMJP, C22, F2; Johnson to Rives and Grooms, Oct. 10, 1967, LVMCF, FMJP, C29, F7; *SDSBS*, Sept. 1967; Order Denying Motion Seeking to Add Parties Defendant, Oct. 12, 1967, LVMCF, FMJP, C30, F1; *RRLR* 12, no. 4 (Winter, 1967): 1841–44.

68. Complaint in Intervention of ASTA, Sept. 2, 1967, LVMCF, FMJP, C30, F2; Memorandum in Support of Motion for Leave to Intervene, Sept. 16, 1967, LVMCF, FMJP, C22, F2; Solomon Seay Jr., *Jim Crow and Me: Stories from My Life as a Civil Rights Lawyer* (Montgomery: New South, 2008), 89–98; Seay interview; Burrell-Slater PTA to Johnson, Sept. 11, 1968, LVMCF, FMJP, C25, F11.

69. Opinions and Decrees (2), Nov. 3, 1967, LVMCF, FMJP, C30, F1; *RRLR* 12, no. 4 (Winter 1967): 1835–40; Wisdom to Johnson, Aug. 28, 1967, LVMCF, FMJP, C29, F3.

70. Lee v. Macon County BOE, affirmed *sub nom* Wallace v. United States, 389 U.S. 215; United States v. Jefferson County BOE cert. denied 389 U.S. 840; *WP*, Dec. 5, 1967; Belknap, *Civil Rights, the White House, and the Justice Department, 1945–1968*, vol. 17, 75–80; Landsberg, *Enforcing Civil Rights*, 140–41; Bass, *Unlikely Heroes*, 307.

71. Green v. New Kent County BOE, 382 F.2d 326 (4th CCA, 1967); Belknap, *Civil Rights, the White House, and the Justice Department, 1945–1968*, vol. 17, 75–80; Landsberg, *Enforcing Civil Rights*, 140–41.

72. Memorandum from Doar to the Solicitor General, Dec. 19, 1967, Memorandum from Pollack to the Solicitor General, Feb. 23, 1968, in Belknap, *Civil Rights, the White House, and the Justice Department, 1945–1968*, vol. 17, 5–9; *WP*, Dec. 5, 1967.

73. Seay, *Jim Crow and Me*, 89–95; Seay interview.

74. Seay, *Jim Crow and Me*, 89–95; Seay interview.

75. Joe Payne to Ernest Stone, Sept. 20, 1967, Payne to Johnson, Jan. 19, 1968, LVMCF, FMJP, C24, F18; Ramsey to Johnson, Feb. 20, 1968, LVMCF, FMJP, C26, F4.

76. Johnson to Rives and Grooms, Dec. 29, 1967, Rives to Johnson and Grooms, Jan. 4, 1969, Grooms to Johnson and Rives, Dec. 14, 1967, Johnson to Pollack, Jan. 17, 1968, LVMCF, FMJP, C29, F7.

77. Johnson to Rives and Grooms, Dec. 29, 1967, Rives to Johnson and Grooms, Jan. 4, 1969, Grooms to Johnson and Rives, Dec. 14, 1967, Pollack to Johnson, Feb. 19, 1968, Johnson to Pollack, Feb. 20, 1968, LVMCF, FMJP, C29, F7.

78. Libassi to Stone, Sept. 6, 1967, Stone to Libassi, Sept. 22, 1967, Johnson to Stone and Libassi, Sept. 25, 1967, Rives to Johnson, Jan. 4, 1968, LVMCF, FMJP, C29, F7.

79. Seay interview; R. W. Hollingsworth to C. W. Russell, Director of Public Safety, c.c. Frank Johnson, Sept. 11, 1967, Johnson to John Doar and Ben Hardeman, Sept. 12, 1967, Opinion and Decree, April 1, 1968, LVMCF, FMJP, C19, F4. See also opinion at 283 F.Supp. 19; Depositions of Ernest Stone, John L. Meadows, and William Hayes Hen-

derson, in Summaries of Depositions, March 14, 1968, LVMCF, FMJP, C29, F8; *SDSBS*, April 1968.

80. Lee v. Macon Decree, April 1, 1968, 283 F.Supp. 194; Johnson to Stone, April 9, 1968, LVMCF, FMJP, C29, F7; Proposed Basic Findings on the Dual Athletic Systems Phase, LVMCF, FMJP, C29, F8; *SDSBS*, April 1968.

81. Memorandum Brief for Defendant, Dr. Ernest Stone, March 16, 1968, and Summaries of Depositions, March 14, 1968, LVMCF, FMJP, C29, F8.

82. Merger Plan of the AHSAA and AIAA, May 3, 1968, LVMCF, FMJP, C19, F4; Seay interview; *Birmingham World*, April 10, 1968.

83. U.S. and Carr v. Montgomery County BOE, 289 F.Supp. 647, 649–54; *BN*, Feb. 25, 1967; Fiss, *Injunctions*, 415–81.

84. U.S. and Carr v. Montgomery County BOE, 289 F.Supp. 647, 649–54.

85. U.S. and Carr v. Montgomery County BOE, 289 F.Supp. 647, 654–8; *SDSBS*, Feb. 1968; *BN*, Feb. 25, 29, 1967; *Jackson Daily News*, Feb. 25, 1968.

86. U.S. and Carr v. Montgomery County BOE, March 2, 1968, 289 F.Supp. 657–60; U.S. v. Jefferson County BOE, 372 F.2d 836, 892–4 (5th CCA, 1967).

87. U.S. and Carr v. Montgomery County BOE, 289 F.Supp. 657, 660–1; *SDSBS*, March 1968.

88. Davis v. Board of School Commissioners of Mobile County, 364 F.2d 896, 901 (1966), 393 F.2d 690 (1968).

89. Davis v. Mobile, 393 F.2d 690, 690–94.

90. Davis v. Mobile, 393 F.2d 690, 694–99.

91. *NYT*, April 5, 1968; *BN*, May 27, 29, 1968; *WP*, May 31, 1968.

92. Carter, *Politics of Rage*, 315–22.

93. *BN*, May 17, 18, 1968.

94. *BN*, May 27, 29, June 1, 1968; *WP*, May 31, 1968; *NYT*, June 10, 1968; Richard Pride, *The Political Use of Racial Narratives: School Desegregation in Mobile, Alabama, 1954–1997* (Urbana: University of Illinois Press, 2002), 61–62.

95. *BN*, May 27, 29, 1968; *WP*, May 31, 1968; *NYT*, June 10, 1968; Pride, *Political Use of Racial Narratives*, 57–63; George Altman, "Former State Senator Pierre Pelham Dies," Al.com, Dec. 4, 2009, http://blog.al.com/live/2009/12/former_state_senator_pierre_pe.html.

96. Pride, *Political Use of Racial Narratives*, 57–63.

97. *BN*, May 20, 1968; Pride, *Political Use of Racial Narratives*, 61–63.

98. *BN*, May 20, 1968; Pride, *Political Use of Racial Narratives*, 61–63.

99. *BN*, May 20, 1968; Pride, *Political Use of Racial Narratives*, 61–63.

100. Green v. County School Board of New Kent County, 391 U.S. 430, 437; James Patterson, *Brown v. Board of Education: A Civil Rights Milestone and Its Troubled Legacy* (New York: Oxford University Press, 2001), 145–46.

101. Green v. County School Board of New Kent County, 391 U.S. 430, 437–41; Belknap, *Civil Rights, the White House, and the Justice Department, 1945–1968*, 77–81; Wilkinson, *From Brown to Bakke*, 115–17.

102. *BN*, May 30, 1968.

103. *BN*, June 1, 3, 1968.

104. *BN*, June 8, 1968; *NYT*, June 10, 1968.

105. *BN*, June 8, 1968; *NYT*, June 10, 1968.

106. *BN*, June 8, 1968; *NYT*, June 10, 1968.

Chapter 5. "Depths of Disillusionment"

1. *Lawlessness and Disorder: Fourteen Years of Failure in Southern School Desegregation*, Special Report of the Southern Regional Council (Atlanta: SRC, 1968), 15, in *Facts on Film, 1968-69 Supplement*, Misc. Materials; see this book's chapter 4, note 41 above.

2. *Lawlessness and Disorder*, 15.

3. Ibid., 19-22; *BN*, Feb. 1, 1970; *Modesto Bee*, Dec. 19, 1969. On the northern strategy, see Joseph Crespino, *Strom Thurmond's America* (New York: Hill and Wang, 2012), 6-8; on Whitten and *Green*, see Gary Orfield, *Must We Bus? Segregated Schools and National Policy* (Washington, D.C.: Brookings Institution, 1978), 239, 243; and Joseph Crespino, *In Search of Another Country: Mississippi and the Conservative Counterrevolution* (Princeton: Princeton University Press, 2009), 186-89.

4. *Lawlessness and Disorder*, Southern Regional Council, 15.

5. Memorandum from Pollack to Attorney General, June 28, 1968, in Michael Belknap, ed., *Civil Rights, the White House, and the Justice Department, 1945-1968*, vol. 17, *Administrative History of the Civil Rights Division of Justice During the Johnson Administration* (New York: Garland, 1991), 18-20; Brian Landsberg, *Enforcing Civil Rights: Race Discrimination and the Department of Justice* (Lawrence: University of Kansas Press, 1997), 140-41; *NYT*, June 6, 7, 1968.

6. U.S. Motion for Further Relief, July 15, 1968, LVMCF, FMJP, C30, F6; Appendix A, Brief of U.S. in Support, Aug. 15, 1968, LVMCF, FMJP (1993 Addition, District Court File), C162, F7-8; Plaintiffs' Pre-Trial Memorandum, Aug. 22, 1968, LVMCF, FMJP, C22, F5; Landsberg, *Enforcing Civil Rights*, 140-41.

7. Pollack to Rives, Aug. 28, 1968, Correspondence Attached, Plaintiffs' Pre-Trial Memorandum in Support, Aug. 22, 1968, 2, LVMCF, FMJP, C22, F5; Cooper v. Aaron, 358 U.S. 1 (1958); Monroe v. Board of School Commissioners of the City of Jackson, Tennessee, 391 U.S. 450 (1968).

8. *BN*, Aug. 22, 1968; *WP*, Aug. 23, 1968. On Brewer as "New South," see Gordon Harvey, *A Question of Justice: New South Governors and Education, 1968-1976* (Tuscaloosa: University of Alabama Press, 2002), 17-66.

9. *BN*, June 13, 16, 21, 1968.

10. *BN*, June 13, 16, 21, Aug. 22, 1968; *WP*, Aug. 23, 1968; Lee v. Macon County BOE, Order and Opinion of Aug. 28, 1968, 292 F.Supp 363, 365.

11. Harris v. Crenshaw County BOE, Order of Aug. 8, 1968, C.A. 2455-N (M. D., Ala.); U.S. v. Crenshaw County Unit of the United Klans of America, Aug. 13, 1968, 290 F.Supp. 181 (M. D., Ala.); Franklin v. Barbour County BOE, Order of Aug. 13, Civil Action No. 2458-N (M. D., Ala.); *BN*, July 22, Aug. 8, 11, 13, 1968; *National Observer*, July 22, 1968.

12. Lee v. Macon County BOE, Order and Opinion of Aug. 28, 1968, 292 F.Supp 363, 363-7, LVMCF, FMJP, C163; *BN*, Aug. 29, 1968.

13. *BN*, Aug. 29, 1968; Defendants Petition to Modify, Sept. 25, 1968, LVMCF, FMJP, C30, F4, emphasis in original; Harvey, *Question of Justice*, 25-26; Jeff Wiltse, *Contested Waters: A Social History of Swimming Pools in America* (Chapel Hill: University of North Carolina Press, 2009), 121-80.

14. U.S Motion for Clarification, Sept. 10, 1968, LVMCF, FMJP, C30, F4.

15. *BN*, June 25, 26, July 16, 1968.

16. *BN*, June 25, 26, July 16, 1968.

17. *BN*, July 24, 25, 1968; *LAT*, July 18, 1968; Richard Pride, *The Political Use of Racial Narratives: School Desegregation in Mobile, Alabama, 1954–1997* (Urbana: University of Illinois Press, 2002), 64–68.

18. *BN*, July 30, 1968; Davis v. Board of School Commissioners, Order and Opinion of July 29, 1968, C.A. No. 3003–63.

19. *BN*, July 28; Pride, *Political Use of Racial Narratives*, 73–74.

20. *BN*, Sept. 7, 17, 18, 1968; Pride, *Political Use of Racial Narratives*, 73–74.

21. *BN*, July 14, 1968.

22. *BN*, July 16, 19, Aug. 3, 1968, Jan. 22, 1969; Harvey Burg, "On Being a Civil Rights Lawyer in the 1960s," interview with Shana Burg, http://shanaburg.com/.

23. *BN*, Aug. 11, 1968; J. Mills Thornton, *Dividing Lines: Municipal Politics and the Struggle for Civil Rights in Montgomery, Birmingham, and Selma* (Tuscaloosa: University of Alabama Press, 2002), 365–68.

24. *BN*, Aug. 11, 1968.

25. Orders of Oct. 14 and 23, 1968, LVMCF, FMJP, C30, F4; *NYT*, Oct. 15, 1968; *BN*, Oct. 25, 1968.

26. Order of Oct. 18, 1968, LVMCF, FMJP, C30, F4; *BN*, Oct. 15, 19, 20, 30, 1968.

27. *BN*, Oct. 15, 19, 20, 30, 1968.

28. Docket Report, LVMTR; *BN*, Nov. 8, 22, 1968; Jack Bass, *Taming the Storm: The Life and Times of Judge Frank M. Johnson, Jr., and the South's Fight over Civil Rights* (New York: Doubleday, 1993), 230–31.

29. Carr v. Montgomery County BOE, 400 F.2d. 1, en banc rehearing denied, 402 F.2d 782 (1968); certiorari granted, 393 U.S. 1116 (March 3, 1969); Owen Fiss, *Injunctions* (St. Paul, Minn.: Foundation Press, 1972), 415–81.

30. Landsberg, *Enforcing Civil Rights*, 141–42; David Norman, "The Strange Career of the Civil Rights Division's Commitment to Brown," *Yale Law Journal* 93 (May 1984): 986 ("*Brown* bag"); Crespino, *In Search of Another Country*, 234–35; Kevin M. Kruse, *White Flight: Atlanta and the Making of Modern Conservatism* (Princeton University Press, 2005), 253–58; Dan Carter, *The Politics of Rage: George Wallace, the Origins of the New Conservatism, and the Transformation of American Politics*, 2nd ed. (Baton Rouge: Louisiana State University Press, 2000), 323–49; Dean Kotlowski, *Nixon's Civil Rights: Politics, Principle, and Policy* (Cambridge: Harvard University Press, 2009), 15–16, 30–33; Leon Panetta, *Bring Us Together: The Nixon Team and the Civil Rights Retreat* (New York: Lippincott, 1971).

31. Landsberg, *Enforcing Civil Rights*, 141–42; Crespino, *In Search of Another Country*, 186–89, 234–35; Kruse, *White Flight*, 253–58; Carter, *Politics of Rage*, 323–49; Kotlowski, *Nixon's Civil Rights*, 15–16, 30–33; *Lawlessness and Disorder: Fourteen Years of Failure in Southern School Desegregation*, Special Report of the Southern Regional Council (Atlanta: SRC, 1968), 21–24, in *Facts on Film, 1968–69 Supplement*, Misc. Materials; David C. Carter, *The Music Has Gone out of the Movement: Civil Rights and the Johnson Administration, 1965–1968* (Chapel Hill: University of North Carolina Press, 2009).

32. Carr v. Montgomery County BOE, *sub nom* U.S. v. Montgomery County BOE, 395 U.S. 225 (1969), 225–35; *RRLS* 1, no. 3 (Sept. 1969): 104; *NYT*, June 3, 1969.

33. Plaintiff-Intervenor's Motion for Further Relief, Feb. 19, 1969, Defendant's Motion to Dismiss, March 20, 1969, Order of May 28, 1969, LVMCF, FMJP, C19, F3.

34. Plaintiff-Intervenor's Motion for Further Relief, Feb. 19, 1969, LVMCF, FMJP, C19, F3.

35. U.S.'s Motion for Further Relief, April 30, 1969, LVMCF, FMJP, C23, F2.

36. ASTA v. Alabama Public School and College Authority, 289 F.Supp. 784 (M. D., Ala., 1969), affirmed 393 U.S. 400 (1969); Jim Leeson, "Colleges and Choice," *Southern Education Report*, Oct. 1968, 3–6.

37. Memorandum Transcript of Hearing, May 27, 1969, and Order of Sept. 17, 1969, LVMCF, FMJP, C22, F7–8.

38. Johnson to Rives and Grooms, June 17, 1969, Rives to Johnson, June 21, 1969, LVMCF, FMJP, C30, F7.

39. U.S.'s Motion for Order to Show Cause, July 14, 1969, Order of July 15, LVMCF, FMJP, C30, F8; Johnson's Handwritten Notes from July 29, 1969 Hearing, LVMCF, FMJP, C23, F6; Order of Aug. 6, 1969, *RRLS* 1, no. 4 (Nov. 1969): 129–30; Johnson to Rives and Grooms, June 27, 1969, LVMCF, FMJP, C30, F7; Johnson to Superintendents and Counsel for Certain School Systems, June 27, 1969, LVMCF, FMJP, Cs23-7.

40. Johnson to Rives and Grooms, Oct. 6, 1969, Rives to Johnson and Grooms, Oct. 9, 1969, Grooms to Rives and Johnson, LVMCF, FMJP, C30, F7.

41. Plaintiff-Intervenor's Motion for Order to Show Cause, Aug. 1, 1969; NEA Complaint in Intervention, Aug. 21, 1969; Order of Aug. 21, 1969; LVMCF, FMJP, C30, F8; Johnson to Rives, Aug. 19, 1969, LVMCF, FMJP, C30, F7.

42. *RRLS* 1, no. 5 (Jan. 1970): 204–5; order at LVMCF, FMJP, C30, F8; Johnson to Rives, Aug. 19, 1969, LVMCF, FMJP, C30, F7.

43. Johnson to Ira DeMent, Nov. 5, 1969, LVMCF, FMJP, C30, F7.

44. *NYT*, April 16, 17, 18, Sept. 13, 1969; *WP*, Aug. 25, 1969; *BN*, June 20, 1969; Panetta, *Bring Us Together*; Landsberg, *Enforcing Civil Rights*, 141–42; Crespino, *In Search of Another Country*, 174, 185–89; Harvie Wilkinson, *From Brown to Bakke: The Supreme Court and School Integration, 1954–1978* (New York: Oxford University Press, 1981), 118–20; Jack Greenberg, *Crusaders in the Courts: How a Dedicated Band of Lawyers Fought for the Civil Rights Revolution* (New York: Basic Books, 1994), 384; Carter, *Politics of Rage*, 396–99. See also Joan Hoff, *Nixon Reconsidered* (New York: Basic, 1994), 77–114; and Kotlowski, *Nixon's Civil Rights*, 15–16, 30–33.

45. *NYT*, April 16, 17, 18, Sept. 13, 1969; *WP*, Aug. 25, 1969; *BN*, June 20, 1969; Panetta, *Bring Us Together*; Landsberg, *Enforcing Civil Rights*, 141–42; Crespino, *In Search of Another Country*, 174, 185–86; Wilkinson, *From Brown to Bakke*, 118–20; Greenberg, *Crusaders in the Courts*, 384; Carter, *Politics of Rage*, 396–99; Alexander v. Holmes, 396 U.S. 1219 (Sept. 5, 1969).

46. *NYT*, April 16, 17, 18, Sept. 13, 1969; *WP*, Aug. 25, 1969; *BN*, June 20, 1969; Panetta, *Bring Us Together*; Landsberg, *Enforcing Civil Rights*, 141–42; Crespino, *In Search of Another Country*, 174, 185–86; Wilkinson, *From Brown to Bakke*, 118–20; Greenberg, *Crusaders in the Courts*, 384; Carter, *Politics of Rage*, 396–99; Alexander v. Holmes, 396 U.S. 1219 (Sept. 5, 1969).

47. *NYT*, Oct. 1, 1969; *Baltimore Afro-American*, Oct. 7, 1969; *Milwaukee Journal*, Oct. 3, 1969.

48. *NYT*, Oct. 1, 1969; John Ehrlichman, *Witness to Power: The Nixon Years* (New York: Simon and Schuster, 1982), 227; Kevin J. McMahon, *Nixon's Court: His Challenge to Judicial Liberalism and Its Political Consequences* (Chicago: University of Chicago Press, 2011).

49. Pride, *Political Use of Racial Narratives*, 81.

50. Davis v. Board of School Commissioners of Mobile, 414 F.2d 609 (5th CCA, June 3, 1969); *RRLS* 1, no. 3 (Sept. 1969): 107–8.

51. *BN*, June 12, 26, 1969; *RRLS* 1, no. 4 (Nov. 1969): 158; Pride, *Political Use of Racial Narratives*, 83–89.

52. *BN*, June 12, 26, 1969; *RRLS* 1, no. 4 (Nov. 1969): 158; Pride, *Political Use of Racial Narratives*, 83–89.

53. *BN*, June 12, 26, 1969; *RRLS* 1, no. 4 (Nov. 1969): 158; Pride, *Political Use of Racial Narratives*, 83–89.

54. *BN*, Oct. 27, 1969; Raymond Wolters, *Race and Education, 1954–2007* (Columbia: University of Missouri Press, 2009), 145–50, 145–46.

55. *BN*, Aug. 1, Sept. 7, Oct. 30, 1969.

56. *BN*, Aug. 4, 1969.

57. *BN*, Aug. 2, 4, 5, 6, 9, Oct. 30, 1969; *RRLS* 1, no. 4 (Nov. 1969): 158–59.

58. *BN*, Aug. 15, 31, Sept. 1, Oct. 30, 1969.

59. *BN*, Aug. 31, Sept. 1, Oct. 30, 1969; *Auburn Plainsman*, Sept. 25, 1969.

60. *BN*, Sept. 3, 4, 19, 26, Oct. 21, 30, 31, 1969.

61. Alexander v. Holmes County BOE, 396 U.S. 19; Landsberg, *Enforcing Civil Rights*, 141–43.

62. U.S. v. Hinds County School Board, 417 F.2d 852; *RRLS* 1, no. 5 (Jan. 1970): 203–4.

63. Singleton v. Jackson, 419 F.2d 1211 (Singleton III); *RRLS* 1, no. 5 (Jan. 1970): 203–4.

64. *RRLS* 1, no. 5 (Jan. 1970): 203–4; Carter v. West Feliciana Parish School Board, 396 U.S. 290; Wilkinson, *From Brown to Bakke*, 119–21.

65. *BN*, Jan. 17, 1970.

66. *BN*, Feb. 22, 24, 26, 28, 1970. Brown famously argued in an address in 1967 that violence was "as American as cherry pie," *NYT*, July 28, 1967.

67. *RRLS* 2, no. 1 (May 1970): 11; *BN*, Feb. 3, 1970; Pride, *Political Use of Racial Narratives*, 91–93.

68. *RRLS* 2, no. 1 (May 1970): 11; *BN*, Feb. 3, 1970; Pride, *Political Use of Racial Narratives*, 91–93.

69. *WP*, Feb. 3, March 12, 1970; *BN*, Feb. 3, 1970; *NYT*, March 21, 1970.

70. *WP*, Feb. 3, March 12, 1970; *BN*, Feb. 3, 1970; *NYT*, March 21, 1970.

71. Betsy Fancher, *Voices from the South: Black Students Talk about Their Experiences in Desegregated Schools* (Atlanta: Southern Regional Council, 1970); "Schools: What Blacks Think Depends on Where," *South Today* 2, 7–8; *WP*, March 27, Sept. 9, 1970; *NYT*, Sept. 9, 1970; *BN*, March 13, Sept. 6, 1970; Pride, *Political Use of Racial Narratives*, 94.

72. *RRLS* 2, no. 2 (July 1970): 52–53; *BN*, Feb. 28, March 3, 1970.

73. *RRLS* 2, no. 2 (July 1970): 52–53; *BN*, Feb. 28, March 3, 1970.

74. *RRLS* 2, no. 2 (July 1970): 52–53; *BN*, Jan. 18, Feb. 3, 14, 28, 1970.

75. *BN*, Feb. 2, 3, 4, 5, 8, 9, 11, 12, 25, 1970.

76. *BN*, Jan. 26, 31, Feb. 3, 8, 25, March 27, 1970.

77. *BN*, Feb. 3, 4, 5, 8, 11, 12, 25, 1970.

78. *BN*, Jan. 27, Feb. 21, 1970.

79. *BN*, Jan. 17, 21, 22, Feb. 3, 5, 9, 12, 17, 21, 22, 1970; *RRLS* 1, no. 6 (Feb. 1970): 251; *RRLS* 2, no. 1 (May 1970): 11–12; *Richmond Times-Dispatch*, Feb. 9, 1970.

80. *BN*, Feb. 24, 25, March 5, 1970.

81. *BN*, Feb. 9, 15, 22, 24, 26, 28, 1970.

82. *RRLS* 2, no. 1 (May 1970): 11–12; *BN*, March 5, 13, 18, April 17, 1970; Pride, *Political Use of Racial Narratives*, 25.

83. *RRLS* 2, no. 1 (May 1970): 11–12; *BN*, March 5, 6, 13, 18, 20, 21, 31, April 17, 1970; Pride, *Political Use of Racial Narratives*, 25; Alabama v. U.S. and Davis, Civil Action No. 5935-70-P (S. D., Ala., 1970); *NYT*, March 21, 1970. On violence elsewhere, see *NYT*, March 5, 6, 8, 11, 1970; and *Arkansas Gazette*, Feb. 3, 1970.

84. *BN*, Sept. 10, 1969, April 22, 24, 29, June 29, 1970.

85. *BN*, Sept. 10, 1969, June 29, 1970.

86. *BN*, Dec. 23, 1969, Feb. 3, 1970.

87. *BN*, Aug. 8, 15, 1969, Jan. 11, 13, 26, 30, 31, Feb. 3, 5, 27, 1970.

88. U.S. Bureau of the Census, *1970 Census of Population, Characteristics of Population* (Washington, D.C.: GPO, 1973).

89. Faye L. Doss, "Hoover," *Encyclopedia of Alabama*, http://www.encyclopediaofalabama.org/article/h-2995; U.S. Bureau of the Census, *1970 Census of Population, Characteristics of Population*.

90. *BN*, July 26, Aug. 2, 1970; *RRLS* 2, no. 4 (Nov. 1970): 130.

91. Davis v. Board of School Commissioners of Mobile County, 430 F.2d 883, 889 (5th CCA, 1970), reversed 402 U.S. 33 (1971); *RRLS* 2, no. 3 (Sept. 1970): 92–93; *BN*, June 16, Sept. 1, 1970.

92. *RRLS* 2, no. 3 (Sept. 1970): 91; *BN*, July 2, 1970.

93. Davis v. Board of School Commissioners, 430 F.2d 883, 889 (5th CCA, 1970), reversed 402 U.S. 33 (1971); *RRLS* 2, no. 3 (Sept. 1970): 92–93; *RRLS* 2, no. 4 (Nov. 1970): 129; *BN*, June 16, July 17, 1970, Aug. 20, 1970.

94. Davis v. Board of School Commissioners, 430 F.2d 883, 889 (5th CCA, 1970), reversed 402 U.S. 33 (1971); *RRLS* 2, no. 3 (Sept. 1970): 92–93; *RRLS* 2, no. 4 (Nov. 1970): 129; *BN*, June 16, July 17, 1970, Aug. 20, 1970.

95. Carter, *Politics of Rage*, 385–95; *BN*, Sept. 8, 1970.

96. Carter, *Politics of Rage*, 385–86; Harvey, *Question of Justice*, 17–66.

97. Carter, *Politics of Rage*, 385–95.

98. Ibid.; Harvey, *Question of Justice*, 63–64.

Chapter 6. *Swann* Song

1. *NYT*, Sept. 13, 1970; *WP*, Sept. 9, 15, 1970; *BN*, Sept. 1, 8, 23, 28, 1970; Richard Pride, *The Political Use of Racial Narratives: School Desegregation in Mobile, Alabama, 1954–1997* (Urbana: University of Illinois Press, 2002), 101–2.

2. *NYT*, Sept. 13, 1970; *WP*, Sept. 9, 15, 1970; *BN*, Sept. 1, 8, 23, 28, 1970; Pride, *Political Use of Racial Narratives*, 101–2.

3. *NYT*, Sept. 13, 1970; *WP*, Sept. 9, 15, 1970; *BN*, Sept. 1, 8, 23, 28, 1970; Pride, *Political Use of Racial Narratives*, 101–2.

4. *BN*, Aug. 13, 23, 1970; *Christian Science Monitor*, Aug. 31, 1970.

5. *BN*, June 28, 1970; *NYT*, Sept. 13, 1970.

6. *NYT*, Sept. 9, 13, 1970; *BN*, Sept. 1, 8, 23, 28, Oct. 2, 1970; Pride, *Political Use of Racial Narratives*, 101–2.

7. *NYT*, Sept. 9, 13, 1970; *BN*, Sept. 1, 8, 23, 28, Oct. 2, 1970; Pride, *Political Use of Racial Narratives*, 101–2.

8. *NYT*, Sept. 13, 1970; *BN*, Sept. 11, 12, 13, 15, 23, 28, 1970.

9. *RRLS* 2, no. 4 (Nov. 1970): 129; *BN*, Sept. 14, 15, 17, 1970.
10. *LAT*, Sept. 1, 21, 1970; *BN*, Aug. 31, Sept 1, 2, 1970.
11. *BN*, Aug. 31, Sept 1, 2, 1970.
12. *NYT*, Sept. 5, 1970; *BN*, Sept. 4, 1970.
13. *RRLS* 2, no. 5 (Jan. 1970): 170; *BN*, Aug. 28, Sept. 7, 11, 14, 28, 1970.
14. *BN*, Oct. 28, Dec. 17, 1970, Jan. 31, 1971, Feb. 15, 16, 17, 19, 1971.
15. *BN*, May 4, 23, 1971.
16. Betsy Fancher, *Voices from the South: Black Students Talk about Their Experiences in Desegregated Schools* (Atlanta: Southern Regional Council, 1970), 1–7, 15–28.
17. Ibid.
18. *RRLS* 2, no. 1 (May 1970): 13; Docket Report, LVMTR; *WP*, April 6, 1970; *BN*, March 1, 1970. See plans drafted with the assistance of the Auburn University Center for Assisting School Systems with Problems Occasioned by Desegregation at LVMCF, FMJP, C23–27; Ray Jenkins to Johnson, Oct. 30, 1969, LVMCF, FMJP, C30, F7.
19. Brooks Barganier to Johnson, Sept. 14, 1970 (letter undated; date received at court), *Greenville Advocate* editorial attached, Sept. 10, 1970, LVMCF, FMJP, C24, F4.
20. B. B. Harper to Johnson, Nov. 20, 1968, "literature" attached, LVMCF, FMJP, C25, F2.
21. Henry A. Vaughan to Johnson, May 23, 1970, LVMCF, FMJP, C25, F1; Telegram, A. J. Thomas to Johnson, Sept. 3, 1970, Charles D. Johnston to Johnson, Jan. 30, 1970, Memorandum of Phone Call, William Denham to Johnson, Jan. 14, 1970, LVMCF, FMJP, C26, F16, F19; Johnson to Charles Woods, Nov. 1, 1972, Johnson to Ira DeMent, Oct. 27, 1972, Elizabeth Phillips to Johnson, Nov. 13, 1972, LVMCF, FMJP, C24, F18.
22. *Randolph Press* (Wedowee, Ala.), Aug. 29, 1970, filed in LVMCF, FMJP, C26, F17.
23. Letters to Johnson from Parents, March–May, 1969, Motion to Intervene of the Committee of 100, May 7, 1969, Order Denying Motion to Intervene, June 20, 1969, Order of July 16, 1969, LVMCF, FMJP, C23, F15.
24. *Wilcox Progressive Era* (Camden, Ala.), Sept. 9, 1971; Wilcox County BOE Plan for Desegregation, *Facts on Film, 1971–1972 Supplement*, Misc. Materials.
25. Terminal Order Adopting HEW Plan for Sumter County, June 11, 1970, Docket Report, LVMTR; see also LVMCF, FMJP, C27, F3; *BN*, Aug. 23, 1969; *National Observer*, Aug. 10, 1970.
26. *BN*, Dec. 1, 1969, Aug. 13, 18, 1973; Carla Crowder, "Private White Academies Struggle in Changing World," *BN*, Oct. 27, 2002; John C. Walden and Allen D. Cleveland, "The South's New Segregation Academies," *Phi Delta Kappan*, Dec. 16, 1971.
27. William John Heron, "The Growth of Private Schools and Their Impact on the Public Schools of Alabama, 1955–1975" (Ed.D. diss., University of Alabama, 1977), 61–107; Allen Davis Cleveland, "Alabama's Private, Nonsectarian Elementary and Secondary Schools in 1970" (Ed.D. diss., Auburn University, 1970), 55–59; *NYT*, Nov. 17, 1970.
28. Richard Fields, *The Status of Private Segregated Academies in Eleven Southern States* (New York: NAACP LDF, 1972), 3–7; Walden and Cleveland, "South's New Segregation Academies," 234–39; *LAT*, Sept. 4, 1972.
29. *BN*, Jan. 15, Aug. 8, 1970; *Race Relations Reporter*, July 16, 1971; Heron, "Growth of Private Schools and Their Impact," 61–107.
30. *Alabama Independent School Association 2012–13 Directory* (Montgomery: Alabama Independent Schools Association, 2012), http://www.aisaonline.org/. See also *BN*, Sept. 2, Oct. 3, 1969.

31. Cleveland, "Alabama's Private, Nonsectarian Elementary and Secondary Schools," 144–45; Walden and Cleveland, "South's New Segregation Academies"; Crowder, "Private White Academies Struggle in Changing World"; *Pittsburgh Courier*, Feb. 5, 1972.

32. Engel v. Vitale, 370 U.S. 421 (1962), Abington School District v. Schempp, 374 U.S. 203 (1963); "Tree of Liberty," *The Citizen* 15, no. 11 (Sept. 1971), 2; Joseph Crespino, *In Search of Another Country: Mississippi and the Conservative Counterrevolution* (Princeton: Princeton University Press, 2009), 252; Bessemer Academy, http://bessemeracademy.com/; Edgewood Academy, http://www.edgewoodacademy.org/.

33. Crespino, *In Search of Another Country*, 226–32, 252–53; Green v. Kennedy, 309 F.Supp. 1127 (D. C., 1970); Green v. Connally, 330 F.Supp 1150 (D. C., 1971), affirmed *sub nom* Coit v. Green, 404 U.S. 997 (1971).

34. *BN*, Aug. 29, Sept. 10, Dec. 30, 1969, Jan. 9, 1970, March 30, 1971; *Baltimore Afro-American*, March 30, 1971; Wright v. City of Brighton, 441 F.2d 447 (5th CCA, 1971). See also *RRLS* 3, no. 2 (July 1971), 53–54.

35. Solomon Seay, interview with author, Feb. 1, 2012, digital recording and transcript in possession of the author; Anthony Lee, interview with the author, Nov. 14, 2011, digital recording in possession of the author; Willie Wyatt, interview with the author, Jan. 4, 2012, digital recording and transcript in possession of the author; Crowder, "Private White Academies Struggle in Changing World."

36. David Cecelski, *Along Freedom Road: Hyde County, North Carolina and the Fate of Black Schools in the South* (Chapel Hill: University of North Carolina Press, 1994), 10–11; Adam Fairclough, *Teaching Equality: Black Schools in the Age of Jim Crow* (Athens: University of Georgia Press, 2001), 66.

37. Joseph Bagley, "A Meaningful Reality: The Desegregation of the Opelika, Alabama City School System, 1965–72" (master's thesis, Auburn University, 2007), 46–51.

38. Ibid., 51–53.

39. Billy Cooper, Eugene Ford, and Joe Roy Berry to Johnson, Oct. 16, 1969, Velma Williams, Sept. 19, 1968, LVMCF, FMJP, C24, F12; Hugh Lloyd to Johnson, May 6, 1969, Petitions of "trustees and patrons" of Coxheath Junior High School (2), undated, LVMCF, FMJP, C26, F4; Lemonde Motley to Johnson, Oct. 21, 1968, LVMCF, FMJP, C24, F7.

40. Mrs. Willie M. Kitchen to Johnson, Aug. 3, 1967. See also Mrs. Dorothy Lee Johnson, Aug. 3, 1967, Thomas W. Carroll to Mrs. Lillie V. Jordan, cc: Frank Johnson, petition attached, Aug. 16, 1967, Lillie Jordan to Johnson, Aug. 20, 1968, and Memorandum of Conference, Feb. 25, 1969, LVMCF, FMJP, C24, F16.

41. Memorandum of Conference, Feb. 25, 1969, LVMCF, FMJP, C24, F16; Bagley, "Meaningful Reality," 46–49.

42. *BN*, May 21, 1969. On *Know Alabama* and similar textbooks, see chapter 4 of this book.

43. Charles Grayson Summersell, *Alabama History for Schools* (Birmingham: Colonial Press, 1961, 1965); Malcolm McMillen, *This Land Called Alabama* (Austin, Tex.: Steck-Vaughn, 1968); Melton McLaurin, "State Textbooks: Distorted Image of Negroes Presented in Some Histories," *South Today* (Southern Regional Council) 2 (1970–71): 8. On textbooks, see Kevin Boland Johnson, "Guardians of Historical Knowledge: Textbook Politics, Conservative Activism, and School Reform in Mississippi, 1928–1982" (PhD diss., Mississippi State University, 2014); and Charles Eagles, *Civil Rights Culture Wars: The Fight over a Mississippi Textbook* (Chapel Hill: University of North Carolina Press, 2017).

44. Christian McWhirter, "The Birth of 'Dixie,'" *NYT*, March 31, 2012; Caldwell v. Craighead, 432 F.2d 213 (6th CCA, 1970).

45. *NYT*, May 5, 1969; *LAT*, Oct. 16, 1970; *BN*, Nov. 6, 1969, Jan. 10, 1970.

46. *BN*, Oct. 10, 13, 14, 17, 26, 27, 28, Nov. 17, 18, 1970.

47. *BN*, Oct. 14, 17, Nov. 17, 18, 1970; *LAT*, Oct. 16, 1970.

48. On busing, see especially Gary Orfield, *Must We Bus: Segregated Schools and National Policy* (Washington, D.C.: Brookings Institution, 1978); Matthew Lassiter, *The Silent Majority: Suburban Politics in the Sunbelt South* (Princeton University Press, 2006); Brian Daugherty and Charles Bolton, *With All Deliberate Speed: The Implementation of Brown v. BOE* (Fayetteville: University of Arkansas Press, 2008); Matthew Delmont, *Why Busing Failed: Race, Media, and the National Resistance to School Desegregation* (Berkeley: University of California Press, 2016); Ansley Erickson, *Making the Unequal Metropolis: School Desegregation and Its Limits* (Chicago: University of Chicago Press, 2016); Tracy E. K'Meyer, *From Brown to Meredith: The Long Struggle for School Desegregation in Louisville, Kentucky, 1955-2007* (Chapel Hill: University of North Carolina Press, 2013); Ronald Formisano, *Boston against Busing: Race, Class, and Ethnicity in the 1960s and 1970s* (Chapel Hill: University of North Carolina Press, 2012); Erica Frankenberg and Gary Orfield, eds., *The Resegregation of Suburban Schools: A Hidden Crisis in American Education* (Cambridge: Harvard Education Press, 2012).

49. Swann v. Charlotte-Mecklenburg BOE, 402 U.S. 1 (1971); *RRLS* 3, no. 1 (May 1971): 7-9; James Patterson, *Brown v. Board of Education: A Civil Rights Milestone and Its Troubled Legacy* (New York: Oxford University Press, 2001), 156-57. On *Swann* and busing in Charlotte, see Lassiter, *Silent Majority*.

50. Davis v. Board of School Commissioners of Mobile County, 402 U.S. 33 (1971); *RRLS* 3, no. 1 (May 1971), 9-10; *BN*, April 21, 1971.

51. Pride, *Political Use of Racial Narratives*, 108-10.

52. *BN*, May 27, 1971; Dan Carter, *The Politics of Rage: George Wallace, the Origins of the New Conservatism, and the Transformation of American Politics* (Baton Rouge: Louisiana State University Press, 1995, 2000), 399-402.

53. *BN*, May 27, 1971; Richard Nixon, "Remarks to Southern News Media Representatives Attending a Briefing on Domestic Policy in Birmingham, Alabama," May 25, 1971, American Presidency Project, University of California, Santa Barbara, http://www.presidency.ucsb.edu/ws/index.php?pid=3024.

54. Joseph Crespino, *Strom Thurmond's America* (New York: Hill and Wang, 2012), 6-7; Carter, *Politics of Rage*, 418-24; Harvie Wilkinson, *From Brown to Bakke: The Supreme Court and School Integration, 1954-1978* (New York: Oxford University Press, 1981), 126; Crespino, *In Search of Another Country*, 220-36; Kevin M. Kruse, *White Flight: Atlanta and the Making of Modern Conservatism* (Princeton: Princeton University Press, 2005), 253-55; *BN*, Aug. 13, 14, 1971; *Christian Science Monitor*, Aug. 16, 1971.

55. *BN*, May 4, 23, 1971.

56. NAACP news releases, April 14, May 2, 1971, *PNAACP*, part 29, series B, reel 1.

57. *BN*, Aug. 13, 14, 1971; *Christian Science Monitor*, Aug. 16, 1971.

58. *BN*, Aug. 13, 14, 1971; *Christian Science Monitor*, Aug. 16, 1971.

59. *WP*, Aug. 14, 1971; *NYT*, Sept. 4, 1971; *BN*, Aug. 14, 1971; *Atlanta Constitution*, Aug. 26; *Miami Herald*, Aug. 17, 1971; Order of Aug. 27, 1971, LVMCF, FMJP, C30, F8; "Pointer, Sam Clyde Jr.," in *Biographical Directory of Article III Federal Judges, 1789-Present*, Federal Judicial Center, https://www.fjc.gov/history/judges/pointer-sam-clyde-jr.

60. *NYT*, Aug. 18, 19, Sept. 4, 1971; *BN*, Aug. 13, 1971; Lee v. Macon County BOE and Calhoun County BOE, and Oxford City BOE, 448 F.2d 746 (5th CCA, 1971); Wayne Flynt, *Alabama in the Twentieth Century* (Tuscaloosa: University of Alabama Press, 2004), 327; Claire M. Wilson, "Hobson City," April 5, 2012, *Encyclopedia of Alabama*, http://www.encyclopediaofalabama.org/article/h-3245.

61. *NYT*, Aug. 18, 19, 1971; Lee v. Macon County BOE and Calhoun County BOE, and Oxford City BOE, 448 F.2d 746 (5th CCA, 1971); *BN*, June 30, 1971; *RRLS* 3, no. 4 (Nov. 1971): 130; "McFadden, Frank Hampton," in *Biographical Directory of Article III Federal Judges, 1789–Present*, Federal Judicial Center, https://www.fjc.gov/history/judges/mcfadden-frank-hampton.

62. Lee v. Macon and Calhoun County BOE and Oxford City BOE, 448 F.2d 746 (5th CCA, 1971); *NYT*, Aug. 18, 19, 1971; *BN*, June 30, Aug. 13, 1971; *Charleston News and Courier*, Aug. 21, 1971.

63. *NYT*, Aug. 18, 1971; *RRLS* 3, no. 4 (Nov. 1971), 130.

64. *Gadsden Times*, Aug. 27, 1971; *Florence (Ala.) Times*, Sept. 2, 1971; *Thomasville (Ala.) Times-Enterprise*, Sept. 17, 1971; *Virginian Pilot* (Norfolk), Dec. 4, 1971.

65. *WP*, July 9, 1971; Pride, *Political Use of Racial Narratives*, 111–14.

66. *WP*, July 9, 1971; Pride, *Political Use of Racial Narratives*, 111–14.

67. "The Southerners—The New Klan?," K. L. Buford Files, *PNAACP*, part 29, series A, reel 1; *Henderson (N.C.) Times-News*, March 16, 1972.

68. "The Southerners—The New Klan?"

69. Ibid.; *Henderson (N.C.) Times-News*, March 16, 1972; Newman Douglass, Laura Browder, and Marco Ricci, *The Reconstruction of Asa Carter*, television documentary (Corporation for Public Broadcasting, 2010).

70. Carter, *Politics of Rage*, 320; Douglass, Browder, and Ricci, *Reconstruction of Asa Carter*.

71. Wayne Greenhaw, "Is Forrest Carter Really Asa Carter? Only Josey Wales May Know for Sure," *NYT*, Aug. 26, 1976. Historian Dan Carter wrote a piece in 1991 proving that Forrest was Asa: "The Transformation of a Klansman," *NYT*, Oct. 4, 1991. See also Carter, *Politics of Rage*, 320; Gillis Morgan, "Asa Carter (Forrest Carter)," *Encyclopedia of Alabama*, Aug. 28, 2009, http://www.encyclopediaofalabama.org/article/h-2427; Joseph E. Lowndes, *From the New Deal to the New Right: Race and the Southern Origins of Modern Conservatism* (New Haven: Yale University Press, 2009), 140–54.

72. Stout v. Jefferson County BOE and BOE for the City of Pleasant Grove, 448 F.2d 403 (5th CCA, 1971), *RRLS* 3, no. 3 (Sept. 1971): 90; *It's Not Over in the South: School Desegregation in Forty-Three Southern Cities Eighteen Years after Brown*, Report by the ACHR et al. (1973), in *Facts on Film, 1972–1973 Supplement*, Misc. Materials, 46–47.

73. District Court proceedings quoted in Appellate Court opinion, Stout v. Jefferson County BOE and BOE for the City of Pleasant Grove, 466 F.2d 1213 (5th CCA, 1972), *RRLS* 3, no. 4 (Nov. 1971): 129–30.

74. Stout v. Jefferson County BOE and BOE for the City of Pleasant Grove, 466 F.2d 1213 (5th CCA, 1972), *RRLS* 3, no. 4 (Nov. 1971): 129–30; *Florence (Ala.) Times-Daily*, Sept. 26, 1971.

75. Stout v. Jefferson County BOE and BOE for the City of Pleasant Grove, cert. denied, 411 U.S. 930 (1972).

76. Knight v. Alabama, 458 F.Supp.2d, 1273 (N. D., Ala., 2004), 1286–97.

77. Reynolds v. Sims, 377 U.S. 533 (1964) (M. D., Ala., 1971); Knight v. Alabama, 458 F.Supp.2d, 1273 (N. D., Ala., 2004), 1286–97.
78. Weissinger v. Boswell, 330 F.Supp 615 (M. D., Ala., 1971).
79. Amendment 325, see full text at http://alisondb.legislature.state.al.us/alison/codeofalabama/constitution/1901/CA-888434.htm; *Rural Policy Matters*, May 2011, http://www.ruraledu.org/; Knight v. Alabama, 458 F.Supp.2d, 1273 (N. D., Ala., 2004), 1286–97; Complaint in Lynch v. Alabama, 16–19, at Plaintiffs' Knight & Sims vs. Alabama Website, https://web.archive.org/web/20090106155141/http://knightsims.com/pdf/08_03_20/complaint_filed.pdf.
80. *WP*, May 16, 1972; Carter, *Politics of Rage*, 432–50.
81. *WP*, May 16, 1972; Carter, *Politics of Rage*, 432–50; Knight v. Alabama, 458 F.Supp.2d, 1273 (N. D., Ala., 2004), 1286–97.
82. Patterson, *Brown v. Board of Education*, 177–80; San Antonio Independent School District v. Rodriguez, 411 U.S. 1 (1973).
83. Bradley v. School Board of the City of Richmond, 462 F.2d 1058 (4th CCA, 1972), affirmed *sub nom* School Board of the City of Richmond v. State BOE of Virginia, 412 U.S. 92 (1973); *WP*, Jan. 16, June 9, 1972; *MA*, May 25, 1973.
84. Patterson, *Brown v. Board of Education*, 177–80; Milliken v. Bradley, 418 U.S. 717 (1974).
85. *MA*, April 15, 1973; *It's Not Over in the South*, 45–48.
86. *It's Not Over in the South*, 45–8.
87. Lassiter, *Silent Majority*, 1–3; Kruse, *White Flight*, 258; Thomas Sugrue, *Origins of the Urban Crisis: Race and Inequality in Postwar Detroit* (Princeton: Princeton University Press, 2010), 91, 106, 197; Richard Rothstein, *The Color of Law: A Forgotten History of How Our Government Segregated America* (New York: Liveright, 2017). On housing discrimination, see also Pegues v. Bakane, 445 F.2d 1140 (5th CCA, 1971), also at *RRLS* 3, no. 4 (Nov. 1971): 157–58.
88. *South Today* 4, no. 6 (March 1973): 2–5; *South Today* 5, no. 2 (Oct. 1973), 2; Carter, *Politics of Rage*, 451–58.
89. Knight v. Alabama, 458 F.Supp.2d, 1273 (N. D., Ala., 2004), 1286–97, quoting the *Mobile Press-Register*, Dec. 12, 1971. See also McCarthy v. Jones, 449 F.Supp 480 (S. D., Ala., 1978).
90. Knight v. Alabama, 458 F.Supp.2d, 1273 (N. D., Ala., 2004), 1286–97, quoting Wallace at 1293; Weissinger v. Boswell, 330 F.Supp 615 (M. D., Ala., 1971).
91. Lynch v. Alabama, No. 11–15464 (11th CCA 2014), published in *Justia*, http://law.justia.com/. On the Lid Bills, in general, see Susan Pace Hamill, "An Argument for Tax Reform Based on Judeo-Christian Ethics," *Alabama Law Review*, 54, no. 1 (2002): 20–33; and Allen Tullos, *Alabama Getaway: The Political Imaginary and the Heart of Dixie* (Athens: University of Georgia Press, 2011), 168–70.
92. Knight v. Alabama, 458 F.Supp.2d, 1273 (N. D., Ala., 2004), 1286–99; Weissinger v. Smith, 733 F2d 802 (11th CCA, 1984); Amendment 373 Ratified, *Justia*; Constitutional Reform Project of the Alabama Appleseed Center for Law and Justice, "Alabama's 1901 Constitution: Barriers to Education," Alabama Appleseed, 2009, http://www.alabamaappleseed.org/; Susan Pace Hamill, "A Chance to Build a New Path," https://www.law.ua.edu/misc/hamill/knight.4.pdf; Carol McPhail, "Current Use Loses Millions for Alabama," *Mobile Register*, Dec. 11, 1994.

93. Knight v. Alabama, 1286–99; Amendment 373; Appleseed Center for Law and Justice, "Alabama's 1901 Constitution;" Hamill, "Chance to Build a New Path;" Hamill, "An Argument for Tax Reform Based on Judeo-Christian Ethics," 25–27.

94. Knight v. Alabama, 458 F.Supp.2d, 1273 (N. D., Ala., 2004), 1286–97; "legal scholar": Hamill, "Chance to Build a New Path."

Epilogue. "If Ever Is Going to Happen"

1. Nikole Hannah-Jones, "Segregation Now," *ProPublica*, April 16, 2014, https://www.propublica.org/article/segregation-now-full-text; Jeff Larson, Nikole Hannah-Jones, and Mike Tigas, "School Segregation after Brown," *ProPublica*, May 1, 2014, http://projects.propublica.org/segregation-now; Sean F. Reardon et al., "*Brown* Fades: The End of Court-Ordered School Desegregation and the Resegregation of American Public Schools," *Journal of Policy Analysis and Management* 31, no. 4 (July 2012): 876–904.

2. Hannah-Jones, "Segregation Now"; Larson, Hannah-Jones, and Tigas, "School Segregation after Brown"; Erica Frankenberg and Gary Orfield, eds., *The Resegregation of Suburban Schools: A Hidden Crisis in American Education* (Cambridge: Harvard Education Press, 2012). On PICS v. Community Schools and "vigorous voluntary efforts," see Tracy E. K'Meyer, *From Brown to Meredith: The Long Struggle for School Desegregation in Louisville, Kentucky, 1955–2007* (Chapel Hill: University of North Carolina Press, 2013). On "the opposite," see Ansley Erickson, *Making the Unequal Metropolis: School Desegregation and Its Limits* (Chicago: University of Chicago Press, 2016).

3. *WP*, July 30, 31, Aug. 8, 1973; Joseph Crespino, *In Search of Another Country: Mississippi and the Conservative Counterrevolution* (Princeton: Princeton University Press, 2009), 226–32, 252–53; Runyon v. McCrary, 427 U.S. 160 (1976); Green v. Regan, 670 F.2d 1235 (DC CCA, 1981); Lawrence McAndrews, "Talking the Talk: Bill Clinton and School Desegregation," *International Social Science Review* 79, no. 3/4 (2004): 87–107.

4. *MA*, July 31, 1973; Carla Crowder, "Private White Academies Struggle," *BN*, Oct. 27, 2002.

5. Crespino, *In Search of Another Country*, 226–32, 252–53; Green v. Regan, 670 F.2d 1235 (DC CCA, 1981); Bob Jones University v. U.S., 461 U.S. 574 (1983); Riddick v. School Board of the City of Norfolk, 724 F. 2d 521 (4th CCA, 1986); *WP*, July 30, 1973; "vendetta": Neal Devins, "On Casebooks and Canons or Why Bob Jones University Will Never Be Part of the Constitutional Law Canon," *William and Mary Law School Scholarship Repository*, 2000, 286; McAndrews, "Talking the Talk," 87–107.

6. Oklahoma City v. Dowell 498 U.S. 237 (1991); Freeman v. Pitts 498 U.S. 1081 (1992); Missouri v. Jenkins 515 U.S. 70 (1995); Lawrence McAndrews, "'Not the Bus, but Us': George W. Bush and School Desegregation," *Educational Foundations*, Winter–Spring 2009, 67–82.

7. Motoko Rich and Tamar Lewin, "No Child Left Behind Law Faces Its Own Reckoning," *NYT*, March 20, 2015; Motoko Rich, "'No Child' Law Whittled Down by White House," *NYT*, July 6, 2012; McAndrews, "Not the Bus, but Us."

8. Lyndsey Layton, "Obama Signs New K–12 Education Law That Ends No Child Left Behind," *WP*, Dec. 10, 2015.

9. Wayne Flynt, *Alabama in the Twentieth Century* (Tuscaloosa: University of Alabama Press, 2004), 101–6; Patrick Cotter and Tom Gordon, "Alabama: The GOP Rises in the Heart of Dixie," in *Southern Politics in the 1990s*, ed. Alexander Lamis (Baton Rouge: Louisiana

State University Press, 1999), 221–48. On southern Republicanism, see Earl Black and Merle Black, *The Rise of Southern Republicans* (Cambridge, Mass.: Belknap Press, 2003).

10. Flynt, *Alabama in the Twentieth Century*, 101–6; Cotter and Gordon, "Alabama," 221–48.

11. Kim Chandler, "Republicans in Bombshell Move Push through Bill Giving Tax Credits for Kids at 'Failing' Schools to Go to Private Schools," *Al.com*, Feb. 28, 2013, http://blog.al.com/wire/2013/02/republicans_push_through_bill.html.

12. Kim Chandler, "From 'Historic' to 'Sleaziness,'" *Al.com*, Feb. 28, 2013, http://blog.al.com/wire/2013/02/from_historic_to_sleaziness_re.html.

13. Ibid.

14. Mike Cason, "Many AAA Scholarships Go to Students Not Zoned for Failing Schools," *Al.com*, Dec. 8, 2014, http://www.al.com/news/index.ssf/2014/12/half_of_alabama_accountability.html.

15. Kim Chandler, "Alabama Accountability Act: 78 Schools Listed As Failing," *Al.com*, June 18, 2013, http://blog.al.com/wire/2013/06/alabama_failing_schools_list_2013.html.

16. Ibid.

17. Boyd v. Magee, C.A. 03-CV-2013-901470 (Circuit Court, Montgomery County, May 28, 2014), 10, reversed/remanded as Magee v. Boyd, 1130987 (Supreme Court of Alabama, March 2, 2015), both published in *Al.com*; Mike Cason, "Montgomery County Judge Rules Alabama Accountability Act Unconstitutional," *Al.com*, May 28, 2014, http://blog.al.com/wire/2014/05/montgomery_county_judge_rules.html. On equity funding case *Ex Parte James*, 836 So.2d 813 (2002), see *LAT*, April 4, 1993, March 27, 1994; and John Herbert Roth, "Education Funding and the Alabama Example: Another Player on a Crowded Field," *Brigham Young University Education and Law Journal* 2, no. 10 (Fall 2003): 754–59, http://digitalcommons.law.byu.edu/.

18. Complaint in Marshall v. Bentley, p. 2, published in *Al.com*; Kim Chandler, "Southern Poverty Law Center Files Lawsuit Challenging Alabama Accountability Act," *Al.com*, Aug. 19, 2013, http://blog.al.com/wire/2013/08/southern_poverty_law_center_fi.html.

19. Associated Press, "Federal Judge Dismisses Lawsuit Challenging Alabama Accountability Act," *Al.com*, April 8, 2014, http://blog.al.com/wire/2014/04/federal_judge_dismisses_lawsui.html; Chandler, "Southern Poverty Law Center Files Lawsuit."

20. Mike Cason, "Alabama Accountability Act Upheld by State Supreme Court," *Al.com*, March 2, 2015, http://www.al.com/news/index.ssf/2015/03/alabama_accountability_act_sta.html.

21. Trisha Powell Crain, "Few Alabama Students Use Choice Given under Accountability Act," *Al.com*, Feb. 9, 2017, http://www.al.com/news/montgomery/index.ssf/2017/02/few_alabama_students_use_choic.html; Alabama Department of Education List of Failing Schools as Defined by the Alabama Accountability Act of 2015, https://www.alsde.edu/.

22. Complaint in Lynch v. Alabama, 19–24, at Plaintiffs' Knight & Sims vs. Alabama Website, https://web.archive.org/web/20090106155141/http://knightsims.com/pdf/08_03_20/complaint_filed.pdf.

23. Complaint in Lynch v. Alabama, 19–24; Susan Pace Hamill, "An Argument for Tax Reform Based on Judeo-Christian Ethics," *Alabama Law Review*, 54, no. 1 (2002): 27.

24. City of Mobile v. Bolden, 446 U.S. 55 (1980); Jim Rutenberg, "A Dream Undone: Inside the 50-Year Campaign to Roll Back the Voting Rights Act," *New York Times Magazine*, July 29, 2015; Chandler Davidson and Bernard Grofman, eds., *A Quiet Revolution*

in the Streets: The Impact of the Voting Rights Act, 1965–1990 (Princeton: Princeton University Press, 1994), 62.

25. *Huntsville Times*, April 19, 24, 2011; Brian Lawson, "Federal Judge Rails against Alabama Education System," *Al.com*, Oct. 21, 2011, http://blog.al.com/breaking/2011/10/federal_judge_rails_against_al.html; Brian Lawson, "Federal Appeals Court Rules Alabama Property Tax System Is Not Discriminatory," *Al.com*, Jan. 10, 2014, http://blog.al.com/breaking/2014/01/federal_appeals_court_rules_al.html.

26. Lynch v. Alabama, 2011 U.S. Dist. LEXIS 155012 (N. D., Ala., 2011), 798–800, Lexis-Nexis Academic; *Huntsville Times*, April 19, 24, Oct. 22, 2011.

27. Lynch v. Alabama, 800–803. On San Antonio case, see chapter 6, note 82, above.

28. *Huntsville Times*, Oct. 22, 2011, Dec. 6, 2012; Lynch v. Alabama, No. 11–15464 (11th CCA, 2014), published in *Justia*, quoting from 2, 28.

29. Lynch v. Alabama, No. 11–15464 (11th CCA, 2014), *Justia*, 28, 29.

30. Brian Lawson, "Federal Appeals Court Rules Alabama Property Tax System Is Not Discriminatory," Jan. 10, 2014, *Al.com*; Brian Lyman, "U.S. Supreme Court Rejects Alabama School-Funding Case," *MA*, Oct. 6, 2014.

31. Institute of Education Sciences, National Center for Education Statistics, http://nces.ed.gov/; *2010 Census of Population*, U.S. Census Bureau, http://www.census.gov; Frankenberg and Orfield, eds., *The Resegregation of Suburban Schools*; "sleepwalking": Gary Orfield, *Dismantling Desegregation: The Quiet Reversal of Brown v. BOE* (New York: New Press, 1996), 332, 346; Charles Clotfelter, *After Brown: The Rise and Retreat of School Desegregation* (Princeton: Princeton University Press, 2006); Solomon Seay, interview with author, Feb. 1, 2012, digital recording and transcript in possession of the author.

32. Joseph Bagley, "A Meaningful Reality: The Desegregation of the Opelika, Alabama City School System, 1965–72" (master's thesis, Auburn University, 2007), 81–87; National Center for Education Statistics; *2010 Census of Population*; Alabama Department of Education Public Data Reports, http://alsde.edu/publicdatareports.

33. National Center for Education Statistics; *2010 Census of Population*; Alabama Department of Education Public Data Reports; *BN*, Oct. 27, 2002; *NYT*, July 9, 2011.

34. J. Mills Thornton, *Dividing Lines: Municipal Politics and the Struggle for Civil Rights in Montgomery, Birmingham, and Selma* (Tuscaloosa: University of Alabama Press, 2002), 502–13; National Center for Education Statistics; *2010 Census of Population*. On magnet schools and the value of "'equity' choice" desegregation plans, see David J. Armour, *Forced Justice: School Desegregation and the Law* (New York: Oxford University Press, 1995).

35. National Center for Education Statistics; *2010 Census of Population*; *BN*, Oct. 27, 2002; *NYT*, July 9, 2011.

36. Trisha Powell Crain, "Alabama Commission Approves Two New Public Charter Schools," *Al.com*, June 27, 2017, http://www.al.com/news/index.ssf/2017/06/alabama_commission_approves_tw.html; Trisha Powell Crain, "Alabama Not Attracting Charter Schools, Numbers Show," *Al.com*, May 16, 2017, http://www.al.com/news/index.ssf/2017/05/alabama_not_attracting_charter.html.

37. Brian A. Duke, "The Strange Career of Birdie Mae Davis: A History of a School Desegregation Lawsuit in Mobile, Alabama, 1966–1997," master's thesis (Auburn University, 2009).

38. National Center for Education Statistics; *2010 Census of Population*; Alabama Department of Education Public Data Reports.

39. National Center for Education Statistics; *2010 Census of Population*; *BN*, June 10, 2012, Feb. 26, 27, 2013; Thornton, *Dividing Lines*, 523–24. On education politics and urban education reform, see James E. Ryan, *Five Miles Away, a World Apart: One City, Two Schools, and the Story of Educational Opportunity in Modern America* (New York: Oxford University Press, 2010).

40. National Center for Education Statistics; *2010 Census of Population*; Alabama State Board of Education, *Plan 2020* (Alabama State Board of Education, 2016), https://www.alsde.edu/; *Alabama Education Directory*, 2012–13 ed., Alabama State Board of Education, https://www.alsde.edu.

41. Stout and U.S. v. Jefferson County BOE, Opinion and Order of April 24, 2017, published on *Al.com*; Nikole Hannah-Jones, "The Resegregation of Jefferson County," *New York Times Magazine*, Sept. 6, 2017; Kent Faulk, "Gardendale Will Get to Form Its Own School System If It Abides by Federal Judge's Three-Year Plan," *Al.com*, April 26, 2017, http://www.al.com/news/birmingham/index.ssf/2017/04/gardendale_will_get_to_form_it.html.

42. Hannah-Jones, "Resegregation of Jefferson County"; Kent Faulk, "Gardendale Appeals Ruling on School Formation," *Al.com*, May 23, 2017, http://www.al.com/news/birmingham/index.ssf/2017/05/gardendale_appeals_ruling_on_s.html.

43. Hannah-Jones, "Resegregation of Jefferson County"; Faulk, "Gardendale Appeals Ruling on School Formation"; Kent Faulk, "Court Rules Gardendale Can't Form School System," *Al.com*, Feb. 13, 2018, http://www.al.com/news/birmingham/index.ssf/2018/02/federal_appeals_court_rules_ga.html.

44. Documents from author's email correspondence with Norman Chachkin: Order Dismissing the LDF, May 20, 2014, Memorandum Opinion, June 20, 2014, Briefs of the U.S. and Plaintiffs, May 10, 2014, and Docket Sheet, Hereford v. Huntsville attached; Challen Stephens, "Huntsville Faces Desegregation Fight in Court This Week," *Al.com*, May 20, 2014, http://blog.al.com/breaking/2014/05/huntsville_goes_to_court_this.html.

45. Challen Stephens, "Justice Department Slams Huntsville for Creating 'More Segregated Education Environments," *Al.com*, May 17, 2014; Challen Stephens, "Huntsville Blasts Justice Department One Last Time before Desegregation Showdown," *Al.com*, May 16, 2014, http://blog.al.com/breaking/2014/05/huntsville_blasts_justice_depa.html.

46. Challen Stephens "NAACP Legal Defense Fund Once Again Sides with Huntsville against Feds," *Al.com*, May 17, 2014, http://blog.al.com/breaking/2014/05/naacp_legal_defense_fund_once.html; Challen Stephens, "Timeline: Race and Schools in Huntsville," *Al.com*, March 4, 2014, http://blog.al.com/breaking/2014/03/timeline_race_and_schools_in_h.html.

47. Hannah-Jones, "Resegregation of America's Schools."

48. Ibid.

49. Hannah-Jones, "Resegregation of Americas Schools"; Crain, "Few Alabama Students Use Choice."

50. Michael Klarman, *From Jim Crow to Civil Rights: The Supreme Court and the Struggle for Racial Equality* (New York: Oxford University Press, 2004); Paul Finkelman, "The Centrality of Brown," in *Choosing Equality: Essays and Narratives on the Desegregation Experience*, ed. Robert L. Hayman Jr. and Leland Ware (State College: Penn State University Press, 2009).

51. Seay interview; Solomon Seay Jr., *Jim Crow and Me: Stories from My Life as a Civil Rights Lawyer* (Montgomery: New South, 2008), 97.

INDEX

Aaron, J. Edward, 36
Adams, Hugh, 58–59
Adams, Oscar, 66–67, 107, 153
Alabama A&M University, 4
Alabama Accountability Act (AAA), 219–23 passim, 232
Alabama Baptist, 73–74
Alabama Christian Movement for Human Rights (ACMHR), 35, 37–38, 52
Alabama Coalition for Equity v. James, 221
Alabama Council on Human Relations, 21–22, 29, 49, 98
Alabama Democratic Conference, 168
Alabama Education Association (AEA), 143, 220
Alabama Farm Bureau (Alabama Farmers' Association, ALFA), 213–14, 225
Alabama Forestry Association, 213–14
Alabama High School Athletic Association (AHSAA), 136–37
Alabama Interscholastic Athletic Association (AIAA), 136–37
Alabama National Guard, 57, 68, 73; armories of, 61, 63, 141, 144
Alabama State Board of Education, 23; control over local school boards as established in *Lee v. Macon County Board of Education*, 83–89 passim, 115; efforts to thwart implementation of HEW guidelines, 93–95, 98–99, 104; operation of trade schools and junior colleges, 158; resolution condemning desegregation decisions, 149
Alabama State Department of Education, 84, 86, 103, 115, 118, 121, 191
Alabama state legislature: designation of highways, 227; *Dillard v. Crenshaw County* and, 121; efforts to block or blunt desegregation, 22–29 passim, 50, 79, 83, 91, 163–64, 172–73, 186, 200–201; meeting as "committee of the whole," 125; passage of Alabama Accountability Act, 219–23; passage of Lid Bill Amendments, 210–15, 223–25; reapportionment of, 23–24, 29, 74, 208–9; Republican Party takes over, 219; "super-segregation committee" in, 29–30; Lurleen Wallace addresses, 123–24; white backlash against, 108; mentioned, 33
Alabama State Teachers' Association (ASTA), 131–34, 158, 160, 168, 221
Alabama State University, 4–5, 21, 116, 158
Alabamians Behind Local Education (ABLE), 60
Alden High School, 166
Alexander v. Holmes County Board of Education, 161–67 passim
Allen, Jim, 99, 143–44
Allgood, Clarence, 67, 73–74, 165, 167
Almond, Lindsey, 30, 39
American States' Rights Association, 71, 176
Anderson, Margaret, 87
Anniston, Ala., 15, 98, 103, 155, 197
Anniston Star, 65
Armstrong, Dwight, 63, 65, 67, 69
Armstrong, Floyd, 63, 65, 67, 69
Armstrong, James, 41
Armstrong v. Birmingham Board of Education, 41–42, 45, 60–69 passim; appeals in, 53–56, 88, 153; influence on other cases, 50–51, 57, 79; initial trial in, 47–48; white flight and, 96
Aronson, Henry, 118
Arrington, Richard, 229

Associated Industries of Alabama, 213–14
Atlanta Declaration, NAACP, 14
Atlanta Journal, 27
Auburn University, 4; Center for Assisting School Systems with Problems Occasioned by Desegregation, 267n18; desegregation of, 91, 257n42; satellite campus in Montgomery (AUM), 45, 158
Auburn University Montgomery (AUM), 45, 158
Autauga Academy, 189
Autauga County, Ala., 150, 212; board of education, 127, 148, 189

backlash thesis, 9–10
Bailey, Joe, 183
Baker High School, 50
Baldwin County, Ala., 212, 228
Baltimore Afro-American, 162
Barbour County, Ala., 42, 100, 150
Bargainer, Brooks, 188
Barnes, Reid, 127
Barrett, St. John, 47, 84–85, 115–18 passim, 127, 129
Bass, Ray, 107, 226–27
Bell, Derrick, 129, 132
Bell, Griffin, 55, 122
Bentley, Robert, 220
Bessemer, Ala., 20, 175, 206; *Brown v. Board of Education of City of Bessemer*, 131, 153, 156; CRD and LDF file suit against, 96, 164, 171; files suit against HEW guidelines, 93, 96, 99–101, 106, 131, 153, 156, 167
Bibb County, Ala., 100, 126–28
Bice, Tommy, 220
Big Mules, 23, 181
Billes, Heloise, 82
Billingsley, Orzell, 45; work on *Hereford v. Huntsville Board of Education*, 51, 64; work on *NAACP v. Wallace*, 107–8; work on *Nelson v. Birmingham Board of Education*, 46–48; mentioned, 230
Birmingham, Ala., 15, 59–61, 78, 91; appeals in *Armstrong* case, 54–56, 88; Big Mules from, 23; charter schools in, 228; Citizens' Council recruitment in, 20–22; compulsory assignment in, 164–75 passim, 182–85 passim, 197, 211; failing schools in, 222; impact of *Green v. New Kent* on, 153; impact of *Singleton II* on, 101; *Nelson* case, 45; Richard Nixon in, 199; municipal secession from, 175–76; 1963 SCLC campaign in, 51–53; Fred Shuttlesworth attempts to desegregate schools in, 34–44 passim; Sixteenth Street Baptist Church bombing, 72–76; trial in *Armstrong* and *Nelson* cases, 47–48; George Wallace blocks desegregation of schools in, 63–72 passim; white flight to suburbs of, 96, 154, 212, 228–30; mentioned, 18–19, 26, 30, 33–34, 46, 49, 52, 79, 81–82, 90, 99, 107, 155, 202, 220. See also *Armstrong v. Birmingham Board of Education*; *Shuttlesworth v. Birmingham Board of Education*
Birmingham News, 46, 53, 59, 89, 103, 108, 121, 153, 172–75, 182; ads taken out in, 165, 171; letters to editor of, 71, 76
Birmingham Stalemate, 40–41
Birmingham World, 26, 35
Black, Hugo, 157, 161
Black Belt, 15–16, 77–79, 233; Alabama Accountability Act and "failing schools" in, 220–24 passim; Bourbon leaders in, 20; Citizens' Council organization in, 18–19; economic reprisal in, 96–98; HEW guidelines and, 100; legislative reapportionment and, 23; Lid Bill amendments designed to protect white property in, 208, 213–14; school cases in, 51, 77, 88, 100; white flight to segregation academies in, 95, 106–7, 190–92, 208, 227–28; mentioned, 41–42, 133, 229
black power, 141
Blacksher, James, 223–35, 228
Bloch, Charles, 22, 27
Blount, Winton, 91
Blount High School, 152, 184
Bob Jones University v. U.S., 217

Booker T. Washington Junior High School, 183
Boone, Buford, 99
Boston, 217
Bourbon leaders, 20, 23
Boutwell, Albert, 23, 30; Boutwell Freedom of Choice Plan, 28, 39; creates biracial Community Affairs Committee, 59; criticized by segregationist students, 71–72; criticized by white liberals, 75; mayoral election of, 51; pupil placement law created with help of, 24–25; school closure opposed by, 63; Sixteenth Street Baptist Church bombing and, 72–73; speaks to Citizens' Council, 38
Boutwell Committee, 23, 25, 28
Bowen, ReVonda, 3
Boyd v. Magee, 221–22, 226
Bradley v. Richmond, 210–11
Bremer, Arthur, 210
Brennan, William, 142–43
Brewer, Albert, 99, 123–24, 140–44 passim, 149–51; invokes white rights, 166–68, 174, 187, 213; involvement in litigation, 154–55, 172–73; race against George Wallace, 178–79, 181
Brewton, Ala., 15
Briggs dictum, 27, 37, 117
Briggs v. Elliot, 27
Browder v. Gayle, 32–33, 37
Brown, John (judge), 45, 55–56, 156, 161
Brown v. Board of Education, 1, 48, 216, 224; *Briggs v. Elliott* and, 117; *Browder v. Gayle* and, 32; *Brown II* implementation decree, 25, 55, 142; *Calhoun v. Lattimer* and, 88; efficacy of, 232; federal judges' stance on, 45, 56; *Green v. County School Board of New Kent* and, 142, 156, historiography of, 9–10; *Lee v. Macon* and, 89, 119, 121–22, 132; *Milliken v. Bradley* and, 221; NAACP's efforts to force implementation of, 13–22 passim; Richard Nixon's enforcement of, 156; state legislature's efforts to nullify, 22–28 passim, 79, 109, 130; white flight as result of, 176,

191, 228; mentioned, 7, 35, 38, 42, 53, 75, 87, 99, 205
Brown v. Board of Education of City of Bessemer, 131, 153, 156
Buckley, William F., 87
Buford, K. L., 58, 61–62, 201
Bullock County, Ala., 17–18, 88, 90, 100
Burg, Harvey, 153
Burger, Warren, 166, 211
Burnett, Ladonna, 46–47
Burns, Crawford, 169
Bush, George H. W., 217–18
Bush, George W., 218
busing, 124, 147, 151, 159, 183, 198–204; during Ford and Carter administrations, 216–17; in Mobile, 163–64, 168, 228; white officials condemn, 172, 181, 208–11
Butler County, Ala., 17–18, 107, 188
Butler High School, Huntsville, 197, 231
Byrd, Harry, 27, 116

Calhoun County, Ala., 202–3, 206, 208
Calhoun v. Lattimer, 87–88
Cameron, Ben, 55–56
Carmichael, Stokely, 141
Carr, Arlam, 91
Carr v. Montgomery County Board of Education, 88, 91, 136–37, 143, 146, 156–57, 177
Carter, Asa, 20–22, 35–36, 43–44, 178, 205–6, 270n71
Carter, Janice, 82
Carter, Jimmy, 217
Carter, Robert, 33
Carter v. West Feliciana Parish School Board, 167–68, 170
Cashin, John, 50–51
Cavalry Hills School for Negroes, 46
Central High School, Tuscaloosa, 231–32
Chachkin, Norman, 230–31
Chambliss, Robert, 64, 72, 75
Chambliss, Shirley, 82
Champion, Mac, 190–91
charter schools, 227–28
Chickasaw, Ala., 139, 163, 186
Choctaw County, Ala., 112

Christian, Raymond, 46–47, 185
Christian Science Monitor, 121
Citizen, 90, 114, 192, 198
Civil Rights Act of 1964, 53, 90, 92, 172; backlash thesis and, 9; establishment of Civil Rights Division, 47; HEW guidelines and, 94, 101–4, 116–17; *Lee v. Macon* enforcement and, 121; mentioned, 147
Civil Rights Division, U.S. Department of Justice, 47, 235; *Alexander v. Holmes* and, 166; *Armstrong v. Birmingham* and, 61, 67; Black Belt school cases and, 100, 105; Calhoun County *Lee v. Macon* case and, 202; *Carr v. Montgomery* and, 157; *Davis v. Mobile* and, 151–54, 168, 177, 184; drafting and enforcement of Civil Rights Act of 1964, 53, 90, 92; enforcement of *Lee v. Macon* statewide decree, 126–28, 131, 133–37, 148–51, 154–58; *Green v. New Kent* and, 123–33, 147; *Herford v. Huntsville* and, 230–31; HEW guidelines and, 101; impacted areas cases and, 50, 54; *Lee v. Macon* and, 57–58, 82–86, 89, 107, 115–18, 120–21; Opelika *Lee v. Macon* case and, 194; shift in policy under Nixon, 162–62, 164, 200–202; stand in schoolhouse door and, 52; Talladega *Lee v. Macon* case and, 185; *U.S. v. Jefferson County* and, 170; mentioned, 3, 9, 56, 63, 96, 103
Civil War, 5, 8, 12, 15, 31, 44, 61
Clark, Jim, 81–82
Clark, Ramsey, 148
Clay, Cassius, 178
Cleburne County, Ala., 98
Clemon, U. W., 168, 170–71, 175, 185–86, 202, 204, 211, 229–31
clergy, white, 17, 21, 49, 60, 70–71, 75
Clinton, Bill, 218, 224
Coffee County, Ala., 98, 195
Cole, Nat King, 20, 22
College Street Elementary School, 115
Collins, Addie Mae, 72
Collins, Monty, 186, 200–201, 203
color-blindness, 6, 8, 10, 152, 175, 222; as color-masked, 6, 8, 149, 166, 173, 198, 215, 219
Committee on Constitutional Law and State Sovereignty, 50
Common Core, 218
compulsory assignment, 148–49, 151–53, 173, 179, 182, 193, 208–9, 213; blacks protest, 196–97; in Jefferson County, 164, 174–75; in *Lee v. Macon* systems, 187, 190, 192; in Mobile, 186; as part of northern strategy, 200; outside the South, 216–17; stand in school bus door and, 201; struck down in *Bradley v. Richmond*, 211. *See also* busing
Concerned Parents for Public Education, 165–66, 171–72, 182–83, 185, 199, 204
Confederacy, 12, 31, 191, 196–97, 220; flags of, 37, 69, 71, 82, 92, 185, 197. *See also* Lost Cause mythology
Congress for Racial Equality (CORE), 169–70, 187, 199
Connor, Eugene "Bull," 41, 51, 65
Cooper, A. J., 204
Cooper v. Aaron, 38, 46, 60
Coppinville High School, 115, 195
Cox, Harold, 117–18, 122
Crawford, Vernon, 48–50, 54–95, 65–66, 152, 168–69, 174, 183; mentioned, 223
Crenshaw County, Ala., 105, 107, 150; *Dillard v. Crenshaw County*, 121, 223
Critz, Wesley, 48, 79
Crowder, Gene, 115–16
Cullman County, Ala., 127
Cullman Times, 73
Current, Gloster, 15

Dallas County, Ala., 16, 18, 81, 98, 107. *See also* Selma, Ala.
Daphne, Ala., 212
Darden, J. W., 194
Darden High School, 194–95
Davidson High School, 174, 183, 199
Davis, Dorothy, 60–61, 64–65, 69
Davis, Pamela, 201
Davis v. Board of School Commissioners of Mobile County, 48–51, 54–56, 60, 66, 79, 182–83; appellate rulings in, 88,

139–40, 151, 156, 163, 167–68, 177; Comprehensive Plan for a Unitary System resulting from, 204–5; compulsory assignment proceedings in, 152–54, 162, 164–65, 173–74, 177; impact on other cases, 57, 143, 201, 223; proceedings since 1979, 228; state officials condemn rulings in, 149, 172; Supreme Court ruling in, 198–99; mentioned, 146

Democratic National Convention: 1948 convention, 29; 1968 convention, 150, 156

Democratic Party: Dixiecrats and, 29; national convention, 29, 150, 156; Reconstruction and, 31, 114, 208; southern whites leave, 8, 91–92, 219–20; Supreme Court justices from New Deal era, 45; mentioned, 30, 49, 103, 168, 178, 199, 210

Demopolis, Ala., 95

Dillard v. Crenshaw County, 121, 223

"Dixie" (song), 21, 69, 196–98

Dixiecrats (States' Rights Party), 29, 162

Doar, John, 57–58, 61–62, 66–68, 83; drafting of Civil Rights Act of 1964, 90; enforcement of *Lee v. Macon County Board of Education*, 120, 123, 126–28; *Green v. County School Board of New Kent* and, 132; stepping down to enter private practice, 135

Doyle, Ernest, 18

Druid High School, 231

Dunn, James, 129

Eastland, James, 21

economic reprisal, 15, 17–18, 23, 97, 144, 150; black activists shielded from, 41, 48; Lid Bill Amendments as form of, 214–15; white criticism of, 32; mentioned, 42

Edwards, Jack, 163

Eisenhower, Dwight, 33, 37, 45

Elba, Ala., 98

Elementary and Secondary Education Act (ESEA), 94, 100, 220, 232; as No Child Left Behind (NCLB) and Every Child Succeeds, 218–19

Elmore County, Ala., 212

Engelhardt, Sam, 19–32 passim, 38, 51, 213

Enterprise, Ala., 115, 195

Enterprise High School, 115

equal educational opportunity, 9–11, 168, 216, 226, 232; in *San Antonio Independent School District v. Rodriguez*, 210, 224; United States Office of Education's Division of, 160; U.S. Congress Select Committee on, 186

Escambia County, Ala., 15

Evers, Medgar, 53

Every Child Succeeds, 218–19

"failing" schools, 218–22, 232–33

Fairfield, Ala., 15, 96, 101, 153, 171, 206

Fairhope, Ala., 212

Farley, Michael, 72–73, 75

Federal Bureau of Investigation (FBI), 3, 57, 185, 205; in Birmingham, 63–64, 75; Hoover and, 61; in Mobile, 152; in Tuskegee, 61–62

Fields, Edward, 59–61, 63–65, 69, 71–72, 91

Fifth Avenue Elementary School, 64–65

Finch, Robert, 161, 163–64, 201

Fiss, Owen, 120–22

Florence, Ala., 79, 99

Flowers, Richmond, 51, 53, 62–63, 68, 79–91 passim

Folsom, Jim, 21, 24–30, 41–42, 219

Folsom, Jim, Jr., 219

Ford, Gerald, 216–17

Fort Dale Academy, 188

Fourteenth Amendment: invoked in litigation, 32, 34, 37, 119, 142, 210; invoked in segregationist rhetoric, 44, 166, 173

Frazier, Allen, 136–37

freedom of choice, 94–98 passim, 100–101, 120, 129, 195; courts begin moving away from, 117–22 passim, 130–69 passim; in higher education, 158, 198; laws proposed by state, 172–74, 177, 200, 204; whites invoke as white right, 8, 10, 131, 141–44 passim, 149–53 passim, 157, 164–68 passim, 171, 182–88 passim, 200–206 passim, 210–12, 221, 233

Freedom Rides, 42, 169
Freeman v. Pitts, 218, 230
Fultondale, Ala., 229

Gadsden, Ala., 17, 46, 88, 90, 101
Gadsden High School, 46
Gallion, Macdonald, 39–40, 174
Gardendale, Ala., 229–30
Gardner, John, 114, 129
Gaston, A. G., 65
Gaston High School, 171
Geneva, Ala., 98
Gewin, Walter, 54–55, 60, 156
Givhan, Walter, 16, 19, 25, 73, 95, 209, 227
Godbold, John, 122
Goldwater, Barry, 92
Gomillion v. Lightfoot, 51
Gray, Fred, 1, 32–33, 88; effort to block opening of AUM, 158; effort to block Oxford city secession, 202; as legislator, 200; representing the NAACP, 34; work on *Knight v. Alabama*, 155, 157–58; work on *Lee v. Macon*, 51, 57–58, 66, 77–80, 83–85, 87, 108, 124, 126–28, 130–31, 136, 150; mentioned 194
Graymont Elementary School, 63, 67, 69, 95
Graysville High School, 166, 174, 184
Greenberg, Jack, 50–51, 84, 89, 121–22, 132, 157, 161–62
Greene County, Ala., 97, 105, 107, 191
Greenhaw, Wayne, 206
Greensboro, Ala., 95
Green v. County School Board of New Kent County, 132–33, 142–43, 146–48, 150, 218; *Alexander v. Holmes* and, 161; impact on Alabama school cases, 153, 158–59, 164, 202; Nixon administration walks back, 162; mentioned, 151
Greenville, Ala., 17, 188
Greenville Advocate, 188
Greenville High School, 188
Green v. Kennedy, 192–93, 217
Griffin, Ethel, 18
Griffin v. County School Board of Prince Edward County, 87–88

Grooms, Hobart, 37, 45, 67, 84, 109; adjudication of *Hereford v. Huntsville*, 51, 56, 88–89; adjudication of impacted areas cases, 54; adjudication of *Lee v. Macon*, 119–28 passim, 135, 155, 159–60, 195; case of Hoover Academy, 193; desegregation of University of Alabama, 52; municipal secession and, 171; mentioned, 202
Gully, Jordan, 96–97

Haikala, Madeline, 229–31
Halberstam, David, 19–20
Hale County, Ala., 16, 98, 105, 107
Hall, Revis, 103, 165, 170–71, 186
Hand, Brevard, 228, 233–34
Harris, E. A., 82
Harrison Elementary School, 13–15, 91, 227
Hayneville High School, 97
Head, James, 75
Henderson, Ellen, 82
Hereford, Sonnie, 50–51, 65, 230–31
Hereford, Sonnie, IV, 51, 64–65, 79
Hereford v. Huntsville Board of Education, 50–51, 54, 56–57, 64–65, 79, 230–31
HEW guidelines, 94, 96, 161, 181; anti-guidelines legislation, 105–6, 114; revised guidelines, 100–104, 107–8, 111, 116–19, 128, 133
Hicks High School, 189
Hill, Leon, 142
Hill, Lister, 95, 103, 116–17, 143
Hillcrest Elementary School, 115
Hobdy, Henry, 60–61, 64–65, 69
Hobson City, Ala., 202–3
Hogue, Michael, 230
Homewood, Ala., 96, 154, 175–76, 184, 206–7
Hood, James, 52
Hoover, Ala., 176
Hoover, J. Edgar, 61
Hoover, William, 71, 176, 193
Hoover Academy, 71, 95, 176, 193
Hornsby, Preston, 58, 62, 86
Houston County, Ala., 18

Howe, Harold, 102, 104, 114–16
Hubbard, Mike, 219–20, 222
Hubbert, Paul, 220, 222
Hueytown, Ala., 154, 175, 229
Humphries, Hulond, 2–4
Hunt, Guy, 219
Huntsville, Ala., 44, 79, 90; controversy over Confederate symbology, 197; desegregation via *Hereford* case, 50–51, 56, 88, 101, 228, 230–31; "failing" schools in, 222; impacted areas cases, 46–47, 50, 54; George Wallace interferes with desegregation in, 60, 63–67 passim; mentioned, 4, 78, 214, 224. See also *Hereford v. Huntsville Board of Education*
Huntsville High School, 231
Huntsville Times, 73
Hurley, Ruby, 14–15, 18

impacted areas cases, 46–47, 50–51, 54, 84, 90
Innis, Roy, 169–70, 187
Interim Committee, 23
Internal Revenue Service (IRS), 191–93, 179, 217
interposition, 27–29, 105

Jackson, Ernest, 40–41, 47, 54, 64, 66–67
Jackson, Harvey, 82
Jacksonville, Ala., 118
Jacobs, David, 142
Jacobs, Jacqueline, 142
James, Fob, 219
Jansen, V.R., 50
Jefferson Academy, 71
Jefferson County, Ala., 20, 72, 96; municipal secession from school system, 206–8, 211–12, 229–31; *Swann* and, 206; Wallace's stand in school bus door and, 201–2, 204; whites protest compulsory assignment in, 166, 171–74, 183–87; white violence in, 36, 38; mentioned, 35. See also *Stout and U.S. v. Jefferson County Board of Education*

Jefferson Davis High School, 137–38
John Carroll High School, 91
Johnson, Frank, 10, 32–33, 45–46, 51, 56; adjudication of Black Belt school cases, 100, 150; adjudication of *Carr v. Montgomery*, 156–57; adjudication of *Lee v. Macon*, 56–61 passim, 84, 88–89, 119–22; adjudication of *NAACP v. Wallace*, 107; adjudication of *U.S. v. Wallace*, 67, 80; blacks reach out to, 195; during courtroom proceedings, 77, 109; enforcement of *Lee v. Macon*, 126–39, 148, 150, 154–60 passim, 194, 198; Freedom Riders and, 42; public criticism and distorted understanding of role of, 86, 125, 143, 187–89; Selma-Montgomery march and, 93; George Wallace and, 42, 44, 48–49, 80; Lurleen Wallace and, 123–24; mentioned, 37, 213, 233
Johnson, Lyndon, 156
Johnson High School, Huntsville, 231
John T. Morgan Academy, 189
Jones, Patricia, 82
Jones, Walter, 25, 31–34, 38, 42
Jones, Wilmer, 82
Jones Valley High School, 197
Jordan, Adalberto, 225
Judkins, Carmen, 82
Judkins, Robert, 82, 87
junior colleges, desegregation of, 158, 198

Katzenbach, Nicholas, 52, 251n40
Keith, Alston, 18, 107
Kelly, Guy, 190
Kennedy, John, 53–56 passim, 61, 67–74 passim, 219
Kennedy, Robert, 64, 68–74 passim, 86, 148, 156
Keppel, Francis, 93–94
Kilpatrick, James, 27–28, 87
King, Martin Luther Jr., 39–40, 51–52; murder of, 140; whites mocking, 60, 145, 151–52; mentioned, 73, 95, 205
Knight, Joe, 5–6
Knight v. Alabama, 5–6, 223–24

Ku Klux Klan, 16, 21–22; bombings attributed to, 52, 59, 64, 72; Asa Carter's affiliation with and other violent acts carried out by, 20, 35–36, 43; injunction against, 150; intimidation by, 38–42, 63, 71, 81, 97–98, 106; mythical role in Lost Cause narrative and historical role in Redemption, 31, 113–14; mentioned, 31, 206

Landsberg, Brian, vii, 9, 56, 121
Lanett, Ala., 128–29
Langan, Joe, 60
Lauderdale County, Ala., 99, 116
law and order, 7–10, 49, 53, 73–76, 135, 146–47, 233, 240n34; Brewer invokes, 140, 149, 151, 166, 172, 179; black activists invoke, 48; business moderates invoke, 93, 98; Asa Carter refuses to adopt, 206; Citizens' Council and, 22–23; judges invoke, 52, 60, 74, 136; Ku Klux Klan and, 16, 113–14; Lid Bill amendments and, 215; local whites invoke, 57–59, 63, 71–72, 81, 141, 164; NAACP rejects, 197, 201; Richard Nixon invokes, 162, 200; press invokes, 74, 90, 99; state officials invoke, 91, 111, 140; George Wallace invokes, 65, 140, 181–82, 200, 213
Lawrence County, Ala., 225
Lee, Anthony, 51, 57, 66, 79, 82, 86–87, 91
Lee, Detroit, 51, 86
Leeds, Ala., 172
Lee v. Macon County Board of Education, 2, 10, 51; black disillusionment with rulings, 194–95; *Brown* and, 9; case cited, 5, 121, 211, 233; courtroom proceedings in, 77–78, 84, 109–11, 115–17, 149; implementation of statewide decree, 127–38 passim, 155–60 passim; Frank Johnson's adjudication of, 56, 58, 61; major rulings in, 87–88, 119–22, 150, 154, 198; motions filed in, 66–67, 81, 83, 107–8, 114, 118, 148, 202; municipal secession and, 202; segregationist reaction to rulings and enforcement, 123–27, 149, 151, 187, 190–91; mentioned, 90–91, 95, 99, 100, 103, 143, 146, 166, 185, 216, 226, 233
LeFlore, John, 48–50, 65–66, 91, 141–42, 174, 199
Leonard, Jerris, 162, 164
Libassi, Peter, 128–29, 135
Lid Bill Amendments, 5–8, 10, 210–15, 223–25
Lieberman, Myron, 152
Limestone County, Ala., 201–2
Linden, Ala., 133
Lingo, Al, 60, 62–67 passim, 75, 81–82
Lockhart No. 2 School, 195
Lockridge, Allen, 185
Los Angeles Times, 183
Lost Cause mythology, 31, 44, 196, 205. *See also* Confederacy
Louisville, Ky., 217
Loving v. Virginia, 132
Lowndes Academy, 107, 190, 217, 227
Lowndesboro, Ala., 95
Lowndes County, Ala., 96–97, 100, 107, 190, 221, 226–27; Lowndes Academy, 107, 190, 217, 227
Lucy, Autherine, 18, 20, 28–29, 34, 61
Lynne, Seybourn, 37, 40–48 passim, 52–56, 67–68, 153, 164–78 passim, 185–86, 206

Macon Academy, 70–71, 77, 81, 83–88, 91, 226
Macon County, Ala., 2, 17, 19, 51, 57; initial desegregation in, 69–70, 90–91; local white resistance in, 81–83, 86; state interference in, 61–63, 70, 77–80, 84–85, 88–89; white flight to Macon Academy, 70–71, 83. *See also Lee v. Macon County Board of Education*; Macon Academy; Tuskegee, Ala.
Macon County High School, 77, 79, 80–84 passim
Maddox, Hugh, 106
Madison, Gordon, 77
Madison County, Ala., 47, 50, 54, 88, 90, 101

Madison Pike Elementary School, 46
magnet schools, 217–18, 228, 230–31
Malone, Vivian, 49, 52
Marcus, Patricia, 63, 66, 69
Marengo County, Ala., 16, 98, 104, 107, 133–34, 190, 233
Marion city board of education, 127–28
Marsh, Del, 221–22
Marshall, Burke, 47, 61, 63, 83, 90
Marshall, Thurgood, 211
Marshall Space Flight Center, 46
Marshall v. Bentley, 222, 226
massive resistance, 7–8, 11, 27, 30, 38, 236n18; continuation of, 144, 215, 225, 232–33
Mayhall, Roy, 49, 92
McAdory High School, 175
McClung, Ollie, 90
McFadden, Walter, 202–3
McKay, Charles, 28–29
McNair, Denise, 72
Meadows, Austin, 23, 26–27; in courtroom proceedings, 84, 109–11, 115–16; enjoined by *Lee v. Macon* court, 88; exerting control over local school systems, 39, 77, 86, 92–94, 102–7; focus of plaintiffs' complaints in *Lee v. Macon* trial, 115, 119; on law and order, 91; retirement, 118; mentioned, 99
Merritt, Vernon, 82
Midfield, Ala., 72, 165, 171, 206–7
Midfield High School, 171
Millbrook, Ala., 212
Milliken v. Bradley, 211
miscegenation, 2, 16, 17, 20, 31–32, 41, 44, 111, 189; *Loving v. Virginia* ruling and, 132
Missouri v. Jenkins, 218
Mitchell, John, 203
Mobile, Ala., 17, 48–50, 54–56, 78; black anger and disillusionment in, 169–70, 187; Comprehensive Plan for a Unitary System, 204–5; compulsory assignment/busing in, 151–54, 162–64, 168–69, 173–74, 177, 182–83, 198–99; desegregation under freedom of choice, 60, 68–69, 88, 91, 139–40; "failing" schools in, 222; impacted areas cases, 50; *Lynch v. Alabama* and, 223; state's freedom of choice law originating from, 200–201; George Wallace attempts to block desegregation in, 64–67; white flight from, 212, 228; white resistance to desegregation in, 61, 140–45, 177, 181–83, 205–6; mentioned, 32, 44, 171–72, 185, 208, 214. See also *Davis v. Board of School Commissioners of Mobile County*
Mobile Press, 152
Mobile Press-Register, 184
Mobile Register, 164
Montgomery, Ala., 12–14, 21, 34, 39–40; AUM case, 158; bus boycott in, 18, 21, 28, 32–33; desegregation via *Carr* case, 88, 91, 100, 136–38, 143, 146, 156–57, 177; "failing" schools in, 222; private schools in, 40, 107, 226–27; Selma-Montgomery march, 93, 97; white flight from, 212, 227–28; mentioned, 22, 58, 66, 69, 77, 99, 103, 109, 111, 115, 117, 125–26, 133, 135
Montgomery Academy, 40, 227
Montgomery Advertiser, 31, 65, 89, 108, 138, 217
Montgomery Improvement Association, 39
Moore, Mary, 220
Morgan, Charles, 74–75
Morgan County, Ala., 98
Motley, Constance Baker, 50–51, 54–55, 64
Moton High School, 172
Mountain Brook, Ala., 96, 154, 175–76, 178, 206
Muhammad, Elijah, 178
municipal secession, from county school systems, 154, 175–77, 184–85, 202–3, 206–8, 229–30
Murphy, Harold, 5, 6
Murphy High School, 140; desegregation of, 60, 64–65, 68; recent enrollment at, 228; violence associated with compulsory assignment and, 184, 186; mentioned, 200

NAACP, 7, 12–18, 211; black opposition to, 144, 151, 153, 169–70; state and local organizations, 47–48, 50–51, 58, 131, 196–97; white resistance to activities of, 19–35 passim; mentioned, 9, 42–43, 53, 74, 78, 80, 100, 107, 114. *See also* NAACP Legal Defense and Education Fund; *NAACP v. Wallace*

NAACP Legal Defense and Education Fund (LDF), 1, 33–34, 99, 101; *Alexander v. Holmes* and, 161–62; *Armstrong v. Birmingham* and, 185; *Carr v. Montgomery* and, 156–57; *Davis v. Mobile* and, 49–50, 139, 151–52, 164, 167–68, 174, 177–78, 183, 204; freedom of choice laws and, 201; *Green v. New Kent* and, 132–33; *Lee v. Macon* and, 51, 84, 121–22, 211; *Milliken v. Bradley* and, 211; segregation academies and, 191; *Stout and U.S. v. Jefferson* and, 165–67, 170–71, 177, 185; mentioned, 88, 118

NAACP v. Wallace, 107–8, 110–11, 114, 118–19, 126

National Education Association, 160; AEA, 143, 220

National Observer, 190

National Review, 87

National States' Rights Party (NSRP), 59–61, 63–64, 69, 71–72, 98

Neighborhood Organized Workers (NOW), 141–42, 170

Nelson, Agnes, 45

Nelson, Oswald, 45

Nelson, Theodore, 45

Nelson v. Birmingham Board of Education, 45, 47–48, 51, 53

New Hope Junior High School, 201

New Right, 10–11, 252n45

New York Times, 161–62, 169, 206

Nixon, E. D., 13, 33–34

Nixon, Richard, 8, 156–57; appearance in Alabama, 199–201; establishment of Citizens' Advisory Committees, 182; judicial appointments made by, 201, 210; retreat from desegregation enforcement, 160–66, 176, 181; George Wallace and, 179, 203–4, 209

No Child Left Behind (NCLB), 218–19, 229

Non-Partisan Voters' League, 48

northern strategy, 147, 198, 200; Stennis and, 147, 156–57, 161; Whitten and, 147, 157. *See also* Brewer, Albert; Wallace, George

Northwest Alabamian, 74

Notasulga, Ala., 77–87 passim, 90

nullification, 27–29, 105

Obama, Barack, 218–19, 229–30

Oklahoma City v. Dowell, 217–18

Oliver High School, 171

Opelika, Ala., 98, 194–95, 226

Opelika High School, 194

Operation Implementation, NAACP, 15–18 passim

Operation Snowball, 141

Oxford, Ala., 202–3

Oxford Elementary School, 203

Oxford High School, 202

pairing plans, 148, 163, 168, 170, 194, 203, 231

Panetta, Leon, 161, 201

Parents Involved in Community Schools v. Seattle School District No. 1, 216

Parker, Allan, 58, 62

Parker, Jack, 72

Parker, John, 27, 37, 117

Parker High School, 36

Parks, Rosa, 1, 33

Patterson, Albert, 30

Patterson, John, 30–31, 42; attacks NAACP, 34; support for segregation academy establishment, 38–40; mentioned, 43, 48, 208, 221

Patterson, Robert, 16–17

Patton, W.C., 14, 18, 34, 197

Payne, Joe, 134

Payne, Lamar, 141, 153

Pelham, Ala., 176

Pelham, Pierre, 141, 144, 152, 163, 181

Pell City High School, 197

Perritt, H. H., 76

Persons, Gordon, 24

Phenix City, Ala., 17, 30

Phillips High School, 36, 38, 71–72
Pickens County, Ala., 97, 127
Pittman, Virgil, 107, 109
Pleasant Grove, Ala., 165, 175–76, 184, 189, 206–8, 229
Pleasant Grove School (Randolph County), 189
Plessy v. Ferguson, 38, 226
Pointer, Sam, 202–4, 207–8, 211
Pollack, Stephen, 133, 135, 147–48
Powell, Josephine, 63, 66, 69
Prattville, Ala., 212
Prichard, Ala., 139, 153, 163–64, 181, 184, 186, 228
Prier, Claude, 66
Prince Edward County, Va., 39, 87
private schools, 23–24, 224; Alabama Accountability Act funding for, 220–22, 232; in Birmingham, 211–12; in Black Belt, 95; freedom of association as rationale to attend, 122; *Lee v. Macon* and, 88, 131, 149, 151; in Mobile, 228; George Wallace's support for, 58, 75, 106. *See also* segregation academies; white flight; *and specific schools*
ProPublica, 216
Pruitt, C. A., 57, 62, 66, 77–78
pupil placement laws, 25–28, 41, 50, 79, 94, 99; courts cite unconstitutional application of, 46, 51, 54; courts order nondiscriminatory use of, 55–57, 60; litigation targeting, 35–40 passim, 85, 88

Ramsay High School, 63–64, 66, 69
Ramsey, Fred, 104–5, 133–34
Randolph County, Ala., 2–4, 189
Randolph County High School, 3
Randolph Press, 189
Ray, James Earl, 140
Rea, James, 81–84
Reagan, Ronald, 8, 190, 217, 228
Reconstruction, 5, 28, 31, 44, 113, 200, 205; "Dixie" and, 196; Hobson City and, 202; Lid Bill Amendments and, 208
Redemption, 5, 38, 44, 196, 214
Redstone Arsenal, 46
Reed, Joe, 168

Reed, Thomas, 200
Reese, Gene, 221–22
Reeves, Alene, 229–30
Reeves, Kymiyah, 229–30
Reeves, Ricky, 229–30
Republican Party, 272–73n9; Eisenhower's judicial appointments, 45; Richard Nixon and, 156, 161; Reconstruction and, 5, 113–14; southern strategy, 8; southern whites join, 92, 114, 219–22; mentioned, 33, 58, 103
Reynolds v. Sims, 208
Riddick v. School Board of the City of Norfolk, 217–18
Robertson, Carole, 72
Robinson, Johnnie, 72
Rosedale High School, 175
Ross, Quinten, 221
Runyon v. McCrary, 217
Ryan, Brady, 97

San Antonio Independent School District v. Rodriguez, 210–11, 224
Sand Mountain, 118
Satterfield, John, 116
Scott, Herman, 136–37
Seay, Solomon, Jr., 1–3, 226, 233–34; on Frank Johnson, 56; work on *Knight v. Alabama*, 5–6; work on *Lee v. Macon*, 51, 126–28, 131–34, 136–37, 155, 157–58, 160, 202
segregation academies, 2, 8, 40, 188–93, 217; in Birmingham, 71–72, 95, 176; *Lee v. Macon* and, 119, 189; in Macon County, 70, 71, 77, 81, 83, 88; in Mobile, 183, 186; in recent years, 226–28, 233; tuition grants to attend, 106–7. *See also* private schools; white flight; *and specific schools*
Segrest, John Fletcher, 70
Sellers, Ennis, 58, 61–62, 70–71
Selma, Ala., 9, 15–16; Bloody Sunday and Selma-Montgomery march, 93, 97, 227; Citizens' Council activity, economic reprisal in, 17–19, 38, 95; initial school desegregation in, 98; white flight to segregation academies, 188–89

Selma Times-Journal, 18, 74
Shades Valley High School, 175
Shannon, H. W., 18
Sharpe, Andy, 70
Shaw High School, 199
Sheffield, Ala., 79
Shelby, Richard, 219
Shelby County, Ala., 176, 229
Shelton, Robert, 39, 59, 63–64, 71
Shores, Arthur, 33, 35, 59, 64
Shorter, Ala., 77–84 passim, 90
Shorter High School, 77, 79, 80–84 passim
Shuttlesworth, Fred, 35–41, 51–52, 64, 67
Shuttlesworth, Pat, 36–37
Shuttlesworth, Ricky, 36–37
Shuttlesworth, Ruby, 36–37
Shuttlesworth v. Birmingham Board of Education, 37–41, 46, 51, 88
Simelton, Bernard, 221
Sims, Larry Joe, 72–73, 75
Singleton v. Jackson, 96; *Singleton II*, 101; *Singleton III*, 167
Sixteenth Street Baptist Church bombing, 7, 9, 72–74
Smith, Lynwood, 224–25
Smyer, Sydney, 19, 23, 52
Snellgrove, J. R., 115
Southerners, the, 205–6
Southern Manifesto, 29
Southern Poverty Law Center (SPLC), 221–22
Southern Press Association, 199
Southern Regional Council, 21, 122, 146–47, 170, 187
southern strategy, 8, 200, 237n21
Southside High School, 188
Spanish Fort, Ala., 212
Sparkman, John, 95, 103
Sparks, Henry, 211
Spritzer, Ralph, 133
Stand Together and Never Divide (STAND), 141–44 passim, 151–53, 163–66 passim, 181, 199, 204
State of Alabama v. U.S. and Davis, 177
St. Elmo High School for Negroes, 50
Stennis, John, 147, 156–57, 161
St. James School, 227
Stone, Ernest, 118, 120, 125–27, 134–36, 148, 150–51, 154–60 passim
Stoner, J. B., 59, 69, 72, 91
Stout and U.S. v. Jefferson County Board of Education, 111, 146, 148; appellate decisions in, 117–23, 126, 132–33, 138, 167, 170; cited in other cases, 139, 143, 156; *Green v. County School Board of New Kent* and, 153, 164–65; state officials criticize decisions in, 125; white flight as result of, 154, 175–76. See also Jefferson County, Ala.
St. Paul's Episcopal School, 228
Strange, Luther, 225
student experiences, 111–13
Student Nonviolent Coordinating Committee (SNCC), 50, 97, 168
Sullins, Martha, 82
Sumter Academy, 190, 227
Sumter County, Ala., 190, 225, 227–28
Sunbelt, 8, 149
Supreme Court of Alabama, 34, 83, 221–22
Swann v. Charlotte-Mecklenburg Board of Education, 182–83, 198–207 passim, 210–11, 216

Talladega County, Ala., 185, 205, 224; board of education, 128
Talladega *Daily Home*, 73
Tarrant, Ala., 20, 96, 100, 206
Taylor, Bruce, 68–69
Teacher Choice Act, 130–32
Terrell, H. L., 107
Terry Heights Elementary School, 231
textbooks, racially distorted, 113–14, 196
Thomas, Daniel, 54–56, 67, 141, 151; delaying desegregation in *Davis v. Board of School Commissioners of Mobile County*, 60, 153, 162, 164, 168–69; hung in effigy, 174; meets with angry white parents, 177–78; rulings in *Davis v. Mobile* reversed, 88, 139, 152, 163, 167; sides with CRD, 184; Wilcox County

school case and, 190; mentioned, 154, 204
Thomasville city board of education, 127–28
Thornberry, Homer, 139, 156
Thurmond, Strom, 147
Time magazine, 73, 116, 122
trade schools, desegregation of, 158, 198
Trimmier, Charles, 66
Trinity Presbyterian School, Montgomery, 227
tuition grant laws, 80, 83–85, 95, 106–7, 115; Alabama Accountability Act as, 220–21; court rulings on, 88, 119, 132; 1967 version, 130–31; mentioned, 208
Tuscaloosa, Ala., 19, 53, 58, 60, 81, 106–7, 116; "failing" schools in, 222; resegregation in, 231–32; mentioned, 39, 54, 71
Tuscaloosa *Graphic*, 73
Tuscaloosa High School, 231
Tuscaloosa News, 74, 99
Tuskegee, Ala., 51, 57–71 passim, 77–82, 90–91, 226–27; mentioned, 107, 200. See also *Lee v. Macon County Board of Education*; Macon County, Ala.; Tuskegee Civic Association
Tuskegee Civic Association (TCA), 34, 51, 58, 61
Tuskegee Institute High School, 58, 79, 87
Tuskegee Public High School, 58, 61–63, 66–67, 77–80 passim, 90–91
Tuttle, Elbert, 45, 54–56, 84

UMS-Wright Preparatory School, 228
Union Springs Herald, 74
United Americans for Conservative Government, 65
United States Commission on Civil Rights (USCCR), 49, 98, 161; Alabama Advisory Committee to, 102
United States Congress, 54, 90–94 passim, 186; Alabama delegation, 29, 95, 103, 143; debates surrounding HEW guidelines, 147, 161, 163
United States Marshals Service, 52, 58, 64, 67–68, 82, 120, 152, 184, 186

United States Office of Education (USOE), HEW, 90–98 passim, 100–104, 114–16, 121, 158–63 passim, 187
United States v. Rea, 83–84
United States v. Wallace, 67
United Student Action Movement of Mobile (USAMM), 187
University of Alabama, 4; attempted desegregation by Lucy and "stand in the schoolhouse door," 18, 20, 281; desegregation by Malone, 49, 52–53; desegregation of undergraduates, 9; mentioned, 30, 33, 42, 82, 188, 232
University of Mississippi, 44, 46, 81
U.S. Eleventh Circuit Court of Appeals, 5–6, 223–25, 230–31
U.S. Fourth Circuit Court of Appeals, 132, 198, 207, 210
U.S. Fifth Circuit Court of Appeals: impatience with *Brown* enforcement, 9, 42, 45; judges known as "Fifth Circuit Four," 56; ruling in *Alexander v. Holmes*, 161; rulings in Alabama school cases, 84, 88, 118, 122, 132–33, 138–39, 151–53, 156, 163–68, 174, 177–78, 182–85 passim, 193, 198, 203–8 passim; striking of placement laws, 54; upholding HEW guidelines, 96, 101, 111, 117; mentioned, 123, 176
U.S. Steel Corporation, 229
U.S. Supreme Court, 1; on Bible reading and prayer in schools, 85, 192; *Brown* and *Brown II*, 13–14, 22, 24, 27, 176; on Civil Rights Act of 1964, 90; historiographical debates about, 9–10; landmark school case decisions beyond *Brown* and Alabama, 87–88, 142–43, 146, 148, 149, 161–62, 166–69, 198, 207–8, 210–11, 216–18, 230; on placement laws, 54, 56; on private schools, 198; rulings in Alabama school cases, 6, 38, 118, 132–33, 156–57, 172, 182–83, 199–200, 221–23, 225; silence after *Brown*, 46; on tuition grants, 70; white criticism of, 31, 60, 74, 153; mentioned, 176–77

U.S. v. Hinds County, 167
U.S. v. Scotland Neck City Board of Education, 207–8

Vestavia Hills, Ala., 96, 175–76, 184, 206–7
Vietnam, 105, 125, 156
Vigor High School, 153, 184, 186, 200, 228
Vineyard School, 12–14
violence, 53, 91, 156, 229; advocates of law and order condemn, 21–23, 49, 60, 65–66, 75–76, 80, 99, 206, 235; in Birmingham, associated with compulsory assignment, 174–75; blacks subjected to or threatened with, 9–10, 34–38, 40, 65, 72–73, 86, 97, 112, 150; fears of, 58, 144, 177, 188–89; in Huntsville, associated with compulsory assignment, 197; in Mobile, associated with compulsory assignment, 153, 184–87 passim, 228; white moderates subjected to or threatened with, 71, 86, 125; whites blame blacks for, 7, 44; whites use as excuse, 3, 81

Wadsworth, Mrs. W. T., 70
Walker, Richard, 63, 66, 69
Walker County, Ala., 98
Wallace, George, 8–9, 42; antiguidelines law and, 114; attempted assassination of, 210–11; Brewer and, 149, 155, 172–73, 178–79; criticism of judges and litigation, 48–50, 131, 187; development of northern strategy, 147, 200; encouragement of white defiance, 60, 103–4, 181–82; executive orders issued to block desegregation, 62–69; first inaugural address, 43–4; interference in Macon County, 58–59, 62, 77–78; *Lee v. Macon* and, 78, 80–81, 83–88 passim, 115, 124; Lid Bill Amendments and, 208–9, 213–14; local whites praise, 72, 188; *NAACP v. Wallace* and, 67, 110–11, 114; Richard Nixon and, 199, 201, 203; presidential campaigning, 156, 210–11; pressuring and intimidating local officials, 93–95,
98–108 passim, 125, 130; Sixteenth Street Baptist Church bombing and, 73; stand in school bus door, 200–204; stand in schoolhouse door, 52–53; state legislature and, 91, 186; support for white private schools, 70–71, 75, 84, 106; tunnel named for, 228; Lurleen Wallace and, 103, 118; mentioned, 45, 77, 123, 140, 162, 196, 205–6, 219, 226
Wallace, Gerald, 178, 199
Wallace, Lurleen, 103, 114, 118, 125, 133; address to legislature condemning rulings in *Lee v. Macon* and *U.S. v. Jefferson*, 123–24; death, 140
Wanniski, Jude, 190
Ware, James, 73
Ware, Virgil, 73
Warren, Earl, 25, 142
Warrior Academy, 191–92
Washington Post, 181
Watkins, Keith, 222
Wedowee, Ala., 2–4
Weissinger v. Boswell, 209, 213
Wenonah High School, 170–71
Wesley, Cynthia, 72
West End, Birmingham, 176; West End Parents for Private Schools, 71–72. *See also* West End High School, Birmingham
West End, Tuscaloosa, 232
West End High School, Birmingham, 63, 66, 69, 197
West End Parents for Private Schools, 71–72
Westbrook, William, 144, 151–52, 163, 204
Westfield High School, 170
Wetumpka, Ala., 105
white flight, 2, 8, 10, 212, 224; due to compulsory assignment, 208–9; Lid Bill Amendments and, 5–6; local officials use as excuse, 149; to private schools, 191–92, 227; to suburbs, 96, 228–32; mentioned, 78, 177, 187, 227. *See also* private schools; segregation academies; *and specific schools*

White Rights (organization), 141
Whites Organized for Rights Keeping (WORK), 141
Whitten, Jamie, 147, 157
Wilcox County, Ala., 100, 105, 190, 227
Wilkins, Roy, 34
Williams, J. S., 16
Williams, Willie, 41, 47, 54
Williamson High School, 140, 142, 152, 183
Wilson, Leonard, 61
Winston, Richard, 18
Winston County, Ala., 33
Wiregrass region, 18, 24, 78, 195
Wisdom, John Minor, 44–45, 55–56, 139; adjudication of *Lee v. Calhoun County Board of Education*, 203; adjudication of *U.S. v. Jefferson County Board of Education*, 117–18, 120–22, 130, 206–7
Woodruff, Buddy, 96–97
World War II, 7, 16, 30, 33, 48, 78, 96
Wright, Theo, 47–48
Wright v. City Council of the City of Emporia, 207–8
Wyatt, Willie, 82, 87, 91

Yale Law Journal, 121–22
Yarbrough, George, 84
Young Men's Business Club, 49, 74

Zukoski, Charles, 75

POLITICS AND CULTURE IN THE TWENTIETH-CENTURY SOUTH

A Common Thread: Labor, Politics, and Capital Mobility in the Textile Industry
by Beth English

"Everybody Was Black Down There": Race and Industrial Change in the Alabama Coalfields
by Robert H. Woodrum

Race, Reason, and Massive Resistance: The Diary of David J. Mays, 1954–1959
edited by James R. Sweeney

The Unemployed People's Movement: Leftists, Liberals, and Labor in Georgia, 1929–1941
by James J. Lorence

Liberalism, Black Power, and the Making of American Politics, 1965–1980
by Devin Fergus

Guten Tag, Y'all: Globalization and the South Carolina Piedmont, 1950–2000
by Marko Maunula

The Culture of Property: Race, Class, and Housing Landscapes in Atlanta, 1880–1950
by LeeAnn Lands

Marching in Step: Masculinity, Citizenship, and The Citadel in Post–World War II America
by Alexander Macaulay

Rabble Rousers: The American Far Right in the Civil Rights Era
by Clive Webb

Who Gets a Childhood: Race and Juvenile Justice in Twentieth-Century Texas
by William S. Bush

Alabama Getaway: The Political Imaginary and the Heart of Dixie
by Allen Tullos

The Problem South: Region, Empire, and the New Liberal State, 1880–1930
by Natalie J. Ring

The Nashville Way: Racial Etiquette and the Struggle for Social Justice in a Southern City
by Benjamin Houston

Cold War Dixie: Militarization and Modernization in the American South
by Kari Frederickson

Faith in Bikinis: Politics and Leisure in the Coastal South since the Civil War
by Anthony J. Stanonis

"We Who Believe in Freedom": Womanpower Unlimited and the Black Freedom Struggle in Mississippi
by Tiyi M. Morris

New Negro Politics in the Jim Crow South
by Claudrena N. Harold

Jim Crow Terminals: The Desegregation of American Airports
by Anke Ortlepp

Remaking the Rural South: Interracialism, Christian Socialism, and Cooperative Farming in Jim Crow Mississippi
by Robert Hunt Ferguson

The South of the Mind: American Imaginings of White Southernness, 1960–1980
by Zachary J. Lechner

The Politics of White Rights: Race, Justice, and Integrating Alabama's Schools
by Joseph Bagley

www.ingramcontent.com/pod-product-compliance
Lightning Source LLC
Chambersburg PA
CBHW011720220426
43664CB00023B/2897